T0389529

Auxiliary Selection in Italo-Romance

Linguistik Aktuell/Linguistics Today (LA)

ISSN 0166-0829

Linguistik Aktuell/Linguistics Today (LA) provides a platform for original monograph studies into synchronic and diachronic linguistics. Studies in LA confront empirical and theoretical problems as these are currently discussed in syntax, semantics, morphology, phonology, and systematic pragmatics with the aim to establish robust empirical generalizations within a universalistic perspective.

For an overview of all books published in this series, please see
benjamins.com/catalog/la

Volume 281

Auxiliary Selection in Italo-Romance. A Nested-Agree approach
by Irene Amato

Auxiliary Selection in Italo-Romance

A Nested-Agree approach

Irene Amato
Leipzig University

John Benjamins Publishing Company

Amsterdam / Philadelphia

The paper used in this publication meets the minimum requirements of the American National Standard for Information Sciences – Permanence of Paper for Printed Library Materials, ANSI z39.48-1984.

DOI 10.1075/la.281

Cataloging-in-Publication Data available from Library of Congress:
LCCN 2023033221 (PRINT) / 2023033222 (E-BOOK)

ISBN 978 90 272 1434 8 (HB)
ISBN 978 90 272 4927 2 (E-BOOK)

John Benjamins Publishing Company · https://benjamins.com

To my parents Angela e Roberto

Table of contents

Acknowledgments

This book has been a long journey. I didn't even know what the destination was when I started it. I learned a lot by writing these pages, not only about language, but mostly about myself. I needed patience, perseverance, and passion, but most of all the help of other people. I would like to thank everyone who supported me along the way. I thank Fabian Heck, Anna Cardinaletti, Gereon Müller, and Barbara Stiebels for their scientific advice, for sharing their knowledge, and for believing in me. Thanks to all other members of the Institut für Linguistik of Universität Leipzig that have come and gone over my six years there. Special thanks go to my fellow adventurers: Mike Berger, Christine Marquardt, Hyunjung Lee, Savio Meyase, and Marie-Luise Schwarzer. For their linguistic judgments, I thank Roberta D'Alessandro, Lucia Molinu, Chiara Benetti, Francesca Nocchi, Tania Cortopassi, Clio Antongiovanni, Cora Antongiovanni, and Flavia Lari. For everything else that doesn't fit in a book, I thank Alessandro and my family: Michele, Roberto, Angela, and everyone who came before us.

List of symbols and abbreviations

aux sel	auxiliary selection
cl	clitic
cl cl	clitic climbing
EF	edge feature
NA	Nested Agree
MLC	Minimal Link Condition
PIC	Phase Impenetrability Condition
ppa	past participle agreement
SCC	Strict Cycle Condition
1	first person
2	second person
3	third person
π	person feature
γ	gender feature
#	number feature
φ	person, number and gender features
TAM	tense, aspect, mood
ABS	absolutive
ACC	accusative
APPL	applicative
AUX	auxiliary
COND	conditional
CONJ	conjunctive
DAT	dative
ERG	ergative
F	feminine
FOC	focus
FUT	future
GEN	genitive
GER	gerund
IMPERS	impersonal
IMPF	imperfect
INF	infinitive
M	masculine

NEG	negation
NOM	nominative
NS	nonsubject voice
OBJ	object
PASS	passive
PFV	perfective
PL	plural
POSS	poss
PRF	perfect
PRS	present
PRTC	participle
PST	past
REFL	reflexive
REL	relative
SG	singular
SBJ	subject
TOP	topic

CHAPTER 1

The problem of auxiliary selection

1.1 Introduction

This book deals with the problem of auxiliary selection in natural languages. An *auxiliary* is a verb that expresses functional meaning, such as person specification, tense or aspect features, and does not have an argument structure of its own, unlike lexical verbs. One of these functional verbs is the *perfect* auxiliary, which shows up in the Romance and Germanic perfect periphrases.[1] The present perfect tense expresses events that occurred in the past and have direct implications in the present. It is constituted by an auxiliary in the present tense that bears person and number inflection, and a lexical verb in the form of a past participle. The perfect auxiliary contributes to the morphological realization of the tense and aspect value of the clause. A basic example from English is given in (1).

(1) *Present perfect tense*
    I   have   eaten
    subject perfect auxiliary past participle

The term *auxiliary selection* refers to the alternation between BE and HAVE as perfect auxiliaries in the Romance and Germanic periphrastic perfect constructions (Perlmutter 1978; Burzio 1986; Kayne 1993; Sorace 2000; Bjorkman 2011, 2018).[2] For the perfect auxiliary, some languages have at disposal either only HAVE (e.g., English, Spanish, Swedish, Portuguese, some varieties of Catalan, some

---

1. In Romance languages such as Italian, the perfect always involves perfective morphology and there are no combinations of the perfect with imperfective morphology, as is instead possible in English (Pancheva 2012). For this reason, I refer to the periphrases as in (1) as *perfect*, without entering any discussion about their semantics. In general, the perfect has characteristics of both temporal and aspectual forms. As a tense category, the perfect temporally locates an eventuality relative to some reference point, expressing anteriority (Iatridou, Anagnostopoulou, & Izvorski 2012:153). As an aspectual category, it describes a state that follows from a prior eventuality (Iatridou et al. 2012:154). The perfect should not be confused with the perfective, which is a type of aspect that conveys the meaning that the eventuality in question is completed (whereas the imperfective aspect presents a situation as ongoing (Iatridou et al. 2012:170)). For the difference between perfect and perfective, cf. Bjorkman (2018:326) and references therein.

2. With small caps I indicate the abstract morpheme corresponding to the root of the auxiliary. For instance, the label 'HAVE' stands for each possible occurrence of the verb 'have'.

Italo-Romance dialects), only BE (e.g., Scottish Gaelic, Welsh, few Italo-Romance varieties, some Slavic languages, Shetland English) or both forms in complementary distribution (see McFadden 2007: 2–12 for a cross-linguistic overview). When both auxiliaries are part of the same grammar, the choice of the auxiliary may depend on different factors, such as the argument structure (e.g., Italian, German, Dutch, French, and many other Romance and Germanic varieties; Sorace 2000; McFadden 2007) or the person specification of the subject (e.g., several Southern Italian dialects, such as Ariellese; Tuttle 1986; Kayne 1993; Manzini & Savoia 2005). An example of the former type is German. In (2) is shown that a change of location verb such as *ankommen* 'arrive' selects BE, whereas a verb that indicates a controlled process with agentive subject such as *arbeiten* 'work' requires HAVE.

(2) a. Der Zug ist   spät angekommen.
         the train be.PRS.3SG late arrive.PRTC
         'The train arrived late.'
     b. Kurt hat   den   ganzen   Sonntag   gearbeitet.
         Kurt have.PRS.3SG the.ACC.SG.M all.ACC.SG.M Sunday.ACC.SG.M work.PRTC
         'Kurt worked all day Sunday'   (Sorace 2000: 864, 874)

Languages of this type have *argument-structure-based auxiliary selection* (or, said otherwise, are argument-structure-driven systems). Languages where the form of the auxiliary depends on the person feature of the subject, instead, have *subject-based auxiliary selection* (or, said otherwise, are subject-driven systems). Such a language is Ariellese, an Italo-Romance variety spoken in Abruzzo, where first and second person subjects are always associated with BE, whereas a third person subject determines the use of HAVE. Example (3) shows that auxiliary selection is not dependent on the type of predicate: both BE and HAVE appear with transitive verbs (3a,b) and unaccusative verbs (3c,d).

(3) a. Ji   so'   fatte   na torte.
         NOM.1SG be.PRS.1SG make.PRTC a   cake
         'I have made a cake.'
     b. Esse   a   fatte   na torte.
         NOM.3SG have.PRS.3SG make.PRTC   a   cake
         'She has made a cake.'
     c. Ji   so'   cascate.
         NOM.1SG be.PRS.1SG fall.PRTC
         'I have fallen down.'
     d. Esse   a   cascate.   (D'Alessandro & Roberts 2010: 43, 44)
         NOM.3SG have.PRS.3SG fall.PRTC
         'She has fallen down.'

The aim of this book is to address the following questions: why the perfect auxiliary appears in these two forms within a single language, what drives the distribution of BE and HAVE, and how cross-linguistic data can be accounted for. These questions are highly relevant to Romance linguistics and theoretical linguistics for several reasons.

Firstly, previous studies on auxiliary selection present various problems, as I will discuss in the following section. This is particularly evident when trying to give the same explanation for auxiliary selection in Standard Italian and in those Italo-Romance varieties where auxiliary selection is subject-based, and when more complex structures such as Italian restructuring are considered. Hence, the linguistic theory that is available so far is not sufficient to give a comprehensive and accurate account of this phenomenon. This book aims at filling this gap in the theory, by giving a unified analysis of auxiliary selection for root clauses and restructuring in Italian and in Italo-Romance, which is also compatible with the theory of other relevant syntactic phenomena, such as participle agreement.

Secondly, it is clear that auxiliary selection cannot be lexical, but rather it depends on syntax (as evident in reflexive clauses and in restructuring). Thus, the understanding of this phenomenon sheds light on the architecture of the grammar and the interaction between the modules of syntax, morphology, and the lexicon. Since there is no syntactic account that can explain the exact distribution of the auxiliaries, it is certainly worth taking on the challenge and seeing in which respect we have to change our view of syntactic operations and their interactions. The solution of long-standing problems, such as auxiliary selection, may shed light on important questions, which constitute the background against which these problems become interesting from a scientific point of view. More concretely, a central debate in linguistics is on the locality conditions of operations. This study, by answering these questions about auxiliary selection, addresses the problem of minimality for the operation Agree.

Thirdly, this phenomenon is subject to extremely rich cross-linguistic variation, as evident just by looking at Standard Italian (argument-structure-driven auxiliary selection) and Eastern-Southern Italian dialects (subject-driven auxiliary selection). The new idea developed in this book is to consider these different splits as the output of the same syntactic structure and operations. Syntax is always the same: all these languages (even languages without any split, such as Spanish) have the ability to realize different feature specifications on the perfect auxiliary acquired via the operation Agree. The cross-linguistic variation stems from two points of variation in the lexicon: how the morpho-syntactic features are ordered on the lexical items, and how these features are realized by morpho-phonological exponents. Language variation is reduced to variability in the morpho-phonological features of the lexicon (Chomsky 1995:204,216). Thus, regarding the issue of linguistic variability, this book also contributes to the broader goals of understanding linguistic universals and cross-linguistic variation.

1.2   Gaps and inadequacies in the previous accounts

There are many different existing approaches to auxiliary selection. Semantic-based analyses have been proposed by Sorace (2000, 2004); Legendre (2007). Sorace (2000, 2004) identifies contextual and semantic factors for determining which auxiliary should be used with which verb, when a language has the choice between two lexical items. For intransitive verbs, Sorace (2000:863) proposes the hierarchy of auxiliary selection in Table 1.1, developed by subsequent works (Keller & Sorace 2003; Sorace 2004; Cennamo & Sorace 2007).

Table 1.1 Auxiliary selection hierarchy

change of location	BE
change of state	
continuation of a preexisting state	
existence of state	
uncontrolled process	
controlled process (motional)	
controlled process (non-motional)	HAVE

Verbs that belong to a semantic class at either the top or the bottom of this hierarchy systematically select for a single auxiliary. In contrast, in the central region of the scale auxiliary selection is not a clear-cut process and the choice depends on both aspectual and thematic factors. The cutting point between the two extremes of the scale is language-specific.

Although the hierarchy in Table 1.1 is useful for determining the argument structure of intransitive verbs, the distribution of auxiliaries in Standard Italian is not fully expected under this hierarchy. In particular, unergative verbs that express a controlled process require the use of HAVE (4a), as established in Table 1.1. However, if one of the arguments is reflexive or impersonal, the auxiliary changes to BE (4a,b).

(4)   a.   Teresa ha   risposto   a sua madre.
          Teresa have.PRS.3SG answer.PRTC at her mother
          'Teresa answered her mother.'

    b.   Teresa si=è   rispost-a.
        Teresa REFL.DAT.3SG=be.PRS.3SG answer.PRTC-SG.F
        'Teresa has answered herself.'

    c.   A scuola si=è   risposto   a tutte le domande.
        at school IMPERS=be.PRS.3SG answer.PRTC to all   the questions
        'At school people have answered all the questions.'

Even if one could argue that an unergative clause with a reflexive indirect object is less agentive than an unergative clause with a canonical indirect object, impersonal clauses resist this explanation. Moreover, the same facts hold for transitive verbs, as shown in (5).

  (5) a.   Teresa ha   lavato   le camicie.
           Teresa have.PRS.3SG wash.PRTC the shirts
           'Teresa has washed the shirts.'

         b.   Teresa si=è   lavat-a.
           Teresa REFL.ACC.3SG=be.PRS.3SG wash.PRTC-SG.F
           'Teresa washed herself.'

         c.   Teresa si=è   lavat-a   il vestito.
           Teresa REFL.DAT.3SG=be.PRS.3SG wash.PRTC-SG.F the dress
           'Teresa washed her dress (for herself).'

         d.   In lavanderia si=è   lavato   tutte le camicie.
           in laundry   IMPERS=be.PRS.3SG wash.PRTC all   the shirts
           'In the laundry room people have washed all the shirts.'

         e.   In lavanderia si=sono   lavat-e   tutte le camicie.
           in laundry   IMPERS=be.PRS.3PL wash.PRTC-PL.F all   the shirts
           'In the laundry room people have washed all the shirts.'

Extremely influential is the incorporation analysis developed by Kayne (1993); Cocchi (1995). The underlying intuition is that both possessive and perfect structures contain a dedicated syntactic head BE and an "abstract" nominal or prepositional head D/P. HAVE is the result of incorporation of the D/P head into the BE head. The first problem of these analyses is that they make use of no longer adopted assumptions that can be hardly adapted to current theories.[3] In addition

---

3. Kayne's (1993) analysis makes use of this D/P head, whose semantic content is not clear, it adopts some assumptions (lack of the D/P head with unaccusatives) and mechanisms (movement turns Ā-positions into A-positions) that should be questioned, it relies on the controversial notion of improper movement. Similar problems affect Cocchi's (1995) analysis: the use of improper movement, the presence of AgrS (which is always inactive in Italian, according to the author), the mono-argumental structure of transitive verbs in reflexive and impersonal clauses. Interestingly, Bjorkman (2011) has adopted the spirit of this analysis and rephrased it in a new

to technicalities, the main problem concerns the D/P head: it does not contribute to semantic interpretation, and it must be absent in certain structures, such as unaccusative sentences. Moreover, the empirical coverage for subject-driven auxiliary selection is not adequate: only the distribution BE-BE-HAVE (see Ariellese in (3)) can be derived by Kayne (1993), but many different patterns are attested (see also Coon & Preminger (2012) for the same problem).

There are also transitivity-based approaches, developed for Dutch by den Dikken (1994); Hoekstra (1994, 1999). HAVE is required to "retransitivize" the perfect participle, which is considered a passive participle. The main issue with these accounts is the assumption of a passive structure for perfect clauses, which is not straightforward for Italian. Moreover, it is not clear how to derive indirect reflexive clauses as in (5c). In addition, these approaches cannot be extended to subject-driven auxiliary selection.

A morphological analysis has been proposed by Arregi (2004) for Basque. In this language, auxiliary selection results from the presence or absence of a specific agreement morpheme, Agr_1, which expresses ergative agreement in transitive clauses. HAVE appears in those contexts where Agr_1 is present. Arregi's (2004) approach shares some similarities with the analysis developed in this book: the alternation HAVE/BE is just a morphological phenomenon, and it is related to φ-agreement. However, Arregi's (2004) analysis can be extended neither to argument-structure-driven systems (covering the Italian data in Section 2.2 of Chapter 2), nor to subject-driven systems.

The most recent accounts of auxiliary selection have been proposed by D'Alessandro & Roberts (2010); Bjorkman (2011, 2018). D'Alessandro & Roberts (2010: 51) argue for a rule of auxiliary selection: in Standard Italian, HAVE is inserted when v (which is the functional head that encodes the type of argument structure of the predicate) is non-defective, otherwise BE is chosen. Clearly, if the constraining factor is the argument structure itself, HAVE should show up with every transitive predicate, including transitive verbs with reflexive arguments (5b,c) and with impersonal arguments (5d,e). D'Alessandro & Roberts (2010) are aware of the problem of reflexives, but do not make any concrete suggestion about how to solve it (see footnote 7 in D'Alessandro & Roberts 2010: 51).

Bjorkman (2011, 2018) proposes an agreement-based analysis. HAVE appears when the argument structure of the verb contains an external argument, otherwise BE shows up. If it is the sole presence of the external argument that determines the form of the auxiliary, BE should not be expected in transitive reflexive

---

form within the minimalist framework. I refer the reader to Bjorkman (2011: 165–171) for an insightful discussion of the virtues and limitations of Kayne's (1993) approach.

clauses such as (5b,c), where there is an external argument. Bjorkman (2011, 2018) does not mention the case of reflexives.

The situation becomes even worse by looking at more complex structures. In restructuring configurations, a modal, aspectual or motion verb embeds a non-finite verb (Rizzi 1976; Wurmbrand 2003; Cinque 2004). This configuration is transparent for clause-bounded phenomena, for example movement of the clitic to the modal verb (clitic climbing, see Cardinaletti & Shlonsky 2004). Another characteristic is the possibility of so-called *auxiliary switch*: the auxiliary of the modal may be the one selected by the embedded verb. In (6a,b), we see that when a modal verb takes an unaccusative verb as its complement (Italian unaccusative verbs select BE as their auxiliary), then the auxiliary of the modal can be either BE (as determined by the lexical verb) or HAVE (as is the case when the modal verb selects a transitive verb). The choice seems to be optional, but it is influenced by other transparency effects such as clitic climbing (6c,d).

(6) a. Teresa ha   voluto   andar=ci   ieri.
          Teresa have.PRS.3SG want.PRTC go.INF=there yesterday
     b. Teresa è   volut-a   andar=ci   ieri.
          Teresa be.PRS.3SG want.PRTC-SG.F go.INF=there yesterday
     c. Teresa ci=è   volut-a   andare ieri.
          Teresa there=be.PRS.3SG want.PRTC-SG.F go.INF yesterday
     d. *Teresa ci=ha   voluto/-a   andare ieri.
          Teresa there=have.PRS.3SG want.PRTC/-SG.F go.INF yesterday
          'Teresa wanted to go there yesterday.'

To the best of my knowledge, this phenomenon has never been analyzed before in the literature (with the partial exception of Wurmbrand 2015: 236). In general, works on restructuring are not concerned with the explanation of auxiliary switch (Rizzi 1976; Cinque 2004; Cardinaletti & Shlonsky 2004), whereas works on auxiliary selection do not explain what happens in restructuring. If one tries to apply the analyses mentioned above to these data, it is impossible to explain the pattern in (6), as I will now explain.

The analysis by D'Alessandro & Roberts (2010) leads to wrong predictions. Four different scenarios can be constructed. Firstly, if the modal verb is always selected by a transitive v, HAVE is always inserted. Secondly, if the v selecting the modal verb is always defective, BE is invariably inserted. Thirdly, if the modal verb is not introduced by any v head and the only v is the one selecting the lexical verb (or if there is a matching condition between the higher and the lower v), then only BE should be possible when the modal verb selects an unaccusative verb. Fourthly, if there is optional alternation between a non-defective v and a defective v, then the auxiliary BE should also be possible with transitive verbs.

Bjorkman (2011) mentions the issue of auxiliary selection in restructuring and sketches an analysis based on Wurmbrand (2003). However, the approach by Bjorkman (2011, 2018) runs into wrong predictions. There are two possible scenarios: the subject of the modal verb is either its external argument, or an argument of the lexical verb (under a raising analysis, as assumed in this book). In the former, the expected auxiliary is only HAVE. This is not compatible with the data in (6). In the latter, the auxiliary is only either HAVE or BE. In fact, if the subject is an argument of the lexical verb, it must move to the matrix subject position, where it surfaces. If it has already been raised to matrix Spec,vP when Perf probes, it invariably leads to HAVE insertion. Alternatively, if it has not been raised yet when Perf probes, then the auxiliary of unaccusative verbs is realized as BE, but never as HAVE. In addition, if one assumes that different timings for subject raising give rise to the alternation in (6), then the same alternation is also expected when the modal verb selects a transitive verb, which is not the case. Hence, the pattern in (6) cannot be straightforwardly derived, unless adopting further assumptions.

Moreover, next to the auxiliary selection problem there is the issue of past participle agreement, which may show up in the perfect tense. Most analyses of participle agreement are not concerned with auxiliary selection and are, indeed, incompatible with current analyses of it. I discuss participle agreement in Chapter 6, where I suggest a new analysis that is fully compatible with the theory of auxiliary selection developed in this book.

To conclude, there is no existing analysis that can fully capture the data described in this section (and in Sections 2.2 of Chapter 2, 4.3 of Chapter 4) and can provide an explicit, derivational analysis of auxiliary selection.

1.3   The framework and the assumptions

This study is couched in *Minimalism* (Chomsky 1995, 2000, 2001). Minimalism (or the *Minimalist Program*) is a linguistic generative theory whose goal is to understand what language is and how it works. In this theory, the architecture of grammar is considered modular and derivational. Each module of grammar (syntax, morphology, phonology, semantics and the lexicon) is separated from the other ones, but it is connected via interfaces (*Y-model*). Each module feeds another one (e.g., syntax feeds morphology). Moreover, all operations obey strict cyclicity. For its modular and derivational character, Minimalism is the suitable framework to model the interaction between the components of grammar. In particular, given the division between modules, the framework can restrict the cross-linguistic variation to the morphology and the lexicon, keeping syntax universal.

In the Minimalist Program, syntactic dependencies can be shaped by two core operations: Merge (further distinguished into external and internal Merge) and Agree. Merge is the operation that is involved in building the structure. The operation that transfers information across the syntactic nodes is Agree. I adopt a standard view of Agree, as subject to feature matching, c-command, minimality, downward probing.

Next to Minimalism, for the morphological realization of syntactic structures I adopt *Distributed Morphology* (Halle & Marantz 1993; Harley & Noyer 1999). Syntax only manipulates abstract bundles of morpho-syntactic features. These are then substituted by morpho-phonological exponents that realize a subset or all of those features (in accordance with the *Subset Principle*). Under this architecture of grammar, the choice of the auxiliary is a matter of vocabulary insertion subject to the Subset Principle. This means that languages with a single auxiliary still have at their disposal the same syntactic operation needed for languages with auxiliary alternations, but they have a more restricted vocabulary inventory, which contains just a single exponent that can spell out the perfect head.

1.4 The proposal in a nutshell

1.4.1 Auxiliary selection is person-Agree

The main claim of this book is that auxiliary selection is the result of Agree for the person feature. This allows to reduce auxiliary selection to the independently needed operation Agree and to unify argument-structure-driven splits and subject-driven splits under the same mechanism. It also locates the problem of auxiliary selection completely in the syntax (and not below the selectional requirement of each verb), making the grammar more simple, by exploiting independently needed functional heads (different types of *v*) and the basic operation Agree.

I propose that the perfect auxiliary realizes a functional head Perf (similarly to D'Alessandro & Roberts 2010; Bjorkman 2011) that selects a verbal phrase *v*P, introduces the perfect semantics, determines the morphological form of the lexical verb and can agree for person. Both HAVE and BE realize the syntactic head Perf. Auxiliary selection depends on the presence or absence of additional featural information in the syntactic head that is realized by the perfect auxiliary. I argue that this information is a person feature. The result of Agree is not spelled out as person inflection on the verb, as is the case for example for Agree in T (cf. subject-verb agreement: *she love-s*), but it rather determines the lexical choice of the auxiliary. The vocabulary entries are presented in (7) and must be intended as follows. As long as Agree on Perf has succeeded (i.e., Perf has copied a person feature, no matter which specific value), HAVE will be the chosen auxiliary. Anytime that Agree does not return any value, the less specific exponent BE must be chosen instead, in accordance with the Subset Principle.

(7) a.   HAVE ↔ Perf[π:α]
     b.   BE ↔ Perf elsewhere

1.4.2   Nested Agree

As I have pointed out above, previous analyses of auxiliary selection fail to give a successful account of it. The data in Section 1.2 show that auxiliary selection in Italian depends on the features of the lower argument. In transitive clauses, where there is a direct object, the auxiliary is HAVE. If either there is no object (unaccusative verbs), or the object is φ-defective (reflexive pronouns), the auxiliary suddenly switches to BE. Thus, BE shows up every time that there is some kind of defectiveness in the structure: either v is defective and there is no accusative object (unaccusative verbs), or there is a featurally defective object (reflexive clauses).

Consequently, the head Perf must be sensitive to both the presence or absence of an object and its φ-features. Hence, Perf must contain a person probe that targets the person feature of the object, as it appears on v (after Agree between v and the object). Looking at the structure in (8), the goal for the probe [uπ] on Perf can only be the DP$_{sbj}$, given the minimality condition of Agree. In general, when two matching goals are available in the structure, the highest one should be selected, since it is the first one to be reached and it should be able to stop Agree.

(8)

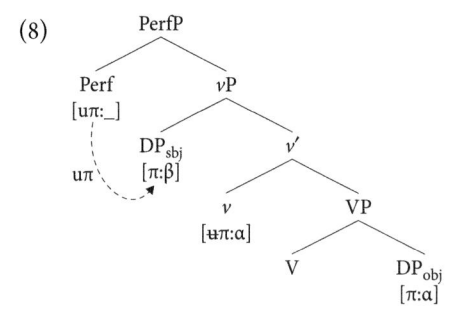

I have just said that the head Perf should Agree with the object (via v) across the subject because the features of the lower argument (reflexive direct or indirect object) influence the realization of the auxiliary. As the structure (8) shows, this operation would result in an anti-minimality configuration. To solve this problem, I introduce the principle of *Nested Agree*, defined in (9).

(9)   *Nested Agree*
  Let F_1 and F_2 be two ordered probes on the same head H. The search space of
  F_1 is the c-command domain of H.
  (i)   *Maximize*: if the Agree operation A_1 for the feature F_1 has targeted the goal
       G, then the subsequent Agree operation A_2 for the feature F_2 must also tar-
       get G.
  (ii) *No-backtracking*: If G is not a goal for F_2, the search space of F_2 is the c-
       command domain of G (not of H).

Nested Agree is a constraint on ordered operations that affects search domains.
Given the assumption that the features on the same head are extrinsically ordered
(Koizumi 1994; Sabel 1998; Heck & Müller 2006; Müller 2009; Georgi 2014),
Nested Agree states that a probe initiating an operation after another probe
located on the same head should pick out the same goal as the preceding probe.
This is expressed by the *Maximize* condition. Thereafter, in case the probe is not
satisfied yet, it must start its search exactly from the goal of the previous operation, without backtracking, as the *No-backtracking* condition prescribes. Nested
Agree stems from the combination of already proposed syntactic principles. In
particular, it can be derived by assuming (i) the Agree-Link theory (Arregi &
Nevins 2012), with the additional idea that an Agree-Link between two heads can
be used for multiple probe-features, (ii) feature ordering, (iii) ban against backtracking, (iv) downward Agree. It also contributes to the ongoing discussion on
the conditions on Agree for multiple probes and on minimality. In fact, Nested
Agree is a new way to deal with intervention effects. As I have just shown, a potential intervener (the subject) lies outside the search domain of the probe ([uπ:_] on
Perf), if its domain has been "reduced" by a previous operation ([uInfl:perf] on
Perf).

  For Standard Italian, the features on Perf are ordered as in (10) (the symbol >
indicates precedence). The derivation (for a transitive verb) is represented in (12)
and (11).

(10)   Perf [uInfl:perf] > [uπ:_]

(11)   Step 1: Agree for [uInfl:perf]

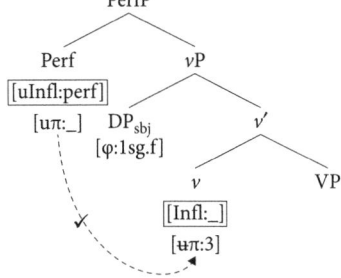

(12)   Step 2: Agree for [uπ:_]

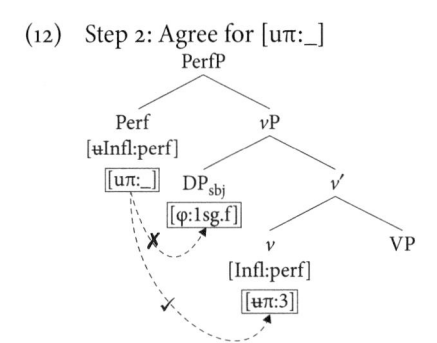

The first feature on Perf to be discharged is [uInfl:perf], as stated in (10). Its search space is the c-command domain of Perf. In (12), the [uInfl] feature on Perf checks the corresponding feature on *v*, which is then spelled out as a past participle. The second feature is a probe for π. The search space of [uπ:_] is not the c-command domain of Perf. In fact, since Perf has already carried out another operation, the domain of a further operation triggered by Perf is dependent on the previous operation. Consequently, as a first step, Perf probes *v* for the π-feature, thereby skipping the subject, as represented in (11). If Agree does not succeed, then the search starts downwards from *v*: the search space of [uπ:_] is the command domain of *v*. The result is that Perf copies the information from *v*, "seeing" both the argument structure type (similar to D'Alessandro & Roberts's (2010) approach) and the features of the lower argument. This results in a cyclic Agree (Legate 2005) configuration, where Perf agrees with the direct object due to the mediation of *v*.

In Standard Italian, the allomorph HAVE (7a) is inserted as long as Perf has succeeded in copying a person feature (as is the case in transitive argument structures). In contrast, BE shows up whenever there is some kind of defectiveness. Translated into Agree, this means either failed Agree (Preminger 2014), or Agree with π-defective items. If *v* is defective, it leads to failed Agree. This is the case of unaccusative clauses. Instead, in the case of reflexive clauses, the reflexive clitic is featurally defective: it enters the derivation with unvalued φ-features, which receive a value via binding (Reuland 2001). At the point when the person probe on v acts, Agree on v fails because the goal still bears unvalued π-features. The failure of Agree on v determines the failure of Agree on Perf, which leads to the insertion of the default allomorph BE, as shown by the vocabulary entries in (7).

An important consequence of this approach is that different orderings of features can account for language variation. In fact, the parametrization of the ordering of features results in the difference in auxiliary selection in Standard Italian and the Southern dialects.

(13) a. Perf [uInfl:perf] > [uπ:_] : π value from v Standard Italian
      b. Perf [uπ:_] > [uInfl:perf] : π value from DP_{sbj} Southern dialects

In Italian (argument-structure-driven auxiliary selection), the first probe [uInfl] restricts the domain of the subsequent probe [uπ] to v and its sister, with the result that v is the only possible goal for Perf. In Ariellese (person-driven auxiliary selection), [uπ] probes as first and its domain is the sister of Perf. In this system, the subject is the highest matching goal, independently of v. An Agree-based analysis has already been proposed by D'Alessandro (2017b) for auxiliary selection in Ariellese, but this idea has never been extended to Italian.

1.4.3 Restructuring

The analysis is also extended to restructuring. I assume that this configuration contains a special head, v_{restr}, which is independently needed to explain other behaviors of restructuring verbs (cf. previous accounts that merge the restructuring verb into a functional head, such as Cinque 2004). This head contains a double [Infl] feature, as indicated in (14). Via the double [Infl] feature, cyclic Agree between the embedded v and Perf takes place.

(14) v_{restr}: [uInfl:non-fin] > [uπ:_] > [Infl:_]

The optionality in auxiliary selection in restructuring derives from different sizes of the complement clause of the modal verb. Different complement sizes determine different search domains for Agree. There is no real optionality for auxiliary selection, but rather for the type of complement of v_{restr}.

1.4.4 Participle agreement

As far as participle agreement is concerned, I argue that in Standard Italian it is licensed by unchecked A-features that require successive cyclic movement (partly following Kayne 1989; D'Alessandro & Roberts 2008; Belletti 2017). This analysis has the advantages of being compatible with the theory on auxiliary selection and of making use of an independently proposed mechanism, edge features (Chomsky 2001; Müller 2010). The new idea here is that edge features are associated with a gender and number probe that targets the moving constituent (a clitic, the object of unaccusative verbs, and so on). Morphological agreement spells out the result of the operation Agree for the features # and γ. Given that auxiliary selection depends on the person feature, whereas participle agreement targets the gender and number features, with the exclusion of the person feature, these two phenomena are independent, as already argued by many previous studies (Loporcaro 1998; Legendre 2010; Belletti 2017).

1.5   Overview of the book

In this book, I propose a new analysis of auxiliary selection because this phenomenon has not yet found a comprehensive explanation in the previous literature, neither for Italian root clauses, nor for Italian restructuring, nor in comparison with other languages with subject-driven auxiliary selection, nor in accordance with other phenomena, such as participle agreement. The present analysis aims at filling this gap, with the broader goal of investigating Agree, the syntactic operation that allows to account for these data. By showing the explanatory adequacy of this operation, this book also contributes to the debate about Agree and its locality domain.

The main achievement of this work is the unification of argument-structure-based auxiliary splits (Standard Italian) and subject-based auxiliary splits (Southern-Eastern Italo-Romance) under the tool of π-Agree. The result is a typology that includes different Italo-Romance varieties and other languages with or without auxiliary selection (for the former, French; for the latter, Spanish). More in general, another important conclusion is the reduction of an apparently unrelated phenomenon (auxiliary selection) to Agree.

The main focus is on Standard Italian and Italo-Romance varieties, but the analysis can be extended to other languages as well. The data for Standard Italian comes from my introspection. I am a native speaker of a variety very close to Standard Italian: Tuscan Italian from the province of Lucca (Viareggio). For the purpose of auxiliary selection, this variety is identical to Standard Italian. My judgments have been compared to those of ten other speakers from the same area. When there is some disagreement, I indicate it with the symbol #, as is standardly done. In general, the core data presented in this book are uncontroversial. Judgments become less neat when I discuss more complex cases, such as restructuring (see Section 4.7), and some cases of participle agreement (see Section 6.6).

For other languages, data comes from the previous literature. The source is always indicated next to the examples.

The structure of the book is as follows. In Chapter 2, I argue for the theoretical proposal of Nested Agree, which is necessary to derive the data of Standard Italian. I present the detailed derivation of the Italian data in Chapter 3, as far as auxiliary selection is concerned. In Chapter 4, I extend my proposal regarding auxiliary selection to the more complex cases of restructuring. Other languages are discussed in Chapter 5. In particular, I present the other main type of auxiliary selection (subject-driven), but I also consider some further cases of argument-structure-driven systems, and other restrictions and interactions. In Chapter 6, I discuss the relevant issue of participle agreement in Italian and I propose an analysis that is compatible with the findings on auxiliary selection. I also briefly discuss other languages. In Chapter 7, I conclude by summarizing the main results of this work.

CHAPTER 2

Nested Agree

2.1 Introduction

In this chapter, I argue for the principle *Nested Agree*, which is a necessary ingredient for a derivational account of auxiliary selection. Nested Agree solves a locality issue that argument-structure-driven auxiliary selection poses. In Standard Italian, the alternation between the perfect auxiliaries BE and HAVE depends not only on the argument structure, but also on the features of the arguments. For this reason, auxiliary selection is modeled as Agree for the person feature. Locality prescribes that the perfect head should only agree with the subject, which is the most local goal for it. However, in Standard Italian the relevant features for auxiliary selection are those of the lower arguments, not those of the subject. Nested Agree justifies the dependency between the perfect head and the lower portion of the clause by regulating the domain of multiple probing. In particular, the dependency between two heads created by a feature is exploited by other features located on those heads. A potential intervener is ignored by a probe if the well-formed dependency created by a previous feature is exploited by this probe.

The structure of this chapter is as follows. In Section 2.2, I introduce the main data analyzed in this book. The claim that auxiliary selection is a form of Agree is stated in Section 2.3. Section 2.4 discusses the background assumptions and the general problem of locality. Nested Agree is introduced in Section 2.5. The relations of this principle with analogous proposals from the previous literature are discussed in Section 2.6. Section 2.7 summarizes the motivations for introducing Nested Agree and its effects.

2.2 Auxiliary selection in Standard Italian

Auxiliary selection is the alternation between the two allomorphs HAVE and BE for the perfect auxiliary in the Romance and Germanic periphrastic perfect constructions. In Standard Italian, this depends on the argument structure (Burzio 1986; Sorace 2000; McFadden 2007; Bjorkman 2011). With transitive verbs, the perfect auxiliary is realized as HAVE (1a), even in the presence of clitic arguments (1b). Intransitive verbs are located along a cline of unaccusativity that ranges between prototypical unergative verbs and prototypical unaccusative verbs. The former exhibit HAVE as the perfect auxiliary (1c), whereas the latter class shows BE (1d). In between there are different verbs that may combine with both auxiliaries (1e).

(1) a. Teresa ha   lavato   la camicia.
         Teresa have.PRS.3SG wash.PRTC the shirt
         'Teresa has washed the shirt.'
     b. Teresa l=ha   lavat-a.
         Teresa ACC.3SG.F=have.PRS.3SG wash.PRTC-SG.F
         'Teresa has washed her/it.'
     c. I   poliziotti hanno   lavorato   fino all'alba.
         the policemen have.PRS.3PL work.PRTC until to.the dawn
         'The policemen worked until dawn.'   (Sorace 2000:874)
     d. Maria è   venut-a   alla   festa.   (Sorace 2000:863)
         Maria be.PRS.3SG come.PRTC-SG.F to.the party
         'Maria has come to the party.'
     e. La pianta è   fiorit-a   / ha   fiorito   due
         the plant be.PRS.3SG blossom.PRTC-SG.F / have.PRS.3SG blossom.PRTC two
         volte quest'anno.   (Sorace 2000:865)
         times this year
         'The plant blossomed twice this year.'

The distribution of auxiliaries presents some further complications. In particular, the auxiliary is realized as HAVE only when transitive or unergative verbs take canonical arguments. If the arguments are reflexive pronouns or impersonal pronouns, the auxiliary suddenly becomes BE, even though the verb is transitive or unergative in the absence of reflexive/impersonal arguments. The reflexive pronoun can be merged as either the direct object (2a) or a dative benefactive argument (2b,c).

(2) a. Teresa si=è   lavat-a.
         Teresa REFL.ACC.3SG=be.PRS.3SG wash.PRTC-SG.F
         'Teresa washed herself.'
     b. Teresa si=è   lavat-a   la camicia.
         Teresa REFL.DAT.3SG=be.PRS.3SG wash.PRTC-SG.F the shirt
         'Teresa washed her shirt (for herself).'
     c. Teresa si=è   rispost-a.
         Teresa REFL.DAT.3SG=be.PRS.3SG answer.PRTC-SG.F
         'Teresa has answered herself.'

Note that if the reflexive argument is not the clitic pronoun *si*, but rather the reflexive phrase *se stess-o/a/i/e*, then the auxiliary is again HAVE (3a,b).

(3) a.   Teresa ha   lavato   se   stessa.
          Teresa have.PRS.3SG wash.PRTC REFL.ACC.3SG self
          'Teresa has washed herself.'

     b.   Teresa ha   lavato   la camicia per se   stessa.
          Teresa have.PRS.3SG wash.PRTC the shirt   for REFL.ACC.3SG self
          'Teresa has washed the shirt for herself.'

BE also emerges in impersonal clauses. These sentences are characterized by the impersonal pronoun *si* as a subject. The predicate can be transitive (4a,b), unergative (4c), or unaccusative (4d).

(4) a.   Ieri   al   ristorante si=sono   mangiat-i   spaghetti.
          yesterday at.the restaurant IMPERS=be.PRS.3PL eat.PRTC-M.PL spaghetti
          'Yesterday at the restaurant people have eaten spaghetti.'

     b.   Ieri   al   ristorante si=è   mangiato spaghetti.
          yesterday at.the restaurant IMPERS=be.PRS.3SG eat.PRTC spaghetti
          'Yesterday at the restaurant people have eaten spaghetti.'

     c.   Ieri   si=è   lavorato   fino all'alba.
          yesterday IMPERS=be.PRS.3SG work.PRTC until to.the dawn
          'Yesterday people have worked until dawn.'

     d.   Ieri   si=è   andat-i   alla   festa.
          yesterday IMPERS=be.PRS.3SG go.PRTC-PL.M to.the party
          'Yesterday people have gone to the party.'

To sum up, HAVE only appears with transitive and unergative verbs when they select for canonical arguments. When one of the arguments is a reflexive clitic or an impersonal clitic, the auxiliary can only be BE. BE is also the only option with unaccusative verbs.

Hence, in argument-structure-driven auxiliary selection not only the type of argument structure counts, but also the features of the arguments. This leads to my main claim: auxiliary selection is an instance of agreement for the person feature.

2.3   Auxiliary selection is π-Agree

In the previous Section 2.2, I have shown that in Standard Italian the choice of the auxiliary depends on both the presence or absence of a direct object (e.g., transitive vs. unaccusative verbs), and the features of the object (e.g., canonical transitive vs. reflexive transitive verbs). This means that the morpho-phonological realization of the perfect auxiliary must depend on the morpho-syntactic features of the object. The necessary conclusion is that the features of the arguments must be taken into account not only in grammars where auxiliary selection is subject-driven (see Example (3) in Chapter 1), but even in grammars where it is argument-structure-driven, as in Standard Italian.

In the Minimalist Program (Chomsky 1995, 2000, 2001), the operation that transfers information along the syntactic spine is Agree. Hence, I argue that auxiliary selection is the result of Agree. In particular, I suggest that the crucial operation is Agree for the person (π) feature for the two following reasons. Firstly, in Italian the auxiliary depends on the features of the arguments (reflexive vs. non-reflexive, and impersonal vs. non-impersonal arguments). This fact can be easily modeled by assuming that different arguments bear different sets of φ-features: defective vs. non-defective. Secondly, in those dialects where auxiliary selection is subject-driven, the auxiliary mainly depends on the person feature of the subject (Loporcaro 2007; Ledgeway 2019).

Following D'Alessandro & Roberts (2010); Bjorkman (2011), I assume that the head Perf, which is the locus of insertion of the perfect auxiliary, is a functional head that selects a vP and it is selected by T. I propose that Perf agrees with v for the person feature. In this way, both the argument structure of the verb and the features of the arguments are taken into account. Depending on the result of this operation, Perf is spelled out by different morpho-phonological exponents (HAVE or BE).

The two verbal roots HAVE and BE realize the same syntactic functional head Perf and are in competition for vocabulary insertion. The auxiliary split results from the availability of two possible allomorphs in the vocabulary inventory of Standard Italian for the morpho-syntactic bundle of features in Perf. Thus, auxiliary selection is a matter of vocabulary insertion.[4]

2.4 Setting the stage

2.4.1 Agree

In the Minimalist Program, grammar is only equipped with two operations: *Merge* (further distinguished into external and internal Merge) and *Agree*. Agree is an operation that establishes a relation between a syntactic head α and a feature F in some restricted search space (Chomsky 2000: 101). Agree is initiated by a type

---

4. Languages with a single perfect auxiliary (such as English, Spanish) only have a single lexical entry at their disposal (see Chapter 5). Languages with split auxiliary selection have a rich system of vocabulary entries: different allomorphs realize different outputs of syntax. This consideration is in line with the idea that language variation should be reduced to variability in the morpho-phonological features of the lexicon (Chomsky 1995: 204,216).

of feature called *probe*, conventionally identified by the prefix *u-*, which targets another feature called *goal*.[5]

Agree is constrained by different conditions. Firstly, it is subject to a *matching condition*. Agree happens under feature identity: the two involved features must be of the same type (Chomsky 2000:122). A second aspect is the *interpretability condition*. Agree is an operation that leads to the elimination of uninterpretable features from syntactic heads for interface reasons (Chomsky 2000:122). The probe is an uninterpretable instance of a feature. The relevant goal is a feature of the same type, but interpretable. Regarding this issue, I go back to the original definition of Agree proposed by Chomsky (2000): being a probe means being uninterpretable, but not necessarily unvalued. Hence, I do not assume that interpretability coincides with valuation (Chomsky 2001:5), following here Pesetsky & Torrego (2007) for the proposal that valuation and interpretability are independent conditions. More concretely, I consider a probe to be any feature of the form *uF*, where the prefix *u-* indicates the ability and the need to start an Agree search. With the term *uninterpretable*, I refer to the activation of a feature in the syntactic derivation (and not to the process of interpretation at the interfaces). The uninterpretability of a feature, indicated by the diacritic [u-], means that the feature can and must trigger an operation and has not done it yet. Hence, uninterpretability is not a semantic property, but rather the signal that the derivation is not completed yet. The uninterpretability is deleted when the operation triggered by that feature is carried out, even when the probe does not find any matching goal. The primary aim of Agree is not valuation, but it is instead the "erasure of uninterpretable features of probe and goal" (Chomsky 2000:122). Hence, Agree can fail in terms of valuation, as proposed by Béjar (2003); Preminger (2014).

The result of Agree is as follows: [uF] →[u̶F]. The more concrete configurations, depending on the make-up of the probe and goal, are schematized in (5).

(5) Agree: [uF]→[u̶F]
    a.   Agree for an unvalued probe [uF:_]
        (i)   if goal [F:α], then probe becomes [u̶F:α]
        (ii) if goal [F:_], then probe becomes [u̶F:_]
        (iii) if no goal, then probe becomes [u̶F:_]
    b.   Agree for a valued probe [uF:α]
        (i)   if goal [F:α], then probe becomes [u̶F:α]
        (ii) if goal [F:β], then probe becomes [u̶F:α][6]

---

5. Probes and goals are *features* that are involved in Agree. However, note that I use these terms in two different ways: I mean both the *features* themselves and the *heads* that bear them (meaning the position they occupy in the syntactic structure). I distinguish these two meanings when relevant (for example, when a single head bears more than one probe).

(iii)   if goal [F:_], then probe becomes [ʉF:α] and goal [F:α]
(iv)   if no goal, then probe becomes [ʉF:α]

Finally, Agree is also subject to *locality*, which can be further distinguished into two conditions. The *directional condition* states that the probe is only allowed to look in its c-command domain. I take this condition on c-command to imply that only *downward Agree* is possible (*pace* Zeijlstra 2012). This may follow from the bottom-up nature of the derivation. As soon as a new head is merged, it is the highest one in the structure and it c-commands the whole search domain. This configuration, in addition to the *Earliness Principle* (Pesetsky 1989), makes downward Agree the natural possibility.[7] The second aspect of locality is the *minimality condition*. This prescribes that the closest goal to the probe (i.e., the highest in the structure) should be chosen, in case of more than one matching goal in the c-command domain. Closeness is defined as follows. For a probe P, its c-command domain is its sister S(P). A matching feature G is the closest one to P if in S(P) there is no J matching P such that G is in S(J) (Chomsky 2000:122). The minimality condition has been formalized in many different ways, for example with the principle of *Relativized Minimality* (Rizzi 1990) and the *Minimal Link Condition (MLC)* (Fanselow 1991; Ferguson & Groat 1994; Chomsky 1995, 2001), given in (6).

(6)   *Minimal Link Condition*   (Chomsky 2001:27)
An Agree operation involving the probe α and the goal β can only apply if there is no δ such that (i) δ c-commands β (ii) δ is c-commanded by α but not by β, (iii) δ bears the relevant feature.

---

6. The configuration with a valued probe encountering a valued goal with a non-matching value has yet to be fully understood. The result of this operation appears to be related to the status of a feature with respect to defective intervention. If a feature F is subject to defective intervention, the result is as schematized in (5b)–(ii): Agree stops when the probe encounters a matching feature, independently of its value. In contrast, if a feature F is not subject to defective intervention, a valued matching feature is invisible for a valued probe. In this scenario, if a probe [uF:α] encounters the possible goals [F:β]/[F:α], then the probe remains [uF:α] and keeps on searching until its domain is exhausted. An operation of this type, where the probe is valued and is not subject to defective intervention, might be case assignment, although further research is needed. If this approach is on the right track, the Agree operations triggered by valued and unvalued probes may have different search requirements: an unvalued probe looks for a matching feature, whereas a valued probe looks for an *unvalued* matching feature.

7. In this analysis, I do not take into consideration the possibility of cyclic upward expansion (Béjar & Rezac 2009), although it might be the case that this happens for certain probes in certain languages. In general, if the aim of Agree is the erasure of uninterpretable features and not their valuation, there is no need to expand the domain upwards when the probe has not found a matching goal.

2.4.2   A problem of minimality

As I have stated in Section 2.3, the head Perf must access the π-feature of the internal argument. However, this information is not local to the head Perf. Even if the π-feature of the object is located on the head v (after a prior Agree operation), at least the subject should be closer than v to the π-probe on the perfect head. The required configuration, illustrated in (7), should be impossible, since it creates a non-local Agree configuration.

(7)   Search of Perf for π-features

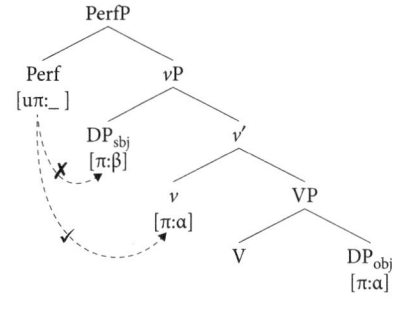

In (7), Agree between Perf and v for [π] violates the minimality condition discussed in Section 2.4.1. When Perf probes for [uπ:_], it should not be able to skip over the subject. Hence, auxiliary selection in Standard Italian poses a problem of minimality. The features of the object on v cannot be copied onto Perf, since there is a competitor that is closer to Perf than the object (namely, the subject).

Minimality is a computational requirement that reduces the search space up to the first matching goal. Although minimality seems to play a role in many cases, it has already been recognized that there exist many scenarios of anti-minimality, such as order-preserving movement and anti-superiority effects (Richards 1997; Starke 2001; Lahne 2012). These "problematic" data are generally accounted for by resorting to other principles or operations such as *Tucking-in* (Mulders 1997; Richards 1997, 2001) or *Equidistance* (Chomsky 2001). Unfortunately, these principles do not offer a straightforward way to account for the grammaticality of the configuration in (7).

Tucking-in constitutes a solution against anti-minimality movement paths, but it is not related to Agree. If applied to Agree, it could eventually give rise to Multiple Agree with both goals (including the non-local goal), rather than to agreement with the lower goal, as required in (7). In the Multiple Agree scenario, where the features of both the object and the subject are simultaneously represented on Perf, one would need an additional system of indices in order to distinguish the different sources of the features, or an "overwriting" mechanism that favors the features of the lower argument.[8] Moreover, Tucking-in violates the strong interpretation of the *Strict Cycle Condition* in (8), as far as I understand.

(8) *Strict Cycle Condition (SCC)*   (Chomsky 1973: 243)
      Within the current cyclic domain α, no operation may exclusively affect positions within another cyclic domain β that is dominated by α.

Since I assume strict cyclicity as a principle of grammar, I do not adopt Tucking-in.

Equidistance does not help here either, since it is defined for multiple specifiers and not for a head and its specifier (as the DP_{sbj} and v are). A principle that favors the head with respect to the specifier (assuming that there is no distinction between the features of the head and those of its projections) is the *A-over-A condition*: an operation can only affect the higher, more inclusive category (Chomsky 1964, 1973; Hornstein 2009; Roberts 2010). The dependency between Perf and v represented in (7) could be derived by resorting to the following specific interpretation of the A-over-A condition: if a probe can be checked either with a head, or with an edge element, it must be checked with the head (Müller 2004: 19). However, this version of A-over-A minimality leads to some wrong predictions. In Section 2.5.3, I discuss in detail why the A-over-A solution does not work for the problem of auxiliary selection.

We are therefore faced with a puzzle. In order to derive the dependency of perfect auxiliary on both the argument structure and the features of the arguments, Perf must *always* skip the subject DP and carry out Agree with v. This violates minimality, though, and no existing principle seems to solve the problem, as discussed here and in the remainder of this chapter. In the next section, I provide an alternative way to deal with this minimality violation. I introduce the principle *Nested Agree*, which follows from the combination of other existing principles of

---

8. The Multiple Agree analysis is not easily feasible for the following reasons. (i) In order to derive BE in impersonal and in reflexive clauses, one would need further assumptions such as that impersonal *si* cannot be agreed with, and that a DP and a bound reflexive object only "count" as a single argument. This is problematic because at the point of the derivation in which Perf probes, the reflexive pronoun has already been bound by the external argument and bears valued φ-features (see Section 3.3.2 in Chapter 3 for details). Hence, the probe on Perf should search not only for π-features, but also for features involved in binding, such as [var] features (Hicks 2009). (ii) Indirect reflexive clauses (*Teresa si è lavata la camicia* in (2b)) still resist this explanation, since there are at least two sets of valued features (one from the external argument, one from the internal argument), but the auxiliary is BE. (iii) Restructuring contexts (see Chapter 4) allow for both auxiliaries with the same number and type of arguments, so auxiliary selection cannot depend on how many arguments are in the structure (but rather on their accessibility).

syntactic theory. By making use of Nested Agree, I offer in Chapter 3 an explicit analysis of auxiliary selection in Standard Italian.

2.5   Nested Agree

Nested Agree is a principle on subsequent applications of Agree. In particular, it restricts the search space of a probe on a head depending on previous operations carried out by the same head. The definition is given in (9).

(9)   *Nested Agree*
      Let F_1 and F_2 be two ordered probes on the same head H. The search space of F_1 is the c-command domain of H.
      (i)   *Maximize*: if the Agree operation A_1 for the feature F_1 has targeted the goal G, then the subsequent Agree operation A_2 for the feature F_2 must also target G.
      (ii)   *No-backtracking*: If G is not a matching goal for F_2, the search space of F_2 is the c-command domain of G (not of H).

Nested Agree prescribes that a probe initiating an operation after another probe located on the same head should pick out the same goal as the preceding probe did. If the probe does not find any matching feature, then it must search the sister of the current node, instead of its sister. Let me now explain the definition in (9) in detail.

   The premise in (9) states the background assumption that if a head triggers more than one operation, then the triggering features on the head are extrinsically ordered (Koizumi 1994; Sabel 1998; Heck & Müller 2006; Müller 2009; Georgi 2014). It also clarifies that the domain of Agree is the structure that is c-commanded by the probe (i.e., its sister). The *Maximize* condition in (9)–(i) expresses the requirement that two (or more) Agree operations triggered by the same head must target the same goal in a sequential fashion. In particular, if a head undergoes more than one search operation, then the second search algorithm starts from the position in the tree returned by the first operation, and so on. The *No-backtracking* condition in (9)–(ii) prescribes that, if the goal-head of the previous operation cannot satisfy the probe because it does not bear any matching feature, then the probe starts its search exactly from this position.[9] In

---

9. The *No-backtracking* condition of Nested Agree might remind the reader of an anti-locality principle (Abels 2003, 2012) in the following scenario. A local goal-feature for the second operation may not be targeted, if the first operation has returned a goal-head that is non-local for the second operation (but is local for the first one). Even though this is an anti-locality effect, I do

other words, a probe cannot go back to already skipped goals, if these have been bypassed by another probe located on the same head. The reason lies in the fact that the probe has already reached a lower position than the syntactic position from which the search originates. Once the probe has arrived to at this position, it cannot backtrack.

I represent the Nested Agree configuration in the following trees. In (10) and (11) we have a structure where the *Maximize* condition leads to successful Agree.

(10) Agree for $[uF_1:\_] \rightarrow [\texttt{u}F_1:x]$ from β

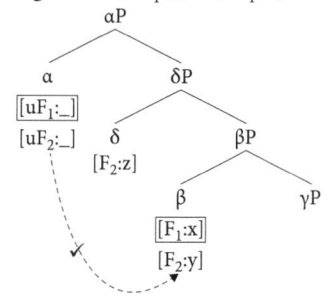

(11) Agree for $[uF_2:\_] \rightarrow [\texttt{u}F_2:y]$ from β

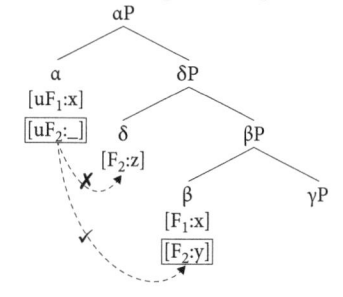

In (10), the features $[F_1]$, $[F_2]$ are ordered on the head α. The search space of the first one to be discharged is the whole c-command domain. $[uF_1]$ targets the highest c-commanded matching goal, F_1 on β. The second operation, triggered by $[uF_2]$, is subject to Nested Agree, since it is preceded by another operation on the same head. Thus, the search space of $[uF_2]$ is reduced: it starts where the previous

---

not consider Nested Agree as an anti-locality principle for two reasons. Firstly, the first Agree operation obeys locality, whereas the second operation would be subject to anti-locality. Since both are Agree operations, the fact that Agree may be subject to either locality or anti-locality is an unwanted contradiction. Secondly, different goals can be anti-local to different extents. The target of the second operation is not the most anti-local goal (i.e., the lower possible goal), but rather the "highest anti-local" goal. This requires some technical implementations and, more importantly, hides a shadow of locality in the anti-locality condition.

operation has stopped. Within its domain, [uF$_2$] targets the highest c-commanded matching goal, as (11) illustrates. In (11), the head β is a matching goal for [uF$_2$]: [uF$_2$] agrees with β, thereby skipping the feature [F$_2$] on δ.

When the "Nested-Agree-goal" does not bear a matching feature, the search proceeds downward from here. In trees (12) and (13), I show the case where the probe cannot be satisfied by the previous goal, and must start a new search within the sister of the current node, according to the No-backtracking condition.

(12)   Agree for [uF$_1$:_] with β

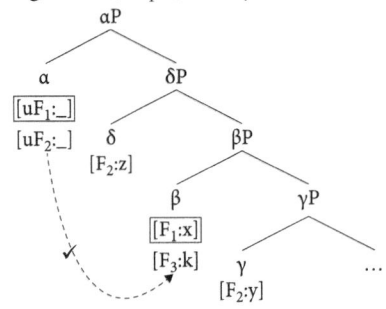

(13)   Agree for [uF$_2$:_] with γ

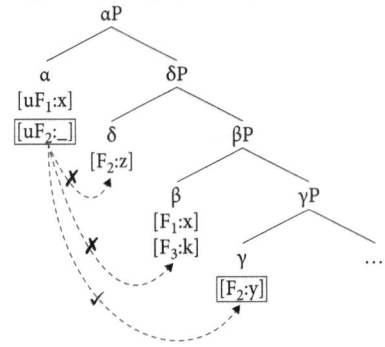

In tree (13), the goal of the previous operation (β) is not a matching goal for the probe [uF$_2$], since it does not bear the feature [F$_2$]. Consequently, the probe goes on downward without backtracking, until it finds a relevant goal (on the head γ in (13)), or until its domain is exhausted.

In case the first operation of a head has failed to return a result, Nested Agree cannot be applied to the subsequent operation, since there is no previous goal to check. Hence, the search domain of this second probe is simply the sister of the probe.

Nested Agree allows to treat minimality violations under a new perspective. In fact, as tree (11) shows, the minimality condition can be circumvented if the target of Agree β is an item that has already been involved in an Agree relation with the probe α, even though δ intervenes. Despite its more embedded position, $[F_2]$ on β is actually the closest possible goal for $[uF_2]$ on α. In fact, δ lies outside the locality domain of $[uF_2]$, since its domain has been "relativized" by the previous operation for $[F_1]$. Nested Agree causes the gradual reduction of the search domain for the features located on the same syntactic position after each operation is carried out: Agree domains are dynamic and interdependent. Note that the relations represented in trees (12) and (13) are all local, but the sequence of operations has produced a representation in which locality is not visible anymore (see also Chomsky 1995: 205 for representations that do not seem local because of sequential application of operations). This means that intervention is not only tied to the featural specification of the involved items, but also to the order of operations they are involved in.

2.5.1   Application of Nested Agree to the Perf head

Let us go back to auxiliary selection. I propose that the head Perf bears two probes: one for the feature [Infl], one for the feature [π]. The Infl-feature is responsible for the morphological realization of the lexical verb as a past participle (see also Bjorkman 2011 for [Infl] on Perf). In particular, I suggest that Perf bears the valued probe [uInfl:perf], which needs to be checked with a feature of the same type, located on v. The probe is located on Perf (and not on v) because it is the higher aspectual/temporal head Perf that determines the form of the lexical verb. Hence, the item that induces the Agree operation is the higher one.[10] The Agree operation triggered by [uInfl:perf] causes v to be realized as a past participle in the morpho-phonology.

The π-probe on Perf is responsible for the dependency of the perfect auxiliary on both the argument structure and the features of the arguments. In fact, there must be some feature that determines auxiliary selection (another alternative is a [D] feature, according to Kayne 1993; Bjorkman 2018). As explained in Section 2.3, I consider [π] to be the relevant feature because argument-structure-driven auxiliary selection is sensitive to featurally defective arguments (reflexive and impersonal arguments), and subject-driven auxiliary selection depends on the person feature of the subject.

In Standard Italian, these features are ordered as in (14).

(14)   Perf: [uInfl:perf] > [uπ:_]

---

10. For similar inflectional dependencies, see the phenomenon of German *status government* (Bech 1955); for a similar implementation of morphological selection in syntax, see Wurmbrand (2012a).

The derivation where Nested Agree operates is given in (15) and (16). When Perf is merged, its Infl-probe checks the corresponding features on *v*, which is the closest matching goal, as represented in (15). After Infl-Agree, the π-probe on Perf starts its search. This operation (π-Agree) is constrained by Nested Agree because there has been a previous operation (Infl-Agree) carried out by Perf, which has given as a result a feature on the head *v*. Due to Nested Agree (Maximize condition), Perf probes *v* for the π-feature, thereby skipping the subject, as (16) shows. If *v* contains a matching feature (as is the case for transitive verbs, see Section 3.2.2 of Chapter 3), the π-probe agrees with *v*. If π-Agree with *v* does not succeed (as is the case for unaccusative verbs, where *v* does not contain any π-value, see again Section 3.2.2 of Chapter 3), then the search continues downward starting from *v*. The search domain of [uπ:_] is the c-command domain of *v*, and no item above *v* can be reached anymore (No-backtracking condition).

(15)   Step 1: [uInfl:perf] → [u̶Infl:perf]

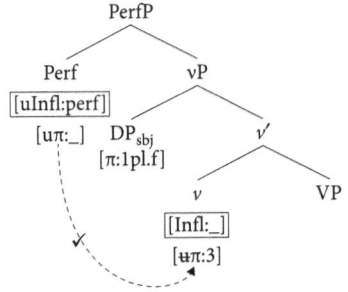

(16)   Step 2: [uπ:_] → [u̶π:3]

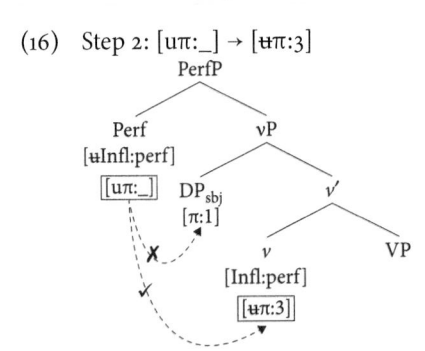

As shown in (16), Perf π-probes either *v* or anything below it (in accordance with the *Phase Impenetrability Condition (PIC)*, Chomsky 2000:108, Chomsky 2001:13, see (4) in Chapter 3), instead of the more local goal DP$_{sbj}$. By agreeing with *v*, Perf "sees" both the argument structure type (similarly to what is suggested in D'Alessandro & Roberts 2010), and the features of the lower argument (as required for reflexive clauses, see Section 3.3.2 of Chapter 3).

The vocabulary entries for auxiliary selection in Standard Italian are given in (17).

(17) a. /HAVE/ ↔ Perf[π:α]
      b. /BE/ ↔ Perf elsewhere

The most specific allomorph HAVE is inserted whenever the π-probe on Perf has copied a person value, whereas BE is inserted if either Agree has failed or the goal is defective as far as the person feature is concerned (for details, see Chapter 3).

This analysis of auxiliary selection as Agree between Perf and the object (via *v*) shares some similarities with the proposal of *cyclic Agree*, a type of long distance agreement (Legate 2005). According to this theory, Agree can apply in an apparently non-local way if it operates in a cyclic fashion, by checking features on every intervening phasal head. For instance, in case of a postverbal nominative object, the head T can agree with the object via mediation of *v*, due to cyclic Agree. In the present case, the features of the object, which are otherwise inaccessible for Perf because of the Phase Impenetrability Condition, are copied first on *v* via Agree, then from *v* to Perf via another Agree operation (specifically, Perf is able to reach *v* because of Nested Agree).

2.5.2   On feature ordering

The assumption of ordered features is a crucial ingredient of Nested Agree. In general, operations triggered by features that enter the derivation at the same time (i.e., on the same head) can either apply simultaneously, or sequentially. Both the simultaneous and sequential approaches require assumptions regarding the structure of syntactic elements and operations. I adopt the sequential view because it fits a strictly derivational view of syntax. If only a single operation can apply at any given stage of the derivation, then features on the same head *have to be ordered*.

The idea that syntactic elements contain sequences of ordered features originally goes back to Koizumi (1994). This author proposes that the head of a phrase with multiple specifiers contains hierarchically ordered features that have to be checked in a certain order (specifically, he deals with hierarchically ordered Top- and Neg-features). The same intuition is also found in Chomsky (1995:179). In particular, Chomsky (1995) proposes that if the features on a lexical item are checked in a certain order, then it is possible to rephrase Baker's (1985)'s Mirror Principle within the Minimalist Program. Sabel (1998:135) also makes use of feature ordering to derive the fact that movement to specifier positions has to precede movement to adjoined positions. Sabel (1998:151) also proposes that C can bear more than one [wh]-feature. These are hierarchically ordered and must be checked in different specifier positions by different wh-phrases.

Evidence for postulating a specific feature ordering comes from two aspects: the interactions between different operations, and the existence of a typology of languages built on different feature orderings. The transparent interactions between operations in terms of feeding and bleeding point at an organization of the features in a fixed order (Georgi 2014: 250), and in particular the ordering is fixed in a language-specific manner (Georgi 2014: 30,129). For instance, Müller (2009); Assmann, Georgi, Heck, Müller, & Weisser (2015) derive the difference between nominative-accusative languages and ergative-absolutive languages by reordering Merge and Agree. For other analyses where Merge and Agree are ordered on a single head, see Bruening (2005); van Koppen (2005); Anand & Nevins (2006); Lahne (2008); Müller (2009); Asarina (2011); Halpert (2012); Richards (2013); Kalin & van Urk (2015); Kučerová (2016); Bjorkman (2018).

Some orders of features might be universal, as has been proposed for the general tendency of probing for person before probing for number (Béjar & Rezac 2003; Preminger 2011; Coon & Keine 2020). In the case of extrinsic orderings, a decisive aspect is crosslinguistic variation, which should arise by reordering operation-inducing features (Heck & Müller 2006; Georgi 2014). Whenever a ranking of features is proposed for a language, if the opposite order is available in another variety, then the analysis is supported by these data. For instance, different dialects of Icelandic are modeled with different orders of operations (Agree on T and raising of dative experiencer) by Sigurðsson & Holmberg (2008). Feature ordering (of agreement features on C) is also used by Ershova (to appear) to model islandhood in West Circassian; dialects that differ on this point have different feature orderings. Optionality within the same language is modeled by assuming variable feature orderings by Puškar (2018). Hence, the existence of a typology of languages built on different orderings legitimates the validity of an analysis based on feature orderings.

This book provides support in favor of extrinsic ordering of features as an explanation for language variation. By ordering the features on Perf, not only do I offer an adequate analysis of auxiliary selection in Italian, but I also allow for cross-linguistic variation. In fact, as I will show in Chapter 5, if the order of the features on Perf that I assume for Standard Italian is reversed, subject-driven auxiliary selection of Southern Italo-Romance dialects is derived. The resulting typology is exemplified in (18).

(18) a. Perf [uInfl:perf] > [uπ:_] (argument-structure-driven auxiliary selection)
      b. Perf [uπ:_] > [uInfl:perf] (subject-driven auxiliary selection)

In Standard Italian and argument-structure-based auxiliary selection in general, [Infl] probes before [π], as stated in (18a). It follows that Perf π-probes v, with the consequence that auxiliary selection depends on the argument structure and, in particular, on the π-feature of the object. In Southern Italian dialects and subject-driven auxiliary selection in general, [π] probes before [Infl], as (18b) indicates. Hence, Perf agrees for [π] with the DP$_{sbj}$: auxiliary selection depends on the features of the external argument.

2.5.3 Against A-over-A type of minimality

As explained in Section 2.5.1, the head Perf is able to probe v for the person feature due to Nested Agree. Other syntactic principles do not lead to this result. I have already touched upon Tucking-in and Equidistance in Section 2.4.2. In this section, I discuss the *A-over-A principle* (Chomsky 1964; Hornstein 2009; Roberts 2010; Preminger 2019).

The A-over-A principle derives from the theory of *Bare Phrase Structure (BPS)* (Chomsky 1964): non-terminal levels of projection (βP and β⁻ in tree (19)) are the same syntactic object as the head (β). They can only be distinguished in relational terms, meaning that a single instance of β dominates or is dominated by another instance of itself. As far as the features are concerned, βP, β⁻ and β cannot be distinguished: they all bear the same featural specification, since they are instances of the same object.

(19) *A-over-A configuration*

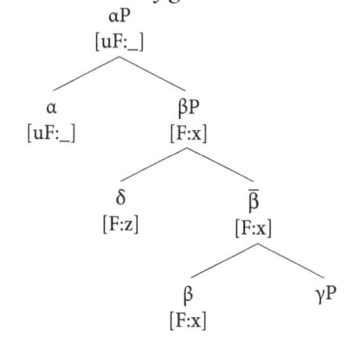

Let us now consider the probe [uF:_] on α in tree (19). Without assuming BPS, the maximal projection βP does not contain any feature (except the categorical feature that allows it to be selected by α) and is "transparent" for Agree. Consequently, the closest possible goal is located in the specifier of the head of that maximal projection (i.e., δ). In contrast, if BPS is assumed, the features on the maximal projection (equal to the features on the head) are the closest possible matching goals for the higher probe. In fact, the probe scans its c-command domain starting from its sister, the maximal projection βP. If this bears the relevant feature, Agree stops. Otherwise, [uF:_] proceeds its search downwards, targeting firstly Spec,β, secondly β, and thirdly Comp,β.

Coming back to auxiliary selection, A-over-A minimality (i.e., XP is closer than X for a higher probe) seems to offer a simple way to let the head Perf probe v, thereby skipping the DP_{sbj}. This happens if Perf probes vP as the closest goal, and this bears the same features of v (because of BPS). However, this analysis faces various problems and leads to some wrong predictions.

First of all, such an account can be hardly adapted to cross-linguistic variation. Since it is based on a general principle of the syntactic theory (BPS), in order to account for cross-linguistic differences it should be assumed that BPS is an active principle in one language (e.g., Standard Italian), but is not in another language (e.g., Ariellese). Hence, A-over-A cannot straightforwardly account for the difference between subject-based and argument-structure-based auxiliary selection, which can be easily derived by Nested Agree (see discussion in this chapter around (18), and Chapter 5).

Another wrong prediction concerns object agreement. Under the A-over-A principle, a language like English is expected to exhibit object agreement on T, which is of course not the case. In fact, assuming that v bears a π-probe that is valued by the object, this probe is projected onto vP. When the probe on T looks for π-features, it is satisfied by vP, which is the closest possible goal, thereby leading to object agreement instead of subject agreement. Hence, we should conclude that the A-over-A principle is not active in English. For Standard Italian, we should say that the head Perf agrees in accordance with the A-over-A principle, whereas the head T agrees without following it (since T agrees with the DP_{sbj} rather than with vP). This is of course a prediction that imposes the rejection of the A-over-A principle.

Another problem related to auxiliary selection is found with unaccusative predicates (see Section 3.3.5 of Chapter 3 for the complete analysis). In general, it is necessary for the derivation of unaccusative sentences (exhibiting BE) to be different from that of transitive sentences (exhibiting HAVE). I model this requirement as failed Agree in the former, and successful Agree in the latter. Assuming A-over-A minimality, however, both derivations result in successful Agree. Let me explain how.

According to the vocabulary entries in (17), HAVE is inserted when Agree succeeds, and BE when it does not. This means that in the derivation with unaccusative verbs Perf should fail to copy a person value, leading to insertion of the allomorph BE. The general idea is that unaccusative verbs combine with a defective v, which bears no π-probe. However, in this syntactic configuration A-over-A minimality leads to successful agreement on Perf, and consequently, to the insertion of the allomorph HAVE. In fact, the probe [uπ:_] on Perf starts its search from the sister of Perf, i.e. vP. The maximal projection vP does not bear the relevant feature, since the defective head v does not bear any person feature. Consequently,

Perf goes on searching within the next highest node. It gets to Spec,*v*, where the DP is located.[11] Perf successfully π-probes this DP, acquiring a valued person feature, which causes it to be spelled out by the exponent HAVE.

One might think that there are ways out of this problem. For example, the unaccusative DP could be raised by an EPP-feature [•D•] on Perf, before Perf probes *v*. If Perf bears [•D•], the subject gets out of the way, and there is no possible goal in the sister of Perf. The π-probe on Perf cannot find a matching feature, and the elsewhere form BE must be inserted at Spell-out. This is exactly what we were aiming at. However, there is a problem with this derivation. The required feature ordering on Perf ([•D•] > [uπ:_]) violates the Strict Cycle Condition (see (8)). The SCC prohibits any operation that excludes the current cyclic domain. When the feature [•D•] is discharged creating the specifier, the current cyclic node is *v*P. Instead, π-probing involves the head and the complement, with the exclusion of the specifier. Strict cyclicity dictates that [•D•] must be the last feature to be discharged because it affects the head and the specifier position. Hence, the feature ordering that one would need to get the right result under the A-over-A configuration is independently excluded by the SCC.

Moreover, there can be other arguments between Perf and *v*, nullifying the effect of the EPP-feature. For example, the quantitative (partitive) clitic *ne* or a dative clitic pronoun can be found in dependence of an unaccusative verb, as in sentences (20a,b).

(20) a. Ne=sono   arrivat-e   molt-e.
          of=be.PRS.3PL arrive.PRTC-PL.F many-PL.F
          'Of them, many have arrived.'

      b. Le=sono   capitat-e   molt-e   cose.
          DAT.3SG.F=be.PRS.3PL happen.PRTC-PL.F many-PL.F thing.PL.F
          'Many things have happened to her.'

---

11. The unaccusative object is located in Spec,*v* under the assumption that *v* (including unaccusative *v*) is a phase (see also Section 3.2.3 of Chapter 3). Since unaccusative *v* does not assign accusative case (Chomsky 2001), the internal argument must move out of the complement of *v* in order to remain accessible for higher case assigners (i.e., T). Consequently, when Perf enters the derivation, the unaccusative object is located in Spec,*v*. Evidence for Spec,*v* as the intermediate landing site of this movement is the position of the floating universal quantifier, as shown in (i).

(i) Le ragazze sono   tutt-e   arrivat-e.
     the girls   be.PRS.3PL all-PL.F arrive.PRTC-PL.F
     'All the girls have arrived.'

Both the unaccusative subject and the clitic are located on the path of Agree, intervening as possible goals for Perf. The EPP-feature on Perf cannot solve the problem of more than one intervening DP. In this case, A-over-A minimality cannot prevent successful agreement: Perf agrees either with the clitic (if it is in the inner specifier of v) or with object DP (if the clitic is in the outer specifier of vP), causing HAVE insertion.

For all these reasons, I do not adopt the A-over-A principle: the only features that are projected onto the maximal projections are categorical features. Having excluded A-over-A minimality, only Nested Agree can account for auxiliary selection.

2.6   Ingredients for Nested Agree

Nested Agree can be derived from the combination of independently motivated principles of syntactic theory, with a few further assumptions. In particular, it can be reformulated within the *Agree-Link* theory (Arregi & Nevins 2012), with the additional idea that an Agree-Link can and must be reused for multiple probe-features. In addition, it shows some similarities with specificity-driven principles such as *Maximize Matching Effects* (Chomsky 2001: 15), *Multitasking* (van Urk & Richards 2015: 132), *Feature Maximality* (Longenbaugh 2019: 21), *Economy condition on multiple probe satisfaction* (Pesetsky 2021: 28). The main difference with these principles is due to the assumption of feature ordering. In this section, I show how Nested Agree can be rephrased into other previous theories of Agree. The upcoming discussion mainly concerns the *Maximize* condition of Nested Agree. The *No-backtracking* condition must be taken as an additional assumption, instead. In fact, after the Maximize option has failed, the probe-head could in principle start its search once again from its sister, which is its original search domain. Nonetheless, I believe that the ban against backtracking is an intrinsic characteristic of downward direct probing.

2.6.1   Agree-Link

The core idea of Nested Agree is that an "Agree-channel" that has been opened must be reused, if possible. Nested Agree makes use of the link established by a previous dependency and exploits it again for a different probing operation, minimizing the number of independent Agree-channels. This consideration can be framed within a proposal developed by Arregi & Nevins (2012), *Agree-Link*.

Under this theory, Agree is split into two operations: *Agree-Link* and *Agree-Copy*. The two steps of Agree are defined as follows (Arregi & Nevins 2012: 86).

(21)　a.　*Agree-Link*: In the syntax, P has unvalued φ-features that trigger Agree
　　　　　with G (possibly more than one). The result is a link between P and G.
　　　b.　*Agree-Copy*: In the Exponence Conversion module, the values of the φ-
　　　　　features of G are copied onto P linked to it by Agree.

The first operation (21a) results in the creation of a "pointer" between two heads.
The derivation stores this link between the probe-head and the goal-head, and not
only the relation between the probe-feature and the goal-feature. The probe copies
the features in a subsequent step of the derivation, Agree-Copy (21b). Hence, the
result of the first component of Agree is simply a syntactic dependency between
two heads (Baker & Souza 2020). At the point of Agree-Copy, all the features can
be transferred from the head-goal to the head-probe.

Within this theory, Nested Agree can be stated as follows: given two ordered
features $F_1 > F_2$, the Agree-Link established for the feature F_2 must be, if possible,
the Agree-Link already established for the feature F_1. If an already existing Agree-
Link dependency can be exploited for more than one Agree-Copy operation, then
it should be used as such.

In this scenario, minimality is computed only on Agree-Link, but not on
Agree-Copy. Once an Agree-Link respects minimality for the feature that has created it, it does not matter for the other features, since they do not create any
new independent Agree-Link, but rather they are parasitic on the previous channel. The first probing operation has opened a channel of communication (an
Agree-Link) that can be parasitically used by other features, thereby circumvent-
ing any eventual violation of the minimality condition by a new Agree-Link. For
instance, in the case of auxiliary selection, the minimality violation of person-
Agree between Perf and v across the subject is avoided by using an already established well-formed Agree-Link (Perf-v), which bypasses the offending intervening
feature (on the DP_{sbj}).

The Agree-Link theory can be used to justify the principle Nested Agree
because it offers an independent motivation to assume that there is something like
a formal link that exists independently from the actual valuation procedure. Once
the two heads P and G enter a relation for a feature F_1, an Agree-Link between
P and G is created. It is true that the existence of such a link does not guarantee
that another probe-feature on the same probe-head must, or even can, make use
of this previous link, without establishing a new one. This is the new part introduced by Nested Agree, which must be stipulated within the Agree-Link theory.

2.6.2   Specificity-driven derivations

Nested Agree can also be derived from the combination of other principles that have already been independently proposed. In a nutshell, Nested Agree is equal to a specificity-driven principle plus the assumption that features are ordered (these two pieces give the *Maximize* condition), plus the *No-backtracking* condition. With the term *specificity-driven* I refer to those syntactic derivations where elements that are more "specific" in their featural inventory (meaning that they carry more features, or more articulated values of these features) are preferred by the probe-feature over less specific elements (Lahne 2012).

Principles that favor this kind of derivation are *Maximize Matching Effects* (Chomsky 2001), *General Specificity Principle* (Lahne 2012), *Multitasking* (van Urk & Richards 2015), *Feature Maximality* (Longenbaugh 2019), and *Economy condition on multiple probe satisfaction* (Pesetsky 2021). I will now discuss these principles, highlighting the differences with Nested Agree, which mainly stem from the assumption of feature ordering.

2.6.2.1   *Maximize matching effects*

Maximize Matching Effects states that when two heads enter a relation, they should check together as many features as possible. The definition is given in (22).

(22) *Maximize Matching Effects (MME)*   (Chomsky 2001: 15)
      If local (P, G) match and are active, their uninterpretable features must be eliminated at once, as fully as possible.

According to (22), if a head H bears the probe-features $[P_1, P_2]$, H should not spare one of its probe-features P_2 for a lower goal G_2 if P_2 could have been checked by a higher goal G_1 (which also checks P_1 on H). MME prescribes that each probe must target the highest matching goal, as soon as possible, in accordance with the Earliness principle (Pesetsky 1989).

Actually, MME does not belong to the class of specificity-driven principles because it does not favor the operation that satisfies more features at the same time (differently from the principles discussed below). This is an effect of minimality. In fact, if there is a higher goal for a probe, this should be chosen instead of a lower one, even when the lower goal would satisfy multiple probes. Nonetheless, I have included it in the present discussion because it has partially inspired the other specificity-driven principles.

MME is similar to the Maximize condition of Nested Agree: Nested Agree *maximizes* the matching relations between the probe-head and the goal-head (although it *minimizes* the number of distinct Agree-Link dependencies). However, the sequentiality that characterizes Nested Agree (which is an effect of feature ordering) makes it partly opposed to MME: depending on the feature ordering, Nested Agree might allow a probe-feature to skip the most local goal-feature.

2.6.2.2 *Multitasking*

Multitasking compares the competing operations A and B triggered by a head H and favors the operation that involves the simultaneous satisfaction of more features.[12]

(23) *Multitasking (MT)*   (van Urk & Richards 2015: 132)
      At every step in a derivation, if a probe can trigger two operations A and B,
      and the features checked by A are a superset of those checked by B, the gram-
      mar prefers A.

In the definition in (23), the word *probe* stands for the syntactic head that bears the two probe-features triggering the operations A and B. If a head bears more than one probe-feature, the operation that satisfies the highest number of probe-features is preferred and must be carried out first. For this reason, MT is different from MME. MT compares the effects of discharging different features, and chose to discharge the feature that brings about more consequences. For instance, if feature A provokes movement to a position where feature B is also satisfied, whereas the satisfaction of feature B does not have any consequence for the satisfaction of feature A, then feature A is discharged first (and feature B is discharged as a consequence of feature A). The satisfaction of different features proceeds by following subset/superset relations, as the definition in (23) states.

Multitasking was designed to account for cases where there are two operations and two items, and only one of them can undergo both operations. This is exemplified with data from the Nilotic language Dinka. Example (24) illustrates that the recipient DP *Ayén* cannot move to Spec,*v* (to the position in (24b), where it normally moves) when there is a wh-phrase *yeŋó* that competes for movement to the same position (even though this surfaces in first position, it must move through Spec,*v*).

---

12. Multitasking has inspired many other principles. One of these is Feature Maximality.

  (i) *Feature Maximality (FM)*   (Longenbaugh 2019: 21)
     Given head H with features $[F_1] \dots [F_n]$, if XP discharges $[F_i]$, XP must also discharge
     each [F] that it is capable of.

According to Longenbaugh (2019: 26), FM is like Multitasking, its difference being that it affects both Merge and Agree. For the general discussion of FM, I refer the reader to the discussion of Multitasking in this section. More specifically, FM is introduced by Longenbaugh (2019) to model participle agreement (I briefly discuss his analysis in Section 6.3 of Chapter 6). Since my approach to participle agreement is very different from his analysis, evaluating how Nested Agree could derive those data is not straightforward.

(24) *Dinka*
    a. Yeŋó cíi   môc   yiên Ayén?
       what PRF.NS man.GEN give Ayen
    b. *Yeŋó cíi   môc   Ayén yiên?   (van Urk & Richards 2015:131)
       what PRF.NS man.GEN Ayen give
       'What did the man give Ayen?'

Assuming that *v* bears the probes [uwh] and [ucase], if in its c-command domain there are two DPs (Ayén and Yeŋó), which both need case, but only one of them is of the wh-category (Yeŋó), then only the wh-phrase (Yeŋó) will be moved, since its movement satisfies both probes at once. In (24a), the recipient DP (Ayén) cannot move to Spec,*v* because this operation would satisfy only a single feature. Sentence (24b) is not grammatical because it requires an additional movement step that is not necessary in (24a).[13]

The interaction of Multitasking with minimality is not discussed in detail by van Urk & Richards (2015). On the one hand, van Urk & Richards (2015:122) state that movement is not subject to the same minimality conditions as Agree is. For instance, in the derivation of (24) the [ucase] feature attracts the direct object across the indirect object, probably involving a minimality violation. On the other hand, movement is considered to be always feature-driven (van Urk & Richards 2015:131). If this is the case, then movement is (indirectly) subject to minimality as well. In fact, there must be some kind of locally restricted Agree operation that licenses movement operations.

The differences between Multitasking and Nested Agree are various. Firstly, Nested Agree is not specificity-driven (see Section 2.6.3). Secondly, it is not transderivational (see Section 2.6.4). Thirdly, it acts in accordance with minimality during the derivation, although it can result in anti-minimality configurations (see Section 2.5).

Multitasking (and ECoMPS below) can be combined with another principle that may allow for the emergence of anti-minimality: the *Principle of Minimal Compliance (PMC)* (Richards 1998:601). This principle regulates the application of other grammatical constraints. Given a syntactic structure and a constraint C that must be evaluated on that structure for a dependency D, if C is respected by that dependency D, then the constraint C does not need to be satisfied anymore by the subsequent dependency D'. Hence, the PMC allows the derivation to "ignore" local violations, once a previous well-formed dependency is established

---

13. The reader may wonder if Nested Agree can rule out (24b). The most straightforward way to do so is to assume that in Dinka the order of the probe-features is [uwh] > [ucase]. The wh-phrase in the lower position is the goal for the first operation; Nested Agree restricts the domain of the second operation [ucase] to the same goal.

and the relevant constraint is respected at another stage of the derivation. As far as the Minimal Link Condition is concerned, the PMC permits a minimality violation if minimality has been satisfied by a previous relevant syntactic dependency.[14] Roughly speaking, it can be said that the *Maximize* condition of Nested Agree is equivalent to the combination of Multitasking, PMC, and feature ordering. Multitasking forces multiple probe-features to be satisfied by the same goal-head; the PMC "includes" minimality violations that may arise in this process; feature ordering ensures sequentiality and its consequences (no specificity-driven derivation, no transderivational approach, possible emergence of apparent anti-minimality).

2.6.2.3 *Economy condition on multiple probe satisfaction*

The Economy condition on multiple probe satisfaction is very similar to Multitasking, both in its effects and in its spirit. The definition is given in (25).

(25) *Economy condition on multiple probe satisfaction (ECoMPS)* (Pesetsky 2021: 28)
When two probes can satisfy their requirements with a single operation, this option blocks any alternative derivation in which the same pair of requirements are satisfied with two distinct operations.

This principle was introduced to favor a more economical derivation over an alternative one that involves more operations. This case is exemplified by (26).

(26) a. Mary seems to have solved the problem.
b. It seems that Mary has solved the problem.   (Pesetsky 2021: 14)
c. Mary, who seems to be the best candidate, ...
d. *Mary, who it seems to be the best candidate, ...   (Pesetsky 2021: 26–27)

In English, raising verbs like *seem* can be merged either with the raised subject of the infinitive (26a) or with an expletive pronoun (26b). These two options cease to be in free alternation when the sentence contains a wh-phrase: now the only option is raising of the wh-phrase (26c), and the expletive-derivation is not possible anymore (26d).

---

14. The Principle of Minimal Compliance can be applied to the problem of auxiliary selection. With respect to the dependency between Perf and *v*, minimality is violated by [π]-probing, but it is respected by [Infl]-probing. Since the previous [Infl]-Agree has respected minimality on the portion of structure between Perf and *v*, the minimality violation introduced by π-Agree on the same path can be ignored. The PMC has a very similar effect to Nested Agree. The two principles are, however, very different. Even though in the case of auxiliary selection Nested Agree has the effect of allowing for a subsequent non-local Agree relation, the rationale behind Nested Agree is not the regulation of any other syntactic constraint.

According to Pesetsky (2021), this has to do with the principle in (25). The v head that selects the verb *seem* bears an EPP-probe. This feature may target either the subject (in (26a), Mary) and raise it to Spec,v, or the CP as a whole (in (26b), [$_{CP}$ to have solved the problem]), merging then the expletive it in Spec,v. However, the situation is different when there are other features involved. In (26c,d), the subject is also a wh-phrase. Now the v head must also be equipped with a wh-probe. The only possible goal of this wh-probe is the wh-subject. In the derivation of (26c), a single operation (raising of the wh-phrase to Spec,v) satisfies both probes on v: raising of who avoids the separate satisfaction of the EPP-probe by it-CP, and of the wh-probe by who. The derivation in (26d) (where the EPP-probe targets the CP, and the wh-probe the subject who) is blocked because of ECoMPS.[15]

Similarly to MME, ECoMPS is subject to minimality: if there is a higher goal, this is targeted instead of a lower one, even if the latter would satisfy more than one probe. For instance, if in (26) there is a higher DP such as an indirect object, then the EPP-probe raises this higher DP and the wh-probe raises the wh-phrase subject (*Mary, who I've been assured to be the best candidate...*, Pesetsky 2021: 25). No alternative derivation is possible.

Hence, the ECoMPS favors a single operation that can satisfy multiple probes over multiple less specific operations. Nested Agree differs from it for the same reasons it differs from Multitasking. Moreover, since ECoMPS is subject to minimality, it comes into play only in cases where two goals are equidistant; this is not the case for Nested Agree.

2.6.2.4 *General specificity principle*

There is another principle that generalizes the "maximizing" effect despite potential minimality violations: the General Specificity Principle.

(27) *General Specificity Principle (GSP)*   (Lahne 2012: 2)
      A Probe undergoes a syntactic operation with the most specific matching goal. Specificity is determined by cardinality of morpho-syntactic features: a set Q is more specific than a set H iff $|Q| > |H|$.

---

15. Nested Agree can account for the data derived via ECoMPS. The feature ordering [uwh] > EPP can generate the data in (26). The sentence with the indirect object (*Mary, who I've been assured to be the best candidate...*, below in this section) is also derived, by considering that the indirect object (which is an argument of the higher v) also has to move to the specifier of the phase because of its unchecked case (since passive v does not assign case). In this sentence, both the wh-probe and the EPP-feature target the lower wh-phrase due to Nested Agree, whereas the indirect object moves for independent reasons.

This constraint leads to specificity-driven derivations: when the search domain of a probe contains more than one potential goal, the probe agrees with the goal that bears the highest number of matching features, regardless of minimality. GSP is equivalent to Multitasking without being subject to the Minimal Link Condition.

In its effects, the General Specificity Principle goes close to what Nested Agree does, although the logic behind the two principles is completely different: Nested Agree is not specificity-driven, and is not transderivational (see Sections 2.6.3 and 2.6.4). Moreover, GSP is similar just to the first step of Nested Agree, *Maximize*. Nested Agree acts on search domains and contains a ban against backtracking, as stated by the *No-backtracking* condition.

2.6.3   Nested Agree is not a specificity-driven principle

Nested Agree is not a constraint that favors the most specific goal in its c-command domain, in contrast with MT, ECoMPS and GSP. It does not require that two heads should match as many features as possible, but rather that an existing dependency is exploited as much as possible as the first step in any new search. As independent of specificity, Nested Agree can also lead to anti-specificity effects. Let me illustrate this point with different configurations: two equally specific goals, a specific lower goal, and a specific higher goal.

If the search domain of a head equipped with multiple probe-features contains two goals that are equally specific, as in tree (28), different scenarios may arise depending on feature ordering.

(28)   Equally specific goals

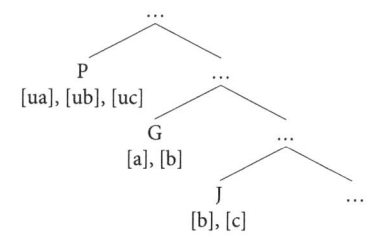

The probe [ua] can either copy [a] from G, or fail. The former happens if [ua] goes first or if it is ordered after [ub] but before [uc], the latter if [ua] goes after [uc] (which, targeting J, excludes G from the search domain of any subsequent probe on P). The probe [ub] can either copy [b] from G (if it goes first, or after [ua]), or from J (if it goes after [uc]). The probe [uc] copies [c] from J, regardless of its order with respect to [ua] and [uc].

The following conclusions can be drawn from this discussion. The probe-feature whose relevant goal is only present on the lower head ([c] on J) is never subject to intervention because G is not a possible goal for it (*strict relativized minimality*). Since Nested Agree prescribes that the search can go on downwards without backtracking when the "Maximize-goal" is not a matching one (see *No-backtracking* in (9)), a lower matching goal is always reached (if accessible because of the Phase Impenetrability Condition).

The probe-feature whose relevant goal is only present on the higher head ([a] on G) may fail to agree depending on the feature ordering, *even though there is no intervener* for [ua]. This is a kind of opacity due to the timing of operations, but totally independent from the locality configuration (in tree (28), there is and there was no intervener between P and G). The general result is that the higher item can be skipped under some circumstances. This is a kind of *relativized anti-locality* effect induced by feature ordering, but it is not absolute anti-locality (G can be itself in a licit position that does not violate anti-locality). For the time being, it remains an empirical question to determine whether this configuration (failed Agree for [a] in (28)) is attested, or whether the feature orderings that cause it can be independently excluded.

That specificity does not play a role for Nested Agree is also evident from the other two asymmetric scenarios, where one goal is more specific than the other. In these cases, the result is similar to what has been illustrated for tree (28). The configuration where the higher goal is more specific is given in (29).

(29)   Specific higher goal

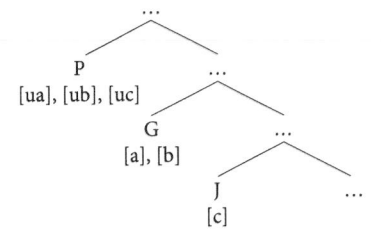

Depending on the order of the probes on P, the probe [ua] either copy [a] from G, or fail; the probe [ub] either copy [b] from G, or fail; the probe [uc] copies [c] from J. Once again, the lower item is always found, if accessible because of the PIC. In addition, if the two goals stand in a subset relationship (i.e., if in tree (30) J contains [a] or [b] rather than [c]), everything is copied by the highest one (G).

In tree (30), the more specific goal is the lower one. Depending on feature ordering on P, the probe [ua] either copy [a] from G, or fail; the probe [ub] copies [b] from J; the probe [c] copies [c] from J. If they stand in a subset relationship (i.e., if in tree (30) J contains [a]), [a] comes either from G or from J (depending on feature ordering), and the other features always come from J.

(30) Specific lower goal

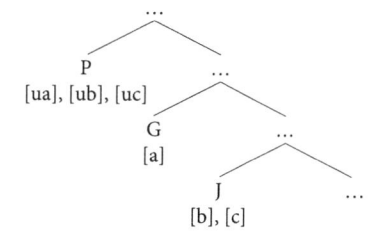

2.6.4 Nested Agree is not a transderivational principle

The other main difference between Nested Agree and MT, ECoMPS and GSP again stems from feature ordering. MT, ECoMPS and GSP are transderivational constraints: a derivation is evaluated in contrast with other possible derivations and it is preferred if it is specificity-driven.[16] When a head bears two features F_1 and F_2, there are different ways in which these features can be checked: among others, a derivation A, where F_1 is checked with X and F_2 with Y, and a derivation B, where F_1 and F_2 are checked with a single head X. MT, ECoMPS and GSP compare A and B, giving preference to the derivation B. This is possible if different structures are evaluated at the end of the syntactic derivation or at the end of a cyclic domain via cyclic optimization. However, this possibility should be ruled out in a derivational approach, such as the one adopted in the present study and advocated by Minimalism. For each step of the derivation, only one option should be possible, in accordance with the principles of syntax.

Nested Agree does not compare competing derivations. It only determines that a probe must start its search from the last inspected head, as an obligatory consequence of the ordering of features. The previous operation sets the upper boundary for the next one. There is no alternative derivation which is better or worse than another one. Hence, Nested Agree has a different computational status with respect to the other principles: it is exactly derivational.

---

16. According to van Urk & Richards (2015: 132), Multitasking is not necessarily a transderivational constraint. Multitasking refers to the "set of possible operations one head can trigger, so that it [the reference set] is evaluated locally, without the need to compare derivations." I do not see how this set could be evaluated without looking at the entire structure, since the economy of the operations does not only depend on the features themselves, but also on their distribution in the structure. Even though Multitasking does not compare complete derivations, it considers some aspects of different structures, whatever these aspects may exactly be (representations, sequences of derivational steps, etc.). Hence, I treat Multitasking-like principles as transderivational and inherently optimizing (and, consequently, compatible with a theory such Optimality Theory, rather than Minimalism).

The other problem of transderivational approaches is the issue of look-ahead, which is relevant in the case of minimality. How does the probe know that it is allowed to skip a closer, less specific goal, if there is a better matching goal lower in the structure? Look-ahead is avoided either by ignoring minimality (GSP), or by excluding anti-minimality configurations (MME and ECoMPS). Nested Agree has the advantages of doing what the GSP allows (and even more: see anti-specificity derivation in Section 2.6.3, and cross-linguistic variation in Section 2.5.2) and to be subject to minimality without incurring any look-ahead problems. In the case of Nested Agree, an apparent anti-minimality configuration (such as π-Agree between Perf and v) does not involve any minimality violation if the new domain of Agree does not contain the intervener anymore.

2.7   Summary

In this chapter, I have introduced the principle *Nested Agree*. Nested Agree regulates ordered applications of Agree, determining the domain of Agree operations when multiple triggers share the same syntactic position. Under the assumption that the features on the same head are ordered, the domain of an operation is reduced by the result of a previous operation. I have motivated my proposal by showing its differences and similarities with previous approaches to minimality violations and specificity effects.

Nested Agree is necessary to account for auxiliary selection in Standard Italian. I have started with the claim that auxiliary selection is a form of Agree, based on the fact that in Standard Italian the distribution of auxiliaries depends on both the argument structure and the type of arguments in the sentence. I have shown that, if this is the case, a problem of minimality emerges. In fact, the choice of the perfect auxiliary depends on both the presence and the type of features of the internal argument. However, at least the external argument is more local to the head that is realized by the perfect auxiliary (Perf) than the internal argument is. I have introduced Nested Agree as a way to deal with this apparently non-local configuration. If Agree operations are ordered, the domain of a subsequent operation may exclude an apparent intervener, depending on the result of the previous operation.

In the next chapter, I offer the detailed derivations of auxiliary selection in Italian, showing that Nested Agree can correctly account for the distribution of the perfect auxiliaries in Standard Italian.

CHAPTER 3

Auxiliary selection
The analysis

3.1 Introduction

In this chapter, I provide the syntactic derivations that lead to the emergence of the perfect auxiliaries BE and HAVE in Standard Italian. I start with some assumptions on the syntactic structure, in particular about the heads and the features that I consider relevant for the analysis (Section 3.2). Having set the stage, I go on with the derivations for transitive clauses (3.3.1), transitive verbs with a reflexive direct object (3.3.2), transitive verbs with a reflexive indirect object (3.3.3), unergative verbs (3.3.4), unaccusative predicates (3.3.5), intransitive verbs that appear with both auxiliaries (3.3.6), passive clauses (3.3.7), quirky verbs (3.3.8), and impersonal clauses (3.3.9). The account of auxiliary selection developed here will be then extended in three directions: it is applied to restructuring contexts (Chapter 4), it is used to explain the cross-linguistic variation in auxiliary selection (Chapter 5), and it is paired with a new analysis of participle agreement (Chapter 6).

3.2 Some notes on the syntactic structure

3.2.1 The perfect head

Various syntactic representations have been proposed for auxiliaries so far. For example, the auxiliary can be either the head of a related functional projection FP (Tenny 1987; Cinque 1999), the head of its own phrase AuxP selected by a semantically-interpreted functional projection (Kayne 1993; Rothstein 2004), or the head of one of some nested vPs (D'Alessandro & Roberts 2010). For the perfect auxiliary, I adopt the syntactic representation in (1), in line with D'Alessandro & Roberts (2010); Bjorkman (2018).[17]

---

17. Bjorkman (2011) proposes a morpho-syntactic account of auxiliaries: the auxiliary is inserted to support inflectional material that is otherwise unable to combine with the main verb. This is what happens when the perfect projection is merged into the structure. In fact, the

(1)

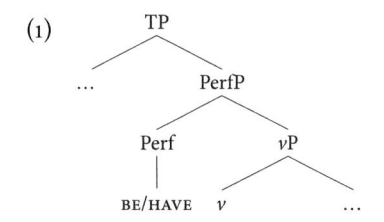

Perf is a functional head that belongs to the Infl-domain, the area where verbal morpho-syntactic features are manipulated. This functional projection is located between TP and *v*P. In particular, it is the first temporal functional projection outside the *v*P (Bjorkman 2018:330). The position of Perf between *v* (or eventually Asp) and T is supported by the semantic analyses in Iatridou et al. (2012); Pancheva (2012). Perf should also be higher than *v* because the perfect auxiliary co-occurs with the passive auxiliary and it is higher than it (Bjorkman 2018:333).

Perf bears the same categorical feature as the heads *v* or Voice, since it is selected by T.[18] Perf also moves to T via head movement instead of the lower *v* (forming the two complex heads V-*v* and Perf-T). In fact, when there is no auxiliary person inflection is realized on the lexical verb, as shown in (2a). This is a consequence of head movement of *v* to T. When there is a perfect auxiliary, person inflection appears on the auxiliary rather than on the lexical verb, which is realized as a participle and remains in the lower position, as illustrated in (2b).

(2) a. Mangio   la mela.
         eat.PRS.1SG the apple
         'I eat the apple.'
     b. Ho   mangiato la mela.
         have.PRS.1SG eat.PRTC the apple
         'I have eaten the apple.'

The function of Perf is the introduction of perfect semantics. I propose that this is encoded in the syntax by a probe of the type *[Infl]*, valued as *perf* : *[uInfl:perf]* (see also Section 2.5.1 in Chapter 2). I follow here Bjorkman (2011), among others:

---

intervening head Perf prevents V from moving to T and combining with the inflectional features on T. This approach provides a unified explanation for auxiliaries of different types. However, it still needs to refer to a syntactic position for the insertion of the auxiliary.

18. Even though Perf bears the category [*v*], it is different from the head *v* for various reasons. Firstly, it is not a phase head, as *v* is (see Section 3.2.3). Even though the analysis would not change if it were a phase, there seems to be no evidence for this claim. Secondly, it contains a valued instance of the [Infl] feature, whereas the other *v* heads host an unvalued [Infl] feature. Thirdly, it takes a phrase headed by another *v* head as its complement (but it shares this property with Voice, which also takes the *v*P as a complement).

inflectional heads bear inflectional features of the type [Infl], which can have different values (such as [Infl:past], [Infl:impf], [Infl:pass]). The peculiarity of my proposal is that the feature [uInfl:perf] is a valued probe: it needs to be checked against a feature of the same type. Such a matching feature is present on the head *v* in the form of an unvalued feature, [Infl:_], which can either remain unchecked, or receive a value by a probe. The former case happens when the structure does not contain any inflectional probes (e.g., in the present tense). The latter scenario takes place when *v* receives a value from another inflectional head, like Perf or passive Voice. This value is then interpreted and spelled out on *v* (the verb is in fact realized as a participle, as shown in (2b)).

3.2.2   The other heads

It is widely assumed that the head responsible for the argument structure is *v*. This head comes in different flavors. There is a non-defective, agentive *v* with full argument structure (*v** in Chomsky 2001) and a defective *v*. The head *v** assigns accusative case to the internal argument of the lexical verb ([ucase:acc]), and contains a probe for person ([uπ:_]).[19] This functional head is used with transitive and ditransitive verbs. I assume that it is also used with unergative verbs. For these verbs, I adopt the following standard assumption originally proposed by Hale & Keyser (1993): they are underlyingly transitive and they merge with a covert cognate object. Evidence for considering unergative verbs as transitive verbs, especially for the purpose of auxiliary selection, comes from the fact that there is no Romance variety where transitive and unergative verbs diverge in the choice of the auxiliary (Loporcaro 2001: 463, Loporcaro 2007: 180).

I also make use of a quirky *v*, similar to non-defective *v*, with the difference that it assigns dative case instead (Chomsky 2001).

Defective *v* combines with unaccusative verbs. These are monoargumental verbs where the sole argument is merged as the internal object of the verb. The syntactic difference between unergative and unaccusative verbs can be traced back to the *Unaccusativity Hypothesis* (Perlmutter 1978; Burzio 1986). Under this proposal, the split of intransitive verbs into two classes depends on the semantics

---

19. Following Chomsky (1995), I consider object Agree to be universal, the cross-linguistic difference lying in the morphological realization of Agree, i.e. in agreement. However, the specific interaction of *v* with the internal object, i.e. the kind of probes that *v* bears (uφ, uπ, u#...), is language specific, as evidenced by the growing amount of studies on Agree. In addition, even though object agreement is not morphologically realized in Italian, the presence of person-related phenomena involving the φ-features of the internal arguments, such as the *PCC (Person Case Constraint)*, may show that there is indeed object Agree in Italian (see for instance the analysis of the PCC by Coon & Keine 2020, among others).

of those verbs. This difference is represented in the syntax by means of different Merge positions of the sole argument. In particular, the verb is unaccusative if its argument is base-merged as the internal argument, while it is unergative if its argument is an external argument. The diagnostics are different and language-specific: passivization, *ne*-cliticization, reduced relatives, formation of deverbal agent nouns, auxiliary selection.[20]

All types of *v* bear an Infl-feature, which determines the morphological inflection that will be realized on the verb. This is given by higher inflectional heads that need to agree with a head bearing an Infl-feature in order to discharge their own [uInfl]-feature.

In addition to *v*, there are other types of functional heads that bear an Infl-feature. These are different instances of Voice, such as $Voice_{pass}$ and $Voice_{impers}$. The former is the head responsible for the passive interpretation, which is encoded by the value *pass* for the probe [uInfl]. The head $Voice_{pass}$ bears both the valued probe [uInfl:pass] and an unvalued instance of [Infl]. The latter head is present in impersonal clauses. Its peculiarity is the presence of an unvalued person feature that licenses the impersonal argument (for details, cf. Section 3.3.9)

The features on the inflectional heads are listed in (3). They are ordered as they appear in the list. With the bullet symbol [•F•] I indicate features that trigger Merge (external or internal, i.e. Move), and with the notation [uF:_] I indicate features that trigger Agree.

(3) a. defective *v*: [Infl:_]
     b. *v*: [Infl:_], [ucase:acc], [uπ:_], [•D•]
     c. quirky *v*: [Infl:_], [ucase:dat], [uπ:_], [•D•]
     d. $Voice_{pass}$: [uInfl:pass], [Infl:_]
     e. $Voice_{impers}$: [Infl:_], [π:_], [•D[π:_]•]
     f. Perf: [uInfl:perf], [uπ:_]

The featural inventory of these heads is a fundamental issue for the present analysis. Since auxiliary selection depends on the presence or absence of a π-feature on *v* (as proposed in Chapter 2), it is crucial to draw a line between a full *v*, which contains, among others, a person probe, and a defective *v*, which does not host any person feature.

---

20. Auxiliary selection cannot be used here as a test for unaccusativity. My main claim is that the different forms of the auxiliary are not lexically selected, but instead they are the result of Agree, which is influenced by the argument structure. If HAVE surfaces, it means that the sentence is a transitive clause with fully-valued arguments, otherwise the default BE emerges. Hence, the argument structure of a verb cannot be determined based on its auxiliary.

3.2.3 Phases

Phases are computational chunks of syntactic structure. I assume that every v is a phase (Legate 2003; Richards 2005; Müller 2010, 2011; Abels 2012; Heck 2016). The phasal status of the head v is relevant because of the Phase Impenetrability Condition, whose definition is given in (4).

(4) *Phase Impenetrability Condition (PIC)* (Chomsky 2000:108)
In a phase α with head H, the domain of H is not accessible to operations outside α, only H and its edge are accessible to such operation.

The PIC imposes a locality constraint on syntactic operations. The complement of a phase head is opaque for operations triggered by heads outside the phase, whereas the head and its specifier(s) remain visible for higher heads, at least until the next phase head is merged in the derivation. If v is a phase, the internal object in its base position is not accessible for anything above the specifier of v (unless it moves, thereby escaping the phase domain). The PIC is the reason why the information from the object is copied by Perf from the head v and not directly from the object. In fact, given the definition of the PIC in (4), the head v remains accessible for operations triggered by the higher head Perf, while the internal argument does not. The assumption that every v is a phase and that the PIC is an active constraint on phases will also be crucial for the analysis of participle agreement in Chapter 6.

3.2.4 φ-features

As far as φ-features are concerned, I assume that person (π), number (#) and gender (γ) are separated, independent branches below the node φ in the feature geometry (Béjar 2003). The different φ-features are not organized in entailment relationships. For instance, it is not the case that a specific φ-feature such as gender entails the presence of the higher node person. Instead, a specific value of a feature only implies the presence of that feature (for instance, [+Auth] requires the presence of the node π, but it is independent of the node γ). Note that, if the person feature is independent of the gender and number feature, a probe for person (as the one on Perf) cannot be satisfied by a gender or number feature.

I also assume that third person counts as a person (Béjar 2003; Bianchi 2006; Nevins 2007; Coon & Keine 2020).

3.2.5 Vocabulary entries

I follow Kayne (1993); D'Alessandro & Roberts (2010); Bjorkman (2011) in considering HAVE as the most specific form, BE as the unmarked form.[21] However, I do not adopt the idea that HAVE results from the incorporation of extra structure into BE (Benveniste 1966; Freeze 1992; Kayne 1993; Cocchi 1995). There are simply two allomorphs in the lexicon of languages with auxiliary selection, which are in competition for the same terminal node Perf. The vocabulary entries that I use for auxiliary selection in Standard Italian are given in (5) (which repeats the entries given in (17) in Chapter 2).

(5) *Vocabulary Items for Perf in Standard Italian*
   a. /HAVE/ ↔ Perf[π:α]
   b. /BE/ ↔ Perf elsewhere

The lexical entries in (5) map the verbal roots HAVE and BE to the syntactic terminal node Perf, depending on the π-feature it bears. In this case, the π-feature is not spelled out as person inflection on the verb (as it happens for example for subject-verb agreement in Standard Italian and English), but it rather determines the lexical choice of the auxiliary.

Lexical insertion is subject to the *Subset Principle* (Halle & Marantz 1993; Halle 1997): the exponents in (5) are in competition for the same terminal node Perf, in such a way that the exponent that realizes the largest subset of features on Perf will be inserted. In particular, HAVE is inserted when the head Perf has agreed in π-features with another head. BE is the default exponent, which is instead inserted when Agree has failed, meaning that no π-value could be copied onto the probe. Agree may fail either because there is no matching goal in the c-command domain of the probe (as is the case for unaccusative verbs), or because the goal is a π-defective item (as it happens with reflexive clitics). The presence of BE always reflects a case of "defectiveness", either in the type of *v* or in the features of the

---

21. The reason why such a lexical inventory has been proposed stems from crosslinguistic comparisons. The main observation is that HAVE always corresponds to BE plus something else. In fact, in possessive, locative and existential structures HAVE is cross-linguistically equivalent to BE plus an oblique/prepositional element (Kayne 1993). Moreover, Estonian and Celtic languages express the perfect with BE plus an aspectual particle that has prepositional content (Bjorkman 2011). The auxiliary BE also occurs as inflectional support when a further auxiliary is needed (cf. overflow pattern of auxiliary use, Bjorkman 2011). Nonetheless, not all analyses assume that BE is the elsewhere form. For Perlmutter (1989: 82), HAVE is the default allomorph. Moreover, in diachrony Latin HAVE has spread through deponent verbs, thereby substituting the periphrastic perfect with BE (Tuttle 1986). In addition, in many languages (Spanish, Sicilian) HAVE has been generalized as the only auxiliary.

arguments. Thus, the insertion of BE is a case of emergence of the unmarked, since the conditions of insertion of the more specific allomorph HAVE are not met.

Note that the entries in (5) are written as metarules for the sake of simplicity. With the term *metarule* I mean an abstraction over the specific Vocabulary Item (VI) rules that precisely illustrate the correspondence between a particular morpho-phonological exponent and the morpho-syntactic bundle of features that it substitutes. HAVE and BE in (5) are just symbols for different exponents that are paradigmatically related. The exact exponents (subject to suppletion depending on the features of T) are given in (6).

(6) a. /a/ ↔ Perf[π]
     b. /av/ ↔ Perf[π] / T[π: +participant, #: −singular]
     c. /son/ ↔ Perf / T[π: +participant +speaker, #: +singular]
     d. /ɛ/ ↔ Perf / T[π: −participant, #: +singular]
     e. /se/ ↔ Perf

The phonological exponents in (6) are then combined with person and number inflection, which substitutes the terminal node T. For inflection, I use the following vocabulary entries. The alternation between more than one allomorph for the same morpho-syntactic bundle (as in (7e,f)) is phonologically-driven and/or depends on the thematic vowel.

(7) a. /o/ ↔ T[π: +participant +speaker, #: +singular]
     b. /i/ ↔ T[π: +participant, #: +singular]
     c. /Ø/ / ↔ T
     d. /jamo/ ↔ T[π: +participant +speaker, #: −singular]
     e. /ete/ ~ /jete/ ↔ T[π: +participant, #: −singular]
     f. /ono/ ~ /on:o/ ↔ T[π: −participant, #: −singular]

When the exponents for Perf and T are combined together, morpho-phonology is responsible for modifying the VI rules in (6) and (7) in such a way that the actual words are created. The resulting paradigm for the present tense is given in Table 3.1.

Table 3.1 Allomorphs of HAVE and BE in the present tense

	1SG	2SG	3SG	1PL	2PL	3PL
HAVE	/ɔ/	/aj/	/ha/	/ab:jamo/	/avete/	/an:o/
BE	/sono/	/sɛj/	/ɛ/	/sjamo/	/sjɛte/	/sono/

3.2.6   Clitic pronouns

Clitics are pronouns with some special characteristics. They do not constitute a phonological word, cannot be stressed, cannot be dislocated nor focused, cannot appear in isolation, have a fixed position in the clause (Cardinaletti & Starke 1999:7). Given these properties, clitics do not surface in the same position as full DPs (for instance, in the internal argument position, in (8a)), but have to move to the tensed verb, as shown in (8b). The symbol t_i indicates the base position of the moved item.

(8)   a.   Teresa mangia   la   torta.
           Teresa eat.PRS.3SG the cake
           'Teresa eats the cake.'
      b.   Teresa la$_i$=mangia t_i
           Teresa ACC.3SG=eat.PRS.3SG
           'Teresa eats it.'

I identify the surface position of clitics with the T head. I assume that clitics move from their base position toward their surface position (Kayne 1975, 1991; Sportiche 1989; Belletti 1999; Matushansky 2006; Bianchi 2006; Cardinaletti 2008).[22] It has been claimed that clitics are simultaneously heads and maximal projections (Kayne 1975; Cardinaletti & Starke 1999; Belletti 1999; Matushansky 2006). In fact, movement of the clitic to T resembles the movement of a maximal projection with respect to locality, but then the clitic adjoins as a head to T (Belletti 1999; Matushansky 2006). The clitic and the verb form a complex head: they cannot be separated by any other material except by other clitics. Moreover, if the verb further moves to C, as in so-called Aux-to-C movement, then the clitic moves together with the verb.

   I model movement of clitic pronouns to T with a selectional feature [•T•] on clitics. This triggers internal Merge (movement) of the head on which it is located with a T head. The clitic moves to T because this selectional requirement cannot be satisfied within the VP. In fact, the clitic (via [•V•] on D) and the verb (via [•D•] on V) mutually select each other; their selectional requirements are satisfied by external Merge. The head T selects for a vP: T is externally merged with the vP that also contains the clitic with its unchecked [•T•] feature. Only at this point the clitic can be internally merged with T. The unchecked [•T•] feature makes the clitic move (as a phrase) to the edge of the phase v via successive cyclic movement because of the PIC, and then to T (as a head) when T is merged. I assume that

---

22. However, there are other theories that propose that the clitics are base-generated in their surface position, such as Sportiche (1996); Monachesi (2005) among others.

cliticization happens as soon as possible (i.e., immediately after external Merge of T) because of the Strict Cycle Condition.

3.2.6.1   *The reflexive clitic pronoun*

In Standard Italian, there are two possible strategies to encode reflexivity: the reflexive argument can be either a reflexive clitic (*se-reflexive*) or a reflexive phrase (*self-reflexive*). The list of pronouns is given in Table 3.2.

Table 3.2 Italian reflexive pronouns

	1SG	2SG	3SG	1PL	2PL	3PL
Reflexive clitics	mi	ti	si	ci	vi	si
Reflexive phrases	me stess-o/a	te stess-o/-a	se stess-o/a	noi stess-i/e	voi stess-i/e	loro stess-i/e

Reflexive clitics show overt morphological inflection for person and number, but they are not inflected for gender, differently from non-anaphoric pronouns that exhibit gender distinctions in the third person singular. Reflexive clitics move to T, as other clitics do. Moreover, they must be bound by a c-commanding antecedent (*Principle A*, Chomsky 1981).

The reflexive phrase is a morphologically heavy pronoun, formed by the weak pronoun in the accusative form (following the definition between clitic, weak and strong pronouns proposed by Cardinaletti & Starke 1999) plus a reflexive component that shows gender and number agreement. This complex pronoun surfaces in canonical argumental positions and does not move to T. Moreover, it needs an antecedent as the reflexive clitic does (although this does not have to be syntactically present, since the phrase can be uttered in isolation: '*Chi ha scelto Teresa? Se stessa.*' 'Who has Teresa chosen? Herself.').

I propose that the two types of reflexive pronouns enter the derivation with a set of φ-features that are differently valued: the se-reflexive has unvalued features, whereas the self-reflexive bears a valued person feature (see Reuland 2001 for a similar distinction in terms of valued/unvalued features).[23] The se-reflexive is morphologically underspecified and referentially defective. It enters the derivation with a set of unvalued φ-features, which are valued by a c-commanding antecedent DP via the process of binding (Fischer 2004; Reuland 2005; Heinat 2006; Kratzer 2009; Rooryck & Vanden Wyngaerd 2011; Sundaresan 2013, 2016). I assume, very generally, that binding is a form of coindexation plus c-command,

---

23. For further discussion of the differences between the two classes of reflexives, see also Reinhart & Reuland (1993); Spathas (2010); Bergeton & Pancheva (2011).

which leads to referential dependency. Binding applies independently of φ-feature valuation, which is a reflex of binding only if one of the involved items carries unvalued φ-features.[24] The unvalued φ-features of the reflexive clitic acquire a value via binding as soon as the antecedent (the external argument, for example) enters the derivation.

In contrast, the self-reflexive pronoun starts the derivation with a valued person feature. The self-reflexive contains a pronominal part that in its use as weak pronominal (i.e. out of the context of the self-reflexive) contains a valued person feature and is not bound by any antecedent (*Principle B*, Chomsky 1981). Nonetheless, the self-reflexive needs to be bound in the very same way as the se-reflexive does, since only a subset of its features is valued (namely, [π], but not [#] and [γ]). In fact, the non-pronominal part *stess-*, which behaves as an agreeing adjective, bears unvalued φ-features and receives gender and number from the binder. Binding establishes the coreferentiality relation via coindexation (Hicks 2009). In addition, the missing features are copied from the c-commanding antecedent. The person feature is not copied from the binder, but it must match because of coindexation. A difference in person feature would lead to a failure to bind, which causes ungrammaticality because of a fatal violation of Principle A.

3.2.6.2 *The impersonal si*

In Standard Italian, impersonal clauses contain the clitic pronoun *si*. There is a large debate in the literature about the morpho-syntactic representation of impersonal *si*.

The main question concerns its argumental status: impersonal *si* is either a syntactic argument, i.e. a referential element with a Theta-role, or a morpheme realizing a functional head. An analysis of the former type has been proposed by D'Alessandro (2004: 39–41): *si* can be merged in every argument position, can bear a Theta-role and a case specification, and is at least partially referential (it refers to an unspecified group of humans including the speaker, Chierchia 1995). An approach of the latter type is developed by Dobrovie-Sorin (1998) for Romanian. The Romanian *si*, marked with accusative case, is a middle-passive mor-

---

24. I assume that binding consists of valuation of the index on the reflexive by the index on the antecedent (or, following Hicks (2009), of the feature [var:_] on the anaphor by the feature [var:i] on the binder). Consequently, the reflexive pronoun and the c-commanding DP bear the same index and form a referential dependency. Binding is in general modeled as an instance of upward Agree (Bjorkman & Zeijlstra 2019) between the antecedent and the anaphor. I do not enter the discussion about the technical implementation, but it could be the case that binding works slightly differently from φ-probing, also because the unvalued features on the anaphor do not behave as standard φ-probes. See also Hicks 2009: 208 for discussion of an alternative to upward Agree.

pheme that signals the suspension of the external Theta-role (Dobrovie-Sorin 1998: 401). The debate on the mixed behavior of *si* between a full argument DP and a passivizing marker goes back to Cinque (1988), who proposes the existence of two types of *si*, one argumental ([+arg]) and one non-argumental ([–arg]).

My position is that impersonal *si* is an argument that can be merged in every argument position. Nonetheless, it is a "special" argument, because it needs to be licensed by the functional head Voice$_{impers}$. This proposal is addressed in detail in Section 3.3.9.

The second main issue about impersonal *si* concerns the features it bears. All the above-mentioned analyses (Cinque 1988; Dobrovie-Sorin 1998; D'Alessandro 2004) share the following claim: *si* does not bear a set of completely valued syntactic φ-features. The reason can be either because it is not an argument at all (Dobrovie-Sorin 1998), because it has underspecified syntactic features (Cinque 1988), or because some of its features are semantic rather than syntactic (D'Alessandro 2004).

Similarly, I also assume that impersonal *si* is featurally defective. In particular, its person feature is not specified at all: [π:_]. This proposal can be traced back to Burzio (1986), where impersonal *si* is considered to have no person feature. Also for Manzini (1986) the person feature on *si* is unspecified. For Cinque (1988), *si* bears a generic person feature, called arb. This arb is something like a syntactic marker for unspecified person, which needs to combine with a personal AgrP. Defectiveness affects the value of the attribute [person] also for Nevins (2007): impersonals are compatible with any antecedent because they are underspecified for [participant] and [author].

Note that it has also been proposed that impersonal *si* is syntactically marked for person. This view is advocated by D'Alessandro (2004): impersonal *si* bears a third person feature. I think that an unvalued person feature is suggested by various facts. Firstly, the impersonal clitic lacks morphologically inflection and is morphologically invariant, differently from other personal pronouns that may inflect for case, person, number, and eventually gender. Secondly, it can include the speakers or not, meaning that it can be semantically associated with different person specifications. This does not have to do with the well-known distinction of inclusive versus exclusive person, but it refers to the interpretation of the pronoun as 1st, 2nd or 3rd person plural. For example, in a sentence such as (9), *si* can be interpreted as 1st or 3rd person plural if the speaker is Italian (1: inclusive interpretation; 3: exclusive interpretation); if the speaker is English and the hearer is Italian, the interpretation of *si* in (9) can be 2nd person plural (*si* refers to a group of people that includes the hearer, but excludes the speaker).

(9) In Italia si=mangia   molti spaghetti.
     in Italy IMPERS=eat.PRS.3SG many spaghetti
     'In Italy people eat a lot of spaghetti.'

Thirdly, impersonal *si* occupies a dedicated position in the string with respect to other clitics (see for instance the data in D'Alessandro 2004: 41).

To sum up, I consider impersonal *si* as an argumental clitic with a defective set of φ-features, in particular with an unvalued [π] feature. This *si* does not need to be bound, but must be licensed by a special Voice$_{impers}$ (see Section 3.3.9).

3.3   Derivations

3.3.1   Transitive verbs

A sentence with a transitive verb in the perfect tense is repeated again in (10). The lexical verb is morphologically realized as a past participle and the perfect auxiliary is a form of the verb HAVE, with person and number inflection controlled by the subject.

(10) Teresa ha   lavato   la camicia.
      Teresa have.PRS.3SG wash.PRTC the shirt
      'Teresa has washed the shirt.'

I now show in detail how the syntactic derivation of a sentence such as in (10) looks like. I assume that a transitive verb is a verbal root that is selected by a full argument structure *v*. This head introduces the external argument, assigns accusative case to the internal argument and contains a person probe that agrees with it (Chomsky 2001).

First of all, the VP is built and merged with a transitive *v*, which has the following feature specification: [Infl:_] > [ucase:acc] > [uπ:_] > [•D•], as shown in (11).[25] All operations are performed exactly in this order. This is represented in (12).

---

25. In the trees here and below in this chapter, I use the symbols α and β to indicate the values for π (person), # (number) and γ (gender) in the feature geometry under the node of φ-features called α or β. In [π:α] and [#:α], α indicates that both values come from the same set of φ-features (i.e., from the same DP). In one case, α stands for a person value for the attribute π; in the other case, for a number value for the attribute #. Note that this is only a notation and not an index. The information about the source of the features is not relevant for the analysis: it does not matter whether various probes find the φ-values on the same DP or distinct DPs.

(11)

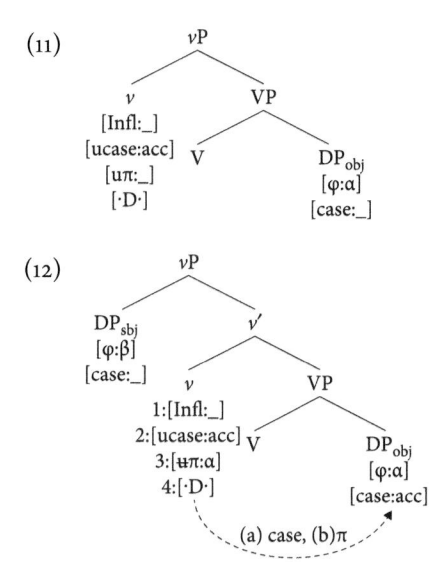

(12)

The first feature on *v* is [Infl:_]. This cannot yet receive a value, since there is no other item that bears [Infl]. In any case, it is not a probe: it does not need to be discharged. Moving on to the second feature, accusative case is assigned to the DP in Comp,V. Thirdly, *v* copies the π-feature from the DP object via Agree. Having acquired a π-feature, *v* can now become a goal for further probes. Finally, *v* introduces the external argument via the selectional feature [•D•] and assigns it the external Theta-role. This precise ordering of features, and in particular the [•D•] feature being the last one, is due to the Strict Cycle Condition (stated in (8) in Chapter 2).[26] This principle states that no operation can target a subpart of the tree with the exclusion of the highest terminal node. This means that a probe feature cannot carry out Agree with some items in the complement after a specifier has been merged. In the present case, the earlier discharge of [•D•], which creates the specifier, would make it impossible to perform Agree on *v* via [uπ:_], since this operation involves the head and its complement with the exclusion of the specifier.

---

26. The Strict Cycle Condition states that "no rule can apply to a domain dominated by a cyclic node A in such a way as to affect solely a proper subdomain of A dominated by a node B which is also a cyclic node" (Chomsky 1973: 243). There are different interpretations of this principle depending on what counts as a cyclic node. Under a strict interpretation, every projection (including minimal projections) is a cyclic domain. As observed by McCawley (1984, 1988), if every projection is a cyclic node, the SCC can predict the order of operations (see also Georgi 2014; Müller 2021). In the present case, the alternative feature ordering [•D•] > [uπ:_] would not comply with the SCC: the earlier discharge of [•D•], which creates the specifier, would make it impossible for *v* to agree for [π] with the internal argument, since this Agree operation involves the head and its complement with the exclusion of the specifier.

Now all operations inside the vP are completed. The features [Infl] on v and [case] on the DP_{sbj} have not been checked yet. The next syntactic head that is merged with vP is Perf, as shown in (13).

(13)

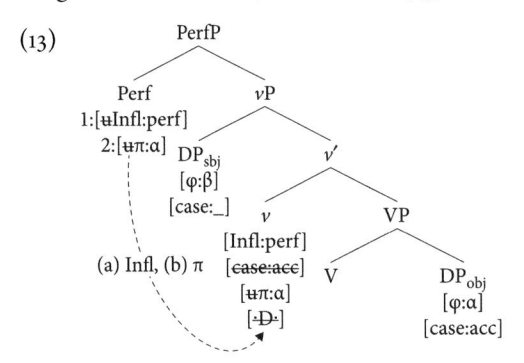

Recall that the features on Perf are so ordered: [uInfl:perf] > [uπ:_]. Perf contains the probe [uInfl:perf] that needs to find another [Infl] to be checked with. The head v contains an instance of [Infl:_], it is accessible (in accordance to the Phase Impenetrability Condition, see (4) in Section 3.2.3), it is c-commanded by the probe [uInfl:perf] and it is the closest matching goal (meaning that there is no other instance of [Infl] that intervenes between the probe on Perf and this potential goal on v).[27] Therefore, Perf agrees with v. The value *perf* is copied onto v, which will be spelled out as a past participle. After this feature has been discharged, Perf goes on with the second one. [uπ:_] is a probe that looks for a matching goal. In the c-command domain of Perf there are two possible matching items, i.e. two syntactic positions with a [π] value: the DP_{sbj} and v (the DP_{obj} is invisible because of the PIC). Crucially, the head Perf has already carried out an operation ([uInfl:perf]) before starting this new search ([uπ:_]). Therefore, the conditions of application of Nested Agree are met. I repeat here again the definition of Nested Agree, discussed in Chapter 2.

(14) *Nested Agree*
Let F_1 and F_2 be two ordered probes on the same head H. The search space of F_1 is the c-command domain of H.
(i) *Maximize*: if the Agree operation A_1 for the feature F_1 has targeted the goal G, then the subsequent Agree operation A_2 for the feature F_2 must also target G.

---

27. With the term *intervention* I refer to the configuration in which a matching feature is c-commanded by the probe and is closer to the probe than the goal is. Intervention is computed via c-command and requires feature matching. The matching feature for a valued probe is the same feature, either unvalued or already valued (see Section 2.4.1 in Chapter 2).

(ii)   *No-backtracking*: If G is not a matching goal for F_2, the search space of F_2 is the c-command domain of G (not of H).

Nested Agree states that this second operation ([uπ:_]) should check as the first possible goal the goal of the previous operation ([uInfl:perf]). The first operation carried out by Perf has found its satisfaction in the feature [Infl] on the head v. Now the second operation ([uπ:_]) must start from the same head v, checking if v bears another feature by which it can be satisfied. In the present case, v contains a value for the person feature. In fact, it has probed for π and has copied a value from the DP_{obj}. Thus, v can satisfy not only the first feature [Infl] on Perf, but also this second person probe.

Note that the DP_{sbj} is actually the goal structurally closest to the probe, but it is invisible for the search of [uπ:_], because Perf is forced to use the open channel that has been established by the previous probe. In other words, the DP_{sbj} lies outside the search domain of Perf[uπ:_] (while it was contained in the locality domain of Perf[uInfl:perf]). There is no intervention, if the domain of Agree is relativized.

The derivation in (14) shows that the head Perf successfully agrees with v for π. In Standard Italian, the dependency of the perfect auxiliary on the argument structure is achieved by Agree of the head Perf with v. The interaction with the features of the direct object is realized by means of cyclic Agree (Legate 2003) between Perf and the DP_{obj}, enabled by the mediation of v.

The derivation proceeds with Merge of T. The T head brings into the syntactic structure the required tense specification by means of a [Tense] feature that can have different values, such as present, past, non-finite and so on. Moreover, it assigns nominative case to the DP_{sbj} in its c-command domain. The second operation it triggers is φ-Agree. Again, there are two different goals in the c-command domain: Perf and the DP_{sbj}. Because of the previous operation of case assignment by T, the φ-probe on T must also target the subject, thereby skipping Perf. This is assured by Nested Agree. After T has copied the φ-values from the DP_{sbj}, it raises it to its specifier via the EPP-feature [•D•]. The tree in (15) represents these operations.

(15)

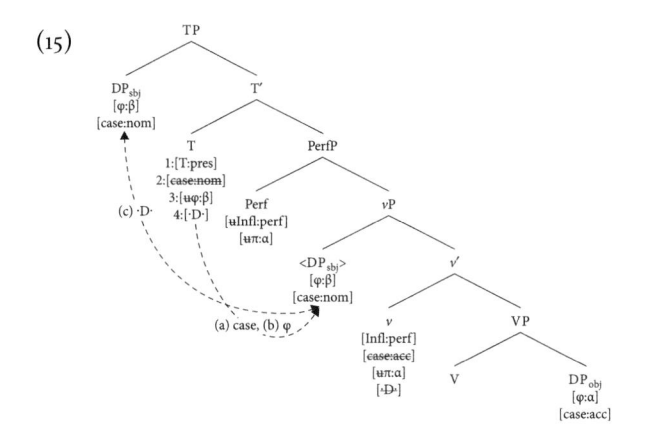

The syntactic derivation is now concluded. Two complex heads are formed via head movement, V+*v* and Perf+T, given in (16) and (17).

(16)

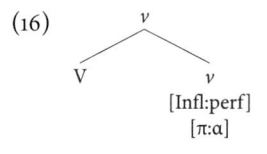

(17)

The head Perf in (17) has copied a π value. At the point of vocabulary insertion, Perf is substituted by HAVE, given the lexical entry (5), repeated here again.

(18) a.   /HAVE/ ↔ Perf[π:α]
      b.   /BE/ ↔ Perf elsewhere

The specific lexical entries for the clause in (10) are as follows.

(19) a.   /la/ /kamitʃa/ ↔ DP[√SHIRT][φ:-part,+sg,+f][case:acc]
      b.   /lavato/ ↔ *v*[Infl:perf][π:-part] + V[√WASH]
      c.   /a/ ↔ Perf[π:-part] + T[T:pres][φ:-part,+sg,+f]
      d.   /teresa/ ↔ DP[√TERESA][φ:-part,+sg,+f][case:nom]

3.3.2   Transitive verbs with reflexive object

In Section 2.2 of Chapter 2, I have said that the auxiliary "switches" from HAVE to BE when a transitive clause contains a reflexive clitic pronoun, as illustrated in (20).

(20) Teresa si=è   lavata.
      Teresa REFL.ACC.3SG.F=be.PRS.3SG wash.PRTC
      'Teresa washed herself.'

Given the vocabulary entries in (5), I consider BE as the default auxiliary. This means that the reflexive object causes a kind of "defectiveness" in the structure, so that the condition of insertion of the more specific auxiliary HAVE is not met and the unmarked BE must be instead inserted. The form of the auxiliary in (20) is the direct consequence of the featural defectiveness of the reflexive clitic *si*.[28] As I have proposed in Section 3.2.6.1, reflexive clitics are featurally deficient: they enter the derivation with unvalued φ-features, which are valued by a c-commanding antecedent DP via binding. In contrast, self-reflexives are morphologically specified for π-features. In fact, recall that reflexive clitics and reflexive phrases determine different realizations for the perfect auxiliary: BE if the predicate merges with the reflexive clitic (as in (20)), HAVE if it merges with the reflexive phrase (as in (21)). The difference in auxiliary selection between these two classes of reflexive pronouns comes about because of the features of the pronouns.

(21) Teresa ha   lavato   se=stess-a.
      Teresa have.PRS.3SG wash.PRTC REFL.ACC.3SG=REFL.ACC.3SG.F
      'Teresa washed herself.'

I take the presence of the auxiliary HAVE in (21) as a hint for the transitive argument structure of both reflexive sentences. In fact, the semantics of the two sentences in (20) and (21) is equivalent. Hence, the auxiliary BE in (20) is not due to the argument structure itself.

    I adopt the transitive-unergative analysis of reflexive clauses, which has been proposed by De Alencar & Kelling (2005); Sportiche (2014); Alexiadou et al. (2015), among others. Although an unaccusative analysis would in principle be possible for (20) and compatible with the present theory of auxiliary selection, the unaccusative analysis cannot be easily extended to indirect reflexive clauses as (22), which contain an internal argument and an external argument that are distinct.[29]

---

28. This intuition is already present in Alexiadou, Anagnostopoulou, & Schäfer (2015). In a footnote, the authors hypothesize that BE-selection is due to the morpho-syntactic properties of the reflexive clitic in combination with clitic movement, although they do not present any analysis (Alexiadou et al. 2015: 102). That the perfect auxiliary BE in reflexive clauses is not tied to intransitivity, but rather to the syntactic presence of the reflexive pronoun, has also been recognized by Schwarze (1998: 103–104).

29. For the unaccusative analysis of reflexive clauses, see Kayne (1975); Grimshaw (1982); Bouchard (1982); Marantz (1984); Pesetsky (1996); Embick (2004). For criticisms, see Reinhart

(22) Teresa si=è   mangiat-a   il panino.
      Teresa REFL.DAT.3SG.F=be.PRS.3SG eat.PRTC-SG.F the sandwich.SG.M
      'Teresa ate the sandwich.'

Since (22) is clearly a transitive clause, the reason why BE shows up in (22) and in (20) cannot be an unaccusative syntactic structure. I treat sentences like (20) and (22) as normal transitive and ditransitive clauses with a φ-defective argument.

   I now provide the derivation for sentence (20). The argument structure in tree (23) is the same as for transitive predicates (see Section 3.3.1). However, the object consists of a φ-defective item. It is also a clitic: it bears a [•T•] feature that must be checked with T. First of all, v agrees with the internal argument. This bears φ-features, although unvalued. Recall that the function of Agree is the erasure of uninterpretable features and not feature valuation (cf. Section 2.4.1 in Chapter 2 for details). Agree is simply the search for a matching feature for syntax-internal and for interface-related reasons. The DP$_{obj}$ is a suitable goal for v: it is in its c-command domain and it contains a matching feature. Even though an unvalued matching feature is not able to provide a value for the probe, it is able to satisfy it. Therefore, v agrees with the DP$_{obj}$ for [π]. The result of this Agree operation is [u̶π̶:_]. Agree is successful, although no π-value has been copied. This can be considered as a case of defective intervention for valuation: an unvalued matching feature causes Agree to stop without successful valuation.

(23)

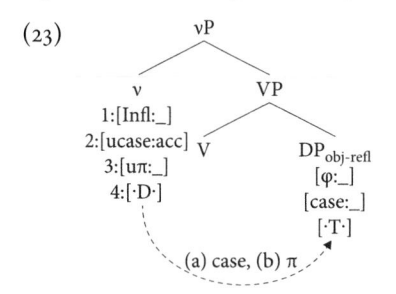

& Siloni (2004, 2005); Doron & Hovav (2007); Schäfer (2008, 2012); Sportiche (2014); Alexiadou et al. (2015).

(24)

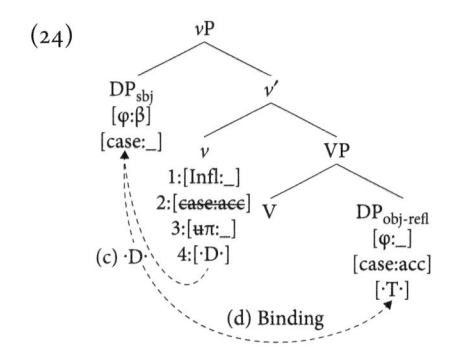

When all operations within the complement of *v* have been carried out, *v* introduces the external argument in its specifier, as shown in tree (24). The operation triggered by the feature [•D•] on *v* must happen after case assignment and π-Agree because of the Strict Cycle Condition (see also Section 3.3.1). After the external argument is merged in the structure, binding takes place: the two DPs are now coindexed. As a consequence of coindexation, the reflexive clitic acquires the same φ-features as the DP$_{sbj}$.

Let me highlight how crucial is the timing of operations. The Strict Cycle Condition assures the earliness of Agree (an operation between the head and its complement) with respect to the introduction of the external argument (an operation that involves the edge of the head). For transitive verbs, Merge of the external argument (and binding) follows π-Agree on *v*. This is a relation of counter-feeding: binding takes place too late for feeding the successful valuation by Agree. Had the external argument been introduced by *v* as the first operation, Agree on *v* would have successfully copied the π-feature of the subject as it stands on the object, since this would have been already bound by the subject. Successful valuation on *v* would have determined the substitution of Perf with the more specific allomorph HAVE, exactly as we saw for transitive verbs with non-defective objects. The feature ordering [uπ:_] > [•D•] on *v* has the consequence of preserving the distinction between an element with a full set of φ-features (i.e., a transitive canonical object, which determines HAVE insertion) from an element that is φ-defective (i.e., a reflexive clitic pronoun, which determines BE insertion). This difference vanishes after binding has taken place, as far as further operations are concerned: from now on, the clitic bears valued φ-features.[30] For instance, binding feeds participle agreement, as the φ-inflection on the past participle in (20) confirms (see Chapter 6).

---

30. Since binding is not feature sharing, but rather coindexation under c-command plus Agree (see Section 3.2.6.1), the featural information on the person probe on *v* is not updated after binding has applied. Agree on *v* has led to failed valuation and the probe remains unvalued, although now the reflexive clitic has its features valued.

At this point, all operations triggered by *v* have been carried out. Before the complement of *v* undergoes Spell-out, unchecked features must move to the edge of the phase (because of the Phase Impenetrability Condition, see (4) in Section 3.2.3). The clitic in the direct object position bears an undischarged [•T•] feature. This [•T•] feature triggers movement of the clitic out of the phase domain because it has to remain accessible for T later. When the clitic moves, it bears valued φ-features (because this happens after binding). These valued π-features cause overt morphological inflection on *v* for number and gender (past participle agreement). Since it is not relevant for the analysis of auxiliary selection, the trees in this section do not contain the PIC-related movement of the reflexive clitic object to an outer specifier of *v*. All details of this movement and of its consequences will be discussed in Chapter 6 on past participle agreement.

In the next step (25), Perf is merged with *v*. As we have already seen for the derivation in (13), Perf checks its [uInfl:perf] feature with *v*. Thereafter, Nested Agree forces the second probe [uπ:_] to exploit the Agree-Link of the previous probe [uInfl:perf]. The head *v* bears a π-feature, although unvalued. The presence of a matching feature on this head is enough for Agree to succeed. The features on Perf become [u̶Infl:perf] and [u̶π:_].

(25)

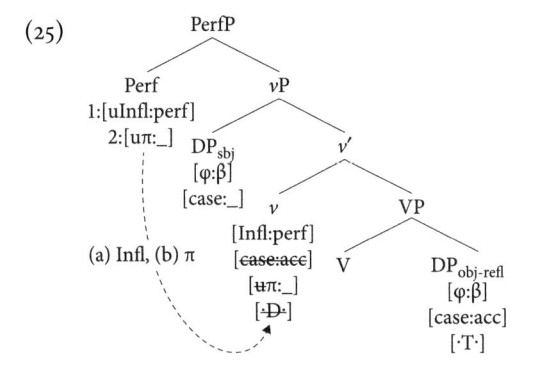

The result of Agree for the person feature on Perf in (25) (and on *v* in (23)) shows that two features match depending on the attribute, not on the value. An unvalued matching feature is a goal and stops Agree by satisfying the probe, since it is an instance of the relevant feature. Even though there is a more specific goal in the structure (i.e., the DP$_{sbj}$ with valued φ-features), it lies outside the search domain of the person Agree operation, due to Nested Agree. In fact, the subject has already been skipped by Perf[uInfl] and cannot be reached anymore by Perf[uπ].

As Agree has lead to failed valuation on *v* in (23), valuation on Perf in (25) fails, too. At Spell-out, the condition for the insertion of HAVE is not met. Even though there is a π-feature on the terminal node Perf, no value is associated with it. Thus, the elsewhere form must be inserted. Note that an unvalued feature is equal to a value within syntax (since it is feature identity that matters), but it is equal to the lack of value for the purpose of vocabulary insertion (since it is the value that matters).

The derivation proceeds with Merge of T with PerfP. As soon as it enters the structure, the clitic moves to T and incorporates into it, forming a complex head. Evidence for clitic placement to T as the first operation to carry out comes for example from raising across an experiencer in Romance: subject raising is only possible if the experiencer undergoes cliticization, thereby leaving the way clear for A-movement of the subject (Rizzi 1986; McGinnis 1998; Heck 2016). The derivation otherwise proceeds as for transitive verbs (see Section 3.3.1).

At the point of Vocabulary Insertion, Perf is substituted by BE because the π-feature on Perf is unvalued. The specific vocabulary entries for sentence (20) are as follows (for substitution of DP_{sbj} and V, see the Vocabulary Items in (19); for participle agreement, see Chapter 6).[31]

(26) a. /ɛ/ ↔ Perf[π:_] + T[T:pres][φ:-part,+sg,+f]
      b. /si/ ↔ DP[φ:-part,+sg,+f]

To sum up, the source of BE in reflexive clauses is Agree with a π-defective item.

Differently from what happens with featurally complete DPs, when the DP_{obj} is featurally defective Perf does not copy any π-value, since valuation on *v* has failed. Therefore, the condition of insertion of the allomorph HAVE is not met and the elsewhere form BE is inserted, in accordance with the Subset Principle.

3.3.3 Transitive verbs with reflexive indirect object

In Section 3.3.2, I have offered the derivation for a transitive clause with a reflexive direct object. The reflexive clitic pronoun can also be merged as the indirect object, with benefactive meaning. An example of a clause with a benefactive reflexive argument is repeated in (27).

(27) Teresa si=è   mangiat-a   il panino.
      Teresa REFL.DAT.3SG.F=be.PRS.3SG eat.PRTC-SG.F the sandwich.SG.M
      'Teresa ate the sandwich.'

---

31. As far as the VI rule for the reflexive clitic *si* is concerned, I think it should be underspecified for case in order to cover both the accusative and the dative reflexives, which correspond to the same lexical entry. The additional difference between the VI entries of the reflexive *si* and of a canonical DP is probably the presence of a referential feature due to binding such as [VAR] (Hicks 2009).

As already discussed in Section 3.3.2, even though an unaccusative analysis has been proposed for direct reflexive clauses as (20), it is much more difficult to accept an unaccusative approach for clauses with a reflexive indirect object, which clearly contain an internal argument and an external argument that are distinct and bear, respectively, patient and agent thematic roles. For this reason, I treat indirect reflexive sentences as transitive clauses with a featurally defective argument.

I assume that the reflexive clitic pronoun bears unvalued φ-features and needs to be bound in the derivation (see Sections 3.2.6.1, 3.3.2). Furthermore, the reflexive pronoun is introduced in the indirect object position by an applicative head *Appl*, which also brings the benefactive semantics and assigns accusative case to the DP object (Marantz 1993; Ura 1995, 2000; McGinnis 1998; Pylkkänen 2008; Anagnostopoulou 2004). The resulting applicative phrase is merged with a special type of *v*, called *quirky v* (see Section 3.2.2). This head is similar to the transitive *v* because it is a full argument structure *v*, but it assigns dative instead of accusative case (Anagnostopoulou 2001; D'Alessandro 2017a).[32] The formulation *quirky* refers to quirky subject constructions in Icelandic (and in Italian), where the thematic subject bears dative case instead of nominative. These structures are created by a dative assigning head, similar to this one (Zaenen, Maling, & Thráinsson 1985; Taraldsen 1995; Sigurðsson 1996; Boeckx 2000; Alexiadou 2003).

The derivation for sentence (27) is as follows. In (28), V is merged with the DP_{obj} and the VP is merged with the Appl head. Appl assigns accusative case to the

---

32. The applicative head might be subject to some cross-linguistic variation for different aspects. In Chapter 5, I show that in Logudorese Sardinian the same type of clause requires the auxiliary HAVE, whereas if the reflexive clitic is the direct object then the auxiliary is BE, as in Italian. I present here Example (29) of Chapter 5.

(i) a.   Maria z=ɛs   samuna:ð-a.   (direct transitive reflexive)
          Maria REFL.ACC.3SG.F=be.PRS.3SG wash.PRTC-SG.F
          'Maria has washed herself.'
     b.   Maria z=a   ssamuna:ðu zal ma:nɔs.
          Maria REFL.DAT.3SG.F=have.PRS.3SG wash.PRTC   the hands
          'Maria has washed her hands.'   (indirect transitive reflexive)

The difference between (27) and (i-b) can be derived in one of the following ways. (i) Sardinian has a high applicative head that selects *v*, while Italian has a lower one that is selected by *v*. (ii) In Sardinian, the applicative head assigns dative to its specifier (rather than accusative to its complement) and combines with a transitive *v* (rather than with a quirky *v*). (iii) In general, unvalued features do not lead to defective intervention, and the difference between Sardinian and Italian is due to the phasal status of the applicative head, which is a phase in Italian, but not in Sardinian. I refer the reader to Section 5.7.1 for discussion.

object and introduces the benefactive DP, which in this structure is also a reflexive clitic.

(28)

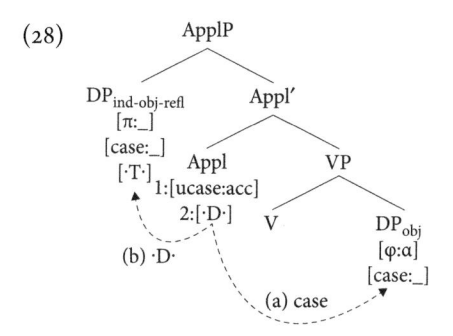

After this step, quirky v is merged into the structure. As tree (29) shows, v assigns dative case to the reflexive clitic *si*. Then, it probes for person. In its c-command domain, the closest matching goal is the reflexive clitic pronoun, which bears the relevant feature [π]. The person probe targets this DP and is satisfied; however, valuation does not succeed. In fact, the clitic is featurally defective: its π-feature is unvalued when it enters the derivation. Via binding, the clitic will acquire a value for its person feature, but at this point of the derivation it has not been bound yet. As already seen in Section 3.3.2, unvalued features lead to defective intervention: Agree stops after having encountered a matching unvalued feature.

(29)

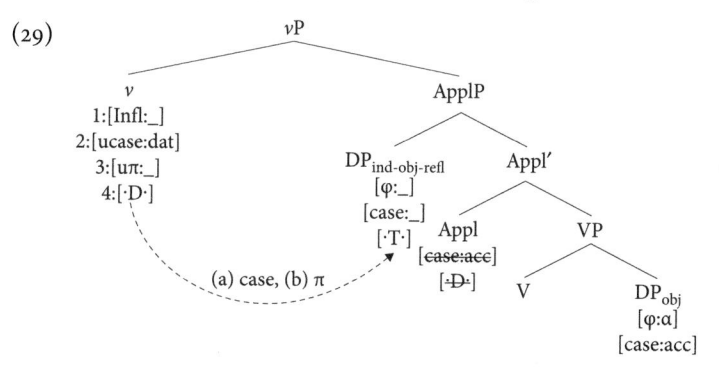

In the next step (30), the external argument is introduced by v. This DP binds the reflexive pronoun: from now on, the reflexive clitic bears valued φ-features. As already discussed in Section 3.3.2, the introduction of the external argument (and binding) takes place too late to lead to successful valuation on v (since Agree has already happened in the derivational step in (29)).

(30)

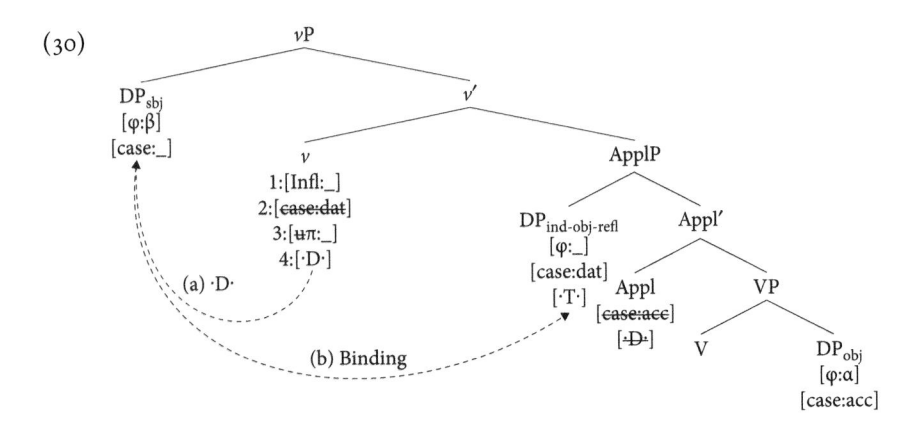

In tree (31), Perf is merged in the structure. It agrees with *v* for [uInfl:perf]. Due to Nested Agree, [uπ] also targets *v*. *v* bears a [π] feature, although unvalued. This is enough to stop the search for [π], resulting in no valuation. Having failed in copying a value for the π-feature on *v* in (29) leads to the same result on Perf. At Spell-out, BE will be inserted because Perf does not contain any valued π-feature.

(31)

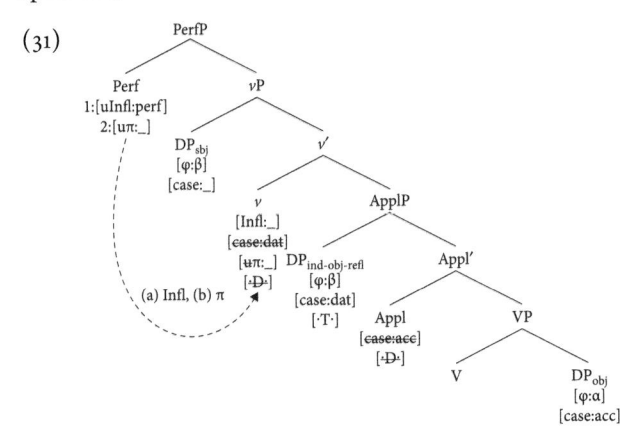

In the next step, T selects PerfP. Cliticization of the reflexive clitic happens as soon as T is merged in the structure (Rizzi 1986; McGinnis 1998; Heck 2016), resulting in a complex head that contains T and the clitic. After cliticization, T assigns nominative case to the subject and agrees with it in φ-features, due to Nested Agree, giving rise to the expected subject agreement. Finally, the DP$_{sbj}$ moves to Spec,T because of the EPP-feature [•D•] on T.

At Spell-out, the terminal nodes are substituted as follows (I repeat here some of the Vocabulary Items already introduced in (19) and (26)).

(32)   a.   /un/ /panino/ ↔ DP[√SANDWICH][φ:-part,+sg,+m][case:acc]
       b.   /mandʒata/ ↔ v[Infl:perf][π:-part] + V[√EAT]
       c.   /ɛ/ ↔ Perf[π:_] + T[T:pres][φ:-part,+sg,+f]
       d.   /si/ ↔ DP[φ:-part,+sg,+f]
       e.   /Teresa /↔ DP[√TERESA][φ:-part,+sg,+f][case:nom]

3.3.4   Unergative verbs

The perfect auxiliary of unergative verbs is HAVE, as shown in (33).

(33)   Teresa ha   risposto.
       Teresa have.PRS.3SG answer.PRTC
       'Teresa has answered.'

As mentioned in Section 3.2.2, I consider unergative verbs as transitive predicates, introduced by a non-defective *v*. Here I follow Hale & Keyser (1993, 2002); Laka (1993); Pineda (2014); Baker & Bobaljik (2017) in considering unergative verbs as universally underlyingly transitive. Unergative verbs merge with an internal argument that has no phonological realization and whose lexical features are the same as the lexical features of the verb. For example, the unergative verb 'dance' corresponds to the transitive structure 'dance a dance'. Unergative verbs differ from transitive verbs only because their object position is not free, but it contains instead a covert cognate object. In addition, I propose that the covert object bears morpho-syntactic features, as other DPs (and even silent arguments such as pro) do. In particular, it bears a valued π-feature with default third person [π:-part].

For the purpose of auxiliary selection, the derivation proceeds exactly as described for transitive verbs in Section 3.3.1. As shown in tree (34), the person feature of the object values the probe on transitive *v*.

(34)

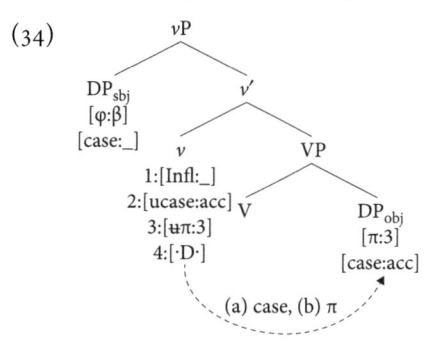

After the step in (34), the π-probe on Perf will copy a valued π-feature from *v*, resulting in HAVE insertion. At Spell-out, the substitutions for the verb and the auxiliary are as follows.

(35) a. /risposto/ ↔ v[Infl:perf][π:-part] + V[$\sqrt{\text{ANSWER}}$]
      b. /a/ ↔ Perf[π:-part] + T[T:pres][φ:-part,+sg,+f]

3.3.5 Unaccusative verbs

The other context where BE shows up as the perfect auxiliary is with unaccusative predicates. An example is repeated in (36).

(36) Teresa è   arrivat-a.
      Teresa be.PRS.3SG arrive.PRTC-SG.F
      'Teresa has arrived.'

As I said in Section 3.2.2, I assume that unaccusative roots are selected by a defective v, which neither introduces the external argument, nor assigns the external Theta-role, nor assigns accusative case The sole argument of these verbs is the internal one, which moves to the subject position. Moreover, I consider defective v to be a phase, as other v heads are (Legate 2003; Richards 2005; Müller 2010, 2011; Abels 2012; Heck 2016).

I propose the following derivation for sentence (36). In tree (37), V selects its internal argument and is selected by defective v.

(37)

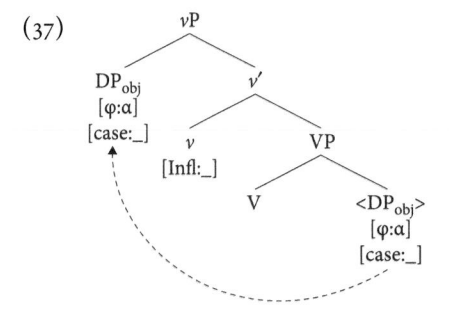

The head v does not interact with the DP: it is neither a case assigner, nor a π-probe. Since the DP has not yet received case, it must move to the edge of the phase for reasons that I will clarify in Chapter 6 (namely, edge feature insertion because of an unchecked feature).

In (38), the head Perf is merged in the structure. Firstly, it checks its [uInfl:perf] on v. Agree between Perf and v is successful: the uninterpretability of [Infl] on Perf goes away and v copies the value *perf* onto the attribute [Infl]. Subsequently, the second feature [uπ:_] on Perf must be discharged.

(38)

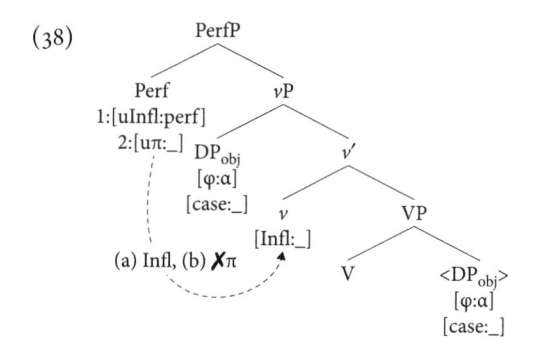

The *Maximize* condition of Nested Agree (see (14)) causes [uπ:_] on Perf to probe *v*. However, in this case *v* does not bear the relevant feature: Perf cannot use the same Agree-Link for the two separate probes it bears. Consequently, a new search must be started, as the *No-backtracking* condition of Nested Agree (see (14)) requires. The new domain for Perf[uπ:_] is not the whole c-command domain of Perf, but only the sister of *v*. In this portion of structure, there is no matching feature. This is due to the phasal status of *v*. In fact, the complement of *v* is opaque for any further syntactic operation because of the PIC. The phase head *v* constitutes the lower boundary for Agree. In addition, there is no possible goal below *v*, since the DP$_{obj}$ has already moved to Spec,*v*. As the No-backtracking condition of Nested Agree assures, it is not possible for Perf to reach the syntactic positions between itself and *v*: once a portion of the tree has been skipped for an operation triggered by a head, this head cannot reach it anymore even for any other operation.

As shown in (38), Agree fails and Perf cannot copy any π-feature. However, this does not cause any derivational crash (Béjar 2003; Preminger 2014). Once the search stops, either because a matching feature has been found, or because the whole domain has been scanned, the uninterpretability of the probe is erased, independently of the result of the operation. If no goal is found, the probe-feature remains unvalued and the elsewhere form is inserted at Spell-out.[33]

In the following step, T is merged into the structure. T assigns nominative to the DP$_{obj}$, probes it for π-features (leading to subject agreement), and triggers its movement to Spec,T.

At Spell-out, the heads V, *v*, Perf and T are substituted as follows.

---

33. According to Béjar (2003); Preminger (2014), a default value is inserted on a probe when Agree fails. I actually depart from this idea: the probe [π:_] on Perf remains unvalued if Agree fails. Nonetheless, I adopt the proposal that the derivation does not crash if Agree fails. The probe can remain unvalued, and the emergence of the elsewhere form is due to lack of valuation, rather than to default valuation.

(39) a. /arrivata/ ↔ *v*[Infl:perf][π:-part] + V[√ARRIVE]
      b. /ɛ/ ↔ Perf[π:_] + T[T:pres][φ:-part,+sg,+f]

To sum up, in unaccusative clauses the unmarked allomorph BE is inserted in the terminal node Perf because π-Agree on Perf has failed. This happens because defective *v* does not bear any π-feature and because there is no other possible goal in the structure. I conclude that the auxiliary BE emerges from the inability to copy a person value, which is due to either the absence of an accessible goal (as is the case for unaccusative verbs), or the presence of a defective goal (as for transitive verbs with a reflexive argument).

3.3.6 Intransitive verbs with both auxiliaries

In Section 2.2 of Chapter 2, I have mentioned that some intransitive verbs may be combined with both BE and HAVE (see (1-e)). When intransitive verbs can appear with both auxiliaries, the choice is influenced by various syntactic and semantic factors, which change the Aktionsarkt and the aspect of the predicate. For example, the verb *correre* 'run' shows up with both auxiliaries, as shown in (40a). However, the auxiliary BE must appear with prepositional phrases (40b), and HAVE with an internal arguments (40c).

(40) a. Maria ha   corso   / è   cors-a   velocemente.
          Maria have.PRS.3SG run.PRTC / be.PRS.3SG run.PRTC-SG.F fast
          'Maria has run fast'.   (Sorace 2000:876)
      b. Maria *ha   corso   / è   cors-a   in farmacia.
          Maria have.PRS.3SG run.PRTC / be.PRS.3SG run.PRTC-SG.F to pharmacy
          'Maria has run to the pharmacy'.   (Sorace 2000:876)
      c. Maria ha   corso   / *è   cors-a   la maratona.
          Maria have.PRS.3SG run.PRTC / be.PRS.3SG run.PRTC-SG.F the marathon
          'Maria has run the marathon'.

For these predicates with mixed behavior, I adopt the view of Sorace (2000): they can be categorized in different positions along a cline of intransitivity (see Table 1.1 in Chapter 1). The lexical semantics of each verb determines the syntactic argument structure in which the verb occurs, and, consequently, the type of *v* head with which it combines. This fact is orthogonal to the present proposal about auxiliary selection. In fact, the syntactic structure (i.e., the *v* head) corresponds to either the one of unergative verbs or the one of unaccusative verbs, thereby conditioning the morpho-phonological realization of the auxiliary. For instance, the verb *correre* 'run' can be selected either by an unaccusative *v* or by an unergative/transitive *v*, which results in the alternation in (40a). A locative prepositional phrase (40b) is possible only with the former argument structure, while an overt object (40c) requires the latter argument structure. Hence, (40b) should be analyzed as an unaccusative clause (cf. Section 3.3.5), (40c) as an unergative clause (cf. Section 3.3.4), and (40a) is ambiguous between these two structures.

Other verbs that combine with both auxiliaries are the so-called *weather verbs*. These are verbs with null valency, referring to atmospheric phenomena. The auxiliary alternation is shown in Example (41).

(41) a. Ha   piovuto molto.
      have.PRS.3SG rain.PRTC a lot
   b. È   piovuto molto.
      be.PRS.3SG rain.PRTC a lot
      'It has rained a lot'

I suggest that this alternation is of the same kind of variation found for other intransitive verbs, as the cline of intransitivity defined by Sorace (2000) describes. These verbs can be categorized with two different v heads: a transitive v (41a), or an unaccusative v (41b). In the former structure (41a), the internal argument is a covert object with valued π-feature [π:3], and the external argument is a quasi-argumental pro. The derivation is exactly as for unergative verbs (Section 3.3.4) Agree between the covert object and v, and, consequently, between v and Perf (with successful valuation), leads to HAVE insertion. In the latter case (41b), the sole argument is a quasi-argumental pro that moves to the subject position. The derivation is as for unaccusative predicates in Section 3.3.5. Perf does not find any π-feature, neither on defective v nor on pro, which is not accessible because of Nested Agree. Therefore, the Perf head will be spelled out by the elsewhere form BE.

3.3.7   Passive predicates

For passive clauses, I make use of a passive Voice$_{pass}$ head, as in all the most recent analyses of the passive (Collins 2005; Bruening 2013; Legate 2014; Alexiadou et al. 2015). Voice$_{pass}$ selects a defective v.[34] As all other inflectional heads, Voice$_{pass}$

---

34. The defectiveness of this head is not inherent, but rather derived. In fact, in Standard Italian it is impossible to passivize unaccusative predicates, as in many other languages. I do not address the question of how a full argument structure v is reduced to the kind of v selected by passive Voice. It could be due to VoiceP (Collins 2005), to a morpho-syntactic operation that prevents the realization of the external argument as an argument (Bruening 2013), to a lexical operation prior to the syntactic computation (Chomsky 1981), or to a structure removal feature (Müller 2016). Note that for the purpose of auxiliary selection it is not relevant whether the person probe is preserved on v or if it goes away together with the ability to introduce the external argument and assigning accusative case. The important point for the analysis is the presence of

bears an [Infl:_] feature, which can either acquire a value via Agree with a higher projection, or remain unvalued. Moreover, it contains a probe [uInfl:pass] that checks the [Infl] feature on v. After Agree with Voice$_{pass}$, v[Infl:pass] is spelled out as a passive participle. A similar inflectional relation between v and Voice$_{pass}$ is also assumed in Collins (2005); Bruening (2013).

In passive clauses, the perfect auxiliary is always realized as BE, as (42) shows.[35]

(42) Teresa è   stat-a   promoss-a.
      Teresa be.PRS.3SG be.PRTC-SG.F promote.PRTC-SG.F
      'Teresa has been promoted.'

I propose the following derivation for passive sentences such as (42). First of all, the passive VoiceP is built in (43). The VP is selected by a defective v, which is then selected by Voice$_{pass}$. Neither v nor Voice$_{pass}$ contains a π-probe. Voice$_{pass}$ agrees with v for [Infl] and this is the only operation between the two heads. The Infl-feature on v receives the value *pass*. The internal argument must also move first to Spec,v, then to Spec,Voice$_{pass}$, because its case feature is not valued and it must remain PIC-accessible to T (more on this in Chapter 6).

---

a passive Voice head, which intervenes because of its [Infl] feature, but lacks a [π] feature. The features on v do not matter, especially under the assumption that v does not move to Voice, as possible intervening adverbs or constituent negation seem to suggest (e.g., *Teresa è stata subito promossa* 'Teresa has been immediately promoted', *Teresa è stata non promossa, ma bocciata* 'Teresa has been not promoted, but rejected').

35. The passive auxiliary is also always spelled out as BE, as shown by the following passive clause in the present tense.

(i) Teresa è   promoss-a.
     Teresa be.PRS.3SG promote.PRTC-SG.F
     'Teresa is promoted.'

This fact can be derived at least in two ways: either there is a specific VI rule (ii-a) that spells out the terminal node Voice$_{pass}$, or BE (ii-b) is inserted as the elsewhere form when there is no person feature on a head of type v, assuming that Voice and v are of the same category.

(ii) a. /BE/ ↔ Voice$_{pass}$
      b. /BE/ ↔ v elsewhere

Note also that there should be a further VI rule that blocks the insertion of the elsewhere form BE for substituting transitive and defective v in simple clauses.

(iii) /Ø// ↔ v / V

The rule (iii) says that v is spelled out as zero when it is adjacent to a V head. This is the case for v because the verbal root undergoes head-movement to the lowest v. It is not the case for Voice$_{pass}$: this is a type of v, but it is not directly adjacent to a V head (because it selects for a vP).

(43)

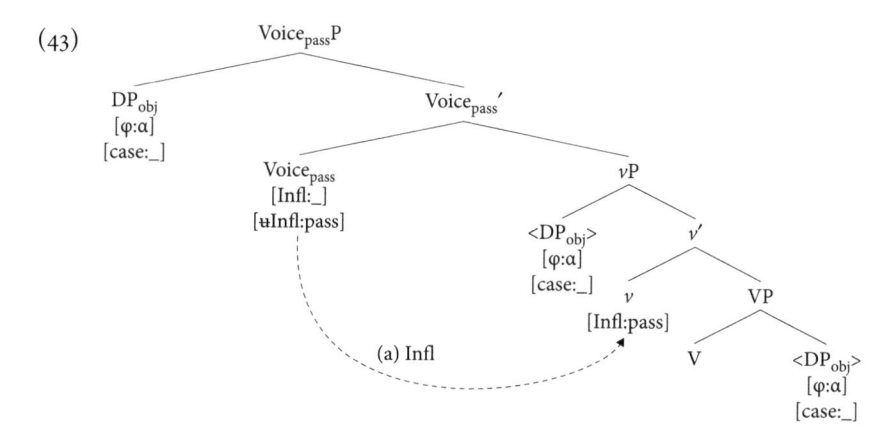

In the next step (44), Perf is merged into the structure. It checks its Infl-feature with Voice_pass. As a next step, Perf probes for person. Due to Nested Agree, Perf must probe Voice for person. However, Voice does not contain any [π]. Consequently, Perf starts its search downward from the sister of Voice. However, since Voice is a phase head, its complement is opaque for Agree, as the PIC prescribes. This means that Perf cannot access anything below the head Voice and Agree stops without any valuation. Moreover, the object has already moved out of its base position. Hence, the person probe does not succeed in finding any goal, and BE will be inserted at Spell-out.

(44)

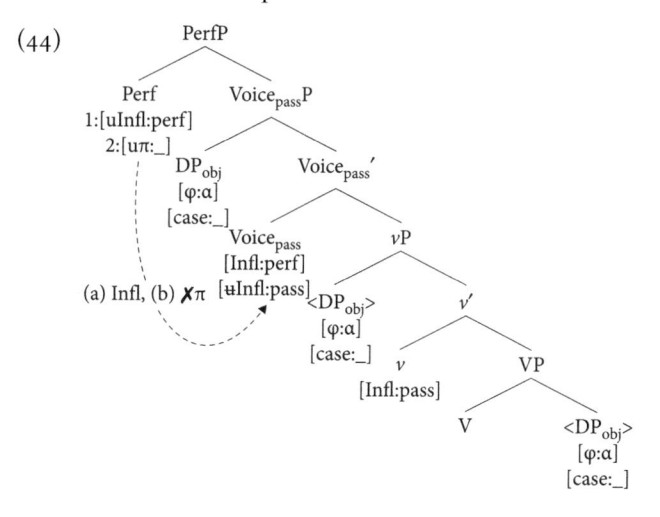

The derivation proceeds with Merge of T, which assigns nominative case to the object, agrees for φ-features with it and raises it to its specifier. This step is identical to the derivation for unaccusative verbs in Section 3.3.5.

At Spell-out, the vocabulary entries for sentence (42) are as follows. The perfect auxiliary BE (*è*) spells out the complex head Perf + T, the passive auxiliary BE (*stat-a*) in the form of a past participle spells out Voice$_{pass}$, and the passive participle of the lexical verb (*promoss-a*) realizes the complex head v + V.

(45)   a.   /promos:a/ ↔ v[Infl:pass] + V[√PROMOTE]
        b.   /stata/ ↔ Voice$_{pass}$[Infl:perf]
        c.   /ɛ/ ↔ Perf[π:_] + T[T:pres][φ:-part,+sg,+f]

To sum up, in passive clauses the perfect auxiliary is always BE because the projection responsible for the passive interpretation Voice$_{pass}$ contains an [Infl] feature, but no [π] feature.

3.3.8   Quirky verbs

Some verbs always combine with the perfect auxiliary BE. These are verbs with psychological meaning that select for two arguments: an internal argument, which bears the Theta-role of theme, is assigned nominative case and agrees with the verb, and an indirect argument, which bears the Theta-role of experiencer and dative case. Sentences with a dative experiencer and a nominative object are called *quirky subject constructions* (Taraldsen 1995; Sigurðsson 1996). An example with the verb *piacere* 'like' is provided in (46).

(46)   A Teresa   sono   piaciut-i   i   panini.
        to Teresa.DAT.3SG.F be.PRS.3PL like.PRTC-PL.M the sandwiches
        'Teresa liked the sandwiches.'

Following Taraldsen (1995); Sigurðsson (1996) (among others), I suggest that these clauses contain a quirky v similar to the v head that is used in the presence of an applicative head (see Section 3.3.3). As proposed by Belletti & Rizzi (1988: 293), I assume that the experiencer is merged as the indirect object within a complex VP, resulting in the double object construction in (47).

(47)   [$_{vP}$ v_{quirky} [$_{VP}$ IO V DO]]

The experiencer IO in Spec,V gets its Theta-role and dative case from quirky v. This quirky v does not introduce any new argument, differently from the quirky v used with benefactive arguments in Section 3.3.3, which selects an applicative phrase and triggers external Merge of a DP. Hence, it can be considered the defective version of the other quirky v. I suggest that quirky v comes in two flavors: full quirky v (to be compared with transitive v), which takes as an argument an ApplP, introduces a new DP and contains a person probe, and defective quirky v

(to be compared with unaccusative v), which selects for a VP, assigns dative case, but does not bear any person probe, similarly to unaccusative v.[36]

The derivation for (46) is as follows. The VP contains one argument in the complement position, and one in the specifier. Quirky v assigns dative case to the higher argument, which is the experiencer in Spec,V, and assigns it the experiencer-Theta-role. Instead, the DP_{obj} remains with unvalued case (it will remain PIC-accessible to T because it moves to the edge of the phase v; see Sections 6.5.5 and 6.6 in Chapter 6 for discussion).

When Perf enters the derivation, it discharges its [Infl] feature with v, which acquires the value *perf*. When it goes to the second feature [uπ:_], Perf must search v because of Nested Agree. This defective quirky v does not contain any π-feature. Perf goes on with its search, scanning the sister of v. However, given the phasal status of v, it is not possible to search into Comp,v. Agree on Perf fails because there it cannot find any suitable goal in the structure, as shown in (48). The result on Perf is [uπ:_], leading to BE insertion.

(48)

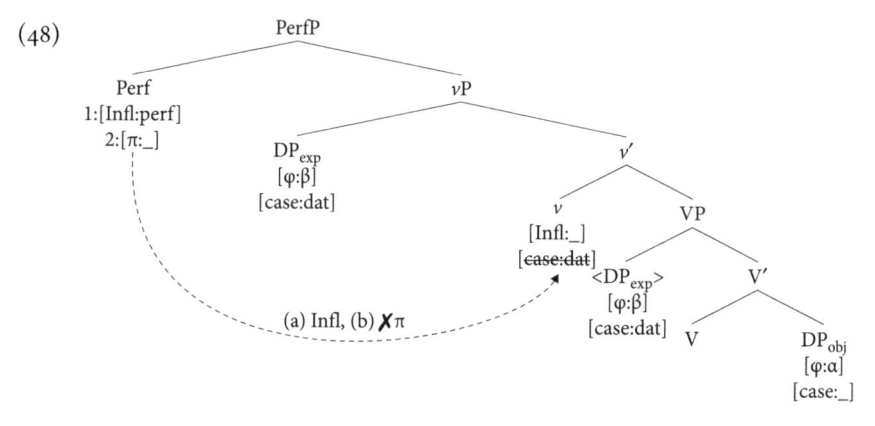

---

36. The person probe on non-defective quirky v cannot be eliminated. In fact, if in a sentence such as (27) in Section 3.3.3 the benefactive argument is not a reflexive clitic, then the auxiliary is again HAVE, as shown in (i).

(i) Teresa gli=ha   mangiato   il panino perchè lui   invece
     Teresa DAT.3SG.M=have.PRS.3SG eat.PRTC-SG.F the sandwich because NOM.3SG.M instead
     voleva   mangiare la pizza.
     want.PST.3SG eat.INF   the pizza
     'Teresa ate his sandwich because he wanted to eat Pizza instead.'

Non-defective quirky v behaves as a transitive v as far as auxiliary selection is concerned, meaning that it should contain a probe for person.

The derivation then proceeds with the T head. This assigns nominative to the DP$_{obj}$ in Spec,v and it φ-agrees with it. The result of this operation at Spell-out will be object agreement on the auxiliary. The vocabulary entries are in (49).

(49) a. /i/ /panini/ ↔ DP[√SANDWICH][φ:-part,-sg,+m][case:nom]
      b. /piaciuti/ ↔ v[Infl:perf] + V[√LIKE]
      c. /sono/ ↔ Perf[π:_] + T[T:pres][φ:-part,-sg,+m]
      d. /a/ /teresa/ ↔ DP[√TERESA][φ:-part,+sg,+f][case:dat]

3.3.9 Impersonal clauses

3.3.9.1 *The structure of impersonal clauses*

Impersonal clauses contain the impersonal clitic pronoun *si*. This pronoun may realize the agent of a transitive verb (50a), the agent of an unergative verb (50b), the patient of an unaccusative predicate (50c), or the patient of a passive verb (50d).[37] The perfect auxiliary is always realized as BE, as illustrated in (50).

(50) a. Ieri   si=sono   mangiat-i   molti spaghetti.
          yesterday IMPERS=be.PRS.3PL   eat.PRTC-PL.M many spaghetti
          'People have eaten a lot of spaghetti yesterday.'

---

37. In contrast, impersonal *si* can never be the object of a transitive verb, as (i) illustrates.

(i) *Teresa si=loda.   (grammatical with the meaning: 'Teresa praises herself.')
     teresa IMPERS=praise.PRS.3SG
     'Teresa praises people.'

To the best of my knowledge, this fact has not yet found a satisfactory explanation. Cinque (1988) argues that *si* needs to combine with a finite T and a personal AgrP, since it is under-specified for the π-feature. However, *si* does move to T because it is a clitic. Maybe a crucial aspect is the incompatibility of *si* with accusative case. However, a least in Romanian the impersonal *si* bears accusative case (Dobrovie-Sorin 1998). The ungrammaticality of (i) and its well-formedness with the reflexive meaning also suggest that the clitic in the object position is bound by the external argument, receiving the reflexive/reciprocal interpretation. This hints at a unified treatment of impersonal *si* and reflexive *si*, the difference being that impersonal *si* cannot be bound. This may be due to the fact that impersonal *si* cannot bear any index, or that it bears [π:arb] instead of [π:_]. If the latter is the case, arb should not count as a syntactic person feature (because it needs to lead to failed valuation on Perf for the purpose of auxiliary selection), but it should be a semantic person feature, in accordance with Cinque (1988). It could also be the case that impersonal *si* must be bound, but only by Voice$_{impers}$, similarly to the Agree relation that is used for expletive Voice in Alexiadou et al. (2015), or to Legate's (2014) predicate restriction (see this section below). As a consequence of this specific binding requirement, impersonal *si* must be the highest DP in the relevant domain, excluding it from the transitive object position.

b. Ieri   si=è   lavorato   molto.
    yesterday IMPERS=be.PRS.3SG work.PRTC a lot
    'People have worked a lot yesterday.'

c. Ieri   si=è   arrivat-i   in ritardo.
    yesterday IMPERS=be.PRS.3SG arrive.PRTC-PL.M in delay
    'People have arrived late yesterday.'

d. Ieri   si=è   stat-i   lodat-i   da tutti.
    yesterday IMPERS=be.PRS.3SG be.PRTC-PL.M praise.PRTC-PL.M by all
    'People have been praised by everyone yesterday.'

I propose that the argument structure of impersonal clauses is created by an impersonal Voice that has passive-impersonal semantics (in accordance with the cline of impersonals elaborated by Legate 2014). I call this head *Voice*$_{impers}$. Importantly, I suggest that Voice$_{impers}$ is associated with a π-feature that semantically restricts the external argument position, but does not saturate it, following Legate (2014: 2). *Saturation* is a semantic operation by which the requirements in the argument position are satisfied through function application or existential closure. *Predicate restriction* is a semantic operation that modifies the argument position by specifying which kind of arguments it can host (Legate 2014: 38, following Chung & Ladusaw 2003). The equivalent of these processes in syntax are Merge of a DP in an argument position (saturation), and a licensing operation (in the form of Agree or c-selection) between argument and functional head (predicate restriction). Following Legate's (2014) approach, I propose that Voice$_{impers}$ bears an unvalued π-feature, which restricts the specifier of Voice$_{impers}$ to arguments that bear an unvalued person feature as well. This is ensured by the presence of $[\pi:\_]$ on Voice$_{impers}$. Because of this feature on Voice$_{impers}$, only an impersonal argument may saturate the external argument position. In fact, the impersonal pronoun bears an unvalued π-feature (see Section 3.2.6.2). No argument with a valued π-feature can occupy Spec,Voice$_{impers}$.[38] The operation that matches the unvalued π-features on Voice and on the impersonal argument is a predicate restriction operation in the form of c-selection. Voice$_{impers}$ bears a $[\bullet D\bullet]$ feature that is relativized to DPs with an unvalued person feature: $[\bullet D[\pi:\_]\bullet]$. The

---

38. This proposal exhibits some similarities with the analysis of reflexively marked anticausatives developed by Alexiadou et al. (2015: 106). These sentences contain an expletive Voice head that projects a specifier, which can only host a se-reflexive. This is because this position can only be occupied by DPs without denotation (given the expletive nature of Voice). A se-reflexive does not express any denotation if it lacks a c-commanding antecedent (Alexiadou et al. 2015: 110). Note that Alexiadou et al. (2015: 99) do not offer any analysis of impersonal clauses, but they suggest that these should involve a Voice projection with an implicit thematic external argument.

impersonal pronoun can be merged either as the external argument of Voice$_{impers}$ (for instance, in transitive clauses), or as the internal argument of the verb, moving to Spec,Voice$_{impers}$ in order to saturate the Voice$_{impers}$ external argument position (for instance, in unaccusative clauses).

The head Voice$_{impers}$ selects a vP. I propose that its complement can be either a defective vP or a full argument structure vP. The different v heads lead to different types of impersonal sentences. In fact, impersonal transitive clauses come in two versions. Either object agreement is realized on both the participle (gender and number agreement) and the auxiliary (person and number agreement), as in (51a) (and in (50a)), or default third person is realized on the auxiliary and participle agreement does not show up, as in (51b).[39]

(51)   a.   Si=sono   mangiat-i   gli spaghetti.
            IMPERS=be.PRS.3PL eat.PRTC-M.PL the spaghetti
       b.   Si=è   mangiato gli spaghetti.
            IMPERS=be.PRS.3SG eat.PRTC the spaghetti
            'People have eaten the spaghetti.'

I argue that the two clauses in (51) correspond to two different structures: (51a) contains a defective v, and (51b) a transitive v. The impersonal clause with agreement is similar to a passive clause, although it is different from a canonical passive; the impersonal clause without agreement is an active impersonal clause.

The difference between the two options is neutralized in the case of unaccusatives. Since unaccusative verbal roots cannot combine with transitive v (while transitive verbs can combine with both: see passivization), the only v that can be selected by Voice$_{impers}$ is the defective one. This is confirmed by the fact that unaccusative clauses do not show any contrast similar to (51a) vs. (51b), as (52) shows.

---

39. The two structures in (51) are not equally distributed across speakers and the variation seems to be idiolectal (D'Alessandro 2004: 56). The clause in (51a) is the standard expression, while (51b) is more marked. Moreover, a difference in the specificity of the object correlates with the availability of the two structures. In particular, (51b) improves if the object is a bare noun: *si è mangiato spaghetti.* I leave the specificity issue out of the discussion because it is not relevant for auxiliary selection: the chosen allomorph is always BE, independently of specificity. In addition, according to D'Alessandro (2004: 60) other sentences that are a mix of the two variants in (51) are also possible for some speakers: *si=è mangiat-i gli spaghetti.* I also leave aside these cases because variation affects participle agreement, but not auxiliary selection.

(52) a. Si=è   arrivat-i   ieri.
          IMPERS=be.PRS.3SG arrive.PRTC-M.PL yesterday
      b. *Si=è   arrivato   ieri.
          IMPERS=be.PRS.3SG arrive.PRTC yesterday
      c. *Si=sono   arrivat-i   ieri.
          IMPERS=be.PRS.3PL arrive.PRTC-M.PL yesterday
          'People have arrived yesterday.'

I will now provide evidence for the claim that Voice$_{imp}$ can select different types of *v*, leading to the different structures in (51). The first observation concerns case. In Italian, pronouns bear overt case inflection. If the DP$_{obj}$ in (51) is substituted with a pronoun, it can be replaced by a nominative pronoun (or by pro) in (51a), and by an accusative pronoun in (51b) (D'Alessandro 2004, 2017a).

(53) a. pro/Essi/*Li   si=sono   mangiat-i.
          PRO/NOM.3PL.M/ACC.3PL.M IMPERS=be.PRS.3PL eat.PRTC-M.PL
      b. *pro/*Essi/Li   si=è   mangiato/-i.
          PRO/NOM.3PL.M/ACC.3PL.M IMPERS=be.PRS.3SG eat.PRTC/-M.PL
          'People have eaten them.'

This suggests that the DP$_{obj}$ bears a different morpho-syntactic case in the two structures in (51). It bears nominative in (51a), as a subject does, and accusative in (51b), as a transitive object does.

Secondly, the DP in (51a) can move to the preverbal subject position, while in (51b) it cannot.

(54) a. Gli spaghetti si=sono   mangiat-i   tutti.
          the spaghetti IMPERS=be.PRS.3PL eat.PRTC-M.PL all
      b. *Gli spaghetti si=è   mangiato tutti.
          the spaghetti IMPERS=be.PRS.3SG eat.PRTC all
          'People have eaten all the spaghetti.'

These data show that the internal argument in (54a) (and in (51a)) behaves as a subject as far as its possible positions are concerned, whereas this syntactic property is unavailable in (54b) (and in (51b)).

The third test concerns depictive secondary predicates. These are adjuncts that are coreferential with an argument of the main verb. In general, they are coreferential with the thematic object in passives, and with the initiator in impersonals (Legate 2014: 96). When applied to (51), this test shows that the depictive phrase refers to the thematic object in (51a), suggesting a passive structure for this sentence. In contrast, in (51b) it refers to the impersonal clitic *si* (which identifies a group of people acting as an agent), indicating an active impersonal structure for (51b).

(55) a. Si=sono   derubat-i   due ragazzi$_i$ [da   ubriachi]$_i$.
          IMPERS=be.PRS.3PL rob.PRTC-M.PL two boys   while drunk
          'People have robbed two boys while drunk.' (the boys were drunk)

      b. Si$_i$=è   derubato due ragazzi [da   ubriachi]$_i$.
          IMPERS=be.PRS.3SG eat.PRTC two boys   while drunk
          'People have robbed two boys while drunk.' (the thieves were drunk)

A fourth piece of evidence comes from the distribution of the by-phrase (i.e., the agent argument in passive clauses). By-phrases should be impossible in the impersonal clauses in (51). If the impersonal sentence with object agreement (51a) is a passive clause and the impersonal pronoun *si* expresses the agent, it should be impossible to add an overt by-phrase because the agent is already present. If the impersonal sentence with object agreement (51b) is an active clause, the agent cannot be expressed with a by-phrase. Example (56) shows that this prediction is born out.

(56) a. *Si=sono   mangiat-i   gli spaghetti dal   cliente.
          IMPERS=be.PRS.3PL eat.PRTC-M.PL the spaghetti by.the customer

      b. *Si=è   mangiato gli spaghetti dal   cliente.
          IMPERS=be.PRS.3SG eat.PRTC the spaghetti by.the customer
          'The customer has eaten the spaghetti.'

In both cases, the impersonal pronoun saturates the external argument position and makes it impossible to merge an agentive by-phrase (as suggested by Legate 2014).

Although impersonal clauses with agreement (as in (51a)) resemble passive clauses, they are not canonical passives. The first point of divergence concerns the form of the by-phrase. In Italian, the agent of a passive predicate is realized as a prepositional phrase (PP). However, *si* is not a PP. This is confirmed by its complementary distribution with DPs (57a) and by its ability to trigger plural agreement when it is base-generated as an object in unaccusative clauses (57b) (PPs cannot control agreement).

(57) a. Si=lavora   molto / Teresa lavora   molto.
          IMPERS=work.PRS.3SG a lot   Teresa work.PRS.3SG a lot
          'People work a lot / Teresa works a lot.'

      b. Si=è   arrivat-i   ieri.
          IMPERS=be.PRS.3SG arrive.PRTC-M.PL yesterday
          'People have arrived yesterday.'

A further difference with passive clauses is that impersonal clauses are also possible with unaccusative verbs, as shown in (57b). Cross-linguistically, unaccusative verbs cannot be passivized, instead.

In addition, passive clauses require an auxiliary that realizes Voice$_{pass}$ (the passive auxiliary BE in (58a)), while in impersonal clauses Voice$_{impers}$ is not morphologically realized (no auxiliary in (58b)). In the perfect tense, passive clauses need two distinct auxiliaries, one for the passive, and one for the perfect (see Example (42)); impersonal clauses only need the perfect auxiliary (see Example (51a)).

(58) a. <u>Sono</u>   mangiat-i   gli spaghetti (da Paolo).
          be.PRS.3PL eat.PRTC-M.PL the spaghetti by Paolo
          'The spaghetti is eaten (by Paolo).'
      b. In Italia si=mangia   gli spaghetti.
          in Italia IMPERS=est.PRS.3SG the spaghetti
          'In Italy people eat spaghetti.'

In the next sections, I illustrate the derivations of the impersonal sentences in (50).

3.3.9.2 Transitive verbs with impersonal si

In this section, I describe the derivation of a transitive impersonal clause with object agreement. I repeat here Example (51a).

(59) Si=sono   mangiat-i   gli spaghetti.
      IMPERS=be.PRS.3PL eat.PRTC-M.PL the spaghetti
      'People have eaten the spaghetti.'

First of all, the VP is built with a transitive verb and a DP complement. This VP is then selected by a defective v, differently from canonical transitive clauses, where the vP is headed by a full argument structure v. Defective v does not interact with anything at this point. In the next step in (60), Voice$_{impers}$ is merged.

(60)

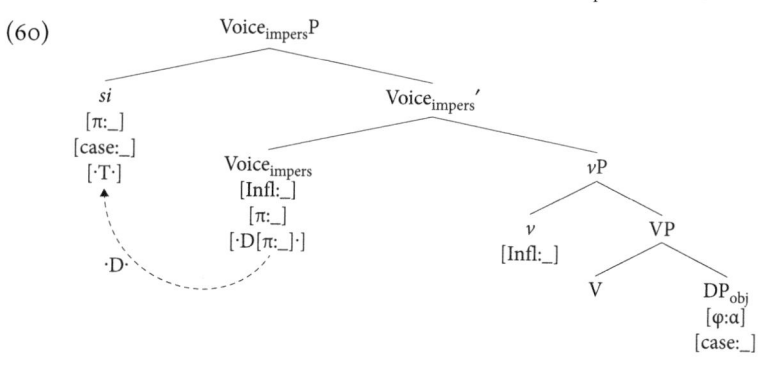

This head contains an unvalued π-feature that restricts the external argument position to an argument that bears the same feature (see 3.3.9.1). I express this requirement with the feature $[\bullet D[\pi:\_]\bullet]$ on $\text{Voice}_{\text{impers}}$. The impersonal pronoun can saturate $\text{Spec,Voice}_{\text{impers}}$, since it bears the right type of feature $(\pi:\_)$. Hence, the impersonal DP *si* is introduced as the external argument, and receives the Theta-role of initiator.

The next head that enters the derivation is Perf, as (61) shows. This checks the [Infl] feature on Voice, which acquires the value *perf*. Consequently, the complex head $V + v + \text{Voice}_{\text{impers}}$ that arises via head movement will be spelled out as a past participle. The [Infl] feature on *v* remains unchecked, but this is not problematic: it is exactly what happens in the present tense, when Perf is not part of the numeration and *v* is selected by T. The next operation performed by Perf is the search for person. Because of Nested Agree, Perf must probe $\text{Voice}_{\text{impers}}$ for π. $\text{Voice}_{\text{impers}}$ is a matching goal for the person probe, since it contains a π-feature, although unvalued. Therefore, Agree stops. The result on Perf is a lack of valuation for the person feature.

(61)

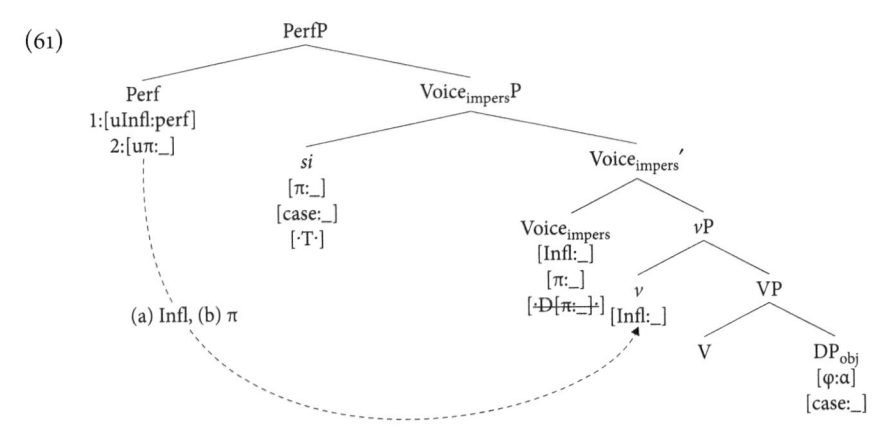

The next derivational steps are shown in (62). As soon as T enters the structure, the clitic *si* incorporates into it, because of its $[\bullet T\bullet]$ feature. The clitic and T form a complex head. From this position, the clitic can neither receive case from T, nor be a target for φ-Agree on T. Hence, the impersonal clitic *si* ends up with an unvalued case feature.[40] Nominative is assigned by T to the internal argument, whose case is still unvalued.[41] Because of Nested Agree, T also probes the DP_{obj} for $[\varphi]$,

---

40. This is in line with Baker's (1988) theory of incorporation, according to which incorporated elements do not need case. Moreover, I follow Bošković (2007) in assuming that case features on a case assigner head (such as T) can remain unchecked without causing any problem in the derivation.

41. The internal object should not be accessible for T because *v* is a phase. I discuss this issue in Section 6.6 of Chapter 6, when addressing participle agreement with in situ objects. When an internal argument controls agreement, this argument should move out of the phase domain in

thereby skipping Voice$_{impers}$. This results in object agreement on the finite verb, as in sentence (59).[42]

(62)

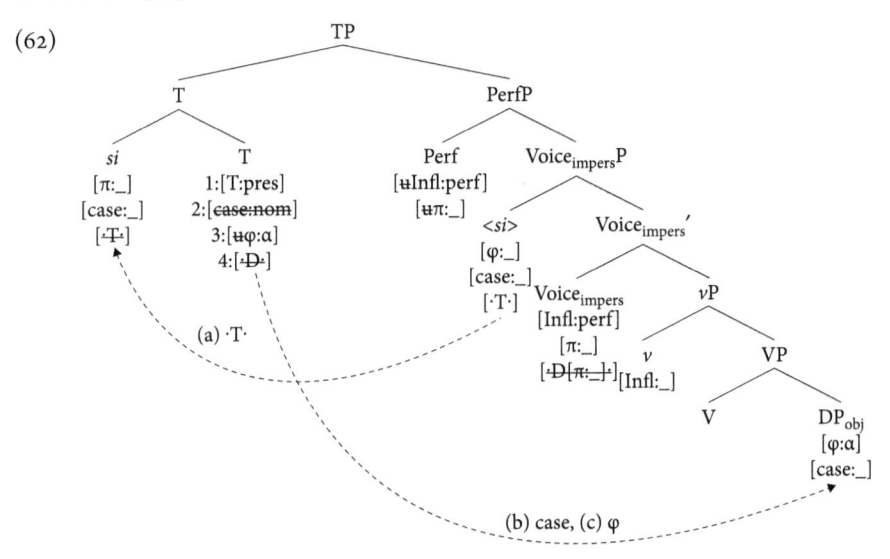

The vocabulary entries at Spell-out are as follows.

(63) a. /gli/ /spaget:i/ ↔ DP[√SPAGHETTI][φ:-part,-sg,+m][case:nom]
      b. /mandʒati/ ↔ v + Voice[Infl:perf][π:_] + V[√EAT]
      c. /sono/ ↔ Perf[π:_] + T[T:pres][φ:-part,-sg,+m]
      d. /si/ ↔ DP[π:_][case:_]

To sum up, the perfect auxiliary is realized as BE because the unvalued π-feature of Voice$_{impers}$ intervenes. It is noteworthy that, in the case of impersonal clauses, the type of argument structure of the verb does not matter for the purpose of auxiliary selection. In all clauses containing an impersonal pronoun the auxiliary is realized as BE because the unvalued person feature on Voice$_{impers}$ always leads to defective intervention. Agree stops without any feature being copied on Perf, resulting in BE insertion.

---

order to remain accessible for higher heads. This movement can be either overt (eventually not visible because of further movement of Voice-v-V to T), or covert (cf. Section 6.6.1 in Chapter 6 for some tests for covert movement).

42. As far as the EPP-feature on T is concerned, it can be satisfied by covert movement of the nominative DP, which can also surface in the subject position, generating the clause *gli spaghetti si=sono mangiat-i* (see also Section 6.6.1 in Chapter 6). Another possibility is that it is satisfied by *pro*, by cliticization, or by movement of the auxiliary to T (Alexiadou & Anagnostopoulou 1998).

This is also evident in the case of impersonal transitive clauses without agreement, as in (51b), repeated again in (64).

(64) Si=è   mangiato gli spaghetti.
      IMPERS=be.PRS.3SG eat.PRTC the spaghetti
      'People have eaten the spaghetti.'

The derivation of (64) is very similar to the one just sketched. The main difference is that in this case *v* is non-defective. The first step of the derivation is shown in (65). Non-defective *v* assigns accusative case to the object, and agrees with it for the person feature. It also introduces the external argument, which in this derivation is the impersonal pronoun. There is no restriction on the type of argument that *v* can introduce in its specifier. However, the derivation would crash at the level of Voice$_{impers}$, if *v* would introduce an element that is featurally different from the impersonal *si*.

(65)

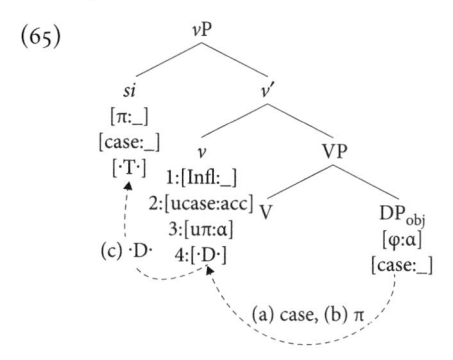

Voice$_{impers}$ is merged in the next step, described in (66). Voice$_{impers}$ restricts its external argument position to a π-defective item. The impersonal pronoun, which was firstly merged as the external argument of *v*, moves to Spec,Voice$_{impers}$, attracted by the [•D[π:_]•] feature on Voice$_{impers}$. No other argument with valued φ-features would be able to satisfy the selectional restriction imposed by Voice$_{impers}$. In this case, the [•D[π:_]•] feature triggers internal Merge instead of external Merge.[43] This is because the numeration does not contain any other DPs that could satisfy this feature.

(66)

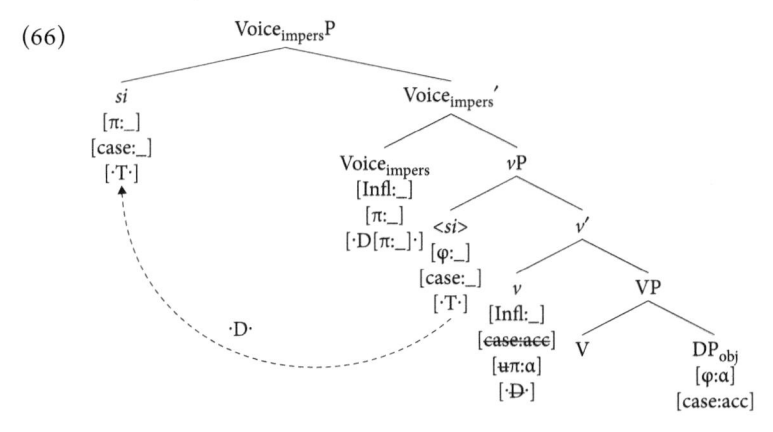

In the next step in (67), Perf is merged with Voice$_{impers}$P. The first operation that Perf carries out is [Infl]-Agree. The highest matching goal is Voice$_{impers}$. The two heads agree for [Infl]. Thereafter, the second probe on Perf initiates its search. Nested Agree forces [uπ:_] on Perf to probe Voice$_{impers}$. This head bears a π-feature, although unvalued. This matching feature stops Agree, independently of its value. The result on Perf is [uπ:_], leading to BE insertion.

---

43. This derivation requires the assumption that Voice$_{impers}$ is a Theta-role assigner only if it combines with a defective vP, namely when it introduces si via external Merge (as in the previous derivation in this section) and not when it raises it (as in the present derivation). Note that this assumption is also needed because otherwise in the derivation of (64) the impersonal si would get two Theta-roles (one from non-defective v, one from Voice$_{impers}$). Moreover, this assumption allows us to rule out the scenario where the numeration contains a further DP, which could be merged in Spec,v instead of si: there is only a Theta-role that is provided by v, and si needs it. A further DP would cause a violation of the Theta-criterion.

(67)

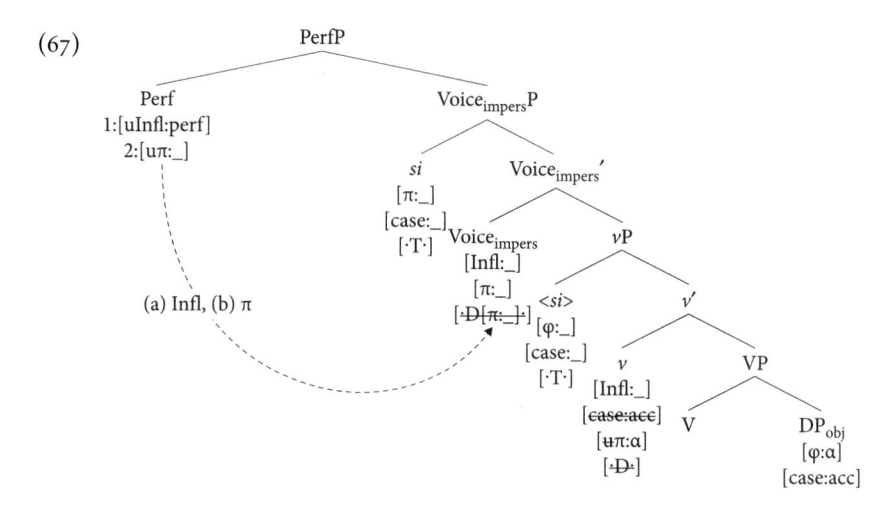

The derivation continues with Merge of T, represented in tree (68). First of all, the clitic *si* moves to T, thereby forming a complex head. Now the clitic is not accessible anymore for operations triggered by T, since it has become part of T itself. When T tries to assign nominative case, there is no possible goal in the structure. In fact, the DP$_{obj}$ has already received case. Consequently, nominative case is not assigned to any DP. Since this operation ([ucase:nom]) does not return any goal, the subsequent operation triggered by T ([uφ:_]) is not constrained by Nested Agree. The probe for person starts its search from the sister of T. It finds Perf, which bears the relevant feature, although unvalued. Hence, T agrees with Perf for [π], without copying any value. At Spell-out, T will be spelled out with default inflection.

(68)

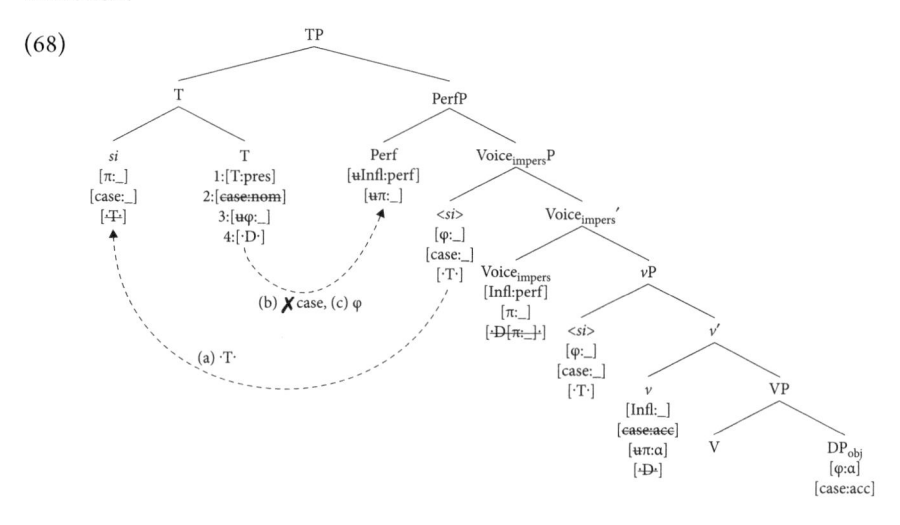

At Spell-out, the vocabulary entries are as follows.

(69) a. /gli/ /spaget:i/ ↔ DP[√SPAGHETTI][φ:-part,-sg,+m][case:acc]
    b. /mandʒato/ ↔ v + Voice[Infl:perf][π:_] + V[√EAT]
    c. /ε/ ↔ Perf[π:_] + T[T:pres][φ:_]
    d. /si/ ↔ DP[π:_][case:_]

3.3.9.3 *Unergative verbs with impersonal si*

An impersonal clause with an unergative verb is repeated in (70).

(70) Si=è   lavorato   molto.
    IMPERS=be.PRS.3SG work.PRTC a lot
    'People have worked a lot.'

The derivation for clauses with unergative verbs is exactly the same as for transitive verbs, based on the assumption that unergative verbs are underlyingly transitive verbs (see Section 3.3.4). In Section 3.3.9.2, I have proposed that there are two possible derivations for transitive predicates, depending on the type of v that is selected by Voice$_{impers}$ (namely, defective v or transitive v). Similarly, Voice$_{impers}$ can also select either a defective v or a transitive v when the verb is unergative.

With a defective v, the derivation is equal to the one proposed for sentence (59) in the previous section. The only difference concerns the internal argument, which is phonologically not realized and bears the following φ-features: [φ: 3,sg,m].

When Perf enters the derivation, it targets Voice$_{impers}$ for person-Agree (after having agreed with it for [Infl]). The person probe on Perf cannot copy any value, leading to BE insertion. When T is merged, *si* incorporates into it; nominative case is assigned to the cognate object and its φ-features are copied onto T. For this reason, the inflection on the auxiliary is third person singular.

Voice$_{impers}$ can also select a non-defective v, as I have proposed in the derivation for the transitive clause in (64). However, the presence of a π-feature on v does not change the result of Agree on Perf. As in the previous case, Perf agrees with Voice$_{impers}$ for [π], without copying any value, thereby leading to BE insertion at Spell-out. As soon as T is merged, *si* incorporates into it. Then, nominative assignment by T fails, since in its c-command domain there is no DP that lacks case. When it comes to [uφ:_], Nested Agree cannot apply because the previous operation has failed: the domain of [uφ:_] on T is the sister of T. As a consequence, the φ-probe targets Perf, without copying any value. At Spell-out, the terminal node T will be substituted by the elsewhere form (third person singular), in correspondence with the unvalued morpho-syntactic feature [φ]. The vocabulary entries for sentence (70) are as follows (I have omitted from the trees the adverbial 'a lot', which is an adjunct to Spec,v).

(71) a.   /molto/ ↔ AdvP[√A LOT]
      b.   /lavorato/ ↔ v + Voice[Infl:perf][π:_] + V[√WORK]
      c.   /ɛ/ ↔ Perf[π:_] + T[T:pres][φ:_]
      d.   /si/ ↔ DP[π:_][case:_]

To sum up, both the derivations with a defective v and with a transitive v lead to the same string: the sentence (70) is ambiguous between two syntactic structures.

3.3.9.4 Unaccusative verbs with impersonal si

In unaccusative impersonal clauses, the perfect auxiliary is always BE in third person singular (and the participle exhibits plural agreement), as shown in (72).

(72) Si=è   partit-i   presto.
      IMPERS=be.PRS.3SG leave.PRTC-M.PL early
      'People have left early.'

Unaccusative verbal roots can combine only with defective v. An unaccusative verb can never be selected by a full argument structure v (whereas transitive verbs can combine with both v heads, see the case of passives). The vP complement can only be built with the defective v. Hence, there is only one option when it comes to the type of v selected by Voice_impers.

      The derivation for (72) proceeds as follows. The unaccusative vP is built as in Section 3.3.5. In this case, the internal argument is the impersonal pronoun si. The head v introduces a phase boundary; the clitic moves to Spec,v, because it bears the unchecked features [case:_] and [•T•] (see Chapter 6). In (73), Voice_impers is merged in the structure. The clitic further moves to its specifier, driven by the [•D[π:_]•] feature on the head. The featural specification of the clitic is compatible with the requirement on Voice ([π:_]).

(73)

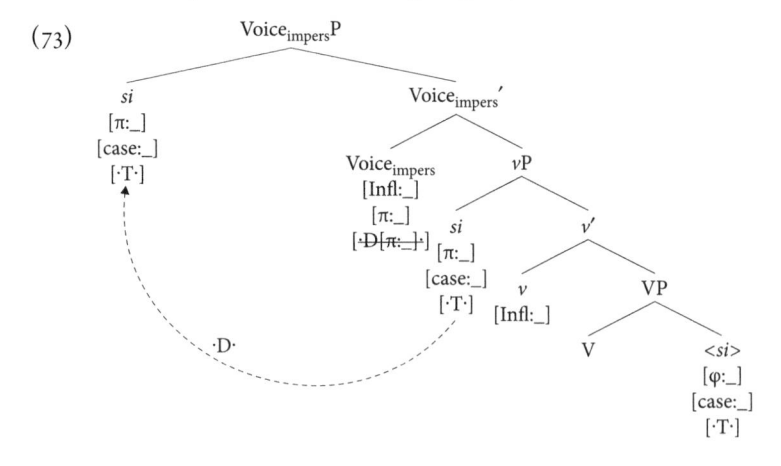

In (74), the head Perf enters the derivation. Perf checks the [Infl] feature on Voice$_{impers}$ and agrees with it for π. However, no value is copied, leading to BE insertion at Spell-out.

(74)

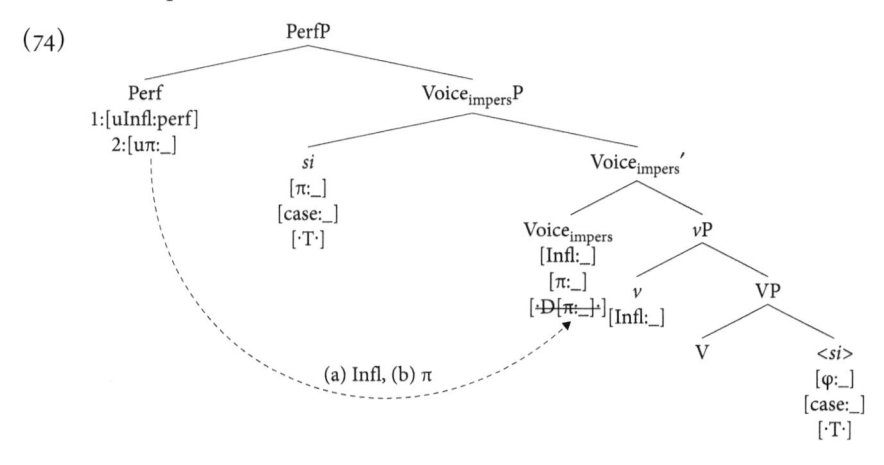

In the next step, T is merged into the structure. The clitic incorporates into it. The head T cannot assign nominative case because there is no possible goal in the structure. The impersonal *si* is the only DP in the structure, and it is not a target for case assignment from T because it is part of T itself. As far as φ-Agree is concerned, T agrees with Perf, which is the closest matching goal in the c-command domain of T, as in the derivation of sentence (64) in Section 3.3.9.2. In this case, φ-Agree is not subject to Nested Agree, because the previous operation of case assignment has failed. Agreement with Perf does not lead to successful π-valuation. At Spell-out, the inflection on T will be realized by default agreement, i.e. third person singular.

At Spell-out, the vocabulary entries for sentence (72) are as follows (I have omitted from the trees the adverbial 'early', which is an adjunct to Spec,*v*).

(75)   a.   /presto/ ↔ AdvP[√EARLY]
       b.   /partiti/ ↔ *v* + Voice[Infl:perf][π:_] + V[√LEAVE]
       c.   /ε/ ↔ Perf[π:_] + T[T:pres][φ:_]
       d.   /si/ ↔ DP[π:_][case:_]

3.3.9.5   *Impersonal passives*

The impersonal argument can also be the patient of a passive clause, as in (76).

(76)   Si=è   stat-i   lodat-i.
       IMPERS=be.PRS.3SG be.PRTC-M.PL praise.PRTC-M.PL
       'People have been praised.'

In this derivation, the impersonal pronoun *si* is merged as the internal argument of a transitive verb with a defective *v*, required in passives. From the internal argument position, the impersonal *si* moves to Spec,*v* because it needs to escape the phase domain (due to its unchecked features). The *v*P is then selected by Voice$_{pass}$, and *v* acquires the value pass for the Infl-feature via Agree with Voice$_{pass}$, determining its realization as a passive participle. The clitic *si* moves to Spec,Voice$_{pass}$. After these operations, Voice$_{impers}$ is merged into the structure. The clitic *si* moves to its specifier, given the [•D[π:_]•] feature. Voice$_{impers}$P is then selected by Perf. Perf probes Voice$_{impers}$ for [Infl], and then for [uπ:_], resulting in failed π-valuation, and, consequently, in BE insertion. When T is merged, cliticization applies. Nominative assignment fails; T probes Perf for φ-features (Nested Agree does not apply because the first operation, nominative assignment, has not returned any result). The default third person singular on the auxiliary in T shows up because, as in the case of unaccusative impersonals, person valuation on T fails, since Perf bears unvalued an π-feature. At Spell-out, the unvalued φ-features on T are realized with the elsewhere form, third person singular.

The vocabulary entries for sentence (76) are as follows.

(77) a.   /lodati/ ↔ *v*[Infl:pass] + V[√PRAISE]
      b.   /stati/ ↔ Voice$_{pass}$[Infl:pass] + Voice$_{impers}$[Infl:perf][π:_]
      c.   /ɛ/ ↔ Perf[π:_] + T[T:pres][φ:_]
      d.   /si/ ↔ DP[π:_][case:_]

3.4   Summary

In this chapter, I have developed a detailed derivation for auxiliary selection in different types of clauses in Standard Italian: transitive, transitive with a reflexive argument (direct or indirect object), unergative, unaccusative, passive, quirky, and impersonal (combined with transitive, unergative, unaccusative, and passive verbs).

Standard Italian is a language where the alternation between BE and HAVE for the perfect auxiliary depends on the argument structure, i.e., it is argument-structure-based. However, the sole dependency on the argument structure cannot account for the distribution of the perfect auxiliaries in different clauses. Auxiliary selection depends not only on the featural make-up of the functional heads, but also on the features of the arguments. The morpho-phonological realization of Perf is determined by both the type of *v* and the π-feature on *v*, valued as a result of a prior Agree relation between *v* and the DP$_{obj}$. The person feature of the internal argument is the decisive factor for auxiliary selection, and this is accessible for

Perf by means of Agree for the [Infl] feature between Perf and *v*. Auxiliary selection in Standard Italian is the result of cyclic Agree between Perf and the DP_{obj}, enabled by the intermediate head *v*.

Whenever *v* successfully agrees for person, Perf also bears a valued person feature. In this case, Perf is spelled out by the more specific allomorph HAVE (in Standard Italian). The default allomorph BE emerges because of morpho-syntactic defectiveness (of either *v* or a DP argument). In particular, if *v* is defective (i.e., it does not inherently bear a person probe), π-Agree on Perf fails and the allomorph BE is inserted. This is the case of unaccusative verbs. Similarly, if Voice contains an unvalued person feature, the probe on Perf remains unvalued. This can be seen in impersonal clauses in Italian. Likewise, if a DP in the complement of *v* is defective, *v* cannot copy any valued person feature. Consequently, the person probe on Perf cannot be valued, causing the insertion of the default allomorph BE. This is the case of reflexive clauses in Italian.

In the next chapter, I extend this analysis to restructuring in Standard Italian, where auxiliary selection seems a very complex phenomenon.

CHAPTER 4

Auxiliary selection in restructuring

4.1 Introduction

In Chapter 2, I have developed an Agree-based theory of auxiliary selection. In Chapter 3, I have derived the distribution of the perfect auxiliaries HAVE and BE in Standard Italian. In this chapter, I extend this analysis to restructuring clauses.[44]

The chapter is structured as follows. First of all, I introduce the phenomenon of restructuring in Section 4.2. The relevant data about auxiliary selection in restructuring are presented in Section 4.3. In Section 4.4, I introduce my proposal about restructuring configurations: these are obligatory monoclausal raising structures with reduced complements of different sizes. In Section 4.5, I propose that auxiliary selection in restructuring is due to two factors: the presence of a special type of v, and the optionality for different sizes of the complement. In Section 4.6, I offer the detailed derivation for all combinations of lexical verbs and complement sizes, thereby providing the first explicit analysis of auxiliary selection in restructuring. I discuss apparently problematic cases of mismatches between clitic climbing and auxiliary switch in Section 4.7. In Section 4.8, I briefly consider the cross-linguistic variation among Italian dialects. In Section 4.9, I touch upon auxiliary selection in other complementation types. Finally, I sum up the results of this chapter in the concluding section (4.10), highlighting their relevance to the theory of auxiliary selection proposed in this book.

---

44. A version of this chapter has appeared as a paper in the journal *Syntax*: Amato (to appear). The present chapter must be considered as a republication of that article. Amato (to appear) also contains the following additional sections. Firstly, it provides supporting evidence for the proposal about different sizes of the complement with new data about operations that are licit or non-licit in the presence of auxiliary switch (as briefly mentioned here in Section 4.4.1). Secondly, the difference between control and raising is discussed with relevant tests (as mentioned here in Section 4.5.4). Thirdly, auxiliary selection with aspectual and motion verbs is given an analysis (here only briefly addressed in Section 4.3.2).

4.2   Restructuring

The term *restructuring* refers to a structure where a modal, aspectual or motion verb takes as its complement a non-finite verb (Rizzi 1976; Wurmbrand 2003; Cinque 2004; Grano 2015). The resulting surface structure is exemplified in (1).

(1) DP_{sbj} restructuring-V [lexical-V]

Even though the syntactic structure in (1) contains two verbs, i.e. the restructuring verb and the lexical verb, it behaves as a single clause equipped with a single verbal extended projection. In fact, this configuration is transparent for some clause-bounded phenomena (which are language-specific). When these syntactic processes apply, they signal the lack of a clause boundary (a CP) between the two verbs. In Standard Italian, the operations that may apply to (1) are clitic climbing, long object movement, and auxiliary switch. The set of restructuring verbs varies depending on the considered operation and it is often subject to intra-speaker variation. Moreover, not every restructuring verb homogeneously allows for all monoclausal behaviors. Instead, restructuring verbs are located along a cline of "monoclausality".

In Standard Italian, clitic climbing is the most widespread restructuring behavior (see de Andrade & Bok-Bennema 2017: 39 for a detailed list of the verbs that allow for clitic climbing). The term *clitic climbing* refers to the placement of a clitic pronoun, which is an argument of the lexical verb, on the restructuring inflected verb. Clitic climbing is in general optional: the clitic can surface either on the verb that selects it (lack of clitic climbing) (2a), or on the restructuring verb (clitic climbing) (2b).

(2)   *Clitic climbing*
    a.   Vorrei   andar=ci   con Maria.
           want.COND.1SG go.INF=there with Maria
    b.   Ci=vorrei   andare con Maria.
           there=want.COND.1SG go.INF with Maria
           'I would like to go there with Maria.'   (Cardinaletti & Shlonsky 2004: 521)

Another clause-bounded process is *long object movement*. In this case, the direct argument of the lexical verb is promoted to the subject position when the restructuring verb is passivized. The verbs that allow for this operation are very few aspectual verbs. An example is given in (3).

(3)   Quelle case   furono   iniziat-e   a costruire negli anni '20.
    those   houses be.PST.3PL start.PRTC-PL.F to build.INF in.the years 20
    'Those houses were started to build in the 20's.' (literally)   (Cinque 2003: 34)

Another transparency effect found in Italian restructuring is *auxiliary switch*. This happens when the form of the perfect auxiliary of the higher modal verb is determined by the lower lexical verb. An example is provided in (4). In (4a), the perfect auxiliary of the modal verb is realized as HAVE; in (4b), the restructuring verb takes the auxiliary BE, which is the auxiliary of the lexical verb (in this example, the unaccusative verb 'go'). Example (4b) is a case of the auxiliary switch. Auxiliary switch is optional, but it is influenced by other transparency effects such as clitic climbing.

(4) a. Teresa ha   voluto   andare al   mare.
         Teresa have.PRS.3SG want.PRTC go.INF to.the beach
         'Teresa wanted to go to the beach.
     b. Teresa è   volut-a   andare al   mare.
         Teresa be.PRS.3SG want.PRTC-SG.F go.INF to.the beach
         'Teresa wanted to go to the beach.'

In the previous literature, there is neither a definition nor a formal analysis of this phenomenon. In this chapter, I show that the distribution of the auxiliaries in (4) is the result of π-Agree in the same way as auxiliary selection in root clauses is π-Agree. I will argue that there is no true optionality, but rather it is the possibility to select complements of different sizes that determines different search domains for Agree, with different results in the valuation of the person probe on Perf.

4.3   Auxiliary selection with restructuring verbs

4.3.1   Modal verbs

As a first rough description, it can be said that the perfect auxiliary of modal verbs is HAVE. This auxiliary emerges in ellipsis contexts and with nominal complementation (Rizzi 1976: 23). In the case of ellipsis, the choice of the auxiliary does not depend on the type of elided complement clause. When the elided verb is the transitive verb *mangiare* 'eat' or the unaccusative verb *andare* 'go', the perfect auxiliary of the stranded modal verb is always HAVE, as shown in (5a,b). Similarly, with nominal complementation the auxiliary is HAVE, as illustrated in (5c).

(5) a. Mangiare la pizza? Non ho   / *sono   potuto Δ!
         eat.INF   the pizza not have.PRS.1SG / be.PRS.1SG can.PRTC
         'Eat pizza? I couldn't!'
     b. Andare al   mare? Non ho   / *sono   voluto Δ!
         go.INF to.the beach not have.PRS.1SG / be.PRS.1SG want.PRTC
         'Go to the beach? I couldn't!'

c.   Ho   / *Sono   voluto   questo.
     have.PRS.1SG / be.PRS.1SG want.PRTC this
     'I wanted this.'

When modal verbs combine with lexical verbs, auxiliary selection is a much more complex phenomenon. I will now present the relevant data in detail. The following examples contain the restructuring modal verb *volere* 'want', but the same behavior is observed with *potere* 'can' and *dovere* 'must'.

If a modal verb selects a HAVE-verb (i.e., a verb whose perfect auxiliary is HAVE: transitive and unergative predicates), then its auxiliary is invariably HAVE (6a,b). This is independent of the position of the clitic pronoun (if present), as (6b,c) show.

(6) a.   Teresa ha   voluto   mangiare la   torta.
          Teresa have.PRS.3SG want.PRTC eat.INF   the cake
     b.   *Teresa è   voluto/-a   mangiare la   torta.
          Teresa be.PRS.3SG want.PRTC/-SG.F eat.INF   the cake
          'Teresa wanted to eat the cake.'
     c.   Teresa ha   voluto   mangiar=la.
          Teresa have.PRS.3SG want.PRTC eat.INF=ACC.3SG.F
     d.   Teresa l=ha   volut-a   mangiare.
          Teresa ACC.3SG.F=have.PRS.3SG want.PRTC-SG.F eat.INF
          'Teresa wanted to eat it.'

In contrast, if the modal verb merges with a BE-verb (i.e., unaccusative verbs, but also transitive predicates with reflexive or impersonal arguments), the perfect auxiliary of the modal can be either HAVE or BE, as shown in (7a,b).[45] The emergence of BE (as in (7b)) constitutes the so-called phenomenon of auxiliary switch, which is optional.

(7) a.   Teresa ha   voluto   andare al   mare.
          Teresa have.PRS.3SG want.PRTC go.INF to.the beach
     b.   Teresa è   volut-a   andare al   mare.
          Teresa be.PRS.3SG want.PRTC-SG.F go.INF to.the beach
          'Teresa wanted to go to the beach.'

---

45. In Standard Italian, *andare* 'go' behaves as an unaccusative verb as far as the following diagnostics are concerned: (i) auxiliary selection, (ii) *ne*-cliticization, (iii) reduced relative clauses, (iv) impossibility of deverbal agent nouns. Other unaccusative verbs are *morire* 'die', *cadere* 'fall', for instance. See Sorace (2000) for a discussion of the cline between unaccusative and unergative verbs.

This optionality is also found if the lexical verb has a clitic argument that does not undergo clitic climbing, as illustrated in (8a,b). However, auxiliary switch is obligatory in the presence of clitic climbing (8c,d).[46]

(8) a. Teresa ha   voluto   andar=ci   ieri.
         Teresa have.PRS.3SG want.PRTC go.INF=there yesterday
     b. Teresa è   volut-a   andar=ci   ieri.
         Teresa be.PRS.3SG want.PRTC-SG.F go.INF=there yesterday
     c. Teresa ci=è   volut-a   andare ieri.
         Teresa there=be.PRS.3SG want.PRTC-SG.F go.INF yesterday
     d. *Teresa ci=ha   voluto   andare ieri.
         Teresa there=have.PRS.3SG want.PRTC go.INF yesterday
         'Teresa wanted to go there yesterday.'

The interaction of clitic climbing and auxiliary switch is very complex. There is a correlation between HAVE and lack of clitic climbing on the one hand (8a), and BE and clitic climbing on the other hand (8c). However, both auxiliaries can be found when the clitic does not climb (8a,b). Instead, clitic climbing and auxiliary switch strongly tend to co-occur (8c,d). I will discuss examples (8b) and (8d) in Section 4.7. For the discussion up to that section, I will concentrate on the most frequent cases, which are (8a) and (8c).

As for clitics, only the locative *ci*, the partitive *ne* and the impersonal *si* can be arguments of unaccusative verbs. An example with the clitic *ne* is given in (9). When it climbs, it triggers obligatory auxiliary switch.

(9) a. Di modelle, hanno   voluto   venir=ne   molte.
         of models   have.PRS.3PL want.PRTC come.INF=of many
     b. ?Di modelle, sono   volut-e   venir=ne   molte.
         of models   be.PRS.3PL want.PRTC-PL.F come.INF=of many
     c. Di modelle, ne=sono   volut-e   venire molte.
         of models   of=be.PRS.3PL want.PRTC-PL.F come.INF many
     d. *Di modelle, ne=hanno   voluto/-e   venire molte.
         of models   of=have.PRS.3PL want.PRTC/-PL.F come.INF many
         'Of models, many of them wanted to come.'

---

46. Note that it is not the clitic pronoun *ci* that changes the perfect auxiliary. In fact, in the case of unergative verbs the auxiliary is invariably HAVE, as (i) shows.

(i) Paolo ci=ha/*ci=è   voluto   lavorare per tre anni.
     Paolo there=have.PRS.3SG/there=be.PRS.3SG want.PRTC work.INF for three years
     'Paolo wanted to work there for three years.'

A similar pattern is found in reflexive clauses. When the reflexive clitic pronoun is the direct or indirect object of a transitive verb, auxiliary switch is always obligatory in the presence of clitic climbing. As (10c,d) illustrates, auxiliary switch is obligatory when the reflexive direct object of the transitive verb climbs. Note also that auxiliary switch without clitic climbing is non-fully grammatical (10b).

(10) a. Teresa ha   voluto   lavar=si   ieri.
          Teresa have.PRS.3SG want.PRTC wash.INF=REFL.ACC.3SG.F yesterday
      b. ??Teresa è   volut-a   lavar=si   ieri.
          Teresa be.PRS.3SG want.PRTC-SG.F wash.INF=REFL.ACC.3SG.F yesterday
      c. *Teresa si=ha   voluto   lavare   ieri.
          Teresa REFL.ACC.3SG.F=have.PRS.3SG want.PRTC wash.INF yesterday
      d. Teresa si=è   volut-a   lavare   ieri.
          Teresa REFL.ACC.3SG.F=be.PRS.3SG want.PRTC-SG.F wash.INF yesterday
          'Teresa wanted to wash herself yesterday.'

The same happens when the reflexive clitic is a dative benefactive argument, in (11).

(11) a. Teresa ha   voluto   mangiar=si   il panino.
          Teresa have.PRS.3SG want.PRTC eat.INF=REFL.DAT.3SG.F the sandwich
      b. ??Teresa è   volut-a   mangiar=si   il panino.
          Teresa be.PRS.3SG want.PRTC-SG.F eat.INF=REFL.DAT.3SG.F the sandwich
      c. *Teresa si=ha   voluto   mangiare il panino.
          Teresa REFL.DAT.3SG.F=have.PRS.3SG want.PRTC eat.INF   the sandwich
      d. Teresa si=è   volut-a   mangiare il panino.
          Teresa REFL.DAT.3SG.F=be.PRS.3SG want.PRTC-SG.F eat.INF   the sandwich
          'Teresa wanted to eat the sandwich for/by herself.'

Impersonal clauses pattern slightly differently. The clitic impersonal pronoun *si* must climb, differently from other clitics. Consequently, auxiliary switch is obligatory. In (12), I present the data for impersonal transitive verbs with object agreement; in (13), for impersonal transitive verbs without object agreement.[47] The same auxiliary distribution emerges in impersonal unergative and unaccusative clauses as well (see also Cinque 1988).

---

47. Note that sentences (12a) and (13a) become grammatical if the clitic *si* is interpreted as benefactive ('they/he wanted to eat the spaghetti for/by themselves/himself'). Sentences (12d) and (13d) are ambiguous between the benefactive and the impersonal interpretations.

(12) a. *Hanno   voluto/-i   mangiar=si   gli spaghetti.
           have.PRS.3PL want.PRTC/PRTC-PL.M eat.INF=IMPERS the spaghetti
      b. *Sono   voluto/-i   mangiar=si   gli spaghetti.
           be.PRS.3PL want.PRTC/PRTC-PL.M eat.INF=IMPERS the spaghetti
      c. *Si=hanno   voluto/-i   mangiare gli spaghetti.
           IMPERS=have.PRS.3PL want.PRTC/PRTC-PL.M eat.INF   the spaghetti
      d. Si=sono   volut-i   mangiare gli spaghetti.
           IMPERS=be.PRS.3PL want.PRTC-PL.M eat.INF   the spaghetti
           'People wanted to eat the spaghetti.'

(13) a. *Ha   voluto   mangiar=si   gli spaghetti.
           have.PRS.3SG want.PRTC eat.INF=IMPERS the spaghetti
      b. *È   voluto   mangiar=si   gli spaghetti.
           be.PRS.3SG want.PRTC eat.INF=IMPERS the spaghetti
      c. *Si=ha   voluto   mangiare gli spaghetti.
           IMPERS=have.PRS.3SG want.PRTC eat.INF   the spaghetti
      d. Si=è   voluto   mangiare gli spaghetti.
           IMPERS=be.PRS.3SG want.PRTC eat.INF   the spaghetti
           'People wanted to eat the spaghetti.'

The summary of the distribution of the two auxiliaries for modal verbs is represented in Table 4.1 (here and in the rest of the chapter, the abbreviation *aux switch* stands for 'auxiliary switch', and *cl cl* for 'clitic climbing').

Table 4.1 Auxiliary selection with modal verbs

	restructuring verb	lexical verb	aux selection	aux switch	cl cl
a.	modal	transitive	HAVE	no	irrelevant
b.	modal	unergative	HAVE	no	irrelevant
d.	modal	unaccusative	HAVE/BE	no/yes	relevant
e.	modal	reflexive	HAVE/BE	no/yes	relevant
f.	modal	impersonal	BE	yes	yes

4.3.2 Aspectual and motion verbs

4.3.2.1 *Aspectual verbs*

In Standard Italian, there are many restructuring aspectual verbs. I mention here some of these verbs: *continuare a* 'keep on', *smettere di* 'refrain from', *cominciare a* 'begin', *iniziare a* 'begin', *prendere a* 'begin', *restare a* 'remain', *rimanere a* 'remain', *stare a* 'stay', *stare per* 'be about to', *solere* 'normally do', *finire di* 'finish'.

The perfect auxiliary of aspectual verbs is HAVE, as illustrated in (14a,b). BE is generally excluded, independently of the presence of a clitic in the structure (14c,d).

(14) a. Teresa ha   cominciato a andare al   mare.
          Teresa have.PRS.3SG start.PRTC to go.INF to.the beach
      b. *Teresa è   cominciat-a   a andare al   mare.
          Teresa be.PRS.3SG start.PRTC-SG.F to go.INF to.the beach
          'Teresa started to go to the beach.'
      c. Teresa ha   cominciato a andar=ci   tre   mesi   fa.
          Teresa have.PRS.3SG start.PRTC to go.INF=there three months ago
      d. *Teresa è   cominciat-a   a andar=ci   tre   mesi   fa.
          Teresa be.PRS.3SG start.PRTC-3SG.F to go.INF=there three months ago
          'Teresa started to go there three months ago.'

Interestingly, auxiliary switch becomes possible under some specific circumstances. The perfect auxiliary of some aspectual verbs (e.g. inceptive aspectuals of the "begin-type" as in (14)–(15), but not conative aspectuals of the "try-type" as in (16)) can be realized as BE if the lexical verb is unaccusative, reflexive or impersonal, and in the presence of clitic climbing, as shown in (15a). Auxiliary switch is optional: the variant without auxiliary switch in the presence of clitic climbing can be found as well, as illustrated in (15b).

(15) a. Teresa ci=è   cominciat-a   a andare tre   mesi   fa.
          Teresa there=be.PRS.3SG start.PRTC-SG.F to go.INF three months ago
      b. Teresa ci=ha   cominciato a andare tre   mesi   fa.
          Teresa there=have.PRS.3SG start.PRTC to go.INF three months ago
          'Teresa started to go there three months ago.'

Auxiliary switch with modal verbs and with aspectual verbs behaves slightly differently. With modal verbs, optionality is only possible without clitic climbing, but it breaks down in favor of auxiliary switch when the clitic climbs (cf. (8d) vs. (15b)). Another difference is that not all aspectual verbs allow for auxiliary switch. Example (16) shows that the perfect auxiliary of *provare* 'try' is never BE, even when clitic climbing has applied.

(16) a. Teresa ha   provato a andar=ci   tre   mesi   fa.
          Teresa have.PRS.3SG try.PRTC to go.INF=there three months ago
      b. *Teresa è   provat-a   a andar=ci   tre   mesi   fa.
          Teresa be.PRS.3SG try.PRTC-3SG.F to go.INF=there three months ago
      c. *Teresa ci=è   provat-a   a andare tre   mesi   fa.
          Teresa there=be.PRS.3SG try.PRTC-SG.F to go.INF three months ago
      d. Teresa ci=ha   provato a andare tre   mesi   fa.
          Teresa there=have.PRS.3SG try.PRTC to go.INF three months ago
          'Teresa tried to go there three months ago.'

Nonetheless, aspectual verbs behave exactly as modal verbs when there is a reflexive argument or an impersonal pronoun. In these cases, all aspectual verbs require
auxiliary switch in the presence of clitic climbing, even those verbs as *provare* 'try',
which in other contexts maintain HAVE. In (17a,b), I show that auxiliary switch
is obligatory when the reflexive clitic climbs. Note that auxiliary switch is impossible when the clitic stays in the lower position (17c,d). The same pattern can be
observed with indirect reflexive objects.

(17) a. *Teresa si=ha   cominciato a lavare.
          Teresa REFL.ACC.3SG.F=have.PRS.3SG start.PRTC to wash.INF
      b. Teresa si=è   cominciat-a   a lavare.
          Teresa REFL.ACC.3SG.F=have.PRS.3SG start.PRTC-SG.F to wash.INF
      c. Teresa ha   cominciato a lavar=si.
          Teresa have.PRS.3SG start.PRTC to wash.INF=REFL.ACC.3SG.F
      d. *Teresa è   cominciat-a   a lavar=si.
          Teresa have.PRS.3SG start.PRTC-SG.F to wash.INF=REFL.ACC.3SG.F
          'Teresa has started washing herself.'

Clitic climbing and auxiliary switch are also obligatory in impersonal clauses. I
present here examples with a transitive verb with agreement (18) and without
agreement (19), but the same pattern is also found with unergative and unaccusative verbs.

(18) a. *Hanno   cominciato a mangiar=si   gli spaghetti.
          have.PRS.3PL start.PRTC to eat.INF=IMPERS the spaghetti
      b. *Sono   cominciato/-i   a mangiar=si   gli spaghetti.
          be.PRS.3PL start.PRTC/PRTC-PL.M to eat.INF=IMPERS the spaghetti
      c. *Si=hanno   cominciato/-i   a mangiare gli spaghetti.
          IMPERS=have.PRS.3PL start.PRTC/PRTC-PL.M to eat.INF   the spaghetti
      d. Si=sono   cominciat-i   a mangiare gli spaghetti.
          IMPERS=be.PRS.3PL start.PRTC-PL.M to eat.INF   the spaghetti
          'People started to eat the spaghetti.'

(19) a. *Ha   cominciato a mangiar=si   gli spaghetti.
          have.PRS.3SG start.PRTC to eat.INF=IMPERS the spaghetti
     b. *È   cominciato a mangiar=si   gli spaghetti.
          be.PRS.3SG start.PRTC   to eat.INF=IMPERS the spaghetti
     c. *Si=ha   cominciato a mangiare gli spaghetti.
          IMPERS=have.PRS.3SG start.PRTC to eat.INF   the spaghetti
     d. Si=è   cominciato a mangiare gli spaghetti.
          IMPERS=be.PRS.3SG start.PRTC to eat.INF   the spaghetti
          'People started to eat the spaghetti.'

To sum up, the possibility of auxiliary switch for aspectual verbs depends on the type of restructuring verb, on clitic placement, and on the type of arguments. As far as I know, the possibility of auxiliary switch for aspectual verbs has remained unnoticed until now. For a tentative analysis of this fact, I refer the reader to Amato (to appear).

4.3.2.2 *Motion verbs*

Standard Italian also presents a last group of restructuring verbs, motion verbs. Restructuring motion verbs are *andare a* 'go to, will', *arrivare a* 'arrive at, even do', *venire a* 'come to, end up', *tornare a* 'come back to, do again'.

With these verbs, the perfect auxiliary is invariably realized as BE. This happens with any lexical verb: unaccusative (20a), transitive (20b), and even in the presence of clitic climbing (20d).

(20) a. Teresa è   arrivata   ad andare in palestra.
          Teresa be.PRS.3SG arrive.PRTC-SG.F to go.INF in gym
          'Teresa got to go to the gym.'
     b. Teresa è   andat-a   a mangiare la torta.
          Teresa be.PRS.3SG go.PRTC-SG.F to eat.INF   the cake
     c. *Teresa ha   andato/-a   a mangiare la torta.
          Teresa have.PRS.3SG go.PRTC/PRTC-SG.F to eat.INF   the cake
          'Teresa went to eat the cake.'
     d. Teresa la=è   andat-a   a mangiare.
          Teresa ACC.3SG.F=be.PRS.3SG go.PRTC-SG.F to eat.INF
          'Teresa went to eat it.'

Reflexive arguments (21a,b) and impersonal *si* (21c) do not provoke any change in the auxiliary. This is expected, since the auxiliary is already BE.

(21) a. Teresa è   andat-a   a lavar=si.
          Teresa be.PRS.3SG go.PRTC-SG.F to wash.INF=REFL
          'Teresa went to eat the cake.'

b. Teresa si=è   andat-a   a lavare.
   Teresa REFL=be.PRS.3SG go.PRTC-SG.F to wash.INF
   'Teresa went to wash herself.'

c. Si=è   andat-i   a mangiare gli spaghetti.
   IMPERS=be.PRS.3SG go.PRTC-PL.M to eat.INF   the spaghetti
   'People went to eat the spaghetti.'

4.4   Restructuring: Raising out of *v*P/TP

4.4.1   *v*P/TP complements

I argue that restructuring configurations are raising clauses of different sizes. This proposal brings together several aspects of the previous literature.

Firstly, I adopt a monoclausal approach to restructuring clauses, as proposed in Wurmbrand 2003, 2004; Cinque 2004; Cardinaletti & Shlonsky 2004; Grano 2015.[48] As is the case in sentences with a single predicate, there is just a single overt subject. However, there must be a lower position than the surface position for the subject because of the semantic interpretation: the DP$_{sbj}$ is interpreted as the subject of the lower lexical verb. Wurmbrand (1999, 2003, 2004) has shown that, cross-linguistically, in restructuring with modal verbs the subject starts out as an argument of the embedded verb, it is interpreted below the modal verb and does not receive any Theta-role from the modal verb. Under this analysis, modal verbs behave as raising verbs.

Secondly, I follow Wurmbrand 2003, 2004; Cinque 2004 for the claim of obligatory functional restructuring: restructuring verbs are functional heads that always create monoclausal configurations. Thirdly, I adopt the idea of optionality with respect to complementation. Restructuring verbs can select different types of complement, as proposed in Cardinaletti & Shlonsky (2004); Wurmbrand (2004, 2014). Differently from Cardinaletti & Shlonsky (2004), I argue that sentences with modal verbs are always restructuring clauses, even when no transparency effect takes place. Differently from Wurmbrand (2014), I argue that in Italian all restructuring verbs (including modal verbs) allow for complements of different sizes, and not only some types of restructuring verbs (lexical restructuring verbs).

---

48. For other monoclausal analyses, see Strozer 1977; Cremers 1983; Picallo 1990; Rochette 1990; Rosen 1991; Haider 1993, 2010; Moore 1994; Kiss 2011. For theories of restructuring that start out with a biclausal structure, see Rizzi 1976; Baker 1988; Sternefeld 1990; Sabel 1996; Koopman & Szabolcsi 2000; Müller 2017; Pesetsky 2021.

I suggest that restructuring verbs can take different types of complements, namely *v*Ps or TPs.[49] In both cases, the complement is reduced and the structure is monoclausal (assuming the presence of a CP boundary as a sign of biclausality).[50] The two possible raising structures are represented in the following trees: (22) consists of raising out of a TP, whereas (23) is an instance of raising out of a *v*P. The modal verb is introduced by a special *v* (v_{restr}) that selects either a TP or a *v*P complement.

(22)   Raising out of TP

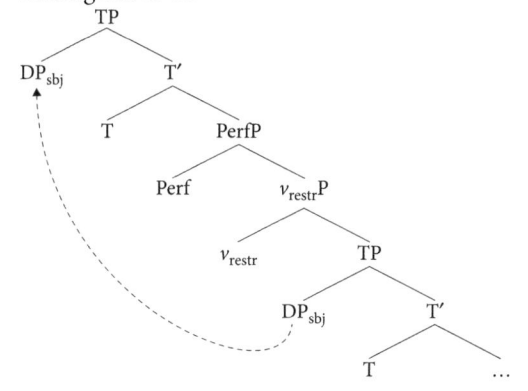

---

49. A similar approach where modal verbs can combine with different types of complements is developed by Wurmbrand (2012b) to explain the morphological realization of the lexical verb in some Germanic languages. In particular, if a modal verb selects a complement as small as a *v*P/VP, then the lexical verb appears as a past participle; if the complement contains a T projection, then the lexical verb is realized as a non-finite form (due to an interpretable T feature on the infinitival head).

50. I do not enter the discussion of nominal complementation. Perhaps when a modal verb (mostly, the verb *volere* 'want') selects for a DP there is some hidden structure, as suggested by Cinque (2004). Alternatively, these verbs can also be categorized as lexical verbs: next to the TP and *v*P complementation (determined by a special restructuring *v*, as discussed below), a DP complementation (with selection by a transitive *v*) is possible too.

(23)   Raising out of *v*P

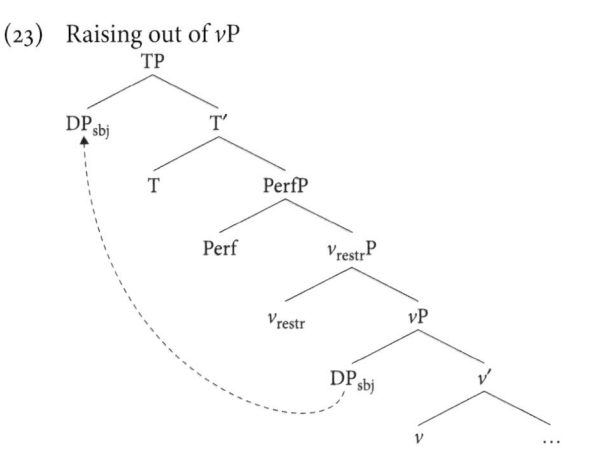

As I will propose in Section 4.5, the presence or lack of transparency effects (clitic climbing and auxiliary switch) is due to the size of the complement selected by the restructuring verb, as represented in (22) and (23). In particular, the structure in (22) determines no auxiliary switch, whereas (23) corresponds to auxiliary switch.

Evidence for the different complement sizes in (22) and (23) comes from the syntactic operations indicated in Table 4.2. These operations are only possible on the clause where the perfect auxiliary is HAVE, but not on the clause with the perfect auxiliary BE, when both auxiliaries are possible, as in Example (4). Since these operations are sensitive to the size of the clause (for instance, negation requires a T head), the results summarized in Table 4.2 can be simply accounted for by assuming a difference in the size of the clause. I refer the reader to Amato (to appear) for the relevant data and discussion.

Table 4.2 Auxiliary switch and operations sensitive to the size of the clause

		BE	HAVE
a.	Perfect complement	✗	✓
b.	Passive complement	✗	✓
c.	Ellipsis	✗	✓
d.	Cleft	✗	✓
e.	Relativization	✗	✓
f.	Clausal negation	✗	✓
g.	Presuppositional negative markers	✗	✓

4.4.2   The T head

The T head of the TP complement in (22) is a "dummy" head because it does not introduce any independent tense. A similar T head is assumed for some type of restructuring verbs (the lexical restructuring ones) in Wurmbrand (2012b, 2014), and for hosting the infinitival marker (zu in German, di, a in Italian) of some restructuring infinitives in Wurmbrand (2003:109).

A semantically vacuous T head is a licit object because mismatches between syntax and semantics are possible. Although "semantic tense is transparently reflected syntactically, syntax does also lead an independent life to some extent, since the lack of tense does not seem to preclude (semantically vacuous) syntactic projections" (Wurmbrand 2014:425). In addition, restructuring infinitives usually lack tense: the tense of the lexical verb is interpreted as referring to a moment that is simultaneous to the time at which the tense of the modal verb refers. It is true that modal verbs (*want* in particular) can combine with future-oriented infinitives (*oggi voglio fare questo domani* 'today I want to do this tomorrow'), but it has been argued that futurity is contributed by a modal element *woll*, rather than by tense (Wurmbrand 2003; Grano 2015). Anterior tense is also possible (*lo potrebbe aver già visto ieri* 's/he may have already seen it/him yesterday'), but in this case there must be an embedded Perf head that contributes to tense/aspect. Hence, these tense interpretations might be introduced by other projections than T.

This T head is also deficient with respect to other morphosyntactic properties. As standardly assumed for non-finite T, it does not bear any φ-probe. In addition, it does not assign case. If it could assign nominative, the raising DP would bear nominative case twice (once assigned from the lower T, once from the higher T).

4.5   Auxiliary selection in restructuring: Cyclic π-Agree

4.5.1   Auxiliary switch: "transparent" π-Agree

In this book, I have considered auxiliary selection as the result of π-Agree. This must be valid, of course, also in restructuring clauses. I argue that auxiliary selection in restructuring is determined by a special v (v_{restr}). In particular, auxiliary switch depends on the joint effect of a small complement and of the probes on v_{restr}.

I suggest that the head v_{restr}, which introduces the modal verb, bears two [Infl] features: a valued one, [uInfl:non-fin], and an unvalued one [Infl:_]. We have already seen an example of a head with a double [Infl] feature in the

case of passives: Voice$_{pass}$ (cf. Section 3.3.7 in Chapter 3). The unvalued [Infl:_]
can either remain unvalued or be valued by a higher inflectional head, such
as Perf. This type of feature is located on every type of *v*. The valued Infl-
feature [uInfl:non-fin] determines that the TP/*v*P complement is non-finite, and
excludes an independent embedded tense interpretation (Wurmbrand 2003;
Grano 2015). Thanks to its double [Infl], this head enables agreement between
the embedded *v* and the matrix Perf, acting as an intermediate agreeing head that
provides a connection between the lower portion of the syntactic tree and the
higher tense extended projection.[51] The function of this head is represented in
trees (24) and (25). The Agree-relations are between the lower *v* and *v*$_{restr}$ in (24),
and between *v*$_{restr}$ and Perf in (25).

(24)

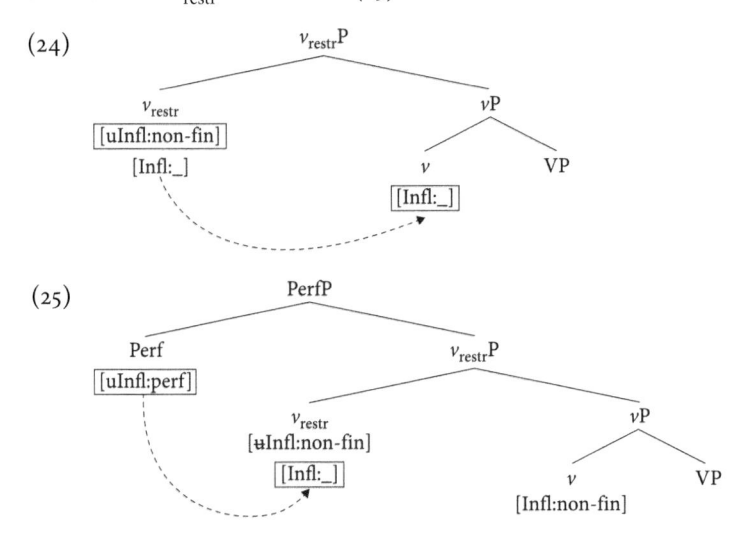

(25)

I propose that the head *v*$_{restr}$ also bears a person probe. Auxiliary selection
depends on the order between the two [Infl] features and the person probe. The
order of the features on the head *v*$_{restr}$ is shown in (26).

(26)   *v*$_{restr}$: [Infl:_] > [uInfl:non-fin] > [uπ:_]

The person probe on *v*$_{restr}$ can access the lower *v*, in accordance with Nested
Agree. Moreover, it can also be accessed by Perf. Consequently, the π-feature
on the lower *v*, which results from both the argument structure (transitive vs.
defective *v*) and the features of the arguments (reflexive/impersonal vs. non-
reflexive/non-impersonal), are copied by Perf via the intermediate head *v*$_{restr}$. This

---

51. I sometimes use the terms *embedded* and *matrix* to refer, respectively, to the lower and the
higher portion of the clause. These labels do not refer to a biclausal structure (see Section 4.4.1).

results in a cyclic Agree configuration (Legate 2005). The whole derivation is schematized in the following trees (27)–(30).

(27)   Step (a): v_{restr} agrees for [Infl]

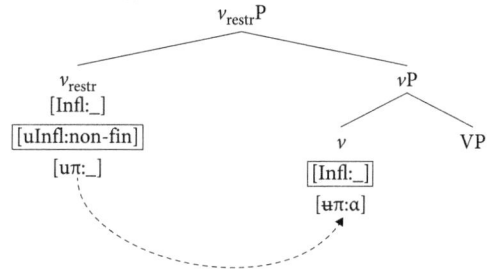

(28)   Step (b): v_{restr} agrees for [π]

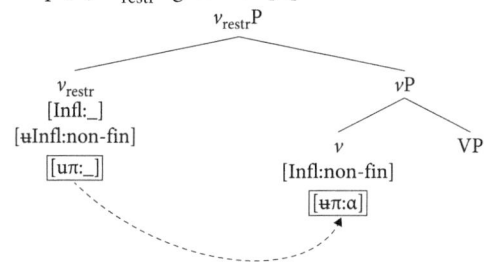

(29)   Step (c): Perf agrees for [Infl]

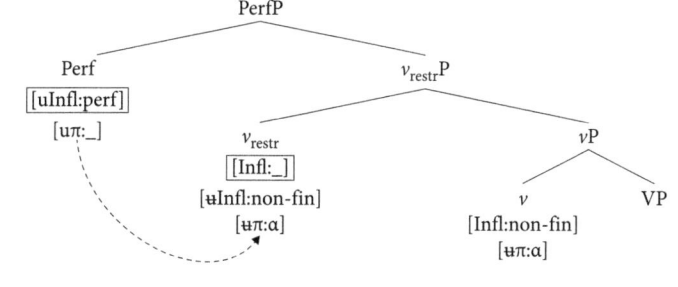

(30)   Step (d): Perf agrees for [π]

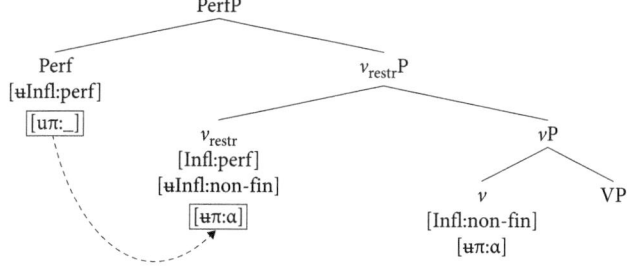

As shown in this derivation, auxiliary selection in restructuring is the result of long distance agreement between the lower lexical v and Perf, thanks to the higher restructuring v. In case of a vP complement, the structure is "transparent": the information about the person feature of the object of the lexical verb reaches the head Perf in the higher portion of the clause, as in root clauses. This results in auxiliary switch if the embedded verb is a BE-verb. Hence, the matrix auxiliary is HAVE with transitive verbs, BE with transitive verbs with a reflexive (in-)direct object, BE with impersonal clauses and BE with unaccusative verbs, as in root clauses. Moreover, clitic climbing is obligatory.[52] In fact, under the assumption that clitics must move to T, when the complement is a vP there is no embedded T head. Hence, the clitic must reach the matrix T head in order to find a host.

4.5.2   Lack of auxiliary switch: "guaranteed" π-Agree

If the features of the lower v are accessible to Perf, then the question is why the perfect auxiliary of the modal verb is not always the "faithful" one, i.e. the one that the lower lexical verb would be combined with. In fact, the syntactic structure should be transparent for auxiliary selection, meaning that an embedded BE-verb should invariably determine the presence of BE on the matrix modal. Instead, we saw that auxiliary switch is optional.

I argue that the difference in auxiliary selection is a reflex of the difference in the size of the complements, as proposed in Section 4.4.1. If the complement is a vP, the clausal auxiliary is realized in accordance with the lexical verb, as explained in Section 4.5.1. In contrast, if the complement is a TP, no transparency effect arises. The reason for the lack of transparency effects is not the presence of a CP barrier.[53] Instead, I suggest that more structure means more possibilities for Agree and for clitic placement. The possibilities for successful Agree increase by enlarging the structure (i.e., the search domain of the probe). In the presence of

---

52. The sentence with auxiliary switch and without clitic climbing is also possible: *Teresa è volut-a andar=ci*, see (8b). I discuss this issue (and the similar case with clitic climbing without auxiliary switch, *Teresa ci=ha voluto andare*) in Section 4.7. For the purpose of the present discussion, I invite the reader to ignore this case, which is marked compared to the standard alternative with auxiliary switch and clitic climbing, *Teresa ci=è volut-a andare*, see (8c).

53. Differently from Cardinaletti & Shlonsky (2004), and similarly to Cinque (2004), I argue that sentences without overt transparency effects are still restructured. In fact, characteristics such as subject raising and dependent tense interpretation are hallmarks of restructuring that indicate the absence of a CP. These characteristics are also present when there are no overt transparency effects in the narrow sense (i.e., clitic climbing and auxiliary switch, indicating the absence of a TP layer; see Section 4.5.1). See Wurmbrand (2003); Grano (2015) for discussion of such properties.

a TP complement, the probe on v_{restr} targets the complex head containing T and the lower v, formed via head movement.[54] Even though v_{restr} targets a subpart of the complex head (v), I assume that the whole complex head is involved. The features of the adjoined parts of the complex head are part of the complex head as a whole (cf. Fanselow 2001 for a similar proposal). After having interacted with the complex T head, v_{restr} can probe the c-command domain of the T head, as stated by Nested Agree, in accordance with the Phase Impenetrability Condition.

As illustrated in (31), v_{restr} agrees for [Infl] with v in the complex head T-v-V.

(31)

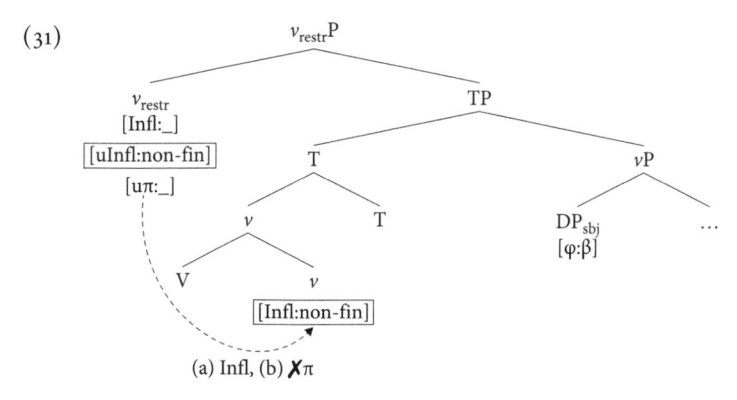

(a) Infl, (b) ✗π

Thereafter, it starts its search for person. If the lower v does not contain any person feature, as in (31) (which exemplifies the case of unaccusative v), the probe goes on scanning the c-command domain of the complex head (according to the *No-Backtracking* condition of Nested Agree, see (9) in Chapter 2). The π-probe agrees with the subject in Spec,v, as shown in (32). Hence, with a TP complement v_{restr} always finds a valued person feature.

---

54. This is valid if head movement happens in the syntax (before, or as soon as, the next phase head is merged in the structure). See Matushansky (2006: 99–101) for the claim that head movement applies (at least partially) in narrow syntax, and Hartman (2011) for evidence in favor of syntactic head movement.

(32)

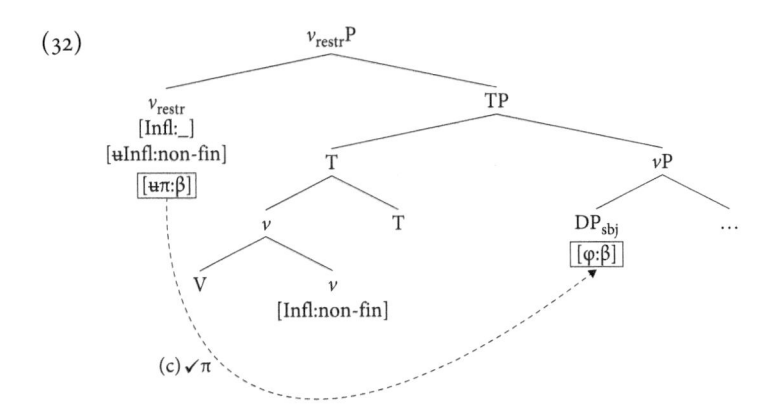

When Perf enters the derivation, it successfully probes v_{restr}, which bears a person feature because it has agreed with the subject, as indicated in (32). π-Agree on Perf always succeeds when the complement of the restructuring verb is a TP, even when the lower v does not contain any person feature. The more specific allomorph HAVE is inserted even when the lexical verb is a BE-verb.[55] In addition, clitics incorporate into the lower T, without reaching the matrix T.

The consequences of the size of complement for auxiliary selection are summarized in (33). If the complement is a vP, auxiliary switch and clitic climbing must take place, if applicable (i.e., if the structure contains a BE-verb and a clitic, respectively). If the complement is a TP, then the result is the lack of auxiliary switch and clitic climbing. Note, however, that there are other more complicated cases that I will address in Section 4.7.

---

55. Let me mention two possible variants of this analysis. In the first alternative option, the T head bears an [Infl] feature, following Wurmbrand (2003); Bjorkman (2011) for the same kind of feature on T and v. In particular, the restructuring T head bears an unvalued Infl-feature [Infl:_], differently from finite, non-defective T, where this feature is specified for different tense values. [Infl:_] acquires the value [non-fin] from v_{restr}. This is also a way to model the tense dependency of the embedded verb on higher heads. Under this scenario, independently of head movement, v_{restr} probes directly T for [Infl], and then the derivation proceeds as just explained. The [Infl] feature on v remains unvalued; the non-finite morphology on the modal verb is achieved via head movement of v to T. Note that this is the version of the analysis adopted in Amato (to appear). Under the second option, the T head bears a person probe that agrees with the subject. That non-finite T can contain a probe for φ-features can be seen from cases of agreeing infinitives in languages such as Portuguese (Raposo 1987). The person feature on T is available for a probe that targets v for person, if either the features of the adjoined parts of the complex head are all accessible for a probe that targets part of the complex head (in a sort of *bag-of-features* model, as stated here in the main text), or T contains [Infl] (as suggested in this footnote about the first alternative analysis).

(33) a. Teresa ha   voluto   andar=ci.   (TP complement)
          Teresa have.PRS.3SG want.PRTC go.INF=there
          'Teresa wanted to go there.'
      b. Teresa ci=è   volut-a   andare.   (*v*P complement)
          Teresa there=be.PRS.3SG want.PRTC-SG.F go.INF
          'Teresa wanted to go there.'

4.5.3   The EPP-feature

The head v_{restr} acts as a "hinge-head" not only in determining the inflectional form of the lower verb and in copying the person feature for the purpose of auxiliary selection, but also by "handing over" the right argument of the lower lexical verb to the higher modal verb. In order to ensure subject raising, v_{restr} must contain an EPP-feature that raises a DP with unchecked case feature to its specifier. Nonetheless, this EPP-feature must be absent when the complement of v_{restr} is defective. To illustrate this point, let us look at participle agreement in restructuring.[56]

As in root clauses, the subject of a transitive verb cannot control participle agreement. This is shown in (33).

(34) Le ragazze hanno   voluto   / *volut-e   / *volut-a
      the girls   have.PRS.3PL want.PRTC want.PRTC-PL.F   want.PRTC-SG.F
      mangiare la   torta
      eat.INF   the cake
      'The girls wanted to eat the cake.'

Given the proposed raising analysis of restructuring, the subject is introduced in the specifier of the lower *v*, which is c-commanded by the position where participle agreement shows up, namely v_{restr} (i.e., the modal verb). When the DP_{sbj} moves across v_{restr}, it should cause participle agreement on it (cf. analysis of participle agreement in Chapter 6). Hence, the absence of participle agreement suggests that this movement is triggered by a feature other than the feature related to participle agreement (edge feature): an EPP-feature.

Hence, I propose that v_{restr} contains an EPP-feature: $[\bullet D_{[case:\_]}\bullet]$. The EPP is a type of Merge feature that moves a DP with unchecked case feature to Spec,v_{restr}. This EPP-feature targets not only a [D] category, but it is also relativized to a [D] category that bears an unvalued case feature: $[\bullet D_{[case:\_]}\bullet]$. The restriction to DPs with an unvalued case feature ensures that the raised element is exactly the subject and not any other DP with already valued case (such as other clitic pronouns).

---

56. For a full understanding of this section, I suggest that the reader first read Chapter 6.

This is a case of relativized probing (Béjar 2003; Béjar & Rezac 2009): the search for internal Merge is relativized to a particular value of a feature.

As just said, the reason why there should be an EPP-feature on v_{restr} is the lack of participle agreement with the subject of a transitive embedded verb. Nonetheless, when the embedded verb is unaccusative, there can be participle agreement on the modal (i.e., on v_{restr}), as shown in (35).

(35)   Teresa è   volut-a   andare al   mare.
       Teresa be.PRS.3SG want.PRTC-SG.F go.INF to.the beach
       'Teresa wanted to go to the beach.'

In order to explain this fact, I suggest that the EPP-feature $[\bullet D_{[case:\_]}\bullet]$ on v_{restr} correlates with the c-selectional feature on v_{restr}, which is also a Merge feature. When v_{restr} selects for a head that does not contain any $[\bullet D\bullet]$ feature (i.e., unaccusative v), it also does not bear the EPP-feature, coming in a defective version. In this case, the subject must be raised by an edge feature, leading to participle agreement. It follows that sentences (34) and (35) must contain two slightly different types of v heads: a full one in (34), and a defective one (lacking the EPP-feature) in (35).

The presence of the EPP-feature $[\bullet D_{[case:\_]}\bullet]$ on v_{restr} correlates with the type of complement of v_{restr} because of the matching condition in (36) (where v^* refers to full-argument-structure v, as defined in Chomsky 2001).

(36) $v_{restr}[\bullet D_{[case:\_]}\bullet] \leftrightarrow v_{restr}[\bullet T\bullet] \lor v_{restr}[\bullet v^*\bullet]$

This is a constraint on the numeration that relates the presence of the EPP-feature on v_{restr} with the type of selected head. It can be seen as a feature co-occurrence restriction between the EPP-feature and the c-selectional feature on v_{restr}. It results in a sort of "matching defectiveness" with respect to the $[\bullet D\bullet]$ feature: v_{restr} contains it when the embedded head also bears it, otherwise it does not.[57] The matching defectiveness is a device to keep track of the defectiveness of the lower part of

---

57. There is only one type of v_{restr} in the lexicon, which is then adjusted in its featural specification by some pre-syntactic operations that act in the numeration and give rise to different flavors of v_{restr}. Note that the numeration should be organized in subarrays that "anticipate" the syntactic structure: a single subset contains only a V, a v, a T and so on (cf. Chomsky 2000 for the notion of phases as lexical subarrays, or chunks of numeration).

the structure.[58] This condition is the reason why in restructuring participle agree-ment patterns as in root clauses.

4.5.4   Against the control analysis

I have proposed that optionality in auxiliary selection in restructuring is a reflex of optionality in the size of the complement clause of the modal verb. An alterna-tive analysis (which is the only previous analysis of auxiliary selection in restruc-turing, as far as I know) has been suggested in Wurmbrand (2015: 236), although only for lexical restructuring and not for restructuring with modal verbs. Option-ality in auxiliary selection is the reflex of ambiguity in the status of the restructur-ing verb. The auxiliary HAVE corresponds to the lexical use of the modal verb, BE to its functional use. The proposal is schematized in (37).

(37)   ✗ auxiliary switch: control
       [DP$_i$ HAVE V$_{modal}$ [$_{CP}$ PRO$_i$ V$_{lexical}$]]

(38)   ✓ auxiliary switch: raising
       [DP$_i$ BE V$_{modal}$ [$_{vP}$ t$_i$ V$_{lexical}$]]

This alternative approach is ruled out by the fact that both the sentences with HAVE and those with BE behave identically with respect to tests for raising and control, summarized in Table 4.3. I refer the reader to Amato (to appear) for the relevant data and discussion. These tests suggest that there is no difference in terms of control and raising depending on the perfect auxiliary of the modal verb. The Spell-out of the perfect auxiliary is independent of the syntactic difference in (37)–(38) and of the "functionality" of the restructuring verb, against Wurmbrand 2015. The raising analysis in (38) can be uniformly adopted for both the sentence with the perfect auxiliary HAVE and the sentence with BE, when both auxiliaries are possible, as in Example (4).

---

58. This defectiveness could be extended to other features of v_{restr}, such as the probe for person. In fact, the presence or absence of a person probe on defective v_{restr} does not change the analy-sis. Indeed, defective v_{restr} should lack the person probe, as the discussion of problematic cases in Section 4.7.2 hints. However, in order to maintain the analysis as simple as possible, I keep the π-probe on defective v_{restr}.

Table 4.3 Auxiliary switch and raising/control diagnostics

		BE	HAVE	raising (seem)
a.	Animacy restrictions	✗	✗	✗
b.	Weather verbs	✓	✓	✓
c.	Passive matrix	✗	–	✗
d.	Same meaning with active/passive	–	✓	✓
e.	High/low scope	✓	✓	✓
f.	Quantifier scope	✓	✓	✓
g.	Case retained	✓	✓	✓

4.5.5 Raising verbs: No auxiliary switch

Since restructuring clauses are raising structures, the reader may wonder whether the raising v could give rise to restructuring, without resorting to an extra v_{restr}. If we look at raising predicates, such as the verb *sembrare* 'seem', auxiliary switch is impossible. As (39) shows, the perfect auxiliary of raising verbs is always BE, independently of the size of the complement (identified by the position of the clitic).

(39) a.   Teresa è   sembrat-a   mangiare la torta.
           Teresa be.PRS.3SG seem.PRTC-SG.F eat   the cake
      b. *Teresa ha   sembrato mangiare la torta.
           Teresa have.PRS.3SG seem.PRTC eat   the cake
           'Teresa seemed to eat the cake.'
      c.   Teresa è   sembrat-a   mangiar=la   tutta.
           Teresa be.PRS.3SG seem.PRTC-SG.F eat=ACC.3SG.F all
      d. *Teresa ha   sembrato mangiar=la   tutta.
           Teresa have.PRS.3SG seem.PRTC eat=ACC.3SG.F all
           'Teresa seemed to eat it all.'

The data in (39) can be derived if the v head involved in raising is a defective one, such as unaccusative v, which only contains an unvalued [Infl:_],

(40) $v_{raising}$: [Infl:_]

The derivation for raising verbs is represented in (41) and (42).

(41)

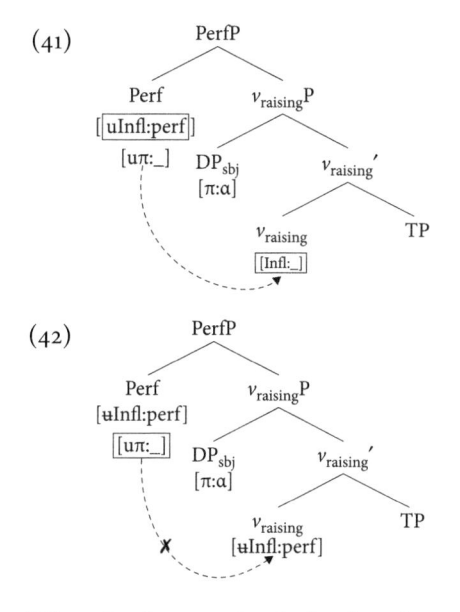

(42)

When Perf enters the derivation, it probes $v_{raising}$ for [Infl]. Then, given Nested Agree, it probes $v_{raising}$ also for the π-feature (thereby skipping the raised argument in Spec,$v_{raising}$). However, it does not find any value on v, since it is defective (i.e., it does not bear a person probe). Since every v is a phase, the probe cannot search into the TP complement of the raising v because of the Phase Impenetrability Condition. In addition, the probe cannot backtrack to any position above $v_{raising}$ due to Nested Agree. Hence, Agree on Perf fails. Raising v leads to BE insertion independently of the embedded syntactic structure, as Example (39) shows.

Differently from raising verbs, modal verbs can exhibit HAVE as the perfect auxiliary and allow for clitic climbing. Thus, the type of v involved in restructuring cannot be the same as the one used in raising configurations. Restructuring clauses cannot be created by a defective, raising v.

As a side note, raising also differs from restructuring for the possibility of having complements of different sizes. The complement of $v_{raising}$ must be a TP, as confirmed by the impossibility of clitic climbing out of the embedded complement.

(43) *Teresa l=è   sembrat-a   mangiare tutta.
       Teresa ACC.3SG.F=be.PRS.3SG seem.PRTC-SG.F eat   all
       'Teresa seemed to eat it all.'

4.6   Analysis

4.6.1   vP + transitive verb

I start with the analysis of small complements (*v*Ps) containing transitive verbs. When a modal verb selects a transitive verb, the auxiliary is always HAVE. If the clause does not contain any clitic, there is no cue for the structure of the complement (whereas for unaccusative verbs auxiliary switch constitutes a way to disambiguate the size of the complement). Hence, Example (44a) is ambiguous between a TP and a *v*P structure. Instead, Example (44b) shows that the embedded complement does not contain a T position, because the clitic undergoes clitic climbing.

(44) a. Teresa ha   voluto   mangiare la torta.
Teresa have.PRS.3SG want.PRTC eat.INF   the cake
'Teresa wanted to eat the cake.'

b. Teresa l=ha   volut-a   mangiare.
Teresa ACC.3SG.F=have.PRS.3SG want.PRTC-SG.F eat.INF
'Teresa wanted to eat it.'

I consider (44) to contain a small complement (a *v*P), as is clear in (44b) and possible in (44a) (cf. Section 4.6.4 for the alternative TP derivation for (44a)). The derivation is as follows.

First of all, the transitive *v*P is built as in root clauses (cf. Section 3.3.1 in Chapter 3). Transitive *v* agrees with the object for person. The *v*P contains the external argument with unchecked case feature in its specifier. If the object is a clitic, it moves to the edge of the *v*P (see Section 6.5.1 of Chapter 6; however, participle agreement on the lexical verb does not show up, since this *v* will not end up bearing the feature [Infl:perf], which is responsible for the morphological realization of *v* as a past participle).

At this point, a modal verb introduced by v_{restr} enters the derivation, as shown in (45). In the trees in this section, I locate the modal verb in a V head, selected by v_{restr}. An alternative representation considers the restructuring verb as the morphological realization of v_{restr}, specified for different modalities by a higher modal projection (to obtain the meanings 'want, can, must').[59] When v_{restr} is merged, it

---

59. The discussion of problematic cases in Section 4.7 and of auxiliary switch for aspectual verbs in Amato (to appear) might suggest that the solution with two distinct heads V and v_{restr} is superior. Instead, an advantage of the alternative option is that the selectional and featural restrictions on v_{restr} are easy to model. I leave this question open, since it is not directly relevant to auxiliary selection.

agrees with the lower v for [Infl]. This creates the first Agree-Link between the two heads. Subsequently, by means of Nested Agree, v_{restr} agrees with v also for [π], as shown in (45) (cf. Chapter 2 for the discussion of the principle and its application to solve the minimality problem posed by auxiliary selection in Standard Italian, where the π-probe on Perf needs to skip the subject in Spec,v).

(45)

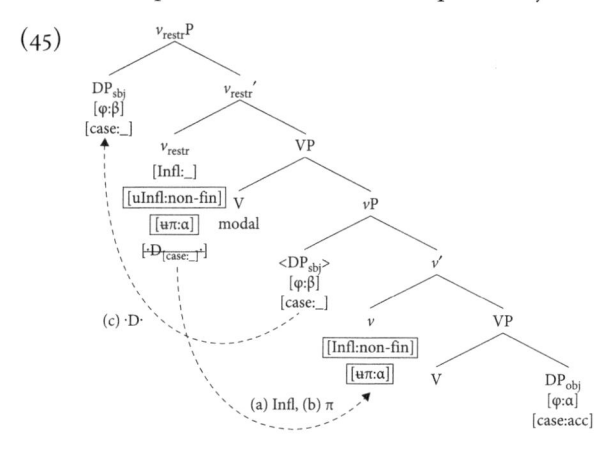

The restructuring v in (45) is a non-defective one equipped with a $[\bullet D_{[case:\_]}\bullet]$ feature (because the embedded v is non-defective, as established by the matching condition in (36)). This EPP-feature attracts a DP with unvalued case feature to Spec,v, as illustrated by the arrow (c) in (45). The EPP-feature ensures the raising behavior of restructuring modal verbs, and in particular that only the external argument will be raised. In tree (45), after v_{restr} has agreed for [Infl] and [π], its $[\bullet D_{[case:\_]}\bullet]$ feature is discharged, and the subject DP introduced by the lexical verb is raised to Spec,v_{restr}. Note that the EPP-feature is not subject to Nested Agree, otherwise it could not reach the DP in Spec,v, once v_{restr} has agreed with v for [Infl] and [π]. This is probably because the EPP-feature contains two components, one of which is discharged first, before the other probes on v_{restr} target v.[60]

---

60. The idea here is that the EPP-feature is composed of two ordered parts: an Agree probe and a Merge feature. The Agree component ($[uD_{[case:\_]}]$) goes first, before [uInfl:non-fin] and [uπ:_]. It agrees with the item that should be moved. This is temporarily removed from the structure and is stored in a separate workspace before being remerged in the tree by means of the Merge feature. The Merge-EPP-component ($[\bullet D_{[case:\_]}\bullet]$) is discharged when all other Agree operations between the head and the complement have been performed. It merges the DP$_{[case:\_]}$ in Spec,v_{restr}. I thank Fabian Heck (p.c.) for discussion of this point.The separate workspace is a proposal by Heck & Himmelreich (2016); Heck (2016). It is a way to deal with intervention effects: it can account for those configurations where the intervener will move out of the way at a later derivational step. Nested Agree can also cover additional cases, namely intervention effects by a specifier or a head that would not move at all. Such an example is

Another alternative solution is that Nested Agree does not constrain Merge operations (but this option needs to be evaluated with further studies).

After all operations have been carried out, any clitic (if there is one) must move to the edge of v_{restr} via edge feature insertion, since v_{restr} is a phase. This is why we see participle agreement on the modal verb in (44b) (I refer the reader to Chapter 6).

The head Perf is now merged in the structure, as indicated in tree (46).

(46)

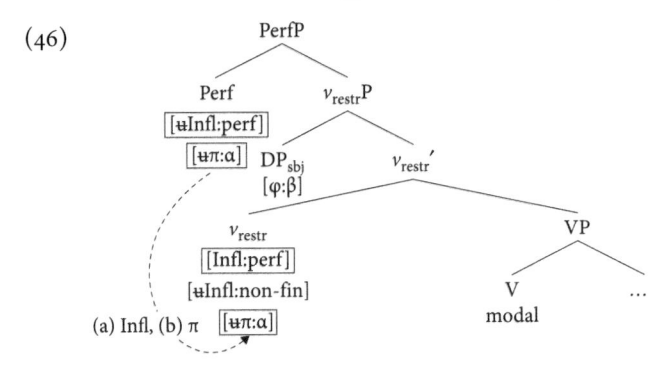

In (46), Perf checks its Infl-feature with v_{restr}, as v_{restr} did with the lower v. Then, it probes it for person, because of Nested Agree. As the representation in (46) shows, Agree succeeds because the head v_{restr} contains a person value. At Spell-out, Perf will be realized by the allomorph HAVE.

When T enters the derivation, if there is a clitic in Spec,v_{restr}, it immediately incorporates into T, since the condition for discharging its feature [•T•] is met (cf. Section 3.3.2 of Chapter 3). Then, T assigns nominative case to the external argument in Spec,v_{restr}, copies its φ features and moves it to its specifier. The φ-probe on T can reach the φ-features of the subject, thereby skipping the φ-features on the Perf head, because of Nested Agree. This is possible if nominative assignment precedes φ-agreement (cf. Section 3.3.2 of Chapter 3).

At the end of the derivation, there are three complex heads: V(lexical) + v, V(modal) + v_{restr}, and Perf + T, represented in (47), (48), and (49).

Agree between Perf and v across the subject in Spec,v (T comes too late in order to resort to the separate workspace explanation; in addition, Merge of the external argument cannot be procrastinated, because the subject binds the reflexive object before this moves to the edge of v, as explained in Section 6.5.2 of Chapter 6). Since the separate workspace approach is compatible with Nested Agree and cannot account for (at least some of) the cases where Nested Agree is needed, I will not discuss this approach any further.

(47)

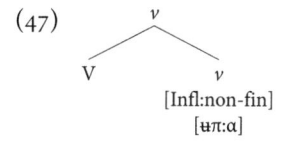

(48)

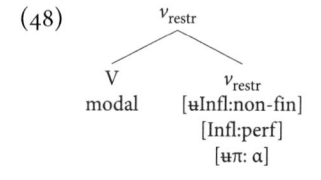

(49)

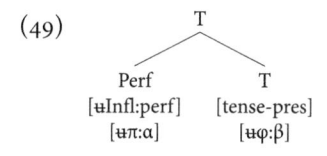

The Vocabulary Items assumed for v are given in (50) (I will introduce and discuss them in (17) and (18) in Chapter 6).

(50) a.   /re/ ↔ v
    b.   /t/ ↔ v[Infl:perf]
    c.   /participle agreement/ ↔ v[γ:α],[#:α] / [Infl:perf]
    d.   /o/ ↔ v / [Infl:perf]

In the complex head V + v in (47), the lexical verb substitutes the terminal node V and is spelled out as a non-finite form. This is due to the value *non-fin* for the feature [Infl]. However, the same realization would have taken place with an unvalued feature, since the non-finite form of the verb is the elsewhere form in Italian, as the VI in (50a) indicates.

    In the complex head V(modal) + v_{restr} in (48), the modal verb is realized as a past participle, since v_{restr} bears [Infl:perf]. This feature leads to the insertion of the more specific verbal form of the participle in (50b). Note that the head v_{restr} contains two instances of the Infl-feature. The realization of [Infl:non-fin] corresponds to the insertion of the elsewhere form (50a), whereas the feature [Infl:perf] requires the more specific form for the past participle (50b). Given the Subset Principle, the latter form is preferred. Next to the past participle suffix, there can be morphological inflection for gender and number if the head v bears a gender and number value, expressed by the exponent in (50c). In the complex head in (48), there are no gender and number values, but only a person value. Hence, the exponent (50d) will be inserted, as in the corresponding clause in (44a) there is no participle agreement. However, if there is a clitic in the structure as in (44b), participle agreement will be realized in accordance with the lexical entry in (50c).

In the complex head Perf + T in (49), the Perf head is realized by HAVE, since it bears a valued person feature. The vocabulary entries for Perf are repeated in (51).

(51)   a.   /HAVE/ ↔ Perf[π:α]
       b.   /BE/ ↔ Perf elsewhere

The φ-inflection on the auxiliary is given by the person and number values copied by T from the DP$_{sbj}$.

To sum up, if the complement of v_{restr} is a transitive vP, the auxiliary is always realized as HAVE, since the lower transitive v probes the object for π and it is probed by the matrix v_{restr}, which is successively probed by Perf. This cyclic Agree configuration allows Perf to copy the person feature of the object.

4.6.2 vP + reflexive verb

When the sentence contains a reflexive pronoun, the clausal auxiliary is BE, as in root clauses. Examples (52a,b) show the case of a reflexive direct object, Examples (52c,d) of a reflexive indirect object. The position of the reflexive clitic on the modal verb indicates that the complement is a vP.

(52)   a.   Teresa si=è   volut-a   lavare.
            Teresa REFL.ACC.3SG.F=be.PRS.3SG want.PRTC-SG.F wash.INF
       b.   *Teresa si=ha   voluto/-a   lavare.
            Teresa REFL.ACC.3SG.F=have.PRS.3SG want.PRTC/-SG.F wash.INF
            'Teresa wanted to wash herself.'
       c.   Teresa si=è   volut-a   mangiare un panino.
            Teresa REFL.DAT.3SG.F=be.PRS.3SG want.PRTC-SG.F eat.INF   a   sandwich
       d.   *Teresa si=ha   voluto/-a   mangiare un
            Teresa REFL.DAT.3SG.F=have.PRS.3SG want.PRTC/-SG.F eat.INF   a
            panino.
            sandwich
            'Teresa wanted to eat a sandwich by/for herself.'

The reason why BE shows up in the sentences in (52) is because Agree on the lower v fails (and, consequently, on the higher v_{restr} and on Perf). The derivation is as follows.

The vP is built as for reflexive root clauses. I refer the reader to Section 3.3.2 of Chapter 3 for details. The main idea is that the reflexive pronoun is φ-defective until it is bound by the external argument (Reuland 2001, among others). Crucially, when v probes the internal argument for [π], the external argument has not been introduced yet (because of the Strict Cycle Condition, Chomsky 1973). Binding has not taken place yet, and the internal argument still bears unvalued φ-features. Hence, person-Agree on v fails. This is shown in (53). The external argument is then introduced. The reflexive clitic is bound by the external argument. The φ-features of the reflexive clitic are now valued as the φ-features of the external argument are, as shown in (54). The π-probe on v has already been discharged, so it remains unvalued.

(53)

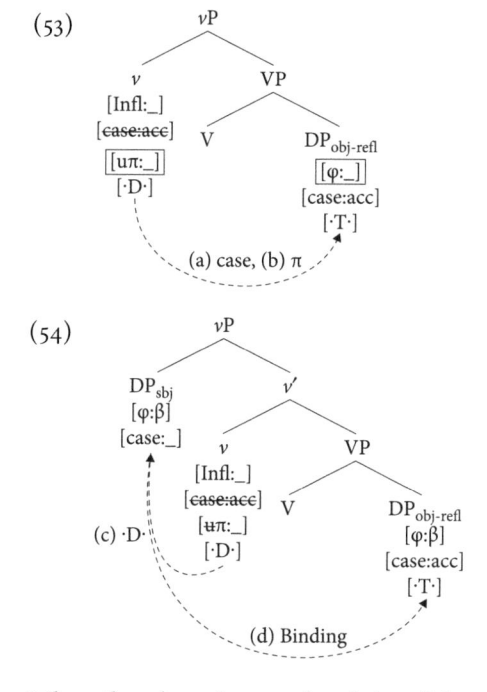

(54)

When the phase is completed the clitic must escape the phase domain because its [•T•] feature has not been checked yet. An edge feature is inserted on v (see Section 6.5.2 of Chapter 6). The result of this operation is movement of the clitic to an outer specifier of v, causing gender and number agreement on v. However, these features will not lead to participle agreement because v does not bear [Infl:perf]. They will be also ignored by v_{restr} because the probe looks for person, and not for gender or number.

The head v_{restr} enters the derivation in its non-defective version, since the vP complement is non-defective (as ensured by the matching condition (36)). The structure is shown in (55). The head v_{restr} checks its Infl-feature with the lower v. Then, it probes for person. Given Nested Agree, it must start its search from v. This is a matching goal because it bears the relevant feature, although unvalued.

Hence, Agree stops because the probe has found a matching goal. However, valuation is not possible because the goal is unvalued.

(55)

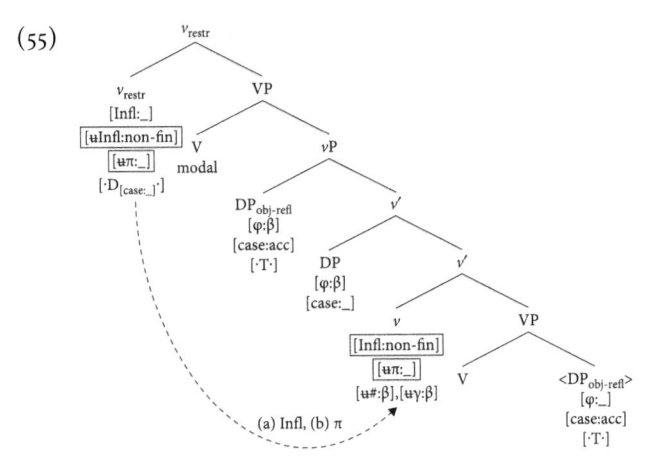

After the person probe has carried out Agree, the $[\bullet D_{[case:\_]}\bullet]$ feature raises the DP subject to its specifier. At this point the phase is completed. The clitic object, bearing the unchecked feature $[\bullet T\bullet]$, is moved by an edge feature. This EF copies the gender and number values of the clitic on v_{restr} and moves it to Spec,v_{restr}. At Spell-out, the gender and number features on v_{restr} will be realized as participle agreement.

The derivation then proceeds exactly as in the previous case. Perf enters the derivation and probes v_{restr} for Infl. By means of Nested Agree, it also probes it for person. v_{restr} bears a person feature, although unvalued. Agree stops and Perf cannot copy any value. The tree is very similar to the tree (46) for a transitive verb. The difference with the previous derivation in Section 4.6.1 is that the unvalued person feature on v_{restr}, due to the unvalued person feature on the lower v, causes the person feature on Perf to remain unvalued as well. In addition, there is also a clitic in Spec,v_{restr}, which will cliticize to T as soon as it enters the derivation.

At Spell-out, Perf is substituted by the elsewhere form BE because the π-feature on Perf is unvalued. Participle agreement is overtly realized, since v_{restr} bears both [Infl:perf] and a valued number and gender feature (because of edge feature insertion).

4.6.3   vP + unaccusative verb

When the modal verb combines with an unaccusative verb, the clausal auxiliary is either BE or HAVE. In Section 4.5, I have proposed that this alternation is a consequence of the size of the complement. I take clitic climbing as the hallmark for a complement smaller than a TP (since it should not contain any T position into which the clitic can incorporate). In the presence of clitic climbing, auxiliary switch is obligatory, as shown in Examples (56) (but cf. Section 4.7 for the dubious acceptability of (56b)). Moreover, participle agreement on the modal verb is obligatory.

(56) a. Teresa ci=è   volut-a   andare ieri.
          Teresa there=be.PRS.3SG want.PRTC-SG.F go.INF yesterday
      b. *Teresa ci=ha   voluto/-a   andare ieri.
          Teresa there=have.PRS.3SG want.PRTC/-SG.F go.INF yesterday
          'Teresa wanted to go there yesterday.'

The derivation for a clause as (56a) is given here below; the derivation for a clause without the clitic (e.g., *Teresa è volut-a andare al mare* 'Teresa wanted to go to the beach') is the same as this one, just simpler.

The vP complement is built as in root clauses (see Section 3.3.5 of Chapter 3). The head v is defective: it is neither a π-probe, nor a case assigner. Its complement contains a DP internal argument and a higher locative clitic, which I situate in Spec,V. Both the locative clitic and the DP_{obj} must move to the edge of the phase, since they bear two unchecked features, respectively [•T•] and [case:_]. Therefore, an edge feature is inserted on v. This EF moves the two DPs to the edge of the phase, and the subset of relevant φ-features (namely, gender and number of the item moved last, cf. 6.5.5 of Chapter 6) are copied onto v. In this specific case, the gender and number features will not be morphologically expressed at Spell-out because this v will not end up being realized as a past participle.

The resulting vP is then selected by v_{restr}. Because the head v is defective, the head v_{restr} is also defective, meaning that it is not equipped with the EPP-feature [•D$_{[case:\_]}$•]. As I said, this is the result of a matching condition on the featural specification of the functional head v_{restr} in the numeration (cf. Section 4.5.3). The derivation is represented in tree (57). The head v_{restr} checks the Infl-feature on v. Then, it probes for person. Given Nested Agree, it must start from the v position, thereby skipping any item in Spec,v. The unaccusative v does not contain any π-feature (it does contain gender and number because of the edge feature, but not person): it is not a matching goal for the person probe on v_{restr}. Since the probe on v_{restr} is not satisfied by v, it can go on searching downwards. However, given the PIC, it cannot look inside the complement of vP (which is, anyway, empty). Hence, person-Agree on v_{restr} fails.

(57)

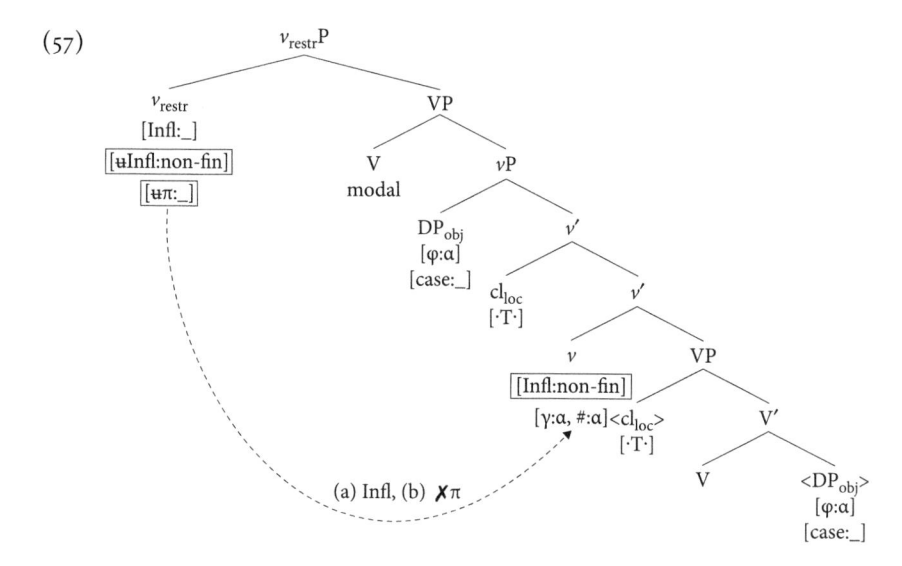

After this operation, the phase is completed. The two unchecked features in the complement of v_{restr}, [•T•] on the clitic and [case:_] on the DP$_{obj}$, trigger the insertion of an edge feature on v_{restr}. This moves the two elements to Spec,v_{restr}. Moreover, the gender and number features of the object are copied on v_{restr}, but not its person value. These features will be realized at Spell-out as participle agreement on the modal verb.

When Perf enters the derivation, it checks the [Infl] feature on v_{restr}. As a second step, it probes v_{restr} for person. This head contains a matching goal, but unvalued. Agree stops, resulting in lack of valuation. Note that, anyway, Perf can neither go back to already skipped goals (the specifiers of v_{restr}) because of Nested Agree, nor go downwards into v_{restr}P, because of the PIC. Hence, no person feature is copied on Perf, as (58) shows.

(58)

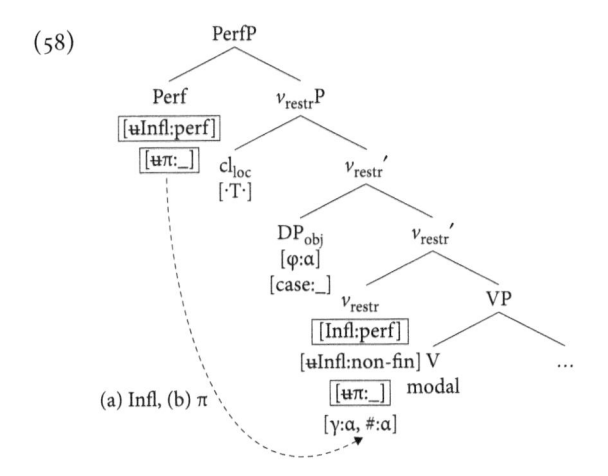

At Spell-out, Perf will be substituted by the allomorph BE.

To sum up, in the case of an unaccusative vP complement both clitic climbing and auxiliary switch are obligatory. The former happens because of the lack of a T position in the embedded complement, the latter because of the lack of π-feature on the lower defective v. For transitive vP complements, the auxiliary is always HAVE because of the presence of a person feature on the lower v, which is copied onto v_{restr} and, consequently onto Perf (cf. Section 4.6.1).

4.6.4   TP + transitive verbs

Modal verbs can also select TP complements. In the clause in (59a), the complement of the modal verb could be either a vP or a TP. In the former case, the derivation is as in Section 4.6.1. In the latter case, the derivation is presented in this section. The same applies to (59b), where the placement of the clitic pronoun on the non-finite verb indicates that the complement contains a T head.

(59) a. Teresa ha   voluto   mangiare la   torta.
         Teresa have.PRS.3SG want.PRTC eat.INF   the cake
         'Teresa wanted to eat the cake.'
     b. Teresa ha   voluto   mangiar=la.
         Teresa have.PRS.3SG want.PRTC eat.INF=ACC.3SG.F
         'Teresa wanted to eat it.'

For the sake of simplicity, I now propose the derivation for a clause without clitics, such as (59a). The derivation with the clitics contains the additional complication of edge features that move the clitic to the specifiers of the phase heads, as described in the previous section. The only difference with the derivation in

Section 4.6.3 is that clitics incorporate into the lower T head in the complement of v_{restr}.

The transitive vP is built as in the previous derivation in Section 4.6.1. The vP is then merged with a T head, as shown in tree (60). I assume that this T head is defective and does not contain any feature (but see footnote 12 in Section 4.5.2 for other suggestions).

(60)

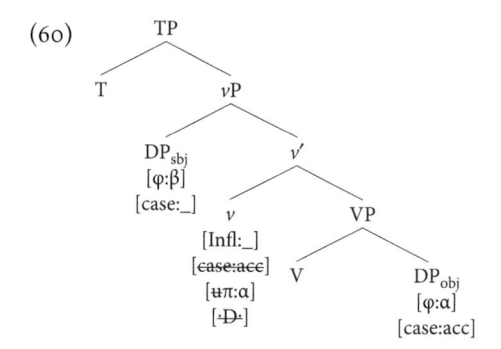

As a next step, head movement takes place, forming the complex head V + v + T. Thereafter, v_{restr} in its full version (namely, with a $[\bullet D_{[case:\_]}\bullet]$ feature) takes the TP as its complement. The head v_{restr} probes v for [Infl], and then for person. Agree succeeds for both features. The DP is also raised to Spec,v_{restr} by the EPP-feature $[\bullet D_{[case:\_]}\bullet]$. The operations are represented in tree (61).

(61)

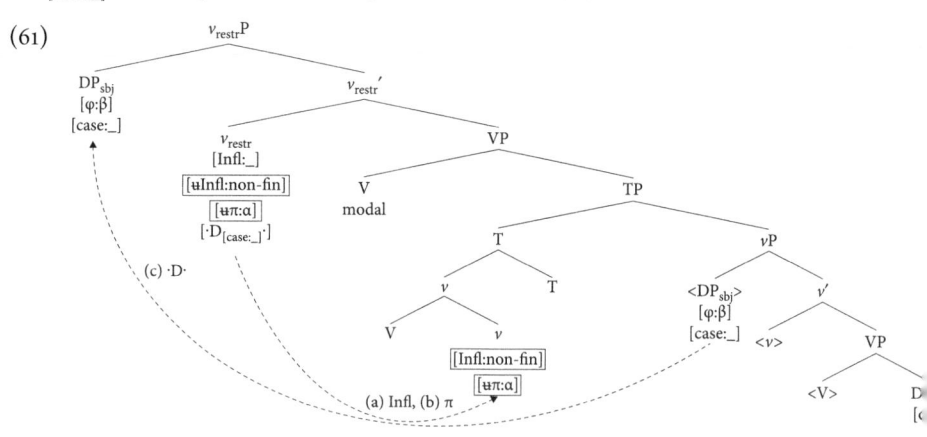

The result of π-Agree on v_{restr} is the same, whether it takes a transitive v as its complement, as in tree (45), or it selects a TP, as in (61). In both cases, v_{restr} successfully probes the embedded v for person. Consequently, the result on Perf will be the same as well: it will probe v_{restr} both for the Infl-feature and for person, resulting in successful valuation, both with a vP complement and with a TP complement. Hence, the allomorph HAVE is always inserted.

This means that sentence (59a) corresponds to two syntactic structures (TP/vP) that cannot be disambiguated when there are no clitics in the clause. Even though the exact structure cannot be detected in this case, I think that it should always be possible to have either a vP or a TP complement, even when this alternation is not visible on the surface, as in transitive clauses without clitic arguments. Nonetheless, a way to avoid the structural ambiguity in (59a) would be to assume a constraint that requires choosing the simpler complement when possible. A principle that prescribes to minimize the structure is *Economy of Representations*, proposed in Cardinaletti & Starke (1999: 47). However, such a principle leads to wrong predictions if applied to restructuring (at least under the present assumptions). On the one hand, this principle should avoid the construction of a TP structure when there is no clitic that would need the T head. Consequently, the auxiliary HAVE should not be possible with an unaccusative verb without a clitic, which is not the case (see Example (56)). Similarly, if this principle imposes the presence of a T head when there is a clitic, clitic climbing should never take place because the complement of the modal verb would already contain a host for the clitic (but cf. Example (44b)). On the other hand, if this principle always imposes a vP complement, lack of clitic climbing and lack of auxiliary switch should never be expected (contrary to Example (65)).

To sum up, in the case of transitive verbs the perfect auxiliary of the modal verb is always realized as HAVE. This is because Perf acquires a valued person feature from v_{restr}, which has copied it from the embedded transitive v, independently of the size of the complement.

4.6.5   TP + reflexive verbs

When the restructuring clause contains a reflexive clitic pronoun that is placed on the lexical verb, the perfect auxiliary is always realized as HAVE, as shown in (62).

(62) a.   Teresa ha   voluto   lavar=si.
          Teresa have.PRS.3SG want.PRTC wash.INF=REFL.ACC.3SG.F
      b.   *Teresa è   volut-a   lavar=si.
          Teresa be.PRS.3SG want.PRTC-SG.F wash.INF=REFL.ACC.3SG.F
          'Teresa wanted to wash herself.'

The position of the clitic indicates that the modal verb selects a TP as its complement. The derivation is as follows. The vP is built as in Section 4.6.2. Agree for person on v fails, as already explained above. The vP is then selected by the T

head, as shown in tree (63). When the T head enters the derivation, the reflexive
clitic incorporates into it, thereby satisfying its [•T•] feature.

(63)

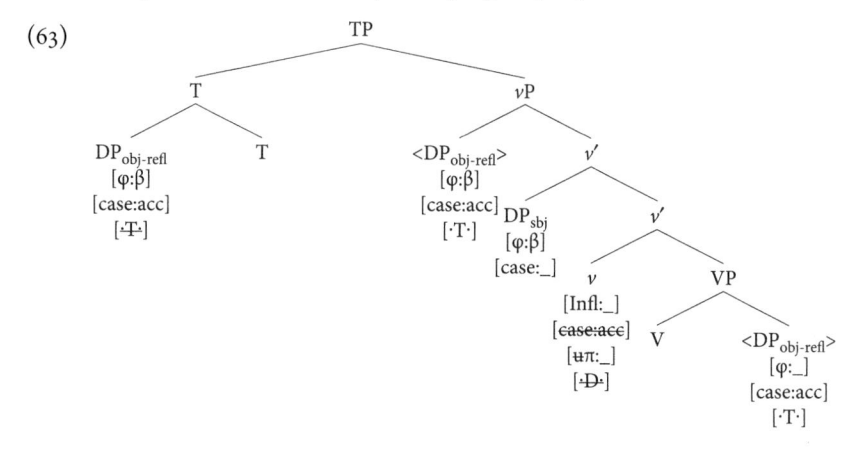

In the next step, the TP is merged with the head v_{restr}. The complement of v_{restr}
contains the complex head T + v + V (plus the clitic), created via head movement.
The head v_{restr} probes the embedded v for [Infl]. After this operation, it probes for
person. Due to Nested Agree, it must target again v. This head is contained in the
complex head formed by V, v, T and the reflexive clitic (which now bears valued
φ-features, acquired via binding). As I said in Section 4.5.2, I assume that all the
features on the subparts of a complex head are simultaneously represented as on a
simple head. For this reason, the features of the complex head are all accessible for
a probe that targets a part of the complex head. This means that the π-probe on
v_{restr} can also access the valued φ-features of the clitic, in addition to the unvalued
π-feature on v. I suggest that in this case of equidistance the valued goal is preferred over the unvalued goal. The π-probe on v_{restr} is valued by the π-feature of
the reflexive clitic pronoun in T. The relevant part of the derivation is illustrated
in tree (64).

(64)

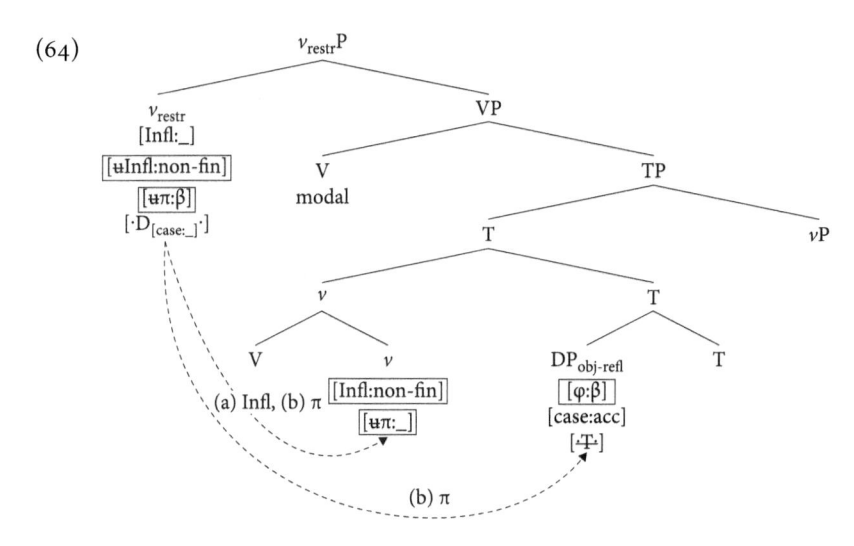

As shown in (64), v_{restr} ends up bearing a valued π-feature after Agree with the reflexive clitic. When Perf enters the derivation, it probes v_{restr} for both [Infl] and [π], thereby succeeding in copying a valued π-feature. At Spell-out, Perf will be substituted by HAVE. Thus, the T head paves the way for new possibilities for Agree on v_{restr} (and, consequently, on Perf).

In addition to the analysis just suggested, there are other possible ways to ensure that a valued π-feature is targeted by v_{restr} in this context. One alternative explanation, which I have sketched in Section 4.5.2, consists of the presence of an unvalued Infl-feature on the T head. In this scenario, v_{restr} would agree with T for [Infl]. It would also probe T for person, without finding a π-feature. The π-probe on v_{restr} would then go on searching its c-command domain (cf. *No-backtracking condition* of Nested Agree in (9) of Chapter 2), and it would agree for person with the subject in Spec,v (or with the clitic, if the probe can access the whole complex head, as just discussed). Another possible analysis makes use of a φ-probe on non-finite T, as in finite clauses. Under this approach, the T head in the complement always agrees with the subject, thereby providing the relevant features both for [Infl] and [π] on v_{restr}, independently of v.

4.6.6 TP + unaccusative verbs

In Section 4.6.3, I have shown that there is no possible goal for the π-probe on v_{restr} when the complement of v_{restr} is a defective vP. In this case, the clausal perfect auxiliary corresponds to the one that the embedded verb would select, namely BE. If instead the complement is a TP, the T head provides a goal for the π-probe on

v_{restr}. Let us now see the derivation for the sentence in (65). Once again, the position of the clitic constitutes evidence for the TP size of the complement.

(65)   Teresa ha   voluto   andar=ci   ieri.
       Teresa have.PRS.3SG want.PRTC go.INF=there yesterday
       'Teresa wanted to go there yesterday.'

Unaccusative verbs are selected by a defective v, which is not a probe for person, nor a case assigner. Once the vP is built, it is merged with a T head, resulting in the TP in tree (66).

(66)

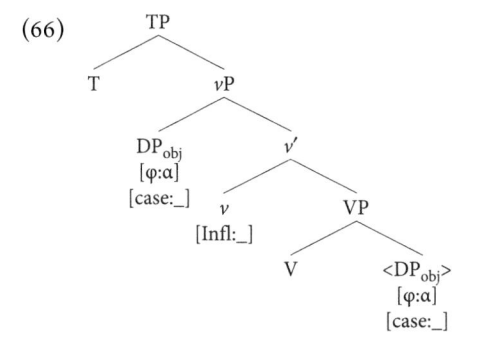

This TP is then selected by v_{restr}. In tree (67), v_{restr} probes v for [Infl]. Then, it discharges its person probe, searching again v because of Nested Agree. The unaccusative v does not contain any person specification. In addition, there is no relevant feature on the complex head that contains v. Hence, the probe proceeds its search downwards, in accordance with Nested Agree (see definition (9) in Chapter 2). It finds a matching π-feature on the internal argument in Spec,v. The person probe on v_{restr} is valued by this feature, as shown in (67).

(67)

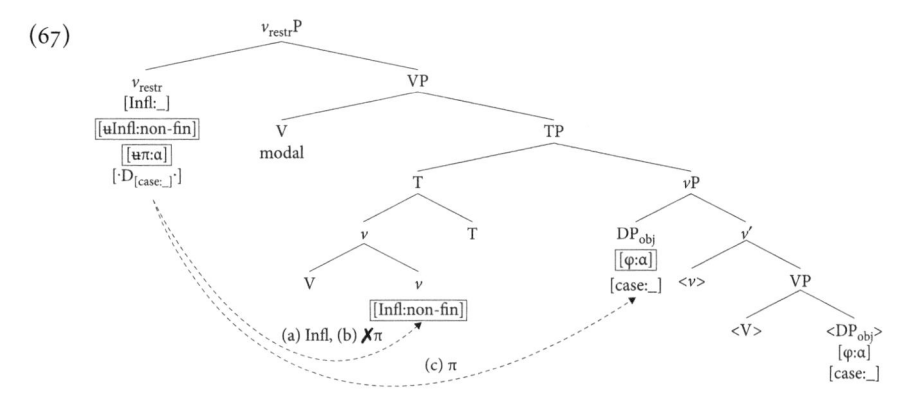

When Perf enters the derivation, it probes v_{restr} for [Infl], and, subsequently, for person. Perf can copy a valued person feature, since v_{restr} has copied it from the subject in Spec,v. For this reason, the auxiliary HAVE will be inserted. In general, more structure means more Agree possibilities for v_{restr}, and, consequently, for Perf. Whenever the complement contains a T head, Agree on Perf always succeeds. T behaves as a "repair" to the defectiveness of the embedded v: its position in the structure makes the lower subject an accessible goal for Agree on v_{restr}.

4.6.7 Impersonal clauses

As shown in Section 4.3, when a restructuring verb selects an impersonal complement there is no optionality for auxiliary selection. The auxiliary is invariably BE and clitic climbing is obligatory. The relevant data are provided in (12) and (13) in Section 4.3. A further example is given in (68).

(68) Si=sono   volut-e   mangiare tutte le   torte.
      IMPERS=be.PRS.3PL want.PRTC-PL.F eat.INF   all   the cakes
      'People wanted to eat all the cakes.'

In Section 3.3.9 of Chapter 3, I have argued that the emergence of BE in impersonal clauses is due to the presence of an impersonal Voice$_{impers}$. The head Voice$_{impers}$ bears an [Infl] feature and an unvalued person feature. The head Perf agrees with Voice$_{impers}$ for both the Infl-feature and the π-feature, due to Nested Agree. The unvalued person feature on Voice$_{impers}$ causes Agree to stop, with the consequence that the person probe on Perf remains unvalued and BE is inserted.

   As always, v_{restr} selects either a vP or a TP complement. In impersonal clauses, the vP option actually consists of a VoiceP (considering Voice as a type of v). In fact, the complement of the modal verb must be at least a Voice$_{impers}$P because impersonal clauses require the presence of a Voice head. If v_{restr} selects a VoiceP complement, the relevant portion of the clause for a transitive impersonal as in (68) is represented in tree (69). The transitive verb is selected by a defective v, and the impersonal clitic si is introduced by Voice$_{impers}$ (cf. Section 3.3.9.1 in Chapter 3). Both the impersonal clitic and the impersonal Voice contain an unvalued person feature.

(69)

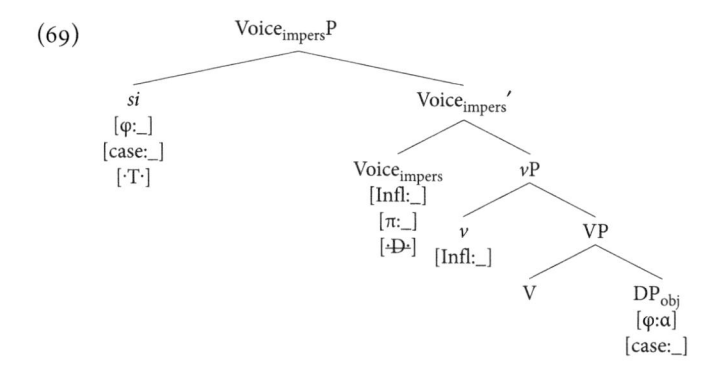

This Voice$_{impers}$P is selected by v_{restr} (assuming that Voice and v are of the same category).[61] In (70), v_{restr} agrees for [Infl] with Voice$_{impers}$, which is the highest matching goal. Successively, it probes it for person, due to Nested Agree. Voice$_{impers}$ bears a person feature, although unvalued. Hence, Agree stops and the result on v_{restr} is [ʉπ:_].

(70)

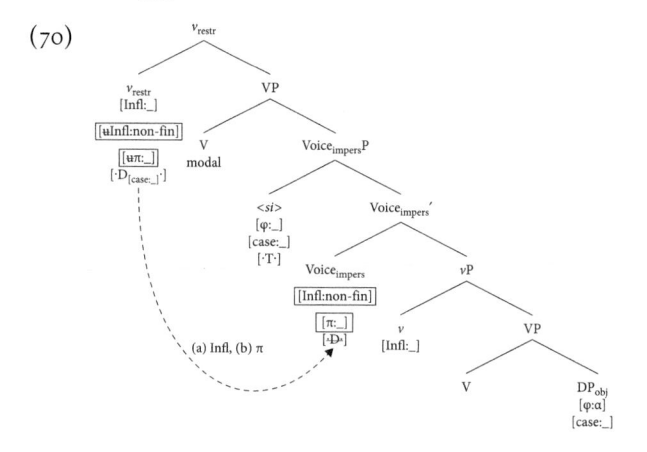

In the next step, Perf is merged into the structure. It probes v_{restr} for both [Infl] and person (because of Nested Agree). As the unvalued person feature on Voice$_{impers}$ has caused defective intervention for π-Agree on v_{restr}, now the same scenario is again repeated on Perf: [ʉπ:_] on v_{restr} leads to defective intervention, resulting

---

61. Note that there is an EPP-feature [•D$_{[case:\_]}$•] on v_{restr}. In fact, when v_{restr} selects a VoiceP equipped with a [•D•] feature, it must come in its non-defective version, equipped with an EPP-feature. [•D$_{[case:\_]}$•] raises the impersonal clitic. Movement of the internal argument is realized via EF-insertion. For this reason, there is participle agreement with the internal argument. Participle agreement is a consequence of the type of v selected by Voice$_{impers}$; if the lower v is defective, the internal object does not receive case from v, so that it must escape the phase (overtly or covertly, cf. Section 6.6 in Chapter 6), thereby triggering participle agreement.

in Perf[ʉπ:_]. Consequently, at Spell-out the elsewhere form BE is inserted for the terminal node Perf.

The other option for v_{restr} is to select a TP complement. As I said above, clitic climbing is obligatory in impersonal clauses. I suggest that the restructuring T head cannot host the impersonal clitic, resulting in obligatory clitic climbing. Perhaps this is a consequence of the fact that impersonal *si* needs to incorporate into a T head that assigns nominative case. This peculiarity might be due to the fact that the impersonal argument does not receive case, as I have proposed in Section 3.3.9.2 of Chapter 3. In Section 4.4.2, I have suggested that the T head involved in restructuring does not assign nominative case. Hence, it is not a suitable host for the impersonal clitic, which needs a non-defective T head.[62]

With a TP complement, the structure is as in (71). Note that the impersonal clitic *si* cannot cliticize to a non-finite T that does not assign nominative case.

(71)

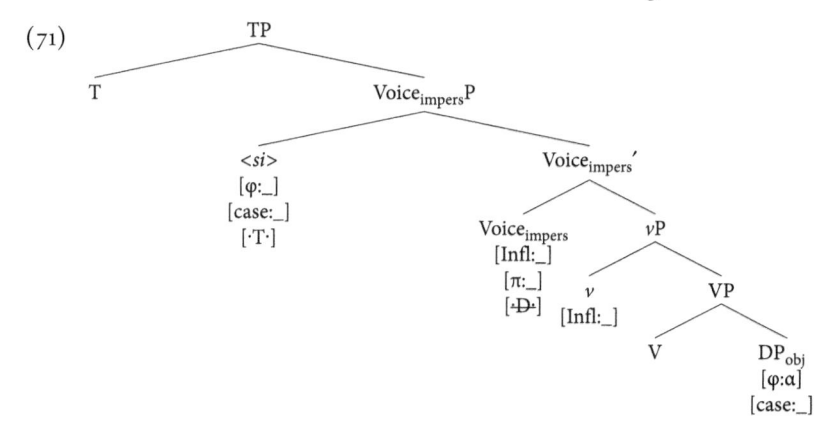

Successively, v_{restr} enters the derivation, as shown in tree (72).

---

62. Restructuring with impersonal clauses requires further research because the data are quite complex. For instance, see Cinque (1988) for the special readings and the distributional restrictions of impersonal *si* in non-finite clauses.

(72)

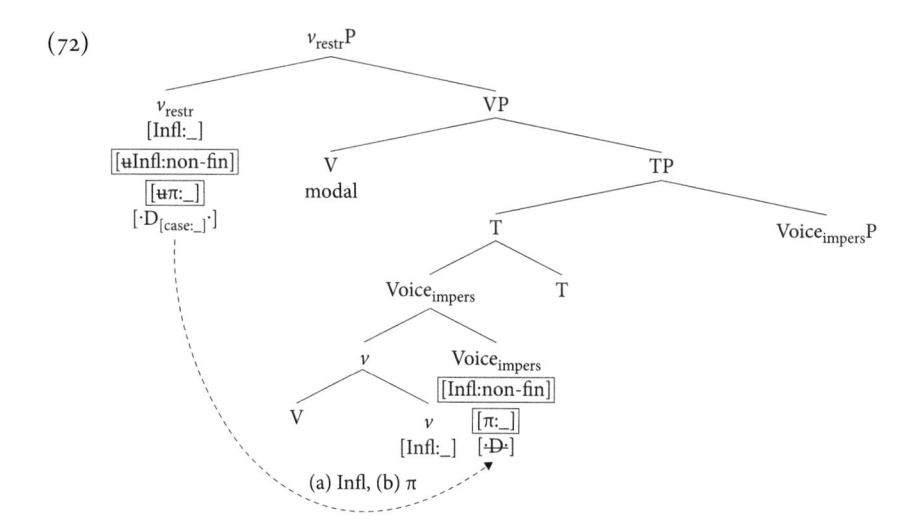

The head v_{restr} probes the complex head T-Voice$_{impers}$-v-V. Agree for [Infl] and [π] target Voice$_{impers}$. The complex head does not contain any valued person feature, with the consequence that the person probe on v_{restr} does not copy any value.[63]

When Perf enters the derivation, it probes v_{restr} for [Infl] and for [π]. Since v_{restr} bears an unvalued person feature, the person probe on Perf remains unvalued as well, with the consequence that BE will be inserted at Spell-out.

To sum up, in both derivations (VoiceP/TP complement) Perf agrees with an item that bears an unvalued person feature (Voice$_{impers}$), leading to BE insertion. Moreover, the clitic must reach matrix T, since there is no other T head available for incorporation (there is no T head in the VoiceP complement, and the T head in the TP complement is not a proper host for this clitic).

---

63. There is actually a case where person Agree on v_{restr} could succeed, leading to HAVE insertion. In the derivation for impersonal root clauses (Section 3.3.9.1 of Chapter 3), I said that Voice$_{impers}$ can select either a defective v or a transitive v. This alternation gives rise to impersonal sentences with and without participle agreement (*si=sono mangiat-i gli spaghetti* vs. *si=è mangiato gli spaghetti*). In the present discussion, I have offered the derivation with a defective v. However, if the embedded v is transitive, then v_{restr} would succeed in copying a valued π-feature within a TP complement. In fact, if in tree (72) v contains a valued person feature, this should be found by the probe on v_{restr} (and, consequently, by Perf). A possible solution is to exclude the TP derivation, also in light of the fact that clitic climbing is obligatory. Perhaps the T head that is found in the complement of a restructuring verb cannot select a Voice$_{impers}$, maybe because it could not host the impersonal argument for case-related reason. Hence, a structure as in (72) is never generated. I leave this issue to further research.

4.7   Some problematic cases

According to the analysis just presented, both auxiliary switch and clitic climbing depend on the size of the complement. This means that these two phenomena (when applicable) should always go together, as (73) summarizes.

(73) a. TP: HAVE + no clitic climbing
      b. *v*P: BE + clitic climbing

However, the picture in (73) is an approximation of the real data. The correlation between the two transparency effects does not always take place. Indeed, it is possible to find the crossed distribution of the two phenomena: HAVE in the presence of clitic climbing, and BE with the clitic in the lower position.

(74) a. TP(?): HAVE + clitic climbing
      b. *v*P(?): BE + no clitic climbing

Although sentences of the type in (74) (especially (74a)) are quite marginal, they are attested. In this section, I suggest some possible ways to account for these exceptions.

Nonetheless, marginal sentences such as (74) might also be the result of some performance errors. More generally, it could also be the case that clitic climbing must be simply dissociated from auxiliary switch. Maybe clitic placement does not necessarily identify a TP layer, but there are extra positions in the clause, similarly to what has been suggested in Cardinaletti & Shlonsky (2004).

4.7.1   HAVE + clitic climbing

In Sections 4.3 and 4.6.3, I said that clauses containing an unaccusative verb with clitic climbing and without auxiliary switch are ungrammatical (cf. sentence (8d) and (56b), repeated in (75)). Nonetheless, this sentence might be accepted by some speakers, as the sign # indicates.

(75) #Maria ci=ha   voluto   andare ieri.
      Maria there=have.PRS.3SG want.PRTC go.INF yesterday
      'Maria wanted to go there yesterday.'

According to the present analysis, (75) should be ungrammatical because it is a blend of two structures in contradiction: the auxiliary HAVE with an unaccusative verb is only compatible with a TP complement, and the clitic in the matrix position only with a *v*P. Under the assumption that clitic climbing is only possible out of a *v*P complement, it cannot be the case that Perf successfully probes for person with an unaccusative *v*P complement, as we saw in Section 4.6.3. Perf can successfully copy a person feature in the case of a TP complement (see Section 4.6.6). However, the position of the clitic shows that there is no T head embedded. How can a sentence like (75) be generated?

First of all, let me highlight that the clause in (75) is ungrammatical according to my own judgment and to the speakers I consulted, and the same is true for Cinque (2004: 153) (where the judgment is: *?) and for Cardinaletti & Shlonsky (2004: 522) (where it is ungrammatical). It should also be noted that such sentences are considerably degraded with other clitics than *ci*. Differently from (75), the auxiliary HAVE is impossible when the lexical verb is unaccusative and a dative clitic moves out of the *v*P complement, as shown in (76).

(76) a. *Il bambino gli=ha   voluto   scappare   dalla
          the child   DAT.3SG.M=have.PRS.3SG want.PRTC run.away.INF from.the
          vista.
          sight

      b. Il bambino gli=è   voluto   scappare   dalla
          the child   DAT.3SG.M=be.PRS.3SG want.PRTC run.away.INF from.the
          vista.
          sight
          'The child wanted to run away from his sight.'

The same can be said with the partitive clitic *ne*.

(77) a. *Di ragazze, ne=hanno   voluto/-e   venire   molte.
          of girls   of=have.PRS.3PL want.PRTC/-PL.F come.INF many

      b. Di ragazze, ne=sono   volut-e   venire   molte.
          of girls   of=be.PRS.3PL   want.PRTC-PL.F come.INF many
          'Of girls, many of them wanted to come.'

Lack of auxiliary switch in the presence of clitic climbing is also impossible with reflexive clitics (cf. the completely ungrammatical *Maria si=ha voluto lavare ieri* 'Maria wanted to wash herself yesterday' in (10c) in Section 4.3) and with impersonal clitics (cf. Example (13c) in Section 4.3, *si=ha voluto mangiare gli spaghetti* 'people wanted to eat the spaghetti').

I conclude that the combination HAVE + clitic climbing with unaccusative verbs is indeed not possible. I propose that the partial acceptability of Example (75) is due to the "special" status of the clitic *ci*. A sentence such (75) might be generated if the complement is a TP and the clitic *ci* is base-generated in a higher position, namely outside the complement TP.[64] In Example (75), *ci* originates in

---

64. The base-generation hypothesis might be favored by the different functions that the clitic *ci* can perform. According to Cruschina (2012), it is a pro-argument in the existential construction, a pro-predicate in the inverse locative and deictic locative construction, a lexicalized item

the matrix clause. Its placement is independent of the size of the complement, which can be a TP (determining HAVE insertion).

4.7.2   BE + no clitic climbing

The auxiliary BE can also appear with the clitic in the lower position. This is shown in sentence (78), which is accepted by some speakers.

(78) #Maria è   volut-a   andar=ci   ieri.
      Maria be.PRS.3SG want.PRTC-SG.F go.INF=there yesterday
      'Maria wanted to go there yesterday.'

Such sentences are sporadically attested in corpora.[65] They are also discussed in the literature. Cardinaletti & Shlonsky (2004) consider sentence (79), which is the equivalent of (78), as degraded when the auxiliary is BE.

(79) Avrei/?Sarei   voluto   andar=ci   con Maria.
      have/be.COND.PRS.1SG want.PRTC go.INF=there with Maria
      'I would have liked to go there with Maria.' (Cardinaletti & Shlonsky 2004:521)

Rizzi (1978:136, fn.26) provides the sentence *Maria è dovuta venirci molte volte* 'Maria had to come there many times', but he notes that its acceptability is degraded if the subject is not third person (for unclear reasons). Cinque (2004:169, fn.18) gives an example from a literary source. Another sentence is found in Burzio (1986:367): *Maria sarebbe volut-a andare a prender=li lei stessa* 'Maria would have wanted to go to fetch them herself.' However, this contains a motion verb, which always imposes BE as its auxiliary.

    The present analysis predicts that sentences such as (78) are ungrammatical, because they correspond to two conflicting structural requirements, as is the case for the similar sentence in (75). In (78), the auxiliary BE can only arise with a *v*P complement, but the position of the clitic indicates a TP complement. How can a sentence like (78) be generated?

---

in the presentational construction. In existential uses it can acquire its locative meaning by coindexation with a null locative argument (Cruschina 2012). In such cases, it can be base-generated in the matrix clause.

65. The marginality of sentences as (78) is confirmed by a corpus search that I have performed on 20/02/2020 on the online corpus of *Repubblica*, available at *https://corpora.dipintra.it*. For sentences with unaccusative verbs without clitic climbing (as (78)), in 5.6% of the cases the auxiliary is BE, and in 94.4% HAVE. Note that with reflexive clitics the examples with BE and without clitic climbing are very rare (0.73%). I take this as a sign of their ungrammaticality, confirming the judgments that I have collected with speakers.

Mismatches of this type remain an open question. I believe that the theory developed in this book can account for all the core data, and that marginal cases can receive independent explanations. I tentatively suggest that the emergence of BE in (78) is due to a defective v_{restr}. Speakers who produce (78) use a defective v_{restr} for selecting a TP when the embedded v is defective, instead of the non-defective v_{restr}, as indicated in (80).[66]

(80)   <u>defective</u> v_{restr} - T - defective v

In particular, the defective v_{restr} in (80) should lack the person probe, like the unaccusative v (cf. discussion in Section 4.5.3). In this case, cyclic Agree between the person feature on the embedded T and matrix Perf (described in Section 4.6.6) is interrupted by the lack of a person probe on v_{restr}. Since the PIC prevents Perf from looking inside v_{restr}P, Agree on Perf fails. Consequently, BE must be inserted even with a TP in complement, resulting in examples as (78). Note that the assumption of no π-probe on defective v_{restr} does not make any difference in the analysis so far.

Crucial evidence for having a defective v_{restr} in (78) is participle agreement, which is present independently of the position of the clitic. This means that the DP_{sbj} is not raised by the EPP-feature, as it happens with a fully-fledged v_{restr}, but rather by an edge feature, which is possible with a defective v_{restr}. Hence, v_{restr} can be defective even when it selects a TP, if the lower v is defective.

4.8   Restructuring in other varieties

In this chapter, I have shown how the optional effect of auxiliary switch arises in Standard Italian. In particular, auxiliary switch takes place given two conditions: a special v_{restr} that acts as a hinge for person Agree, and a small complement for the modal verb (vP, but not TP). The optionality for different sizes of the complement leads to the optionality for different transparency effects.

In other Italo-Romance varieties, optionality for auxiliary selection and for placement of the clitic tends to disappear (Egerland 2009). As far as clitic placement is concerned, in Northern varieties the lower position in enclisis on the lexical verb is preferred, while in Southern varieties clitics tend to be placed on the higher auxiliary. As far as auxiliary selection is concerned, the former exhibit HAVE in restructuring (as expected), while the latter tend to have obligatory aux-

---

66. This change may happen categorically, meaning that some speakers always perform auxiliary switch, or it could be optional. More research should shed light on this point.

iliary switch. However, this only happens in languages where auxiliary selection is argument-structure-driven, as in Standard Italian. For languages where auxiliary selection is subject-driven, the size of the complement does not matter and the auxiliary is realized according to the person feature of the subject, as in root clauses. I will now provide two examples.

In the Northern dialects, the auxiliary in root clauses behave similarly to Italian (with some variation with reflexives, cf. Chapter 5 for details). An example of a Northern variety is Paduan (Cennamo & Sorace 2007). In Paduan, the auxiliary in restructuring can only be HAVE and clitic climbing does not take place. When Paduan speakers are asked to translate Italian restructuring clauses that contain BE and clitic climbing, these are translated with HAVE and with the clitic in the lower position (Pegoraro 2018). Examples (81b,d) are the Paduan translations of the Italian sentences (81a,c).

(81) *Paduan*
    a. Siamo   potut-i   uscire da lì   solo dopo un po'.
         be.PRS.1PL can.PRTC-PL.M exit.INF from there only after a   little
    b. Ghemo   podesto ussire da lì   soeo dopo un poco.
         have.PRS.1PL can.PRTC exit.INF from there only after a   little
         'We could get out of there only after a while.'
    c. Lo=voglio   fare   entro domani.
         ACC.3SG.M=want.PRS.1SG do.INF by   tomorrow
    d. Vojo   far=lo   entro doman.   (Pegoraro 2018: 20–22)
         want.PRS.1SG do.INF=ACC.3SG.M by   tomorrow
         'I want to do it by tomorrow.'

These facts can be easily explained if Paduan restructuring verbs always select TP complements, independently of the features of v_{restr}. Hence, in those Northern varieties where auxiliary selection is argument-structure-driven, restructuring verbs can only take TP complements, and may or may not be selected by the special v_{restr} that I have introduced for Standard Italian.

In many Southern dialects, the auxiliary is dependent on the features of the subject (subject-based auxiliary selection, cf. Chapter 5 for details). Such a language is Ariellese (D'Alessandro & Roberts 2010; D'Alessandro 2017b). Here, auxiliary selection in restructuring is based on the person feature of the subject and does not change depending on the type of the lexical verb. For example, in root clauses the perfect auxiliary is always BE with first person subjects. As (82) shows, the same happens in restructuring. The auxiliary exclusively depends on the person feature of the subject of the restructuring verb, without any variation or optionality.

(82)   *Ariellese*
    a.   So   vulute   ij   a lu mare.
        be.PRS.1SG want.PRTC go.INF to the beach
    b.   *Aje   vulute   ij   a lu mare.
        have.PRS.1SG want.PRTC go.INF to the beach
        'I wanted to go to the beach.'
    c.   Ci=so   vulute   ji   da sole.
        there=be.PRS.1SG want.PRTC go.INF by myself
    d.   *C=aje   vulute   ji   da sole.   (R. D'Alessandro, p.c.)
        there=have.PRS.1SG want.PRTC go.INF by myself
        'I wanted to go there by myself.'

This distribution can be explained with the analysis of subject-driven auxiliary selection that I propose in Chapter 5. In subject-driven auxiliary selection, the person probe on Perf is not constrained by Nested Agree because it is ordered before the [uInfl] probe. Hence, it targets the raised subject in Spec,v_{restr}, which is the highest matching goal in its search domain. In this case, both the type of complement and the features on v_{restr} are irrelevant: the auxiliary is always the same as in root clauses (for Ariellese, BE-BE-HAVE). Auxiliary switch of the Italian type is impossible in languages with subject-driven auxiliary selection because Perf invariably probes the subject.

As Example (82) shows, clitic climbing is obligatory: the clitic must be located in the higher position. This fact indicates that in Southern varieties the complement of a modal verb can only be a *v*P. In languages of this type (with obligatory clitic climbing and subject-driven auxiliary selection), restructuring verbs can only take *v*P complements, and may or may not be selected by the special v_{restr}, with any effect on the form of the perfect auxiliary.

The behavior of clitic placement and auxiliary selection in dialects confirms that the two phenomena are independent. In general, these data show that the correlation between restructuring and transparency effects cannot be absolute, and their absence does not necessarily imply the lack of restructuring. These cross-linguistic differences naturally follow from different sizes of the complement, as summarized in (83).

(83)   a.   Southern dialects (Ariellese): *v*P complement
        – clitic climbing,
        – auxiliary switch not applicable (subject-driven auxiliary selection)
    b.   Northern dialects (Paduan): TP complement
        – lack of clitic climbing,
        – lack of auxiliary switch

There is also an interesting implication between the different transparency effects, which finds an explanation in the analysis of auxiliary switch that I have proposed in this chapter. According to a study performed by Egerland (2009) on speakers from different geographic areas (Vallebona, Brescia, Reggio Emilia in Northern Italy; Gallipoli, San Martino in Pensilis, Catanzaro in Southern Italy; Cagliari in Sardinia), if an informant accepts auxiliary switch with a restructuring verb, s/he also accepts clitic climbing with it.

(84)   a.   If auxiliary switch → clitic climbing
  b.   If no clitic climbing → no auxiliary switch

The implication (84), proposed by Egerland (2009), states that if auxiliary switch is possible, clitic climbing must also take place. Under the present analysis, auxiliary switch and clitic climbing can apply if the complement of the restructuring verb is a vP. However, auxiliary switch requires more specific conditions than clitic climbing does. The former depends on both the size of the complement and the features on v_{restr} (in languages where auxiliary selection is argument-structure-based), whereas the latter only depends on the size of the complement. If clitic climbing is excluded, auxiliary switch is impossible because the complement is a TP. If clitic climbing takes place, it means that the complement is a vP. In this case, if auxiliary switch is not possible, this is either because of independent reasons (as is the case for subject-driven varieties), or because the head v_{restr} is missing.

4.9 Outside restructuring: Biclausal structures

'In Standard Italian, in biclausal sentences with subordination the matrix auxiliary is in general HAVE. This is the case, for instance, with *say*-verbs, as shown in (85a,b).

(85)   a.   Teresa ha   detto [$_{DP}$ una bugia].
    Teresa have.PRS.3SG say.PRTC a lie
  b.   Teresa ha   detto [$_{CP}$ di sentir=si   bene].
    Teresa have.PRS.3SG say.PRTC to feel.INF=REFL.ACC.3SG.F well
  c.   Teresa ha   detto [$_{CP}$ che si=sente   bene].
    Teresa have.PRS.3SG say.PRTC that REFL.ACC.3SG.F=feel.PRS.3SG well
    'Teresa has said a lie / to feel well / that she is feeling well.'

The internal argument of the matrix verb in (85) can be either a DP or a CP (in (85b), the CP projection is identified by the possibility of topicalized arguments before the particle *di*). The matrix clause in these structures is transitive, as the presence of the auxiliary HAVE confirms. Recall, in fact, that Perf can be realized as HAVE only in the presence of a valued π-probe on *v*, which is the case with a non-defective *v* (in the absence of any defective argument), as I have illustrated in Chapter 3. Hence, biclausal structures contain a non-defective *v*. The matrix clause behaves as a transitive root clause, leading to HAVE as the matrix auxiliary. The auxiliary is HAVE even when the embedded verb is unaccusative, as shown in (86).

(86) a. Teresa ha   detto   [$_{CP}$ di andare via   presto].
          Teresa have.PRS.3SG say.PRTC   to go.INF away early
      b. Teresa ha   detto   [$_{CP}$ che va   via   presto].
          Teresa have.PRS.3SG say.PRTC   that go.PRS.3SG away early
          'Teresa has said to leave early / that she is leaving early.'

This confirms the transitive argument structure of the matrix verb. Further evidence comes from auxiliary switch to BE when the matrix clause contains a reflexive indirect object (87) or an impersonal external argument (88), exactly as it happens for transitive root clauses.

(87) a. Teresa si=è   dett-a   [$_{DP}$ una bugia].
          Teresa REFL.DAT.3SG.F=be.PRS.3SG say.PRTC-SG.F   a   lie
      b. Teresa si=è   dett-a   [$_{CP}$ di
          Teresa REFL.DAT.3SG.F=be.PRS.3SG say.PRTC-SG.F   to
          sentir=si   bene].
          feel.INF=REFL.ACC.3SG.F well
      c. Teresa si=è   dett-a   [$_{CP}$ che
          Teresa REFL.DAT.3SG.F=be.PRS.3SG say.PRTC-SG.F   that
          si=sente   bene].
          REFL.ACC.3SG.F=feel.PRS.3SG well
          'Teresa has said herself a lie / to feel well / that she is feeling well.'

(88) a. Ieri   a lavoro si=è   detto   [$_{DP}$ una bugia].
          yesterday at work IMPERS=be.PRS.3SG say.PRTC   a   lie
      b. Ieri   a lavoro si=è   detto   [$_{CP}$ di
          yesterday at work IMPERS=be.PRS.3SG say.PRTC   to
          sentir=si   bene].
          feel.INF=REFL.ACC.3SG well
      c. Ieri   a lavoro si=è   detto   [$_{CP}$ che
          yesterday at work IMPERS=be.PRS.3SG say.PRTC   that
          ci=si=sente   bene].
          IMPERS=REFL.ACC.3SG=feel.PRS.3SG well
          'Yesterday at work people have said a lie / to feel well / that people feel well.'

These facts can be derived if the person probe on matrix transitive *v* always finds a valued person feature in the internal argument position (on either the DP or the CP, assuming that the C head bears φ-features), unless a reflexive or impersonal clitic higher than the DP/CP intervenes.[67]

Unaccusative verbs can also select clausal complements. An example is the verb *parere* 'look like'. Its complement can be a DP, as in (89a), or a CP, as in (89b) and (89c) (in (89b), the complement should be smaller than a CP in order to allow for raising, but also be bigger than a TP, since the non-finite subordinate clause can contain preverbal topicalized elements, see Rizzi 1997).

(89)   a.   Teresa è   pars-a   [$_{DP}$ una vera campionessa].
            Teresa be.PRS.3SG look.like.PRTC-SG.F   a   real champion
       b.   Teresa è   pars-a   [$_{TP}$ vincere tutte le gare].
            Teresa be.PRS.3SG look.like.PRTC-SG.F   win.INF all the competitions
       c.   È   parso   [$_{CP}$ che Teresa abbia   vinto   tutte
            be.PRS.3SG look.like.PRTC   that Teresa have.SUBJ.PRS.3SG win.PRTC all
            le gare].
            the competitions
            'Teresa looked like a real champion / to have won all the competitions.'

With matrix unaccusative verbs, the perfect auxiliary is invariably BE, even in the presence of a CP complement. This is expected with a defective *v* (see also Section 4.5.5 on raising). In fact, if the *v* associated with the unaccusative verb does not contain any person probe, Agree on Perf always fails, independently of the type of complement, leading to the emergence of the unmarked form BE.

To sum up, in the case of biclausal subordination transitive verbs are selected by a transitive *v*, while unaccusative verbs are selected by a defective *v*. Transitive *v* causes the perfect auxiliary to be realized as HAVE, whereas defective *v* determines the realization of the perfect auxiliary as BE.

---

67. The presence of φ-features on C can be due to different reasons. One possibility, which goes back at least to Stowell (1981), is that CPs are embedded under a nominal shell. These clausal complements are DPs with a covert definite determiner, which selects a CP as its complement. I suggest that the covert D head can host (default) φ-features. For discussion of the DP-approach, cf. Moulton (2009); Kastner (2015). An alternative is to say that C bears φ-features of its own (Platzack 1986). The φ-features could also be located on T, and be accessible in C because of Agree or head movement of T to C.

4.10   Summary

Restructuring configurations are characterized by apparently optional transparency effects in the choice of the perfect auxiliary associated with the restructuring verb: the auxiliary can be either HAVE, or the one corresponding to the lexical verb (auxiliary switch). In this chapter, I have provided the first formal analysis of auxiliary selection in restructuring, as far as I am aware. I have argued that if one assumes that auxiliary selection is an instance of π-Agree and if the lower portion of the clause can be of different sizes (as there is evidence for), then the distribution of the auxiliaries BE and HAVE is exactly predicted.

The transparency effects in auxiliary selection arise because restructuring configurations contain a special type of v_{restr}, which creates a cyclic Agree configuration. This is possible because of a double [Infl] feature that builds the connection between the higher and the lower portion of the clause. In case of a small complement below this v_{restr}, the clausal auxiliary faithfully corresponds to the one that would be selected by the lower v, since v_{restr} copies the information on the lower v, which is successively copied by Perf. Auxiliary switch consists of the emergence of BE due to failed Agree or Agree with φ-defective items, as we saw for root clauses. Nevertheless, this effect is optional, since it depends on the size of the complement. Different complement sizes determine different search domains for Agree. By enlarging the complement, the lower v is no longer the decisive factor for the realization of the auxiliary. Instead, the presence of a T head neutralizes the difference between the different types of v and suppresses the transparency effect, leading to HAVE insertion, regardless of the type of lexical verb. Hence, there is no real optionality for auxiliary selection, but rather for the type of complement of v_{restr}.

I have also examined the correlation between auxiliary switch and clitic climbing, since they both depend on the size of the complement. In the case of a small complement (a vP), both auxiliary switch and clitic climbing take place, if applicable. In the case of a large complement (a TP), the auxiliary is invariably HAVE and the clitic remains in the lower position. I have also discussed some problematic cases where the correlation is not so neat.

To conclude, the idea that auxiliary selection is π-Agree finds further confirmation in these data about auxiliary selection in restructuring.

CHAPTER 5

Auxiliary selection in other Italo-Romance varieties

5.1 Introduction

In the previous chapters, I have developed a detailed analysis of the distribution of the auxiliaries BE and HAVE in Standard Italian. In this language, auxiliary selection is argument-structure-driven: the auxiliary "signals" the type of argument structure of the lexical verb. I have argued that this is possible if auxiliary selection is the morphophonological realization of syntactic Agree for person.

In this chapter, I consider auxiliary selection in other Italo-Romance varieties. First of all, I describe and analyze the other main type of auxiliary selection: *subject-driven*. In many Central and Southern-Eastern Italo-Romance varieties, the perfect auxiliary depends on the person feature of the subject, without any influence of the argument structure. I will show that subject-driven auxiliary selection can be derived by the same system that I have proposed for Italian. It is the difference in the ordering of features on the head Perf that gives rise to this different type of auxiliary distribution.

After having dealt with subject-driven auxiliary selection, I come back to argument-structure-driven auxiliary selection. I will focus on two aspects: the presence of additional person restrictions, and the variation in reflexive clauses. For the former, I discuss languages where the auxiliary alternation based on argument structure is restricted to specific person specifications (*mixed systems*). In particular, I show that the present analysis offers a theoretical explanation for the attested patterns of this type. For the latter, I explain why argument-structure-driven systems exhibit much variation in the presence of reflexive pronouns, both cross-linguistically and within languages. Finally, I briefly describe other argument-structure-driven languages outside Italo-Romance, such as German and French.

The chapter is structured as follows. In Section 5.2 I illustrate my proposal for subject-driven auxiliary selection, discussing the case of Ariellese (5.2.3). I also describe some various types of splits: systems restricted by tense, aspect or mood (5.3.1), and by number (5.3.2). Languages with a single auxiliary are discussed in Section 5.4. Languages where the auxiliary alternation based on argument structure is restricted to specific person features are analyzed in Section 5.5.

In Section 5.6, I provide an explanation for the possible and impossible interactions between the two types of auxiliary selection (subject-driven and argument-structure-driven). In Section 5.7, I account for the variation in reflexive clauses, both cross-linguistically (5.7.1) and within languages (5.7.2). In Section 5.8, I briefly describe some examples of other argument-structure-driven systems beyond Italian. The concluding Section 5.9 summarizes the main results of this chapter.

5.2   Subject-based auxiliary selection

5.2.1   Distribution based on the features of the subject

Italo-Romance varieties are Romance languages spoken in Italy, closely related to Standard Italian. In many of these languages, the morphological realization of the perfect auxiliary only depends on the person feature of the subject, and not on the argument structure. Languages of this type are mostly found in Central and Southern Italy, but also in Northern Italy (for instance, some Novarese dialects of Piedmont), and outside Italy (some northern Catalan dialects) (Ledgeway 2019:357).[68] The exact distribution of HAVE and BE according to person is language-specific and there is huge variation among the Romance varieties spoken in Italy. In the most frequent pattern, the auxiliary corresponding to first and second persons (local persons, under the terminology proposed by Aissen 1999) is realized differently from the auxiliary of third person. This frequently gives rise to the paradigm BE-BE-HAVE (BBH). An example for the distribution BBH is the variety spoken in Southern Lazio, as shown in (1).[69]

(1)   *Southern Lazio*
  a.   So   maɲˈɲatə.
       be.PRS.1SG eat.PRTC
       'I have eaten.'
  b.   Si   maɲˈɲatə.
       be.PRS.2SG eat.PRTC
       'You have eaten.'

---

68. I use the term *dialect* as a synonym for *language* and *variety*, without committing to any specific sociolinguistic notion.

69. For all the examples in this chapter, I give the string as I found it in the source reference. In most cases, it is a transcription that contains IPA symbols, with different levels of accuracy.

c. A   maɲˈɲatə.
   have.PRS.3SG eat.PRTC
   'S/he has eaten.'

d. 'Sema   maɲˈɲatə.
   be.PRS.1PL eat.PRTC
   'We have eaten.'

e. 'Seta   maɲˈɲatə.
   be.PRS.2PL eat.PRTC
   'You have eaten.'

f. 'Ana   maɲˈɲatə.
   have.PRS.3PL eat.PRTC
   'They have eaten.'   (Cordin 1997: 93)

The reversal distribution HHB is also attested, although more rarely. Examples are the dialects of Pompei (Giammarco 1973) and Aliano (but note that HHB seems to be restricted to unaccusative verbs) (Manzini & Savoia 2005). Moreover, next to splits that separate 1st-2nd person from 3rd person, almost all combinations are possible. For instance, there are languages where 1st and 3rd person pattern together with the exclusion of 2nd person. An example is Bisceglie (HBH-HHH): the 2nd person singular selects BE, whereas 1st and 3rd persons determine HAVE insertion (Loporcaro 2007: 195). Other varieties of this type are Introdacqua (HBHHHH) (Loporcaro 2007: 184) and Canosa Sannita (HBHHBH) (Legendre 2010). In Gioia del Colle (BHBHHH), the auxiliary for 1st and 3rd person singular is different from the auxiliary for 2nd person singular, although the distribution of HAVE and BE for the singular is opposite to the above-mentioned dialects (Loporcaro 2007: 196).[70] There are also cases where just the first person is realized differently from the other persons. Examples are Capracotta (HBB) (Manzini & Savoia 2005: II: 708), Roccasicura (B~H B B B B B) and Canosa di Puglia (B~H H H H H H) (Ledgeway 2019: 363).

Even closely related dialects may be affected by huge variation. In Table 5.1, I represent the distribution of the perfect auxiliaries in the closely related varieties spoken in L'Aquila (Abruzzo), Introdacqua (Abruzzo), Capracotta (Molise),

---

70. It should be noted that the data presented in Manzini & Savoia (2005) contradict this picture. According to that study, the dialects spoken in Bisceglie (Manzini & Savoia 2005: II: 721) and Canosa Sannita (Manzini & Savoia 2005: II: 687) have the pattern BBH. For Introdacqua and Gioia del Colle there is no documentation there. Manzini & Savoia (2005: II: 728) also provide a list of varieties where the 2nd person patterns differently from the other persons: in Vastogirardi, Sassinoro, Ruvo, and Bitetto, the distribution is H~B B H~B. A more precise picture of linguistic variation in auxiliary selection should be assessed with new data. What is relevant for the present discussion is the unquestionable fact that many different combinations are attested.

Sassinoro (Campania) (Giammarco 1973:162–6, Manzini & Savoia 2005:II, 708–9, 719–20).

Table 5.1 Variation in auxiliary selection in Abruzzo, Molise, Campania

	1SG	2SG	3SG	1PL	2PL	3PL
L'Aquila	B	B	H	B	B	H
Introdacqua	H	B	H	H	H	H
Capracotta	H	B	B	H~B	H~B	H
Sassinoro	H~B	B	H~B	H~B	H~B	H~B

To sum up, the splits according to person range from the frequent pattern BBH to the opposite HHB, to free variation, to splits that single out just the second person or only the first person (for data, cf. Loporcaro 2001, 2007, 2016; Manzini & Savoia 2005, 2007; Legendre 2010; Ledgeway 2019).

In addition, other factors may influence the distribution of the perfect auxiliaries. For instance, in some varieties (e.g., Bisceglie) the alternation is attested with singular subjects, whereas in the plural there is less variation. Moreover, in the pluperfect and in the counterfactual (future-oriented conditional perfect/pluperfect subjunctive) a single auxiliary is often generalized: such an example is San Benedetto del Tronto, where the pattern BBH is replaced by BE in the counterfactual perfect (Cocchi 1995:124, Manzini & Savoia 2005:II: 682–683, Ledgeway 2019:356). I will discuss these further factors in Section 5.3.1.

5.2.2   Subject-driven auxiliary selection is Agree for person

Given the astonishing cross-linguistic variation in the distribution of the perfect auxiliaries, even among closely related dialects, I propose that the specific realization of the auxiliary must be due to the morpho-phonological component of the grammar. The variation described in Section 5.2.1 depends on the specific vocabulary entries of each variety. The same conclusion has already been drawn in D'Alessandro 2017b. Evidence in favor of this view also comes from the choice of the elsewhere form. When one form is generalized in some parts of the paradigm, for example in the plural or in the pluperfect, dialects that otherwise share the same pattern make opposite decisions. Examples of this type are the languages spoken in Pescocostanzo and Giovinazzo: the former generalizes BE in the plural, the latter HAVE, although they have identical auxiliary patterns in the singular (Ledgeway 2019:361). Hence, the fine-grained distinctions must be due to language-specific VI (Vocabulary Items) inventories. Nonetheless, the dependency on the person feature (realized at Spell-out by the vocabulary entries) must be due to syntax, since it is encoded in the morpho-syntactic feature of person [π].

I claim that auxiliary selection in subject-driven systems is the result of person-Agree on Perf, as is the case in Standard Italian. A similar proposal has been developed by D'Alessandro (2017b), although only for the subject-driven varieties spoken in Abruzzo and not for Standard Italian.[71] Under the present theory, the dependence on the person feature of the subject is obtained if the order of the probes on Perf is switched with respect to Italian. In subject-driven systems, the feature ordering on the head Perf is as in (2a), opposite to the Italian ordering in (2b).

(2) a. Perf [uπ:_] > [uInfl:perf]   subject-driven
     b. Perf [uInfl:perf] > [uπ:_]   argument-structure-based

If the person probe goes first, its search domain is the whole c-command domain of the head Perf, which includes the DP subject as the highest matching goal (also the unaccusative subject, assuming that every v is a phase). Hence, the person probe on Perf targets the DP subject in Spec,v. After person Agree, the second operation triggered by the probe [uInfl] is subject to Nested Agree: its search domain starts from Spec,v (where the goal of the previous operation is located). The DP$_{sbj}$ is not a matching goal for [Infl]. Instead, the head v bears the relevant feature and is contained in the search domain of [uInfl:perf]: Perf successfully agrees with v for [Infl]. The syntactic operations for the subject-driven type (2a) are illustrated in trees (3) and (4).

---

71. Agree-based analyses like the one proposed here and the account by D'Alessandro (2017b) are flexible enough to derive all the patterns described in Section 5.2.1. Other previous analyses of person splits tend to focus on the typical pattern BBH (Tuttle 1986; Kayne 1993; Cocchi 1995; Manzini & Savoia 2005; D'Alessandro & Roberts 2010; Coon & Preminger 2012; Steddy & van Urk 2013). In general, BBH is explained by referring to the particular properties of the different person features. For this reason, these approaches cannot be easily applied to those patterns where the split is not between first/second person vs. third person. One of the few previous analyses that consider various splits is proposed by Legendre (2010). Subject-driven auxiliary selection is analyzed within Optimality Theory, making use of constraints that correlate a person scale to an auxiliary scale. However, in order to account for all the possible interactions with tense, aspect, mood, and argument structure, the number of ad hoc constraints must be very high, considerably increasing the number of possible languages (and the picture becomes more complicated if one tries to account for both argument-structure-driven and subject-driven systems at the same time; see the constraints in Legendre 2007, 2010).

(3) Step 1: Agree for [uπ:_]

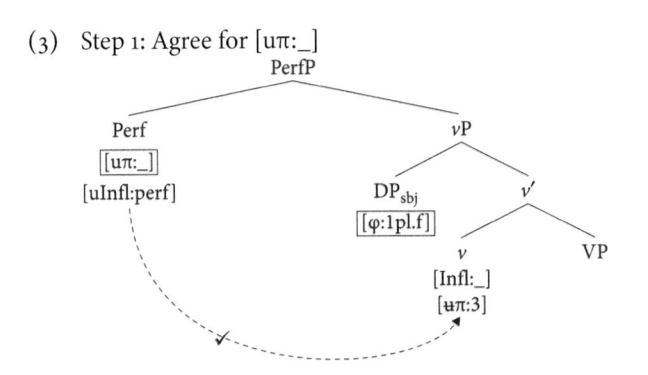

(4) Step 2: Agree for [uInfl:perf]

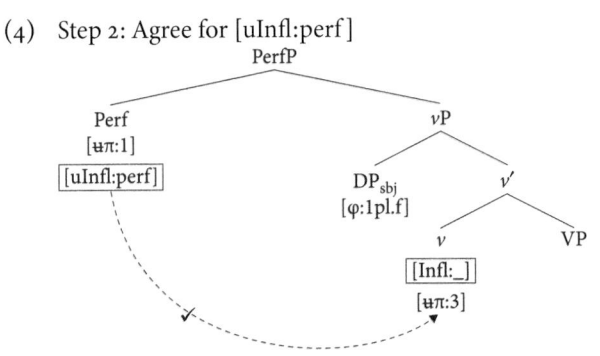

One prediction stems from this analysis: subject-driven systems are never sensitive to the person feature of the object. In fact, Perf targets the subject for π-Agree, which is always a matching goal because it bears φ-features. This means that the person-probe on Perf can never reach either *v* or the object. This is due to minimality. As a consequence, the same perfect auxiliary is expected in both canonical transitive clauses and reflexive transitive clauses. As far as I know, this prediction is borne out (for instance, see Ariellese in Section 5.2.3). I am not aware of any case of subject-driven auxiliary selection where the person feature of the object determines the form of the auxiliary. It is true that there are some varieties that seem to be person-driven, where reflexive clauses pattern differently from transitive clauses (as is the case in Standard Italian). However, I will argue in Section 5.5 that these varieties are instances of argument-structure-driven auxiliary selection, with additional person restrictions.

To sum up, in subject-driven auxiliary selection (2a) the π value comes from DP$_{sbj}$. In argument-structure-driven auxiliary selection (2b) the π value is copied from *v*, thereby tracking both the argument structure type and the feature of the object. The syntactic implementation of the variation in auxiliary selection lies in the feature ordering. This is in line with recent proposals that see cross-linguistic variation as the result of different extrinsic ordering of features (Heck & Müller

2006; Müller 2009; Georgi 2014; see also Section 2.5.2 in Chapter 2). The different ordering in (2), together with Nested Agree as a principle on ordered operations, shapes the typological difference between argument-structure-based and subject-driven auxiliary selection. All other fine-grained distinctions depend on the morpho-phonological realization due to different vocabulary entries, which can also be sensitive to other morpho-syntactic factors, such as the features on T or the features of reflexive pronouns, as we will see throughout this chapter.

In the next section, I illustrate the proposal for a BBH variety, Ariellese.

5.2.3   Ariellese

Ariellese is an Italo-Romance variety spoken in Abruzzo. The perfect auxiliary is BE for first and second person subjects, whereas a third person subject determines HAVE insertion. Example (5) shows the pattern BBH for transitive (5a,b), unergative (5c,d) and unaccusative predicates (5e,f).

(5) a. Ji   so'   fatte   na torte.
         NOM.1SG be.PRS.1SG make.PRTC a   cake
         'I have made a cake.'
     b. Esse   a   fatte   na torte.
         NOM.3SG have.PRS.3SG make.PRTC a   cake
         'She has made a cake.'
     c. Ji   so'   fatijate.
         NOM.1SG be.PRS.1SG work.PRTC
         'I have worked.'
     d. Esse   a   fatijate.
         NOM.3SG have.PRS.3SG work.PRTC
         'She has worked.'
     e. Ji   so'   cascate.
         NOM.1SG be.PRS.1SG fall.PRTC
         'I have fallen down.'
     f. Esse   a   cascate.
         NOM.3SG have.PRS.3SG fall.PRTC
         'She has fallen down.'   (D'Alessandro & Roberts 2010: 43–44)

Importantly, the pattern BBH is also found in reflexive clauses. Examples (6) contain a reflexive direct object, Examples (7) a reflexive indirect object.

(6) a. Me=so   llavate   jire   sere.
         REFL.ACC.1SG=be.PRS.1SG wash.PRTC yesterday night
         'I washed myself last night.'

b. Marije s=a   llavate   jire   sere.
    Maria REFL.ACC.3SG.F=have.PRS.3SG wash.PRTC yesterday night
                                             (R. D'Alessandro, p.c.)
    'Maria washed herself last night.'

(7) a. Me=so   llavate   li vistite da sole.
      REFL.DAT.1SG=be.PRS.1SG wash.PRTC the clothes by myself
      'I washed my clothes by myself.'

    b. Marije s=a   llavate   li vistite da sole.
      Marije REFL.DAT.3SG.F=have.PRS.3SG wash.PRTC the clothes by herself
      'Maria washed her clothes by herself.'   (R. D'Alessandro, p.c.)

These examples show that in Ariellese the features of the direct or indirect object do not matter. This is expected if the probe on Perf always targets the subject. Hence, the distribution BBH holds across all clausal types. In addition to reflexive clauses, passive predicates (8) and quirky verbs (9) exhibit the same perfect auxiliaries.

(8) a. Ji   so   statə   nvitatə.
      NOM.1SG be.PRS.1SG be.PRTC invite.PRTC
      'I was invited.'

    b. Marije a   statə   nvitatə.
      Marije have.PRS.3SG be.PRTC invite.PRTC
      'Maria was invited.'   (R. D'Alessandro, p.c.)

(9) a. A me   m'a   piaciutə lu paninə.
      to DAT.1SG REFL.DAT.1SG have.PRS.3SG like.PRTC the sandwich
      'I liked the sandwich.'

    b. A Marije j'a   piaciutə lu paninə.
      to Marije DAT.3SG have.PRS.3SG like.PRTC the sandwich
      'Maria liked the sandwich.'   (R. D'Alessandro, p.c.)

In Ariellese, impersonal clauses are possible with the generic meaning. The perfect auxiliary is HAVE, as shown in (10).

(10) A la casa mè s=a   sembre magnite li spaghitte.
     at the home my IMPERS=have.PRS.3SG always eat.PRTC the spaghetti
     'At my place, people have always eaten spaghetti.'   (R. D'Alessandro, p.c.)

The auxiliary HAVE indicates that the impersonal argument in Ariellese is marked for third person, differently from Italian. Alternatively, this could suggest that the elsewhere form in Ariellese is HAVE, rather than BE, as suggested below in (12).

According to the proposal developed in Section 5.2.2, the distribution of the perfect auxiliaries in Ariellese is derived if the order of features on the head Perf is [uπ:_] > [uInfl:perf]. As for the lexical entries, there are two possible inventories. In (11), the elsewhere form is BE, as in Standard Italian, and HAVE is the more specific allomorph, which can only be inserted in the presence of a 3rd person feature. In (12), instead, HAVE is the elsewhere form and BE is specified for local persons.

(11) *Vocabulary Items for Ariellese (option 1)*
    a.   /HAVE/ ↔ Perf[π:-part]
    b.   /BE/ ↔ Perf elsewhere

(12) *Vocabulary Items for Ariellese (option 2)*
    a.   /BE/ ↔ Perf[π:+part]
    b.   /HAVE/ ↔ Perf elsewhere

Both (11) and (12) are possible lexical inventories of Ariellese. In fact, in many closely related dialects the elsewhere form is either BE or HAVE (Ledgeway 2019).

Ariellese has also a complex pluperfect. With first and second person, two auxiliaries are present: the higher one follows the BBH pattern, and the lower one is always HAVE (13a). In third person, there is just a single auxiliary, realized as HAVE (13b).

(13) a. (ji)   so   ve'   magnatə/cagnatə/fatijatə.
          NOM.1SG be.PRS.1SG have.IMPF.PST eat/change/work.PRTC
          'I had eaten/changed/worked.'
    b. (essə)   ave'   magnatə/cagnatə/fatijatə.
          NOM.3SG.F have.IMPF.PST eat/change/work.PRTC
          'She had eaten/changed/worked.'   (D'Alessandro 2017b: 20)

One way to model this fact is with a further aspectual projection, Asp, lower than Perf. This head Asp is realized by the lower auxiliary, always HAVE. Perf is realized according to the rules in (11) or (12), with an additional rule: a null exponent is inserted when Perf is marked for third person and c-commands Asp.

This analysis finds additional support in the phenomenon of restructuring. In restructuring, a lexical verb is the argument of a modal verb in a monoclausal configuration (cf. Chapter 4). In Standard Italian, when the lexical verb is an unaccusative or reflexive verb the perfect auxiliary can be either HAVE or BE. For instance, the sentence 'I wanted to go to the beach' has the following two translations: *ho voluto andare al mare* (with HAVE) and *sono voluta andare al mare* (with BE). The Ariellese equivalent of this sentence in (15a) requires the auxiliary BE, because the subject is first person. Restructuring sentences follow the pattern

BBH, as shown in (14). No other realization is possible. This is also independent of clitic placement.

(14) a. So   vulute   ij   a lu mare.
          be.PRS.1SG want.PRTC go.INF to the beach
          'I wanted to go to the beach.'

      b. Ci=so   vulute   ji   da sole.
          there=be.PRS.1SG want.PRTC go.INF by myself
          'I wanted to go there by myself.'

      c. *C=aje   vulute   ji   da sole.
          there=have.PRS.1SG want.PRTC go.INF by myself
          'I wanted to go there by myself.'

      d. Marije a   vulute   ji   a lu mare.
          Maria have.PRS.3SG want.PRTC go.INF to the beach
          'Maria wanted to go to the beach.'

      e. Marije c=a   vulute   ji   da sole.
          Maria there=have.PRS.3SG want.PRTC go.INF by herself
          'Maria wanted to go there by herself.'   (R. D'Alessandro, p.c.)

BBH also emerges when the lexical verb is transitive (15), and reflexive (16).

(15) a. Li=so   vulute   fa   da sole.
          ACC.3SG.M=be.PRS.1SG want.PRTC do.INF by myself
          'I wanted to do it by myself.'

      b. Marije l=a   vulute   fa   da sole.
          Maria ACC.3SG.M=have.PRS.1SG want.PRTC do.INF by myself
          'Maria wanted to do it by herself.'   (R. D'Alessandro, p.c.)

(16) a. Me=so   vulute   allava'   da sole.
          REFL.ACC.1SG.F=be.PRS.1SG want.PRTC wash.INF by myself

      b. *M=aje   vulute   allava'   da sole.
          REFL.ACC.1SG.F=have.PRS.1SG want.PRTC wash.INF by myself
          'I wanted to wash me by myself.'

      c. Marije s=a   vulute   allava'   da sole.
          Maria REFL.ACC.3SG.F=have.PRS.1SG want.PRTC wash.INF by herself
          'Maria wanted to wash her by herself.'   (R. D'Alessandro, p.c.)

The distribution of the perfect auxiliaries for the modal verb is BBH, as in root clauses. Auxiliary selection does not depend on the argument structure of the lower verb, but only on the person feature of the subject (which in restructuring raises to the subject position). This is expected if in Ariellese the person probe on Perf always targets the subject, differently from Italian.

5.3   Not only person

5.3.1   Tense, aspect and mood variation

So far, we saw that auxiliary selection may depend either on the argument struc-
ture, or on the features of the subject (or on both, as I will show in Section 5.5).
In this section, I discuss the influence of temporal, aspectual or modal restrictions
(TAM).

In many varieties, auxiliary alternations are confined to particular mood or
tense specifications. TAM restrictions may contribute to more fine-grained distinctions, as exemplified in the graph in (17).

(17)   TAM restrictions

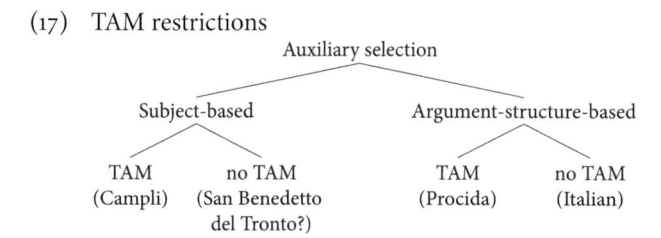

A very frequent case of tense restriction is when the two auxiliaries alternate in
the present perfect tense, but the elsewhere form is found outside this context.
An example of a subject-driven system restricted by tense is the dialect spoken in
Campli (Abruzzo), where the pattern BBH is only found in the present and counterfactual perfect, whereas BE is generalized in the pluperfect (Manzini & Savoia
2005: II: 685–686, Ledgeway 2019: 357).

Subject-driven systems that are not restricted by any TAM specification are
rare, instead (Manzini & Savoia 2005: II: 729).[72] There seems to be no tense
restriction in the dialect spoken in San Benedetto del Tronto (Marche). Here, the
subject-based split is maintained in the pluperfect (Manzini & Savoia 2005: II:
682–684). However, it has also been reported that the person split has progres-
sively been suppressed from the pluperfect and counterfactual paradigms (Cocchi
1995: 124, Ledgeway 2019: 360). Another example for the lack of temporal restrictions is Ariellese: here the split is found in both the present perfect and the pluperfect. However, there are some mood restrictions: only HAVE is found in the past
subjunctive/conditional (D'Alessandro 2017b: 11).

---

72. Perhaps this fact can be explained if there are further aspectual projections that block Agree
between Perf and the DP_{sbj}. Alternatively, it could show that the dependency on the feature of
the subject is realized by contextually sensitive vocabulary entries that spell out Perf in the context of particular features on T (similarly to what is proposed for mixed systems in Section 5.5).
I leave this question to future research.

Among the argument-structure-based systems, in the dialect spoken in Procida HAVE alternates with BE in the present perfect, while BE is generalized in the pluperfect and counterfactual perfect (Ledgeway 2000: 624–626). A language with no TAM restrictions at play is instead Standard Italian.

Languages where the auxiliary is exclusively conditioned by TAM categories are quite rare (Ledgeway 2019: 352–353). Within Romance outside Italy, the auxiliary entirely depends on mood in Romanian: it is HAVE in the realis mood, BE in the irrealis mood (Avram & Hill 2007). An Italo-Romance variety of this type is San Leucio del Sannio (Iannace 1983: 72–80, 88–89, Ledgeway 2019: 350–351): the present perfect and the counterfactual perfect exhibit HAVE, whereas the pluperfect has BE. Since languages of this type are few, I follow Ledgeway (2019) in considering TAM-interactions as further restrictions, as schematized in (17), instead of talking of tense-based or mood-based systems.

The influence of TAM categories on the perfect auxiliary is possible either because of head movement, or because of Agree. I propose to model it by means of head movement. When the syntactic structure contains further TAM heads, head movement creates the complex head Asp-Perf-T. The resulting complex head looks like (18) (low aspect) or (19) (high aspect).[73]

(18)   Low TAM projection

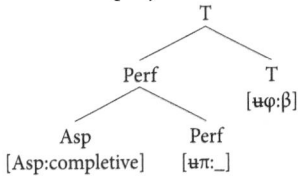

(19)   High TAM projection

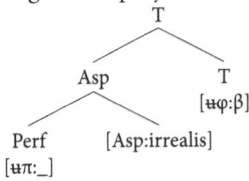

---

73. In the present discussion, I consider tense, aspect and mood restrictions to be introduced by syntactic heads that are local to Perf. It should be noted that if mood is marked on C, then auxiliary selection can be influenced by mood only when there is T-to-C movement. This is confirmed by Romanian. In this language, the perfect auxiliary is influenced by mood. Even if mood is expressed in the C-domain, there is evidence that Perf moves to such a high position. In fact, the auxiliary that occurs in the irrealis mood is realized as a clitic in enclisis on an affix mood marker that is higher than T.

At Spell-out, Perf is realized by a contextually sensitive VI that refers to the presence of the TAM node in the complex head. An example of vocabulary entries for a language where auxiliary selection is influenced by TAM-restrictions is given in (20). In this example, HAVE realizes the perfect auxiliary in sentences with a third person subject (BBH), and in all clauses in the irrealis aspect (counterfactual perfect). A language of this type is the variety of San Benedetto del Tronto.

(20) *Vocabulary Items for San Benedetto del Tronto*
    a. /HAVE/ ↔ Perf[π:-part]
    b. /HAVE/ ↔ Perf / Asp[Asp:irrealis]
    c. /BE/ ↔ Perf elsewhere

Outside of the present perfect, in Central Italy the generalized form is generally BE; in South-Eastern Italy the elsewhere form tends to be HAVE (Ledgeway 2019:356).

5.3.2 Number restrictions

In a considerable number of languages, the number feature of the subject influences the choice of the auxiliary. Singular and plural often exhibit different patterns. Subject-driven splits that are restricted to the singular can be found in Pescocostanzo and Giovinazzo. As is often the case, these two varieties share an identical pattern in the singular, but differ in the arbitrary choice of the elsewhere form in the plural (BE in Pescocostanzo, HAVE in Giovanazzo, Ledgeway 2019:361).

Among argument-structure-based systems, it is not easy to find pure number restrictions. In general, when the valency split is restricted to a specific number, it is also constrained by person. An argument-structure-driven system can be subject to further person restrictions, but it cannot be subject just to number restrictions without any corresponding person restriction. I will talk about these mixed systems in Section 5.5. Examples are the dialects of Secinaro, Zagarolo, Agnone, and Castelvecchio Subequo (Ledgeway 2019:368–370). For instance, the variety of Secinaro exhibits an argument structure distinction only in the 3rd person singular (B~H B H in transitives, B~H B B in unaccusatives); in the plural, there is a person split with some alternations that are unrelated to the argument structure.

It is noteworthy that number restrictions can only depend on the number feature of the subject. This means that the influence of number features can be modeled as φ-Agree on T. In fact, the number value of the subject is always represented on T, which independently φ-agrees with the subject. The number restriction can be implemented via vocabulary entries that refer to the features on T, once Perf head-moves to T. The lexical entries for Pescocostanzo look as in (21).

(21)   *Vocabulary Items for Pescocostanzo*
    a. /HAVE/ ↔ Perf[π:-part] / T[#:+sg]
    b. /BE/ ↔ Perf elsewhere

5.4   Single auxiliary

In some languages, there is just one perfect auxiliary at disposal. Languages where the only auxiliary is HAVE are Sicilian, Spanish, Portuguese, and modern Catalan. The opposite scenario, where the only auxiliary is BE, is quite rare. An example might be the variety spoken in Terracina (Lazio) (Tuttle 1986), but this should be confirmed by new investigations. Outside Romance, we can mention Southern Slavic languages, Scottish Gaelic, Welsh, and Shetland English (McFadden 2007: 676).

Loporcaro (2007) has suggested that languages with a single auxiliary belong to the same class of languages with subject-driven auxiliary selection. This is because the choice of the auxiliary is coherent across different verbal classes. In both cases, a single pattern (BE or HAVE for the former group; BBH or any other split for the latter group) is generalized across all types of argument structure. In contrast, argument-structure-driven auxiliary selection depends on the type of clause.

On the contrary, I suggest that the underlying syntax of languages with a single auxiliary does not have to be the same as subject-driven systems. A language with a single auxiliary can be either a subject-based system, or an argument-structure-driven system. The only relevant fact is the inventory of vocabulary entries: either the lexicon only contains a single Vocabulary Item (see (22) below), or it has an underspecified Vocabulary Item (see (23) below), whose conditions of insertion are always met. Only in the latter case the language has to be a subject-driven system. I will now explain this point in more detail.

In general, a single auxiliary means that the result of Agree is neutralized on the surface. This can be due either to the presence of a single vocabulary entry, or to a morpho-syntactic-context that is always met. If there is a single vocabulary entry, it does not matter whether auxiliary selection depends on the argument structure or on the person feature of the subject: there is simply no choice in the lexicon. For example, the lexical entries needed for Sicilian are in (22).

(22)   *Vocabulary Item for Sicilian (option 1)*
    /HAVE/ ↔ Perf

Alternatively, a language exhibits a single auxiliary if the conditions of insertion of a specific allomorph are always met. A uniform condition for insertion is either lack of Agree on Perf, or successful Agree on Perf. The former is achieved if there is no π-probe on Perf: the featural make-up of functional heads can also be subject to lexical variation. Nonetheless, I prefer to keep the syntax uniform. The latter happens in subject-driven systems, where Perf always finds the person feature on the subject. In this type of language, the generic context of insertion "presence of a valued person-feature on Perf" is always met, whereas this is not the case for argument-structure-driven systems (where valuation via Agree may succeed or not succeed, depending on the type of v and on the features of the arguments). In this scenario, the vocabulary entries for Sicilian are as in (23). Note that with such a lexicon Sicilian must have subject-driven auxiliary selection (i.e., [uπ:_] > [uInfl:perf] on Perf).

(23)   *Vocabulary Items for Sicilian (option 2)*
    a.   /HAVE/ ↔ Perf[π:α]
    b.   /BE/ ↔ Perf

Hence, varieties with a single auxiliary can be either subject-driven systems, or argument-structure-based systems. It all depends on their lexicon.

5.5   Mixed systems

There are also languages where the perfect auxiliary follows a person split, but only in a particular type of argument structure. Loporcaro (2007) calls this type of language *mixed systems*, and places them in the group of subject-driven systems. I also call these languages mixed systems (for consistency with the previous literature), but I consider them as argument-structure-driven systems with additional person restrictions. In what follows, I will explain why.

    An example of mixed system is the variety spoken in Tufillo (Abruzzo), where the person split is only found with transitive/unergative verbs (24a,b,c), but not with unaccusative verbs (24d,e,f).[74]

(24)   *Tufillo*
    a.   Sɔ   par'læ:tə.
         be.PRS.1SG talk.PRTC
         'I have talked.'

---

74. As already said in Section 3.2.2 of Chapter 3, there is no Romance variety where transitive and unergative verbs diverge in the choice of the auxiliary (Loporcaro 2001: 463, Loporcaro 2007: 180). For this reason, these two classes are always kept together in this chapter.

    b.   Si   par'læ:tə.
          be.PRS.2SG talk.PRTC
          'You have talked.'

    c.   ɣa   par'læ:tə.
          have.PRS.3SG talk.PRTC
          'S/he has talked.'

    d.   Sɔ   mmə'eutə.
          be.PRS.1SG come.PRTC
          'I have come.'

    e.   Si   mmə'eutə.
          be.PRS.2SG come.PRTC
          'You have come.'

    f.   ε   mmə'eutə.
          be.PRS.3SG come.PRTC
          'S/he has come.'   (Manzini & Savoia 2005: II: 690)

The auxiliary distribution is summarized in Table 5.2. On the one hand, there is a person split that is only visible for transitive/unergative verbs, whereas for unaccusative verbs the same auxiliary is generalized for all persons. On the other hand, there is an argument-structure split that is only present for 3rd person, while 1st and 2nd person show the same auxiliary.

Table 5.2 Auxiliary selection in Tufillo (Manzini & Savoia 2005: II: 690–691)

	unaccusatives	transitives, unergatives
1st SG	B	B
2nd SG	B	B
3rd SG	B	H
1st PL	B	B
2nd PL	B	B
3rd PL	B	H

There are two different approaches to these data, and to mixed systems in general. Auxiliary selection is either subject-driven, but restricted to a particular argument structure, or it is argument-structure-driven, but this distinction is only possible for a particular person feature. I propose that auxiliary selection in mixed systems is argument-structure-based, although it is further constrained by the features of the subject, as they appear on the syntactic head T (as will become clear throughout this section). Whenever there is a dependency on argument structure, even if it is confined to some cells of the paradigms (or even to a single cell), auxiliary selection must be dependent on the argument structure. In fact, any influence of the argument structure is excluded in subject-driven systems because of minimality (see Section 5.2.2).

Further evidence for the treatment of mixed systems as argument-structure-driven systems, rather than subject-driven systems, comes from the behavior of reflexive clauses. In subject-driven systems, the auxiliary in reflexive clauses and transitive clauses is the same (e.g., in Ariellese, see Examples (5)–(7)). In argument-structure-driven systems, the auxiliary in reflexive clauses is not the same as in transitive clauses; instead, it is the same as in unaccusative clauses (cf. Examples (2), (3) in Chapter 2 for Italian). In mixed systems, transitive verbs with reflexive arguments behave as in argument-structure-based systems in selecting the same auxiliary as unaccusative verbs. For example, in the variety of Tufillo the auxiliary of reflexive and unaccusative verbs is the same, as shown in (25).

(25) *Tufillo*
    a.   Mə   sɔ   arraˈvæːtə.
          REFL.ACC.1SG be.PRS.1SG wash.PRTC.SG
          'I have washed myself'
    b.   Tə   si   arraˈvæːtə.
          REFL.ACC.2SG be.PRS.2SG wash.PRTC.SG
    c.   Ts   ɛ   arraˈvæːtə.
          REFL.ACC.3SG be.PRS.3SG wash.PRTC.SG
    d.   Tʧə   sɛmə   arraˈviːtə.
          REFL.ACC.1PL be.PRS.1PL wash.PRTC.PL
    e.   Və   sɛːtə   arraˈviːtə.
          REFL.ACC.2PL be.PRS.2PL wash.PRTC.PL
    f.   Ts   ɛ   arraˈviːtə.
          REFL.ACC.3PL be.PRS.3PL wash.PRTC.PL

(Manzini & Savoia 2005: II: 690)

Thus, auxiliary selection in mixed system is argument-structure-driven (as in Standard Italian). This means that the features on Perf are ordered as follows: Perf [uInfl:perf] > [uπ:_] (see Section 5.2.2). After Agree, which happens as in Standard Italian (see Chapter 3 for details), the features on the complex head Perf + T are as in (26).

(26)   Complex head Perf + T in argument-structure-based systems
     (i)   Unaccusative, reflexive verbs

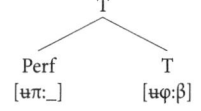

(ii)   Transitive, unergative verbs

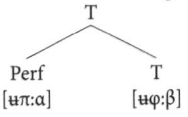

In unaccusative and reflexive clauses, the features on the complex head T + Perf are as in (26)–(i). As explained for Standard Italian in Chapter 3, in argument-structure-based systems the probe on Perf remains unvalued in unaccusative and reflexive clauses (cf. Sections 3.3.5, 3.3.2, respectively). In the former, this happens because unaccusative v is not a probe for person; in the latter, because transitive v has undergone Agree with an item with unvalued φ-features (the reflexive pronoun). The head T contains a [uφ:_] probe that targets the DP_{sbj} in Spec,v, invariably leading to subject agreement.

In transitive and unergative clauses, the features on the complex head T + Perf are as in (26)–(ii) (where the symbols α and β indicate that the features can be different). Perf has successfully agreed with v (which had agreed with the object), while T has agreed with the subject.

The peculiarity of mixed systems lies in the lexicon. In languages where the argument-structure-based split is limited to some cells, the vocabulary entries make reference to the person specification of the subject that is present on T after φ-Agree. In fact, the head Perf moves to T to combine with finite inflection, thereby forming the complex head Perf + T, as illustrated in (26). The head T independently agrees with the subject for φ-features, causing subject agreement on the finite verb. Given the syntactic structures in (26), the following Vocabulary Items are needed to derive the Tufillo data in (24).

(27)   *Vocabulary Items for Tufillese*
    a.   /HAVE/ ↔ Perf[π:α] / T[φ:3sg]
    b.   /BE/ ↔ Perf elsewhere

The vocabulary entries in (27) are typical of argument-structure-driven systems because the person feature on Perf is not specified for any particular value (cf. Italian VIs in (5) in Chapter 3). In addition, they make reference to a specific person feature on another subpart of the complex head, the head T. This type of lexicon, together with the feature ordering [uInfl:perf] > [uπ:_] on Perf (which leads to the structures in (26)), gives rise to mixed systems. In the specific case of Tufillo, the rules in (27) indicate that HAVE is inserted in transitive/unergative clauses with third person subjects, while BE surfaces everywhere else, in accordance with the data in (24).

Auxiliary selection in mixed systems can be quite complex. Other examples of mixed systems are the dialects of Lanciano, Scanno, and Pietransieri (Abruzzo) (Giammarco 1973; Loporcaro 2001). In Table 5.3, I illustrate the distribution of auxiliaries for the dialect of Pietransieri.

Table 5.3 Pietransieri (Loporcaro 2007: 198)

	unaccusatives	transitives, unergatives
1st SG	B	B
2nd SG	B	B
3rd SG	B	H
1st PL	B~H	H
2nd PL	B~H	H
3rd PL	B~H	H

In Pietransieri, auxiliary selection depends on the argument structure: transitive/unergative verbs pattern differently from unaccusative verbs. In addition, both classes exhibit a dependency on the person and number features of the subject. The vocabulary entries that can explain the data of Pietransieri are listed in (28).

(28) *Vocabulary Items for Pietransieri*
    a.   /HAVE/ ↔ Perf$[\pi{:}\alpha]$ / T$[\#{:}\text{pl}]$
    b.   /HAVE/ ↔ Perf$[\pi{:}\alpha]$ / T$[\pi{:}3]$
    c.   /HAVE/ ↔ Perf / T$[\#{:}\text{pl}]$ (optional rule)
    d.   /BE/ ↔ Perf elsewhere

The more specific allomorph HAVE is inserted when two conditions are met: Perf has successfully agreed for person (i.e., in transitive/unergative clauses, see representations in (26)), and the subject is either plural (28a), or 3rd person (28b). In addition, HAVE can also be inserted in unaccusative clauses with plural subjects (see free variation B~H in the plural of unaccusatives in Table 5.3). This is modeled with the optional rule (28c), which inserts HAVE when the subject is plural, independently of the person feature on Perf. Rule (28c), which constitutes a generalization of rule (28a), must be optional because there is free alternation in unaccusative clauses with plural subjects. Moreover, in transitive clauses the rule (28c) is blocked by the more specific rule (28a), which leads to obligatory HAVE insertion.

    In addition to the dialect spoken in Pietransieri, in many other mixed systems there is optionality in auxiliary selection in some areas of the paradigm. As just said, I model free variation by means of optional rules in the lexicon.[75] An optional rule emerges when speakers have at their disposal more than a single grammar at a time, so that they can generate different outputs depending on which grammar is used. Note that optionality affects contextually sensitive rules. These are complex rules that make reference to the features on T for substituting Perf. Their complexity perhaps makes them more subject to optionality.

Interestingly, mixed systems provide evidence against those analyses that treat local person splits (first/second person vs. third person) as person ergativity splits, as indicated by Loporcaro (2007). In ergative languages, there are processes that distinguish between 1st and 2nd person pronouns and 3rd person pronouns (and other nominal DPs). Similarly, it has been argued that auxiliary distributions where 1st and 2nd person pattern differently from 3rd person (e.g., BBH/HHB) might also be due to split ergativity (Kayne 1993; Manzini & Savoia 1998; D'Alessandro & Roberts 2010; Coon & Preminger 2012). However, mixed systems have this split only in some clausal types. This means that such languages would simultaneously have an active/inactive alignment in transitive clauses, and an absolutive/ergative split in unaccusative and reflexive clauses. In addition, if mixed systems do not have an ergativity alignment, then it is also very unlikely that an ergativity alignment is active in the closely related variety of Ariellese. Languages with mixed systems and subject-driven systems of auxiliary selection are very closely related, both genetically and spatially. Hence, they should not differ in ergativity.

To sum up, I propose that auxiliary selection in mixed systems is argument-structure-based and not subject-driven. In addition, the Vocabulary Items of mixed systems are further constrained by the features of the subject as they appear on T. Hence, there are two major classes of systems with person specifications: either pure subject-based systems, or argument-structure-based systems influenced by the features of the subject (mixed systems).

---

75. Free variation can also result from different processes. For example, free variation in subject-driven systems seems to have another source, as I will explain in Section 5.6. In subject-driven systems, the information on T is redundant because both Perf and T bear the same π-feature. However, it can play a role when the lexicon of a language contains vocabulary entries that spell out the same feature on Perf and on T in different ways, as in (i-a,b). These rules generate free variation.

(i)   a.   /HAVE/ ↔ Perf[π:3]
       b.   /BE/ ↔ Perf / T[π:3]

5.5.1 The Sardinian type

In the previous section, I said that in mixed systems reflexive clauses behave as unaccusative clauses, like in Italian. To be more precise, the pattern does not seem to be exactly as in Standard Italian, but rather as in Logudorese Sardinian (Loporcaro 2007: 190–191). In Sardinian, auxiliary selection is argument-structure-driven. Differently from Italian, not all reflexive clauses pattern as unaccusative clauses, but there is a split within reflexive clauses. Indirect transitive reflexives (i.e., transitive clauses with a reflexive dative argument) trigger the same auxiliary of transitive verbs, whereas the other reflexive clauses cause the same auxiliary of unaccusative verbs. I provide the Logudorese Sardinian data in (29), although I will deal with reflexives in Section 5.7.

(29) *Logudorese Sardinian (Bonorva)*
    a. Maria ɛs   palti:ð-a.   (unaccusative)
        Maria be.PRS.3SG leave.PRTC-SG.F
        'Maria has left.'
    b. Maria z=ɛs   samuna:ð-a.   (direct transitive
        Maria REFL.ACC.3SG.F=be.PRS.3SG wash.PRTC-SG.F   reflexive)
        'Maria has washed herself.'
    c. Maria z=ɛr   rispɔst-a.   (indirect unergative
        Maria REFL.DAT.3SG.F=be.PRS.3SG answer.PRTC-SG.F reflexive)
        'Maria has answered herself.'
    d. Maria z=a   ssamuna:ðu zal ma:nɔs.   (indirect
        Maria REFL.DAT.3SG.F=have.PRS.3SG wash.PRTC   the hands   transitive
        'Maria has washed her hands.'   reflexive)
    e. Maria a   mmaniɣaðu (za minɛstra).   (transitive)
        Maria have.PRS.3SG eat.PRTC   the soup
        'Maria has eaten (the soup).'   (Loporcaro 2007: 190–191)

In mixed systems, the same auxiliary is found in unaccusative, direct transitive reflexive, and indirect unergative reflexive clauses. Instead, indirect transitive reflexive sentences have the same auxiliary as transitive and unergative clauses. The distribution of the two auxiliaries is exactly as in Sardinian in Example (29). This is schematized in Table 5.4, where the symbols x and y stand for different distributions. For example, for the dialect spoken in Pietransieri x represents the distribution B B H H H H, and y the distribution B B B B~H B~H B~H.

An example of mixed system that follows the Sardinian split is the dialect of Altamura, exemplified in Table 5.5. Here there is free variation with 1st and 2nd person, while with 3rd person there is alternation depending on the verbal class (unaccusative B, transitive B~H). Reflexives patterns as in Sardinian: the cutting

Table 5.4 Mixed systems as "Sardinian" types

	unaccus.	dir. trans. refl.	indir. unerg. refl.	indir. trans. refl.	trans., unerg.
Standard Italian	B	B	B	B	H
Logudorese Sardinian	B	B	B	H	H
Mixed systems	x	x	x	y	y

point is between indirect transitive reflexives on one side, and indirect unergative reflexives and direct transitive reflexives on the other side.

Table 5.5 Altamura (Loporcaro 2007: 203–204)

	unaccus.	dir. trans. refl.	indir. unerg. refl.	indir. trans. refl.	trans., unerg.
1st SG	B~H	B~H	B~H	B~H	B~H
2nd SG	B~H	B~H	B~H	B~H	B~H
3rd SG	B	B	B	B~H	B~H
1st PL	B~H	B~H	B~H	B~H	B~H
2nd PL	B~H	B~H	B~H	B~H	B~H
3rd PL	B~H	B~H	B~H	%B~H	H

The fact that mixed systems are always of the Sardinian type, as highlighted by Loporcaro (2007), requires more research. At this point, I cannot provide any data against, or in favor of, this generalization. I also do not have a good explanation for why the cutting point between the two auxiliaries should always set apart indirect transitive reflexives from other reflexives. The fact that indirect transitive reflexives pattern as transitive clauses must be due to the syntactic structure: the reflexive argument is introduced higher in the structure, lying outside the domain of the person probe on *v*. I will come back to this issue in Section 5.7.1. What is important for the present discussion is the fact that in mixed systems the perfect auxiliary of (some) reflexive clauses is different from the auxiliary of transitive clauses. This constitutes evidence for treating auxiliary selection in these languages as argument-structure-driven. If in mixed systems the features of the object play a role for auxiliary selection (i.e., similarly to Italian, differently to Ariellese), we expect reflexives to pattern differently from transitives, as is the case.

5.6 Relations between subject-driven and argument-structure-driven systems

Argument-structure-based auxiliary selection can be further influenced by person asymmetries (see Section 5.5), or modal and temporal restrictions (see Section 5.3.1). On the contrary, subject-based systems may be influenced by modal and temporal restrictions, but not by argument structure-related restrictions (Ledgeway 2019: 352–353). The relations between the different types are represented in the graph in (30).

(30) Restrictions

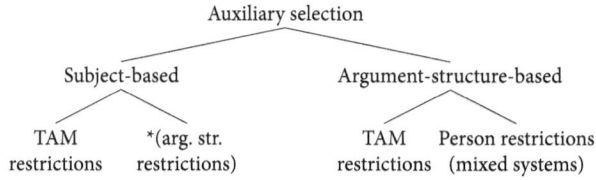

Auxiliary selection
— Subject-based
— Argument-structure-based
TAM restrictions — *(arg. str. restrictions)
TAM restrictions — Person restrictions (mixed systems)

This is expected under a theory where the person probe on Perf can exclusively target either the DP$_{sbj}$ in Spec, v, which is the higher matching goal, or the head v, due to Nested Agree. If Perf agrees with the DP$_{sbj}$, the information on v and on the object is not accessible anymore because of minimality. For this reason, subject-driven systems are not compatible with argument structure restrictions. In contrast, argument-structure-driven systems may also be sensitive to the features of the subject. As already seen in the discussion of mixed systems (cf. Section 5.5), there is a further possible point of variation for argument-structure-driven auxiliary selection: if Perf π-agrees with v, thereby skipping the DP$_{sbj}$, the information about the DP$_{sbj}$ is still available on T, which independently agrees with the subject. I will now explain this point in more detail.

Head movement leads to complex heads in trees (31) and (32), which represent the case of transitive/unergative verbs, respectively in argument-structure-driven and subject-driven auxiliary selection.

(31) Argument-structure-driven systems

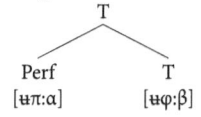

T
— Perf [uπ:α]
— T [uφ:β]

(32) Subject-driven systems

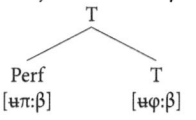

T
— Perf [uπ:β]
— T [uφ:β]

In argument-structure-driven systems (31), Perf has agreed with *v* (and, consequently, with the object), whereas T copies the features of the subject (via Nested Agree; see Section 3.3.1 of Chapter 2). Depending on the φ-features of the arguments, the heads Perf and T may end up bearing different person features. When the complex head contains different person features, as in (31), it is possible to achieve further distinctions if the lexical entries that substitute the terminal node Perf make reference to the featural content of another subpart of the complex head (i.e., T). If the vocabulary entries do not make any reference to T, as in (33), we have a pure argument-structure-based system. Instead, if the vocabulary entries refer to T, as in (34), we have a mixed system, which is an argument-structure-based system with additional person restrictions.

(33) Argument-structure-based systems
     a. /HAVE/ ↔ Perf[π:α]
     b. /BE/ ↔ Perf elsewhere

(34) Mixed systems
     a. /HAVE/ ↔ Perf[π:α]
     b. /HAVE/ ↔ Perf / T[π:3]
     c. /BE/ ↔ Perf elsewhere

The same scenario also takes place if the clause is unaccusative or reflexive. In this case, *v* does not contain any person value, whereas T contains the person feature of the subject (see Sections 3.3.2 and 3.3.5 in Chapter 3). Hence, the Vocabulary Items can make reference to the φ-features on T, similarly to (34).

This possibility is instead excluded in subject-based splits because the complex head contains the same value of the person feature on both terminal nodes Perf and T. In tree (32), both Perf and T bear the same person feature because both have agreed with the subject. If the Vocabulary Items are of the type in (33) or (34) (i.e., with a generic value α on Perf), auxiliary selection always results in the same allomorph (for example, HAVE), since in these languages Agree for [uπ:_] on Perf always succeeds in finding a value on the DP_{sbj} in Spec, *v* (see also Section 5.4). Instead, if the vocabulary entries realize specific person values, as is generally the case for subject-driven systems, then the additional information on T cannot add any new information for realizing more fine-grained distinctions. The different vocabulary entries are given in (35). The relevant syntactic structure is in (32), which emerges in subject-driven systems.

(35) Subject-driven systems
     a. /HAVE/ ↔ Perf[π:3]
     b. /HAVE/ ↔ Perf / T[π:3]
     c. /HAVE/ ↔ Perf[π:2] / T[π:3]
     d. /BE/ ↔ Perf / T[π:3]

The Vocabulary Item (VI) in (35a) simply states that the auxiliary HAVE must be inserted when the subject is 3rd person. We have already seen many examples of vocabulary entries of this type (see Example (11) for Ariellese). A VI such as (35b) makes reference to the same person value as (35a), but on a different subpart of the complex head. This rule is as specific as (35a) and corresponds to the same context of insertion. Hence, (35b) is redundant. The condition of insertion of a VI such as (35c) is never met, since Perf and T bear the same value for the feature [π] (because they both probe the DP$_{sbj}$ if the feature ordering on Perf is [uπ:_] > [uInfl:perf]). The VI (35d) is in competition with (35a) since they refer to two subparts of the same context (Perf[π:3] / T[π:3]), but they map to two different allomorphs. There are two possible scenarios here. First of all, the competition between (35a) and (35d) can give rise to free variation. The result is a subject-driven system with free variation according to some person value, without any argument structure restrictions. For instance, the specific rules in (35) result in the distribution B B B~H (found with plural subjects in Poggio Imperiale, Castelpetroso, and Gallo Matese, Manzini & Savoia 2005: II: 728). A second possibility is that the VI that realizes the feature of the terminal node itself (here, (35a)) is more specific than the one referring to other parts of the complex head (here, (35d)), which are less local to the node to be substituted. In this case, the VI in (35a) is chosen over (35d). The result is a pure subject-driven system.

In Table 5.6, I represent the different types of auxiliary selection according to the feature ordering on Perf and to the different types of Vocabulary Items (VIs).

Table 5.6 Systems of auxiliary selection

VIs make reference to:	Perf: [uInfl] > [uπ]	Perf: [uπ] > [uInfl]
underspecified π on Perf	argument-structure-driven	single auxiliary
specific π on Perf	✗	subject-driven
underspecified π on Perf + φ on T	mixed systems	subject-driven
specific π on Perf + φ on T	✗	subject-driven
Tense/Aspect/Mood on T	TAM-restricted	TAM-restricted
not important: only one entry	single auxiliary	single auxiliary

Argument-structure-driven systems derive from the order [uInfl] > [uπ] on Perf, and a lexicon where there is a distinction between the lack vs. the presence of a person feature on Perf, independently of its specific value. Argument-structure-driven systems where the Vocabulary Items refer to specific values of the person feature do not seem to be attested. In such languages, the auxiliary would depend on the particular value of the person feature of the transitive object. Unfortunately, I do not have any explanation for this gap in the typology.

Mixed systems are languages that exhibit an argument-structure-based split with additional person restrictions related to the features of the subject. Under the present analysis, whenever a language shows a dependency on argument structure, the head Perf must have the feature ordering [uInfl] > [uπ]. In addition, the Vocabulary Items refer to the person feature of the subject expressed on the head T.

Subject-driven systems arise from the ordering [uπ] > [uInfl]. No further restrictions based on argument structure are possible, because Agree is constrained by minimality: Perf agrees with the subject and cannot reach v. Moreover, there cannot be any subject-driven system that makes reference to the person feature of the object, because of minimality. This prediction seems to be borne out, since in these languages transitive clauses and reflexive clauses show the same auxiliary distribution, differently from what happens in argument-structure-driven systems and mixed systems. Whenever a particular value of the person feature is specified in the Vocabulary Item, the subject-based split emerges. In this case, the person feature on T can never affect auxiliary selection, since it constitutes redundant information (both Perf and T agree with the subject). If the lexicon of such a language contains vocabulary entries that spell out the same feature on Perf and on T in a different way (as (35a) and (35d)), either the VIs specified for Perf is used, or they give rise to free variation.

Languages that are sensitive to tense/aspect/mood (TAM) restrictions have Vocabulary Items that make reference to these features on the T head.

Languages exhibit a single auxiliary either if they have a single Vocabulary Item for Perf, or if the ordering of features is as in subject-driven systems and the Vocabulary Items are not specified for a particular value of the person feature.

5.7   Reflexive clauses in argument-structure-driven auxiliary selection

An advantage of treating argument-structure-based splits as the result of Agree for person is the possibility to model the distribution of the two auxiliaries in reflexive clauses. Interestingly, it is exactly the area of reflexive clauses that exhibits much cross-linguistic variation among argument-structure-based systems (see Section 5.7.1). In addition, if a language with argument-structure-driven auxiliary selection exhibits free variation, it is always in the area of reflexive clauses (see Section 5.7.2) (Loporcaro 2007, 2016).

The reasons for variation in reflexive clauses may be various. Firstly, it could be that reflexive pronouns are merged in different positions (for instance, inside a big VP in a double object construction, or introduced by a high or a low applicative head at different levels of attachment, and so on). Secondly, they could be more or less heavy as far as the syntactic layers are concerned (KP vs. DP/D). Thirdly, they could acquire the features via binding at different stages of the derivation. Fourthly, they could enter the syntactic structure with already valued features (see Section 3.2.6.1 of Chapter 3).

All these factors have an effect on Agree on v (and, consequently, on Perf). The reflexive pronoun may lead to failed valuation of the π-probe on Perf for different reasons. Either the matching feature on the reflexive pronoun is not a reachable goal because of its position outside the domain of the probe, or the matching feature is not visible because of the presence of further structure, or the matching feature is not valued (as in Italian; see Section 3.3.2 of Chapter 3). These different possibilities must be carefully evaluated for each language. For the present discussion, the crucial point is that languages can differ with respect to one or more of these factors. In addition, languages that show optionality of auxiliaries with reflexive pronouns may have different strategies at their disposal.

5.7.1 Cross-linguistic variation

To facilitate comparison with previous literature on auxiliary selection in reflexive clauses, I consider the clausal types used in Loporcaro (2007: 187): transitive sentences with a reflexive direct object (direct transitive reflexive), unergative clauses with an indirect reflexive object (indirect unergative reflexive), and transitive sentences with an indirect reflexive object (indirect transitive reflexive). These are exemplified in (36) for Standard Italian, and in (37) (which repeat Example (29)) for Logudorese Sardinian.

(36) a. Maria è   partit-a.   (unaccusative)
          Maria be.PRS.3SG leave.PRTC-SG.F
          'Maria has left.'

      b. Maria si=è   lavat-a.   (direct transitive
          Maria REFL.ACC.3SG.F=be.PRS.3SG wash.PRTC-SG.F   reflexive)
          'Maria has washed herself.'

      c. Maria si=è   rispost-a.   (indirect unergative
          Maria REFL.DAT.3SG.F=be.PRS.3SG answer.PRTC-SG.F   reflexive)
          'Maria has answered herself.'

      d. Maria si=è   lavat-a   le mani.   (indirect
          Maria REFL.DAT.3SG.F=be.PRS.3SG wash.PRTC-SG.F the hands   transitive
          'Maria has washed her hands.'   reflexive)

      e. Maria ha   mangiato (la minestra).   (transitive)
          Maria have.PRS.3SG eat.PRTC the soup
          'Maria has eaten (the soup).'

(37) *Logudorese Sardinian (Bonorva)*
  a. Maria ɛs   palti:ð-a.   (unaccusative)
    Maria be.PRS.3SG leave.PRTC-SG.F
    'Maria has left.'
  b. Maria z=ɛs   samuna:ð-a. (direct transitive
    Maria REFL.ACC.3SG.F=be.PRS.3SG wash.PRTC-SG.F reflexive)
    'Maria has washed herself.'
  c. Maria z=ɛr   rispɔst-a. (indirect unergative
    Maria REFL.DAT.3SG.F=be.PRS.3SG answer.PRTC-SG.F reflexive)
    'Maria has answered herself.'
  d. Maria z=a   ssamuna:ðu zal ma:nɔs. (indirect
    Maria REFL.DAT.3SG.F=have.PRS.3SG wash.PRTC the hands transitive
    'Maria has washed her hands.'   reflexive)
  e. Maria a   mmaniɣaðu (za minɛstra). (transitive)
    Maria have.PRS.3SG eat.PRTC the soup
    'Maria has eaten (the soup).'   (Loporcaro 2007: 190–191)

In Standard Italian, the perfect auxiliary for all reflexive clauses is BE. Instead, in Logudorese Sardinian the perfect auxiliary of indirect transitive reflexive clauses is HAVE (37d), as in transitive clauses (37e).

 In addition to the Italian and the Sardinian types, many distinct distributions of auxiliaries are possible within reflexive clauses. As already recognized by Loporcaro (2007: 193), the distribution of the perfect auxiliaries among different reflexive clauses is organized in accordance with the implicational hierarchy shown in Table 5.7.

Table 5.7 Hierarchy of reflexive clauses for languages with two auxiliaries (Loporcaro 2007, 2016)

unaccusative	BE
direct transitive reflexive	
indirect unergative reflexive	
indirect transitive reflexive	
transitive, unergative	HAVE

 The cline in Table 5.7 determines that there are no "non-continuous patterns of auxiliary selection": if the clausal types are ordered in this way, there is no variety where the distribution is BE-HAVE-BE or HAVE-BE-HAVE. Table 5.8 shows the different cutting points in the distribution of BE and HAVE for various languages. It also illustrates that some patterns of auxiliary selection are impossible. In particular, the cutting point between the two auxiliaries within the category of reflexives can be as in rows (a), (b), (c), (d), but not as in rows (e), (f), (g).

The different patterns represented in Table 5.8 are expected under the present theory. In Minimalism, different argument structures involve different feature specifications: a full argument structure v is featurally different from defective v (Chomsky 2001). Hence, it is expected that the opposite poles of the cline (unaccusative and transitive verbs) may exhibit different auxiliaries. In addition, the features of the reflexive argument play a role with a full argument structure v, which is exactly the type of v involved in reflexive clauses (transitive or unergative). Variation within the transitive/unergative argument structure (whose v bears a person probe) is expected if auxiliary selection is due to Agree for the person feature.

Table 5.8 Splits in auxiliary selection (data from Loporcaro 2007: 189,193, Loporcaro 2016: 814)

		unaccus. =(36a)	dir. trans. refl. =(36b)	indir. unerg. refl. =(36c)	indir. trans. refl. =(36d)	trans., unerg. =(36e)
a.	Italian	BE	BE	BE	BE	HAVE
b.	Sardinian	BE	BE	BE	HAVE	HAVE
c.	Picernese	BE	BE	HAVE	HAVE	HAVE
d.	Engadinian	BE	HAVE	HAVE	HAVE	HAVE
e.	*variety x	HAVE	BE	HAVE	BE	HAVE
f.	*variety y	BE	BE	BE	HAVE	BE
g.	*variety z	BE	HAVE	BE	HAVE	HAVE

When the lexicon of a language has two vocabulary entries for the perfect head, the two opposite poles of the scale in Table 5.8 are distinguished by the two auxiliaries, as in rows (a), (b), (c) and (d). The cutting point across the class of reflexives is language-specific. Instead, it is impossible to find the same auxiliary both with unaccusatives and transitives, but the other one with reflexives, as shown by the impossibility of varieties x and y in Table 5.8. This fact is predicted by the present analysis. In a language where transitive and unaccusative verbs have the same auxiliary, it means that the vocabulary entry for Perf is insensitive to the presence or absence of a person feature on Perf. Hence, the same vocabulary entry must also be inserted in reflexive clauses, since it is not sensitive to the person feature. For this reason, varieties x and y are impossible.

In order to rule out variety z, we must first consider the possible structures of reflexive clauses. Direct transitive reflexives are reflexive clauses where the reflexive pronoun is merged in the internal argument position, as shown in (38). For auxiliary selection, there are two possibilities. If the reflexive pronoun has an unvalued person feature, as in Italian, the verb patterns as an unaccusative verb and BE is inserted (Perf[ᴜπ:_]). Instead, if it bears a valued feature, then the verb behaves as a canonical transitive verb and the auxiliary is HAVE (Perf[ᴜπ:α]). This is what happens in Engadinian (row (d) in Table 5.8).

(38) Direct transitive reflexive (cf. (36b))
      structure: $[_{vP} {}^{v}trans[uπ:\_] [_{VP} V DP_{refl}]]$
      auxiliary: if $DP_{refl}[π:\_]$, then BE; if $DP_{refl}[π:α]$, then HAVE.

Indirect unergative reflexives (39) have a covert cognate object. The reflexive dative argument is either introduced in the VP as an indirect object (option (39a)), or by an Applicative head, either lower or higher than v (options (39b) and (39c)).[76] If the reflexive is in a position lower than v, then Agree must behave as in (38): the person feature on the reflexive DP stops the probe from going on searching (leading to defective intervention if unvalued). If it is higher than v, then the clause patterns as a transitive one and the auxiliary is HAVE, since v successfully probes the covert object that bears φ-features valued as default.

(39) Indirect unergative reflexive (cf. (36c))
      a. structure: $[_{vP} v_{trans}[uπ:\_] [_{VP} DP_{refl} V DP_{covert}]]$
          auxiliary: if $DP_{refl}[π:\_]$, then BE; if $DP_{refl}[π:α]$, then HAVE.
      b. structure: $[_{vP} v_{trans}[uπ:\_] [_{ApplP} DP_{refl} Appl [_{VP} V DP_{covert}]]]$
          auxiliary: if $DP_{refl}[π:\_]$, then BE; if $DP_{refl}[π:α]$, then HAVE.
      c. structure: $[_{ApplP} DP_{refl} Appl [_{vP} v_{trans}[uπ:\_] [_{VP} V DP_{covert}]]]$
          auxiliary: HAVE.

The same can be said for indirect transitive reflexive clauses (40), where the object is instead overt and can bear different φ-features.

(40) Indirect transitive reflexive (cf. (36d))
      Same possibilities as in (39) (difference: DP_{obj} is not covert).

Variety z in Table 5.8 is excluded because of a contradiction. Assuming that in a given language reflexives are consistently merged with the same featural specification across all cases in (38), (39) and (40), if the direct transitive clause (38) has HAVE, it means that the clitic has valued features, since it behaves as a canonical transitive direct object. If it has valued features, according to (39) it must lead to HAVE insertion there as well, no matter in which position of the clause the reflexive

---

76. The hierarchy of functional heads is illustrated in (i) (adapting Pylkkänen 2008; Nie 2020).

    (i) $[_{HighApplP} HighAppl [_{vP} v [_{LowApplP} LowAppl [_{VP} V]]]]$

is inserted. Hence, it is not possible that the perfect auxiliary is realized as HAVE in direct transitive reflexives, but as BE in indirect unergative reflexives and/or indirect transitive reflexives.

This analysis seems to predict that indirect unergative reflexive clauses (39) and indirect transitive reflexive clauses (40) always pattern together, since the only difference is the phonological status of the direct object. However, we saw that in Logudorese Sardinian the two types of clauses contain different perfect auxiliaries (row (b) in Table 5.8; see also Example (37)). This is possible if in Sardinian indirect unergative reflexive clauses and indirect transitive reflexive clauses correspond to different syntactic structures: the former to (39a), the latter to (39c). In particular, indirect unergative clauses are double object constructions with a reflexive indirect object, where both objects are part of the same VP: $[_{VP}$ IO_{refl} V DO]. The dative is an argument of the verb in the VP-internal indirect object position.[77] Instead, in indirect transitive clauses the dative argument must be introduced higher in the structure by an Applicative head: $[_{ApplP}$ IO_{refl} Appl $[_{vP}$ $v_{trans}[uπ:\_]$ $[_{VP}$ V DO]]]. Here, the dative has a benefactive function that is given by the presence of an Applicative head.[78]

---

77. An alternative possibility (suggested by Fabian Heck, p.c.) is that indirect unergative clauses are built with a quirky v that assigns dative case. Under the assumption that the covert unergative object does not need case (only lexically realized NP must be assigned abstract case; Vergnaud 1977; Chomsky 1980), a single case feature on v suffices to value the case feature of the reflexive indirect object, without any applicative head. Instead, if the second object is overt, and thus needs case, another functional head is needed (i.e., the applicative head). This explains why indirect unergative reflexive clauses and indirect transitive reflexive clauses may have different perfect auxiliaries. It also clarifies why the switched variant of Sardinian (B B H B H) is excluded. In fact, direct transitive reflexives and indirect unergative reflexives can pattern in the same way, as I have just explained for Italian and Sardinian, or the latter can be more complex since it has two arguments, as in Picernese. However, if indirect unergative reflexives behave differently, then also the version with two overt arguments (indirect transitive reflexives) must behave in the same way (leading to Picernese B B H H H, and excluding "inverted-Sardinian" B B H B H).

78. In addition to the high Applicative analysis, there is another possible account of the Sardinian data. There could be cross-linguistic variation in the case feature on the Applicative head. In Italian, the Appl head assigns accusative case and is selected by a quirky v (see Section 3.3.3 of Chapter 3). This quirky v assigns dative to the reflexive pronoun in Spec,v. Successively, it probes it for person, leading to BE insertion because of agreement with the φ-defective reflexive dative pronoun. In contrast, the Sardinian Appl head does not assign accusative but rather dative case, and it is selected by transitive v that assigns accusative, as shown in (i).

(i) $[_{vP}$ $v_{[ucase:acc]}$ $IO_{[case:dat]}$ $[_{ApplP}$ $Appl_{[ucase:dat]}$ $[_{VP}$ V $DO_{[case:acc]}$]]]

The Appl head assigns dative to the reflexive pronoun in its specifier, leaving the DO with unvalued case. Then, transitive v assigns accusative to the DO across the reflexive IO (assuming

Past participle agreement also constitutes some evidence in favor of a higher position of the reflexive pronoun in indirect transitive reflexive clauses in Sardinian. As explained in Chapter 6, I propose that in Standard Italian the inflection on the participle is due to an edge feature on *v*. Participle agreement emerges when a DP with some unchecked features transits in Spec, *v* in order to escape the phase domain. If participle agreement also has the same source in Sardinian, then it should show up when the reflexive pronoun is merged below *v*, but not when it is base-merged in a position higher than *v*. As Example (37) shows, the reflexive pronoun controls participle agreement in direct transitive reflexive clauses (37b) and indirect unergative reflexive clauses (37c), but it does not in indirect transitive reflexive clauses (37d).

If this line of thinking is on the right track, there are two consequences. In Logudorese Sardinian, the reflexive dative arguments have different functions in the two types of clauses, indirect unergative reflexives (37c) and indirect transitive reflexives (37d). In addition, if it is true that the benefactive argument in indirect transitive reflexive clauses is introduced by a high ApplP in Sardinian (37d), and by a low ApplP in Standard Italian (36d), the dative should be interpreted differently in the two languages. So far, I could not find any clear difference between Sardinian and Italian datives. The only context where there seems to be a difference is with verbs such as *tenere* 'hold'. In Italian, the clauses with benefactive dative or without it are equivalent (41a,b). In Logudorese, the verb in the clause with the reflexive dative means 'wear' (41c), and the verb without it 'hold' (41d).

(41) a. Mario ha   tenuto   il berretto.
          Mario have.PRS.3SG hold.PRTC the cap
          'Mario kept the cap (either wearing it or holding it in his hands).'
      b. Mario si=è   tenuto   il berretto.
          Mario REFL.DAT.3SG=be.PRS.3SG hold.PRTC the cap
          'Mario kept the cap (either wearing it or holding it in his hands).'
      c. Mario s=at   muntesu sa zizia.
          Mario REFL.DAT.3SG=have.PRS.3SG hold.PRTC the cap
          'Mario kept wearing the cap.'
      d. Mario at   muntesu sa zizia.
          Mario have.PRS.3SG hold.PRTC the cap
          'Mario kept the cap in his hands.'   (L. Molinu, p.c.)

Further work is needed to establish whether the reflexive dative pronouns in Standard Italian and in Logudorese Sardinian occupy different syntactic positions.

---

that there is no defective intervention for case). Given Nested Agree, *v* agrees for person with the DO, thereby skipping the reflexive IO, leading to HAVE insertion because of agreement with the direct object.

Similarly to Sardinian, in Picernese (row (c) in Table 5.8) HAVE is inserted for both indirect unergative reflexives and indirect transitive reflexives, whereas BE is inserted for direct transitive reflexives. This means that reflexive pronouns have unvalued features and are always merged high in the structure, when they are not the direct object. Participle agreement cannot confirm this hypothesis, since in Picernese it is not present.

To conclude, with the present analysis I provide an explicit answer to the question why the cross-linguistic and intra-linguistic variation in auxiliary selection in reflexive clauses conforms to the cline defined in Table 5.7. I also correctly predict the possible and impossible distribution of auxiliaries represented in Table 5.8.

5.7.2   Triple auxiliation

In some varieties where auxiliary selection is argument-structure-driven, BE and HAVE may stand in free variation in reflexive clauses. This leads to three different possibilities: HAVE, BE or HAVE~BE (hence, *triple auxiliation*, following Loporcaro 2007). Crucially, free variation does not occur across all cells of the paradigm, but it only affects reflexive clauses (Loporcaro 2007: 202). This fact confirms that free variation must be due to the particular features of the reflexive DP. This is expected if auxiliary selection is a form of person Agree.

Varieties of this type (often belonging to Gallo-Romance and Raetho-Romance) are mostly found in Northern Italy, in particular in Piemonte (Castelletto Merli, Castellazzo Bormida, Felizzano), Veneto (Molina di Ledro, Velo, Cazzano) and Friuli (Grizzo, Montereale), but also in Southern Italy (Stigliano, Altomonte) (Manzini & Savoia 2005: II: 649–650). Some distributions of auxiliaries are given in Table 5.9. Free variation can be found in different contexts: in all reflexive clauses (Veneto), or only in some of them (Castrovillari, Macerata, Genova), following the cline discussed in Section 5.7.1.

Table 5.9 Free variation in reflexive clauses (Loporcaro 2016: 817)

	unaccus. =(36a)	dir. trans. refl. =(36b)	indir. unerg. refl. =(36c)	indir. trans. refl. =(36d)	trans., unerg. =(36e)
Castrovillari	B	H~B	H~B	H	H
Veneto	B	H~B	H~B	H~B	H
Genova	B	B	H~B	H~B	H
Macerata	B	B	B	H~B	H
Sardinian	B	B	B	H	H
Italian	B	B	B	B	H

I suggest that this free variation can be derived if reflexive pronouns may enter the derivation either with unvalued features, leading to BE insertion as in Italian, or with already valued features. Next to the series of φ-unvalued reflexive clitics, there is a series of reflexives already marked with valued φ-features, as I have proposed for the Italian reflexive phrase *se stess-o/-a/-i/-e* (cf. Section 3.2.6.1 in Chapter 3). These pronouns determine HAVE insertion as in canonical transitive clauses. Hence, free variation depends on the features of the reflexive clitics. If the reflexive is not valued for φ-features, Agree on *v* fails and the perfect auxiliary is the same as for unaccusative clauses; if its φ-features are already valued, then the clause behaves as a transitive one. Optionality in the featural make-up of reflexive clitics leads to free variation in the perfect auxiliary. In addition, a further factor of variation is constituted by different Merge positions of the reflexive argument (see also Section 5.7.1). Future research can establish the factors that influence free variation in each language.

Free variation with reflexives can also be restricted to some particular person features. An example for free variation depending on person is the dialect spoken in Valdobbiadene, in (42).[79] The distribution is B~H B~H H H B~H H.

(42)   *Valdobbiadene*
   a.   Mi=me=son   petena-da   /
         NOM.1SG=REFL.ACC.1SG=be.PRS.1SG comb.PRTC-SG.F
         mi=me=ho   petenà.
         NOM.1SG=REFL.ACC.1SG=have.PRS.1SG comb.PRTC
         'I have combed my hair.'
   b.   Ti=tu=te=se   petena-da   /
         2SG=NOM.2SG=REFL.ACC.2SG=be.PRS.2SG comb.PRTC-SG.F
         ti=tu=te=ha   petenà.
         2SG=NOM.2SG=REFL.ACC.2SG=have.PRS.2SG comb.PRTC
         'You have combed your hair.'
   c.   Ela=la=s=ha   petenà.
         NOM.3SG.F=REFL.ACC.3SG=have.PRS.3SG comb.PRTC
         'She has combed her hair.'
   d.   Noialtre   s=aven   petenà.
         NOM.1PL.F REFL.ACC.1PL=have.PRS.1PL comb.PRTC
         'We have combed our hair.'

---

79. More in general, in reflexive clauses there can be variation based on the person feature of the subject without necessarily causing free variation. In Paduan, first and second person singular and second person plural select BE, whereas third person and optionally second person plural select HAVE. The pattern is B B H H B~H H (Benincà, Parry, & Pescarini 2016: 204).

e. Voialtre   ve=se   petena-de   / voialtre
    NOM.2PL.F REFL.ACC.2PL=be.PRS.2PL comb.PRTC-PL.F   NOM.2PL.F
    v=avè   petenà.
    REFL.ACC.2PL=have.PRS.2PL comb.PRTC
    'You have combed your hair.'

f. Lore   le=s=ha   petenà.
    NOM.3PL.F NOM.3PL=REFL.ACC.3PL=have.PRS.3PL comb.PRTC
    'They have combed their hair.'   (C. Benetti, p.c.)

Some more examples of free variation in reflexive clauses can be found in the
dialects spoken in Canton Ticino and Valsugana, shown in Table 5.10. As the symbol % indicates, these data are subject to idiolectal variation.

Table 5.10 Free variation with reflexives according to person (Loporcaro 2007: 201)

	unaccus.	refl. 1SG	refl. 2SG	refl. 3SG	refl. 1PL	refl. 2PL	refl. 3PL	trans., unerg.
Torcegno	B	%H~B	%H~B	H	%H~B	%H~B	H	H
Serso	B	H~B	H~B	H	H~B	H~B	H	H
Pergine	B	%H~B	%H~B	H~B	%H~B	%H~B	H~B	H

As shown in Table 5.10 and in Example (42), free variation is not equally distributed across all persons of the paradigm. In particular, it tends not to be present
with 3rd person subjects.[80] This uneven distribution of free variation may depend
on different factors. As I have proposed above, there can be different series of
reflexive pronouns, one with unvalued features, and one with lexically valued features. In addition, I suggest that the paradigm of the valued series can be defective, lacking some forms. The restrictions on reflexive pronouns with valued or

---

80. Free variation restricted to 1st and 2nd person is reminiscent of the case of personal pronouns in Standard Italian as far as participle agreement is concerned. When the direct object
is a 1st, 2nd person clitic (i-a), participle agreement is optional; when it is 3rd person (i-b), the
participle must agree with it.

(i) a. Ci/vi=ha   vist-o/e/i.
        ACC.1PL/ACC.2PL=have.PRS.3SG see.PRTC-DEFAULT/PL.F/M.PL
        'S/he has seen us/you.'

    b. Li=ha   vist-i/*visto.
        ACC.3PL=have.PRS.3SG see.PRTC-M.PL/DEFAULT
        'S/he has seen us/you.'

See Cardinaletti (2008); Manzini (2019) for possible explanations of this asymmetry. Ideally, the
optionality of participle agreement with 1st, 2nd person clitics and the free variation in auxiliary
selection with 1st, 2nd person reflexive clitics should be given the same (or a similar) explanation.

unvalued φ-features to certain person specifications remain a problem to explore in future work.

An important point concerns participle agreement. In the Valdobbiadene examples in (42), the auxiliary BE correlates with the presence of participle agreement, whereas HAVE correlates with lack of participle agreement. This fact is quite common: in other varieties of Veneto and Friuli there is variation in the auxiliary and the agreement on the past participle (Benincà & Vanelli 1984; Kayne 1993). The following examples show some sentences from Central Veneto: direct transitive reflexives in (43), indirect transitive reflexives in (44).

(43) *Central Veneto*
    a. La Maria se=zé   vestì-a   in presa.
       the Maria REFL.ACC.3SG.F=be.PRS.3SG dress.PRTC-SG.F in hurry
    b. La Maria se=ga   vestìo   in presa.
       the Maria REFL.ACC.3SG.F=have.PRS.3SG dress.PRTC in hurry
       'Maria has dressed herself in a hurry.'   (Loporcaro 1998: 89)

(44) *Central Veneto*
    a. La Maria se=zé   finì-a   le paste.
       the Maria REFL.DAT.3SG.F=be.PRS.3SG finish.PRTC-SG.F the pastries
    b. La Maria se=ga   finìo   le paste.
       the Maria REFL.DAT.3SG.F=have.PRS.3SG finish.PRTC the pastries
       'Maria has finished the pastries.'   (Loporcaro 1998: 89)

Similar facts can be observed in Algherese, which is a variety of Catalan spoken in the Sardinian enclave of Alghero.

(45) *Alghero*
    a. Akeʎaz miɲonas sa=son   daɾas   la ma.
       those girls   REFL.DAT.3PL.F=be.PRS.3PL give.PRTC.SG.F the hand
    b. Akeʎaz miɲonas s=an   dati   la ma.
       those girls   REFL.DAT.3PL.F=have.PRS.3PL give.PRTC the hand
       'Those girls have shaken hands.'
    c. Luz miɲóntsi sa=son   mangǎtsi   luz aspagéts.
       the boys   REFL.DAT.3PL.M=be.PRS.3PL eat.PRTC.PL.M the spaghetti
    d. Luz miɲóntsi s=am   mangǎti luz aspagéts.
       the boys   REFL.DAT.3PL.M=have.PRS.3PL eat.PRTC the spaghetti
       'The boys have eaten the spaghetti.'   (Loporcaro 1998: 120)

These data may provide evidence in favor of two distinct versions of reflexive pronouns. When reflexive clitics have lexically unvalued φ-features and acquire them via binding, the derivation is as in Italian, resulting in BE and past participle agreement. If the reflexive clitics bear already valued person features, and in particular, if these are valued as default 3rd person, then HAVE and no participle agreement are expected (although note that lack of participle agreement may also be the result of impoverishment).

The hypothesis of reflexive clitics lexically marked with default φ-features could be confirmed by languages where these two series of pronouns map to different exponents. In the dialect of Conegliano (Veneto), reflexive pronouns exhibit two distinct forms, which correlate with the presence/absence of participle agreement and with the form of the auxiliary (Kayne 1993: 15). In particular, there are two possibilities for 2nd person plural: either the clitic *ve*, morphologically marked for 2nd person plural, or the default form *se*, generally used for third person. The former causes BE insertion and participle agreement, whereas the latter leads to HAVE without participle agreement. Hence, Conegliano confirms that there are two possible series of reflexive clitics (although more data are needed: this observation is reported by Kayne (1993: 15) based on communication with G. Saccon). More generally, in Northern Italy the third person reflexive *se* tends to allow for a wider range of antecedents than in Italian (Kayne 1993: 27). It often appears with 1st person antecedents, for instance in Venetian (shown in (46)), but also in many Southern Italian varieties as well (Benincà & Poletto 2005: 270).

(46) *Venetian*
    a. El   se=ga   meso   i   calzeti.
          NOM.3SG.M REFL.DAT.3SG.M=have.PRS.3SG put.PRTC the socks
          'He has put his socks on.'
    b. Se=gavamo   meso   i   calzeti.
          REFL.DAT.3SG=have.PRS.1PL put.PRTC the socks
          'We have put our socks on.'   (Benincà & Poletto 2005: 270)

To sum up, on the top of the argument-structure-based split there can be some further distinctions depending on the features of the object. Under the present analysis of auxiliary selection, it is expected that variation concerns reflexives, both cross-linguistically (cf. Table 5.8) and within a language (cf. Tables 5.9 and 5.10). The alternation between the two auxiliaries is not only determined by the structure of the clause, its projections or features, but also by the way in which the reflexive pronouns enter the structure.

5.8 Other argument-structure-driven systems

Besides Standard Italian, there are many varieties where auxiliary selection is argument-structure-driven. In this section, I briefly discuss German and French.

In German, auxiliary selection is argument-structure-driven: BE is found with unaccusative (47a), HAVE with transitive/unergative predicates (47b).

(47) a. Der Zug ist   spät angekommen.
     the train be.PRS.3SG late arrive.PRTC
     'The train arrived late.'

   b. Kurt hat   den   ganzen   Sonntag
     Kurt have.PRS.3SG the.ACC.SG.M whole.ACC.SG.M sunday.ACC.SG.M
     gearbeitet.
     work.PRTC
     'Kurt worked all day Sunday'   (Sorace 2000: 864,874)

The main differences with Italian arise in reflexive and impersonal clauses. In German, reflexive clauses behave as normal transitive clauses, with the perfect auxiliary HAVE.

(48) a. Ich   habe   mich   gewaschen.
     NOM.1SG have.PRS.1SG ACC.1SG wash.PRTC
     'I have washed myself.'

   b. Ich   habe   mir   die Antwort gegeben.
     NOM.1SG have.PRS.1SG DAT.1SG the answer give.PRTC
     'I have given myself the answer.'

Note that German does not have genuine reflexives for local person. The pronouns *mich* and *mir* in (48) can also be used in non-reflexive context (*du hast mich gewaschen* 'you have washed me', *du hast mir die Antwort gegeben* 'you have given me the answer'). Moreover, they are weak pronouns, not clitic pronouns. Weak pronouns occur in a position higher than strong pronouns and DPs, but do not need to be adjacent to the verb (Cardinaletti & Starke 1996, 1999; Cardinaletti 2004). German *mich* has the distribution of weak pronouns: *ich habe mich gestern gewaschen* 'I have washed myself yesterday' vs. *ich habe gestern den Hund gewaschen* 'I have washed the dog yesterday'. It also inflects for case, person and number, but not for gender.

The difference between Italian and German (and Dutch) in auxiliary selection in reflexive clauses has been related to the fact that German does not have cliticization (Haider & Rindler-Schjerve 1987). In Section 5.7, I have suggested that reflexive clitics may bear different sets of features in different languages. Similarly, I propose that the reason for this contrast is not the status of the argument (full DP vs. clitic pronoun), but rather its featural inventory (valued φ-features vs. unvalued φ-features). HAVE insertion in (48) can be explained if reflexive pronouns in German behave like the Italian reflexive phrases *se stess-o/-a/-i/-e*: they enter the derivation with valued φ-features.

The same can be said for German impersonal clauses. The impersonal pronoun *man* behaves as other canonical DPs: it causes the insertion of BE with unaccusative verbs, and of HAVE with transitive/unergative verbs, as shown in (47). This can be explained if the impersonal pronoun bears valued φ-features (in particular, default features [φ:3sg]).

(49)   a.   Wenn man   zu spät gekommen ist,   muss   man
           when IMPERS too late arrive.PRTC be.PRS.3SG must.PRS.3SG IMPERS
           sich   entschuldigen.
           ACC.3SG apologize.INF
           'When one was too late, one should apologize.'

         b.   Wenn man   zu viel   gearbeitet hat,   muss   man
           when IMPERS too much work.PRTC have.PRS.3SG must.PRS.3SG IMPERS
           sich   ausruhen.
           ACC.3SG rest.INF
           'When one has worked too much, one should rest.'

Another point of variation between German and Italian concerns some intransitive verbs.

As mentioned in Section 1.2 of Chapter 1, intransitive verbs are located on a hierarchy that goes from unaccusative verbs to unergative verbs (Sorace 2000). The cutting point in the scale is language-specific. For all languages with argument-structure-driven auxiliary selection, if core unaccusative and unergative verbs pattern as in Italian (BE and HAVE, respectively), each intransitive verb along the gradient of unaccusativity can be categorized with a different argument structure than the Italian counterpart. Hence, there are verbs that are categorized as unergative in Italian, but as unaccusative in German (e.g., *avere viaggiato/gereist sein* 'have traveled'), and vice versa (e.g., *essere durato/gedauert haben* 'have lasted').

The same considerations about intransitive verbs also apply to other languages, and to French as well. In this Romance language, BE is found with a smaller subset of verbs than in Italian and German, but auxiliary selection follows the same pattern. As shown in (50), HAVE is used with transitive and unergative verbs, HAVE with unaccusative verbs.

(50)   a.   Anne a   pris   la clé.
           Anne have.PRS.3SG take.PRTC the key
           'Anne has taken the key.'   (Loporcaro 2016: 802)

         b.   Les policiers   ont   travaillé   toute la nuit.
           the policemen have.PRS.3PL work.PRTC all   the night
           'The policemen have worked all night.'   (Sorace 2000: 863)

c. Marie est   arrivé-e   en retard.
    Marie be.PRS.3SG arrive.PRTC-SG.F in delay
    'Marie has arrived late.'   (Sorace 2000: 863,874)

In reflexive clauses, in French the auxiliary is BE as in Italian, as illustrated in (51).

(51) a. Marie s=est   dépeint-e   come l'unique candidate
          Marie ACC.3SG=be.PRS.3SG depict.PRTC-SG.F as   the.sole candidate
          possible.
          possible
          'Marie depicted herself as the only possible candidate.'
      b. Marie et Jeanne se=sont   longuement écrit.
          Marie and Jeanne REFL.DAT.3PL=be.PRS.3PL for.long.time write.PRTC
          'Marie and Jeanne wrote to each other for a long time.'
      c. La veuve s=était   écrit   de fausses lettres.
          the widow REFL.DAT.3SG=be.PST.3SG write.PRTC of false   letters
          'The widow had written herself some fake letters.'   (Loporcaro 2016: 808)

In (51), BE emerges if the reflexive pronouns bear unvalued φ-features at the time
when v probes for person, as is the case in Italian. Note that participle agreement
patterns differently from Italian. In French, is present with direct transitive reflexives (51a), but not in indirect unergative reflexives (51b) and in indirect transitive reflexives (51c). This fact might be explained if datives are never a (possible)
goal for φ-Agree in French. When the reflexive pronoun bears dative case (51b,c),
its features are not accessible for the probe that determines participle agreement.
When it is an accusative direct object, it is a visible goal (51a). This is different
from Italian, where dative DPs cannot control agreement as in French, but dative
reflexive DPs can: *Teresa si=è fatt-a i panini* 'Teresa has made the sandwiches for
herself' (cf. Section 6.5.3 in Chapter 6).

Impersonal clauses work as in German. The impersonal pronoun on behaves
as a canonical DP with φ-features valued as default [φ:3sg.m].

(52) a. On est   arrivé.
          IMPERS be.PRS.3SG arrive.PRTC
          'People arrived.'
      b. On a   mangé.
          IMPERS have.PRS.3SG eat.PRTC
          'People ate'

To conclude, within similar systems of argument-structure-driven auxiliary selection there may be some differences that emerge from the featural specification or
syntactic structure (reflexives in German), or from other independent facts of the
language (lack of agreement with indirect object in French).

5.9 Summary

In this chapter, I have addressed the cross-linguistic and intra-linguistic variation for auxiliary selection, with a focus on Italo-Romance varieties. I have distinguished two main types of auxiliary selection: argument-structure-driven, where the determining factor is the type of clause; and subject-driven, which depends on the features of the subject, but not on the type of clause. I have analyzed these two systems by using two different extrinsic orderings of features on the head Perf: [uInfl:perf] > [uπ:_] for the former, [uπ:_] > [uInfl:perf] for the latter.

Considering auxiliary selection as the result of person Agree allows not only to give a unified explanation that keeps the syntax very similar across different languages and confines the more fine-grained distinctions to the lexicon, but also to account for some specific facts. It is noteworthy that argument-structure-driven systems can be subject to further restrictions: tense, aspect and mood distinctions, but also person/number distinctions (resulting in so-called mixed systems). In contrast, subject-driven auxiliary selection cannot be further constrained by restrictions based on the argument structure or on the person feature of other arguments. This is due to minimality.

In addition, I have argued that those alleged subject-driven systems that make reference to the argument structure (mixed systems) are instead argument-structure-driven systems, with some further distinctions given by the person feature of the subject as it appears on T. Hence, the distance between the two apparently very different systems of Standard Italian and Italo-Romance varieties is reduced not only by the fact that auxiliary selection in Italian is π-Agree in the same way as it is π-Agree in subject-driven systems, but also because many alleged subject-driven varieties are indeed argument-structure-based systems.

In addition, by treating argument-structure-driven auxiliary selection as the result of Agree for person, I could clarify why the area of reflexive clauses shows so much crosslinguistic and intra-linguistic variation within argument-structure-based varieties. These facts can be explained if the features of the object play a role in argument-structure-driven systems, as I have argued throughout this book, and in particular if reflexive pronouns may bear different features and enter different syntactic structures.

CHAPTER 6

Past participle agreement

6.1 Introduction

Auxiliary selection is not the only morpho-syntactic phenomenon that characterizes the perfect periphrasis: past participle agreement can also show up. Past participle agreement consists of overt morphological inflection for gender and number on the perfect participle. In this chapter, I propose an analysis of participle agreement that is compatible with the theory of auxiliary selection developed in this book. The central idea is that participle agreement arises when there is some kind of defectiveness in the structure, which is encoded in the form of unchecked features. Participle agreement is the morphological reflex of syntactic successive cyclic movement, which must apply in case of defectiveness of either functional heads (in the case of the unaccusative object), or arguments (in the case of clitic pronouns). Auxiliary selection and participle agreement are independent phenomena, although they are both sensitive to morpho-syntactic defectiveness.

The chapter is structured as follows. In the next Section 6.2, I present the data on participle agreement in Standard Italian. I briefly discuss previous analyses in Section 6.3. The main proposal is developed in Section 6.4, where I also discuss different aspects of the analysis. The derivations for Standard Italian are provided in Section 6.5. In Section 6.6 I discuss participle agreement with in situ constituents, which apparently seems to be a problem for the present analysis. I move on to other Italo-Romance varieties in Section 6.7. I discuss the relation between auxiliary selection and participle agreement in Section 6.8. I conclude in Section 6.9.

6.2 The distribution of past participle agreement

In Standard Italian, past participles can bear overt inflection for gender and number, but not for person. The past participle shows overt morphological inflection for gender and number in the following cases: with the unaccusative subject (1a), with the accusative clitic object of a transitive verb (1b), with a resumptive accusative clitic in the context of left dislocation (1c), with the reflexive clitic as direct object or indirect object of a transitive verb (1d,e), with the passive subject

(1f), with the theme of a quirky verb (1g), with the object of a transitive impersonal clause (1h), with the subject of an unaccusative impersonal clause (1i), with the partitive clitic object of a transitive verb (1j).

(1) a. Teresa è   uscit-a.
         Teresa be.PRS.3SG go.out.PRTC-SG.F
         'Teresa has gone out.'

    b. Teresa l=ha   lavat-a.
         Teresa ACC.3SG.F=have.PRS.3SG wash.PRTC-SG.F
         'Teresa has washed her/it.'

    c. La camicia, Teresa l=ha   lavat-a.
         the shirt   Teresa ACC.3SG.F=have.PRS.3SG wash.PRTC-SG.F
         'The shirt, Teresa has washed it.'

    d. Teresa si=è   lavat-a.
         Teresa REFL.ACC.3SG.F=be.PRS.3SG wash.PRTC-SG.F
         'Teresa has washed herself.'

    e. Teresa si=è   lavat-a   il vestito.
         Teresa REFL.DAT.3SG.F=be.PRS.3SG wash.PRTC-SG.F the dress
         'Teresa has washed her dress.'

    f. La camicia è   stat-a   lavat-a.
         the shirt   be.PRS.3SG be.PRTC-SG.F wash.PRTC-SG.F
         'The shirt has been washed.'

    g. A Teresa   sono   piaciut-e   le caramelle.
         to Teresa.DAT.3SG.F be.PRS.3PL like.PRTC.PL.F the candies
         'Teresa has liked the candies.'

    h. Si=sono   mangiat-e   le caramelle.
         IMPERS=be.PRS.3PL eat.PRTC-PL.F the candies
         'People have eaten the candies.'

    i. Si=è   arrivat-i   in ritardo.
         IMPERS=be.PRS.3SG arrive.PRTC-PL.M in delay
         'People have arrived late.'

    j. Ne=hanno   lavat-e   molte.
         of=have.PRS.3PL wash.PRTC-PL.F many.PL.F
         'Of them, they have eaten many.'

What all the instances of participle agreement in (1) have in common is phrasal movement. In most of the examples in (1), the DP that controls agreement on the participle does not surface in its base position. Examples (1g) and (1h) seem to be an exception, since the participle agrees with the object in situ. However, the object is "special", since it bears nominative case and controls finite agreement on T. In Section 6.6, I will argue that the object is only apparently in situ and undergoes cover movement. Considering now the examples in (1), they all involve movement of the argument that controls agreement on the participle. In fact, the unaccusative argument and the passive argument move to the subject position for case assignment, whereas the clitics move to the inflected verb because of a Merge feature (see Section 3.2.6 in Chapter 3). These are all instances of A-movement, namely movement triggered by case assignment, φ-Agree or Merge features (for the A vs. Ā distinction, cf. Mahajan 1990; Müller 1995; van Urk 2015; Safir 2019). Hence, the following implicational relation between movement and past participle agreement (ppa) can be drawn from the data.

(2) a. A-movement → ppa
     b. no ppa → no A-movement

The generalization in (2) states that if an XP moves because of reasons such as case assignment, Merge features, Agree features, then it triggers overt inflectional agreement on the past participle (ppa). Conversely, if there is no overt inflection on the participle, then movement driven by an A-feature has not taken place. Note also that the correlation in (2) does not say anything about Agree when nothing moves. We will see in Section 6.6 that it is possible to have participle agreement also with constituents that seem to be in situ (cf. Examples (1g) and (1h)).

I exclude from the discussion all instances of Ā-movement, such as wh-movement, focus, topicalization, and so on, since they do not trigger participle agreement in Standard Italian (but they do in other languages; an example is relativization in French, Kayne 1989: 85–86, Branigan 1992: 36). There is no participle agreement with the subject or object of transitive verbs (3a), with the unergative subject (3b), with dative arguments (3c) (unless reflexive: cf. (1e)), with topicalized/focused DPs without resumption (3d), with wh-phrases (3e), with relative pronouns (3f), with the object of a transitive impersonal clause (3g) (in alternation with (1h)).

(3) a. Teresa ha   lavato   la camicia.
         Teresa have.PRS.3SG wash.PRTC the shirt
         'Teresa has washed the shirt.'
     b. Teresa ha   lavorato.
         Teresa have.PRS.3SG work.PRTC
         'Teresa has worked.'
     c. Alla ragazza, le=ho   dato   la torta.
         to.the girl   DAT.3SG.F=have.PRS.1SG give.PRTC the cake
         'To the girl, I have given her the cake.'
     d. La camicia, Teresa ha   lavato   (non la giacca).
         the skirt   Teresa have.PRS.3SG wash.PRTC not the jacket
         'The skirt, Teresa has washed it (not the jacket).'

e. Quante   torte hanno   mangiato i   ragazzi?
   how many cakes have.PRS.3PL eat.PRTC the boys
   'How many cakes have the boys eaten?'

f. La camicia che ho   lavato   è   asciutta.
   the shirt   that have.PRS.1SG wash.PRTC be.PRS.3SG dry
   'The shirt that I have washed is dry.'

g. Si=è   mangiato caramelle.
   IMPERS=be.PRS.3SG eat.PRTC candies
   'People have eaten candies.'

6.3   Previous analyses

That participle agreement is dependent on movement has already been proposed
by Kayne (1985, 1989); Déprez (1998); Belletti (2017); D'Alessandro & Roberts
(2008), among others. However, some of these accounts (Kayne 1985, 1989;
Bouchard 1982; Branigan 1992; Friedemann & Siloni 1997; Belletti 2005) are
framed within a theory that is no longer accepted for its mechanisms, such as
Spec-head-agreement or a dedicated agreeing head (not fully compatible with
the assumptions of this study, couched in Minimalism). Other proposals
(D'Alessandro & Roberts 2008; Belletti 2017; Longenbaugh 2019; Georgi & Stark
2020) make use of downward Agree between the probe on the participle head and
the VP-internal argument, but they are not compatible with the present analysis
of auxiliary selection.

For instance, D'Alessandro & Roberts's (2008) proposal cannot be integrated
with an Agree-based analysis of auxiliary selection as the present one, since it
locates φ-features on both transitive and unaccusative v (or related projections),
thereby undermining the featural distinction between different argument structures. In general, D'Alessandro & Roberts's (2008) approach seems to be incompatible with any analysis of argument-driven auxiliary selection, such as the
theory developed by the same authors in D'Alessandro & Roberts 2010. In addition, it is subject to more severe problems.[81]

The analysis by Longenbaugh (2019) also runs into problems when one tries
to make it compatible with argument-driven auxiliary selection. In fact, it is based

---

81. Georgi & Stark (2020) have identified the following shortcomings of D'Alessandro &
Roberts's (2008) analysis: (i) the crucial assumption that unaccusative v is not a phase, (ii) the
existence of languages, such as French, where the verb does not move to v_{prt}, as it should under
D'Alessandro & Roberts's (2008) approach, (iii) wrong predictions for Ā-movement to Spec,C,
(iv) overgeneration based on the computation of traces/copies, (v) the crucial use of derivational memory.

on the assumption that every *v* triggers both Merge and Agree, thereby ignoring the difference between full and defective *v* that is relevant for auxiliary selection. Moreover, it relies on assumptions that cannot be applied here (e.g., in Italian items marked for dependent case are not accessible for Agree; Merge of the external argument precedes Agree on *v*). It has also some troubles in covering the Italian data, in particular participle agreement with reflexive indirect object clitics. In addition, participle agreement with in situ DPs can only be derived by assuming that the DPs are really in situ (but see Section 6.6.1 for evidence in favor of covert movement), with the additional machinery of an optional EPP-feature or a null expletive.

The work by Georgi & Stark (2020) makes use of two independent mechanisms for generating participle agreement in French: resumption, and φ-agreement between the head *v* and the internal argument in its base position. I do not exclude that participle agreement may emerge from different syntactic processes, as I argue for Old Italian and some Italo-Romance varieties in Section 6.7.2. However, even though the analysis by Georgi & Stark (2020) is probably on the right track for French, it cannot be applied to Italian participle agreement. First of all, it is based on the evidence (provided by Lahousse 2006, 2011) that in situ DPs controlling agreement are really in their base position (Georgi & Stark 2020: 23). However, Italian behaves differently from French: in situ controllers of agreement have some properties that show that they have moved from their base position, as I show in Section 6.6.1. In addition, the evidence that French participle agreement does not pattern as a reflex of DP-movement cannot be tested for Italian, where there is no participle agreement with wh-phrases that can create dependencies across clause boundaries (Georgi & Stark 2020: 25). Hence, Georgi & Stark's (2020) analysis cannot be successfully applied to the Italian data. Moreover, it is incompatible with the analysis of auxiliary selection pursued here (in fact, it only considers a very simplistic analysis of auxiliary selection that does not account for the data, cf. footnote on page 36 of Georgi & Stark 2020).

6.4 Participle agreement is the Spell-out of an edge feature

In this section, I provide an analysis of participle agreement that is fully compatible with the theory of auxiliary selection developed in Chapters 2 and 3. I propose that Italian past participle agreement is a reflex of movement of the controller DP to the edge of the phase head *v*. More precisely, participle agreement spells out an *edge feature* (EF) on *v*.

I consider past participle agreement to be located on the head *v* for two main reasons: *v* is a phase (see Section 3.2.3 of Chapter 3), and is independently realized as a past participle due to the feature [Infl] (see Sections 2.5.1 of Chapter 2, 3.2.1 of Chapter 3). There is no need for an extra head devoted to participle agreement.

Following Chomsky (2001); Müller (2010); Abels (2012); Nunes (2019), among others, I consider movement to the phase edge to be triggered by an edge feature (EF) that must be inserted on the phase head *v*. I suggest that in Italian edge features that target unchecked A-features consist of a Merge feature and a probe for gender and number. The Merge component of EF is a structure-building feature [•uF•] that triggers movement of the unchecked feature to the specifier of the phase head. The probes [uγ:_, u#:_] copy the φ-features of the "to-be-moved XP". These φ-features on *v* will be spelled out as agreement on the verb. The appearance of past participle morphology is due to the value *perf* for the attribute [Infl] on *v*. The analysis is represented in (4), which may exemplify movement of an unaccusative internal argument, for instance.

(4)

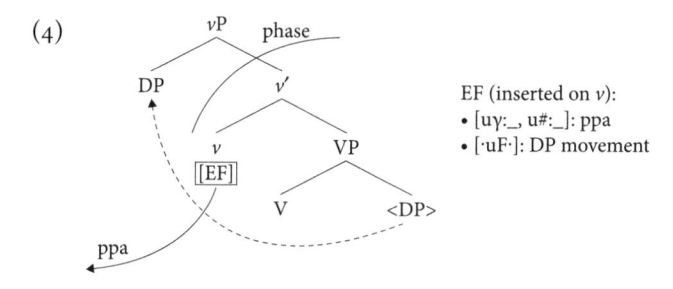

EF (inserted on *v*):
• [uγ:_, u#:_]: ppa
• [·uF·]: DP movement

The present analysis is built on the well-established idea that participle agreement in Standard Italian is dependent on movement (as briefly discussed in Section 6.3). The GB mechanism of Spec-head-agreement is simply rephrased into minimalist terms by making use of phases, successive cyclic movement, and edge features. The main advantage of the present proposal over other accounts based on movement lies in the use of an already proposed technology, namely edge features, independently needed for successive cyclic movement. This makes it possible to avoid the assumption of any further projection activated by phrasal movement, such as AgrOP, or any Spec-head configuration. Agree always applies under c-command, as standardly assumed in Minimalism.

This approach is also in line with the idea that participle agreement and auxiliary selection are independent phenomena (Loporcaro 1998; Bentley & Eythórsson 2004; Manzini & Savoia 2007; Legendre 2010). Even though both auxiliary selection and participle agreement are instances of Agree, in these two cases Agree applies on different heads and for different features (see also Section 6.8).

In the next sections, I discuss the various aspects of this analysis.

6.4.1 Successive cyclic movement

Phases are chunks of syntactic structure that is cyclically sent to the two interfaces LF and PF (Chomsky 2001, 2008). When the phrase of a phase head is built, the complement of the phase head is sent to Spell-out. At this point, the portion of syntactic structure that has been sent to the interfaces is not accessible anymore for further syntactic computations. This is expressed by the PIC, repeated again in (5).

(5) *Phase Impenetrability Condition (PIC)* (Chomsky 2000:108)
In a phase α with head H, the domain of H is not accessible to operations outside α, only H and its edge are accessible to such operations.

The PIC states that the domain (i.e., the complement) of a phase is opaque to any syntactic operation outside the phase, whereas its edge (head and specifier) is not. If a head in the complement is not ready yet to be sent to the interfaces because it bears an unchecked feature, it should remain available for further operations outside the phase. This is achieved if it moves to the edge of the phase. Hence, the PIC forces successive-cyclic movement via phase edges.

In addition to the phase theory, I also adopt a *feature-based* approach to successive cyclic movement (Chomsky 2001; Müller 2010; Abels 2012; Nunes 2019). Under the assumption that each instance of movement is necessarily feature-driven (Chomsky 1995), the intermediate steps of successive cyclic movement via the escape hatches of the phases must be triggered by an appropriate feature: an edge feature.

Note, however, that edge features are not universally assumed as triggers for intermediate movement. Successive cyclic movement can be derived with the interaction of different principles (*phase balance*, Heck & Müller 2000; Müller 2010; *local derivational optimization*, Heck & Müller 2003) or with repel-based mechanisms (*agnostic movement*, Franks & Lavine 2006; see also Bošković 2007; Stroik 2009). The present proposal is halfway between the feature-based account and the repel-based approach: successive cyclic movement is triggered by an edge feature, which is inserted on the phase head if and only if in the phase domain there is an element that must be moved out of it.

6.4.2 The edge feature

As already stated above, I propose that the edge feature not only consists of a Merge feature, but also of an Agree feature for gender and number [uγ:_, u#:_].

To be more precise, I suggest that the edge feature is an array of three ordered features: an Agree feature, a φ-probe for gender and number, and a Merge feature. The components of the EF are represented in (6).

(6) EF: [uF] > [u#], [uγ] > [•F•]

First of all, the phase head has to agree with the unchecked feature. The [uF] component of the EF establishes an Agree relation with the XP that must be moved.[82] This operation simply matches the type of feature that is unchecked, before any valuation or structure-building operation applies (for a similar mechanism, cf. the step of *Agree-Link* in the framework proposed by Arregi & Nevins 2012). This *match-component* of the edge feature is needed because it avoids intervention effects for the following φ-probes. In fact, the [uF] feature creates the Agree-Link that is exploited by the successive φ-probing operation, in accordance with Nested Agree. This means that the subsequent probes [u#], [uγ] target the to-be-moved element and not simply the highest c-commanded item that bears φ-features. Note that the φ-Agree component of the EF results in φ-features on the phase head (i.e., it is not deleted when the EF is discharged). Exactly this set of φ-features is spelled out as morphological inflection on the past participle. After φ-Agree, the Merge feature ([•F•]) moves the XP to the specifier of the phase head. The function of this part of the EF is to create an escape hatch, i.e. a specifier of a phase head (or multiple specifiers), when an XP contained in the complement of the phase head must move out of the Spell-out domain because it bears some unchecked features.

Evidence in favor of edge features comes from movement-related morphology (for a survey, cf. Heck & Müller 2000; van Urk 2016; Georgi 2019). When successive cyclic movement leaves a sign in the form of morphological agreement, there must be a feature responsible for this. These overt signs of intermediate movement have been used to argue that movement is feature-driven by Chomsky (1995); McCloskey (2002); Abels (2012); Georgi (2014); van Urk (2016), among others. Italian past participle agreement is an example of a reflex of A-movement. Similarly, Bruening (2001) has argued that participle agreement in Passamaquoddy is caused by intermediate movement. In this language, Ā-extraction across a verb optionally triggers participial agreement on the verb. This is analyzed as parasitic agreement resulting from the movement to the edge of the phase *v* (Bruening 2001: 209).

---

82. In (6), F stands for a generic feature, but I think that edge features should be category-specific, as suggested in Müller (2010: 38,58). The probe in (6) is actually specified for the kind of unchecked feature that has triggered its insertion: [u[ucase:_]], [u[•T•]], and so on. However, at least for Standard Italian, a generic distinction between A- and Ā-features might be enough (see also Sections 6.5.4 and 6.5.5).

6.4.3   Timing of EF-insertion

I propose that the edge feature is not an inherent feature, but is instead inserted on the phase head when it c-commands an unchecked feature.[83] If the complement of the phase head contains a feature that has not been checked yet (typically, [case:_] for the unaccusative object, [•T•] for clitics), then the phase head receives an edge feature that extracts the unchecked feature, with consequent pied-piping of the whole phrase.

I argue that the EF is inserted on a phase head when all the operations triggered by the head have been exhausted. Concerning the timing of insertion, this proposal is in line with the idea of edge features originally developed by Chomsky (2000:109), (2001:34): EFs (called EPP-features there) are assigned once the phase is completed. The main reason why EF-insertion should be the last operation on a phase head is because of reflexive constructions. Recall that in this case the participle agrees with the reflexive clitic object, as shown in (1d), repeated here again.

(7)   Teresa si=è   lavat-a.
      Teresa REFL.ACC.3G.F=be.PRS.3SG wash.PRTC-SG.F
      'Teresa has washed herself.'

Since the clitic triggers φ-agreement on the participle, it must bear valued φ-features. The clitic receives its φ-features from the external argument via binding. Hence, the external argument must be merged before the EF is inserted. In contrast, if the EF were inserted before the introduction of the external argument, the φ-probe on the EF would not have copied any value from the clitic, because the clitic would not have been bound yet. The necessary conclusion is that the EF must be inserted after the external argument has been introduced and has bound the clitic. Hence, EF-insertion happens after all operations on the phase head have been performed (pace Müller 2010).

---

83. EF-insertion violates the *Inclusiveness Condition* (Chomsky 1995, 2000, 2001), which states that anything that was not contained in the input in the numeration can be added in the output. This is a general problem with feature insertion and does not concern in a particular way the present analysis. I follow here Müller (2010:38): the problem can be circumvented by assuming that the Inclusiveness Condition is violable. Movement out of the phase domain, which is necessary because of the presence of unvalued features, can only take place if a triggering feature is inserted, although under a violation of the Inclusiveness Condition.

6.4.4   Feature insertion and the Strict Cycle Condition

If EF-insertion happens as the last operation within a phase, this seems to violate the Strict Cycle Condition (SCC) (Chomsky 1973: 243), as pointed out by Müller (2010). This principle states that within the current syntactic domain it is not possible to apply an operation to two positions α and β that are contained in another domain that is dominated by the current one (i.e., a smaller sub-domain that excludes the current active node). All operations must apply at the root of the current cyclic node. If the edge feature is inserted as the last operation on the head (after v has discharged its structure-building feature [•D•], introducing the external argument), the current cyclic node for EF-insertion is the maximal projection vP. At least the Agree operations triggered by the subparts of EF (Agree for the unchecked feature, Agree for gender and number) violate the SCC because they involve the head and the complement with the exclusion of the specifier.

To avoid this problem, I propose that feature insertion actually consists of two subsequent processes: Merge of a feature on the maximal projection (which is the current active domain), and activation of the feature on the head that projects the current active domain (because the feature needs to be represented on a head in order to be discharged).[84] Edge feature insertion happens at the level of the maximal projection after all the operation-inducing features on the head have been discharged. Since the EF is inserted when the vP is built, and not when v enters the derivation, the EF is inserted on the vP. This is in accordance with a strict interpretation of the SCC, since it involves the maximal projection vP, which also contains the specifier position and is the current active node. The inserted feature then projects onto the head, in order to be discharged. This is due to a mechanism that I call *downward feature projection*: if a feature is merged on an XP (feature insertion), then it must also be present on the head X. After the EF is inserted on the vP, it automatically projects on v, from where it can be discharged. Everything that happens now on the v level is also represented on the vP level. Since the root node vP is involved, there is no violation of the SCC. Downwards feature projection only applies to inserted features, and is a way to make them participate in the derivation.[85]

---

84. I thank Fabian Heck (p.c.) for suggesting this solution to me.

85. The question about what *feature insertion* is remains open. Feature insertion is not a canonical instance of Merge: a single feature is not a head, its insertion does not discharge a Merge feature [•EF•] on the head on which it is inserted, and this operation does not create a new syntactic object containing two heads or phrases in a sisterhood relation. I consider feature insertion to be a Merge operation between a single feature and a maximal projection, triggered by an unchecked feature within the maximal projection. The result of this operation is the same maximal projection with one more feature on it and on the head that projects it.

6.4.5 Edge features and Agree on Perf

Another consideration concerns the interaction of the EF with auxiliary selection. We saw in the previous chapter (cf., for instance, Sections 3.3.2, 3.3.5) that BE is the selected allomorph when the head Perf has not found any person feature value in the syntactic structure. A question that may arise is why the presence of an edge feature (and, in particular, its φ-probe component) on v does not feed Agree on higher heads. The answer to this question is straightforward and has to do with the kind of features involved. Even though the EF brings a subset of φ-features on v, namely gender and number, it does not contain person, which is the goal for Agree on Perf[uπ:_]. Hence, the EF cannot influence the probe on Perf because these two probes target different features.

6.4.6 Unvalued features

The idea that edge features must be inserted on the maximal projection of the phase head when there is an unchecked feature in its domain raises the question about which kind of operations must be successfully carried out, or else the derivation would crash.

Let us start with Agree features. A feature of type [uF:_] is a probe that has not been discharged yet. Assuming that EF-insertion is the last operation performed on an XP, [uF:_] is always discharged before EF-insertion. A feature of type [uF:_] is a probe that has been discharged, but has failed to copy a value. Here, I assume that failed Agree is possible (cf. Section 2.4.1 in Chapter 2). Hence, an unvalued feature of the shape [uF:_] (in case the probe has failed to find a matching goal) does not require EF-insertion, in the very same way as [uF:α] does not. As far as unvalued features are concerned, such as [Infl:_] on v or [φ:_] on reflexive clitics, they are lexical properties of the heads and are inert features (as the lack of the prefix u– illustrates). Hence, they do not trigger EF-insertion.

If failed Agree is an option for Agree-probes, why can the same not be said for the unchecked features that trigger EF-insertion (i.e., [case:_], [•T•])? I propose that a feature such as [case:_] is different from an Agree probe [uF:_], as the u-prefix highlights. [case:_] is not an active feature that scans its c-command domain searching for a case value. In fact, it cannot be discharged without a case assigner being in the structure. Even though case assignment can be considered an instance of Agree, an unchecked case feature cannot start an operation, but needs to be the target of the operation of case assignment, differently from [Infl:_] or [π:_]. This means that [case:_] cannot be discharged in advance, in order to avoid EF-insertion. Instead, it requires edge feature insertion.

A feature such as [•T•] can initiate Merge. However, it cannot search its c-command domain. This type of feature remains inactive until an item of the right category is selected from the numeration. Similarly, selectional features involved in external Merge are discharged once two heads or phrases are put together, but they do not search the c-command domain. The feature [•T•] of clitics, although able to start an operation, cannot be discharged before T enters the structure, with the consequence that it is not possible to avoid EF-insertion at the vP level.

In general, the present proposal highlights a difference between various operations as far as valuation and activity are concerned. The necessary conclusion is that Agree is different from case assignment and from checking of the clitic-feature [•T•] (and Merge features in general). Unvalued case and non-discharged Merge features trigger the insertion of edge features, while an unvalued probe cannot do so because of the possibility of failed valuation.

6.4.7   Ā-movement does not trigger participle agreement

As illustrated in Section 6.2, in Standard Italian only A-movement causes overt morphological inflection on the participle, whereas other kinds of movement, such as relativization, wh-movement, topicalization, do not give rise to participle agreement. This fact can be explained if EFs are categorically specific (Müller 2010: 38,58, Abels 2012: 59, Georgi 2014: 236, Heck 2016: 48–49), and differ with respect to the φ-probes.

EFs that trigger Ā-movement are of the types EF[wh], EF[top], and so on; EFs that trigger A-movement are of the categories EF[case:_], EF[•T•], and so on. These different types of EF can have different compositions. I have suggested that in Italian EFs for A-movement contain three parts: an Agree probe for the relevant category, a φ-Agree probe, and a Merge feature that builds the specifier. In addition, I propose that in Italian EFs for Ā-movement lack the φ-probes. The difference between the two classes of features is represented in (8), where F_A are features such as [case], [T], while $F_{\bar{A}}$ are [wh], [top], [foc].

(8) *Edge features in Standard Italian*
  A-EF: $[uF_A] > [u\#], [u\gamma] > [•F_A•]$
  Ā-EF: $[uF_{\bar{A}}] > [•F_{\bar{A}}•]$

For languages where participle agreement is related to successive cyclic movement, cross-linguistic variation can be due to the various components of EFs.[86]

---

86. In Standard Italian, there is a correlation between EF and φ-probes: A-EF with φ-probes on the one hand, and Ā-EF without φ-probes on the other hand. This seems not to be the case in French and Passamaquoddy. Looking at French in (10), both case-EFs and wh-EFs contain

For example, French behaves similarly to Italian, but in addition it allows for agreement with wh-phrases and relative phrases (Kayne 1989; Branigan 1992). An example of relativization in French is given in (9).

(9)   les chaises que Paul a   *repeint   / repeint-es
       the chairs that Paul have.PRS.3SG repaint.PRTC / repaint.PRTC-PL.F
       'the chairs that Paul has repainted'   (Kayne 1989: 85–86)

It is not clear whether past participle agreement in French is related to movement to the edge of the phase. Probably, this language has more than one strategy at its disposal at the same time (φ-probe, cliticization), as shown by Georgi & Stark (2020). Establishing which analysis should be adopted for French lies out of the scope of this chapter. Nonetheless, the distribution of participle agreement in French could be modeled with the inventory in (10).

(10)   *Edge features in French*
       case-, T-, wh-EF: [uF] > [u#], [uγ] > [•F•]
       Top-, Foc-EF: [uF] > [•F•]

Another language where Ā extraction optionally triggers participial agreement is Passamaquoddy (Bruening 2001). This phenomenon can be explained by means of the inventory in (11). Optionality derives from the availability of the two different grammars (11a) and (11b).

(11)   *Edge features in Passamaquoddy*
       a.   EF: [uF] > [u#], [uγ] > [•F•]
       b.   EF: [uF] > [•F•]

6.5   Derivations

6.5.1   Transitive verbs with object clitic

The first case I would like to address is past participle agreement with an object clitic in transitive clauses, as in the following sentence.

φ-probes. This could show that EFs must be categorically specific, but this specification does not map to the A- versus Ā-distinction. Under this view, the symmetry of the featural inventory of Italian in (8) is just an accident. However, French does not necessarily prove that the correlation between the type of movement and the composition of the EF does not hold anymore. It could also be the case that in French wh-movement and relativization pattern more similarly to A-movement than they do in Italian. The distinction between A- and Ā-movement is in fact blurry and it consists of different properties that tend to cluster together, but do not always do so. Cf. Mahajan (1990); Müller (1995); van Urk (2015); Safir (2019) for discussion.

(12) Paolo l=ha   lavat-a.
      Paolo ACC.3SG.F=have.PRS.3SG wash.PRTC-SG.F
      'Paolo has washed her/it.'

As far as the auxiliary is concerned, I refer the reader to Section 3.3.1 in Chapter 3, where the derivation for transitive clauses is provided. In Example (12), the object is a clitic pronoun, which causes the additional phenomenon of participle agreement (absent when the object is a full DP, cf. Example (3a)). Gender and number agreement on the lexical verb is due to Agree with the clitic. Agree takes place because the clitic must move out of its base position in order to be able to check its [•T•] feature later in the derivation.

First of all, the VP and the transitive vP are built (cf. tree (12) of Chapter 3). Once all the operations on the head v have been carried out, the VP is sent to Spell-out. However, this would cause a problem because the phase domain (e.g., the VP) contains an unchecked feature: [•T•] on the clitic. This feature [•T•] on the D head of the clitic triggers Merge of the clitic with a T head. This feature cannot be satisfied yet, since there is no such a head in the structure. Therefore, it must escape the phase domain by moving to the edge of the phase (pied-piping the whole DP). Successive cyclic movement to the edge of the vP is caused by an edge feature, which is inserted on v (or on the vP, see discussion in Section 6.4.4). This is represented in tree (13). The external arrow indicates that an edge feature is inserted in the structure.

(13)
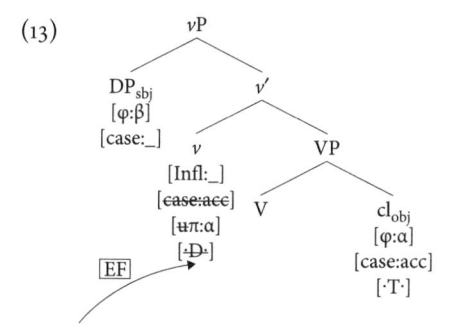

In tree (14), I show the effects of the edge feature. To provide a simpler representation, in this tree I only show the edge feature on v (with its three ordered components) and the involved features on the other heads, but the full sets of features on the heads also contain the features shown in tree (13). The first component of the category-specific edge feature agrees with the unchecked feature [•T•]. The second part of EF agrees for gender and number with the head that bears the unchecked feature. The third part of EF moves the head with the unchecked feature to an outer specifier of v. At the end of the derivational step in (14), v has copied gender and number features from the clitic, which is now located at the edge of the phase in an outer specifier, from where it is accessible for other higher heads.

(14)

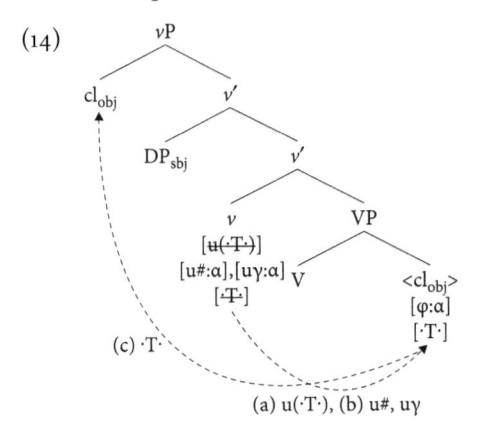

The derivation then proceeds as indicated in Sections 3.3.1 and 3.3.2 of Chapter 3 (the former contains the full derivation for a transitive clause, the latter is relevant for cliticization).

At Spell-out, the complex head V + v (formed via head movement) contains a value for # and γ. Tree (15) exemplifies the case of a transitive v with a clitic object.

(15)

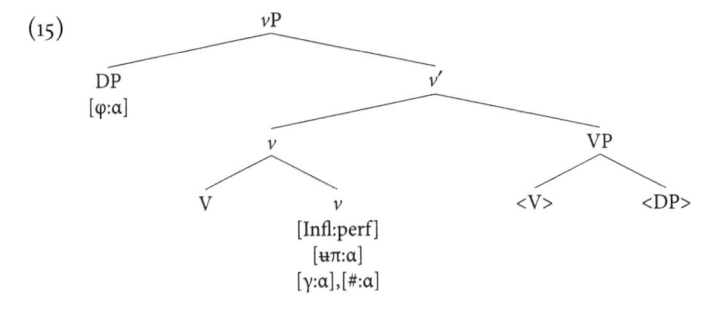

In (15), the person value [π] on v is due to the fact that transitive v is a probe for person (see Section 3.3.1 in Chapter 3). The person feature on v determines the allomorph of the auxiliary on Perf, but it is not spelled out as inflection. The features that are spelled out by overt morphological inflection (but do not influence the morphological realization of Perf, see Section 6.4.5) are the gender [γ] and number [#] values on v. These features are located on v because of the edge feature, as I have explained in this section. The morpho-phonological exponents for the lexical verb *lavare* 'wash' in the form of the feminine singular participle *lavata* are given in (16).

(16) lav   -a   -t   -a
      lexical root - thematic vowel - v[Infl:perf] - v[#:sg],[γ:f]

The Vocabulary Item responsible for participle agreement is expressed by the metarule in (17). The specific lexical entries are represented in (18).

(17) /participle agreement for α/ ↔ v[Infl:perf],[γ:α],[#:α]

(18) a. /t/ ↔ v[Infl:perf]
      b. /a/ ↔ v[γ:f] / [Infl:perf]
      c. /e/ ↔ v[γ:f],[#:pl] / [Infl:perf]
      d. /i/ ↔ v[#:pl] / [Infl:perf]
      e. /o/ ↔ v / [Infl:perf] (elsewhere)

Note that the node v is spelled twice, as (16) shows: once for the feature [Infl], and once for the φ-features. Firstly, the vocabulary entry /t/ (18a) that spells out the [Infl] feature on v is inserted in the terminal node v. Then, Vocabulary Insertion does not stop after this single Vocabulary Item is inserted, but it goes on discharging the next features [γ], [#]. This is due to a mechanism called *Fission*, originally proposed by Noyer (1992). Fission applies when a single morpheme may correspond to more than a single Vocabulary Item, as in (18). In this case, Fission creates an additional position of exponence after one Vocabulary Item is inserted. This operation applies again until all the features of the morpheme have been discharged (Harley & Noyer 1999: 6).[87]

The result of EF-insertion is morphologically realized only in the presence of the head Perf that assigns the right value to the Infl-feature on v, while it is not visible on any other form of the verb (for example, in simple tense clauses). I express this relation by making use of context-sensitive Vocabulary Insertion. The vocabulary entries in (18) only realize the φ-features on v when this head also bears the value *perf* for the feature [Infl]. This is an instance of strictly local allomorphy, since all relevant features are located on the same head (cf. also Georgi & Stark 2020: 37 for the same mechanism).

This derivation leads to past participle agreement in the case of clitic arguments. Clauses where participle agreement is controlled by resumptive clitics (see (1c) in Section 6.2) are generated in the same way. Whatever analysis is assumed for resumption, the idea is that participle agreement is due to the A-dependency

---

87. The alternative solution would be to have two different heads in syntax, as shown in (i).

(i) lav   - a   - t   - a
     lexical root - thematic vowel - v[Infl:perf] - Part[#:sg],[γ:f]

In (i), v is spelled out by the participial morpheme /t/. A further head Part is spelled out as gender/number inflection because of EF-insertion.

with the resumptive clitic that moves to T, as with a canonical argument clitic, and not with the left dislocated DP. In fact, the participle does not agree with a left-dislocated constituent if there is no resumptive pronoun (see (3d) in Section 6.2). The same asymmetry between dislocation with or without resumption can also be observed on the right edge of the sentence (Cardinaletti 2002). Cases such as (1c) can be analyzed as structures where the dislocated DP is adjoined to the matrix clause in the left periphery. The object position just contains a clitic that moves to T, causing object agreement exactly as in the derivation presented in this section.

6.5.2 Transitive verbs with reflexive direct object

An interesting case arises when a transitive verb takes a reflexive clitic pronoun as one of its arguments. In Example (19), the direct object is a reflexive clitic.

(19) Teresa si=è   lavat-a.
       Teresa REFL.ACC.3SG.F=be.PRS.3SG wash.PRTC-SG.F
       'Teresa washed herself.'

The selected allomorph for the perfect auxiliary is BE. As I have explained in Section 3.3.2 in Chapter 3, this is caused by the presence of an unvalued person feature on v, which leads to failed valuation for the feature [π] on Perf. Since the value of the person feature on v derives from Agree with the internal argument, the conclusion is that the φ-features on the reflexive clitic must be unvalued.

On the contrary, participle agreement shows that the φ-features on the clitic pronoun are valued. Since clitics control participle agreement (see Section 6.5.1), and since the external argument is never a controller of participle agreement (Belletti 2017), overt morphological inflection on the lexical verb in (19) is controlled by the clitic pronoun. The conclusion is that the reflexive clitic must bear valued φ-features, contrary to what auxiliary selection suggests.

As already discussed in Section 6.4.3 and Section 3.3.2 of Chapter 3, I propose that the answer to this puzzle lies in the timing of operations. On the one hand, when person-Agree on v is carried out, the reflexive clitic has not been bound yet, with the consequence that Agree fails. On the other hand, when the clitic moves out of the phase domain due to EF-insertion, it has already acquired valued φ-features via binding by the external argument. The two operations target the same item, the reflexive clitic pronoun, but at different derivational stages. Binding feeds EF-Agree (and, consequently, participle agreement) because it precedes it and it creates the conditions for its success. Instead, binding counterfeeds Agree on v (and, consequently, the selection of the more specific allomorph HAVE for the auxiliary), because it takes place too late to create the adequate conditions for successful valuation via Agree.

Tree (20) illustrates how binding happens after Agree on *v* has taken place, leading to failed Agree (the tree is the same as tree (24) in Chapter 3).

(20)

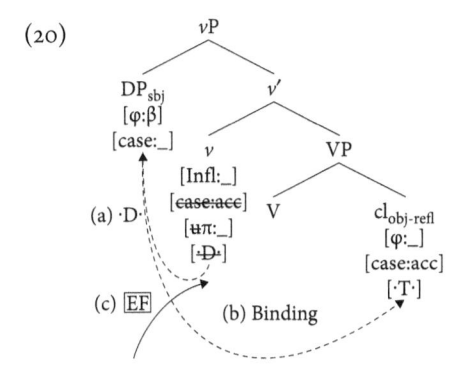

When the external argument is introduced (crucially, after π-Agree on *v*), it binds the reflexive direct object, which acquires valued φ-features. After all operations triggered by the phase head have been carried out, an edge feature is inserted because of the presence of the feature [•T•] on the object. Edge feature insertion is indicated by the external arrow in (20).

In tree (21), I only represent the three components of the edge feature on *v* and the relevant features on the DP object (in order to avoid complicated representations; see Chapter 3 for the detailed derivations). The EF agrees with the clitic via the Agree feature [u(•T•)], which targets the unvalued feature on the clitic. Then, it agrees with it for number and gender. Now *v* bears a subset of valued φ-features that will be realized by overt morphological inflection. After this step, the unvalued feature is moved to an outer Spec,*v*, pied-piping the whole DP.

(21)

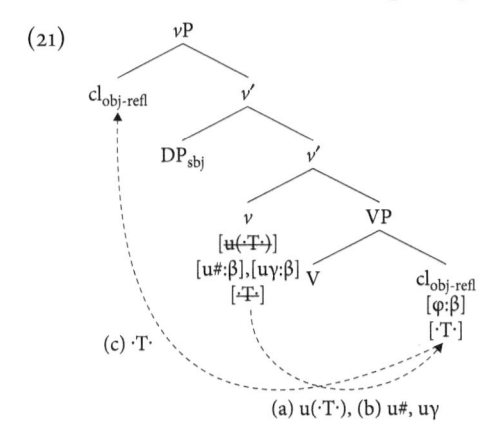

After the step in (21), the derivation proceeds exactly as for transitive clauses in Section 6.5.1 (and in Chapter 3). At Spell-out, overt gender and number inflection is realized on the past participle, since *v* has copied gender and number features from the reflexive clitic (coreferential with the DP_{sbj}) due to EF-insertion. The lexical entries responsible for participle agreement are discussed in Section 6.5.1.

6.5.3   Transitive verbs with reflexive indirect object

The same configuration as in Section 6.5.2 also arises when the reflexive clitic is merged as the indirect object with benefactive meaning. In Example (22), the participle agrees with the dative reflexive clitic in gender and number.

(22)   Teresa si=è   fatt-a   i   panini.
       Teresa REFL.DAT.3SG.F=be.PRS.3SG make.PRTC-SG.F the sandwich.PL.M
       'Teresa has made the sandwiches for herself.'

Note that in Standard Italian participle agreement with a (non-reflexive) dative argument is impossible, as (23) shows.

(23)   Teresa le=ha   fatto   i   panini.
       Teresa DAT.3SG.F=have.PRS.3SG make.PRTC the sandwich.PL.M
       'Teresa_i has made the sandwiches for her_j.'

These data illustrate that the reflexive clitic indirect object does not behave as a canonical dative argument, even though it is merged in the same position (Spec,Appl), it bears dative case and it can be substituted by a prepositional dative (with the relevant changes in position, auxiliary selection, and participle agreement: *Teresa ha fatto i panini a/per se stessa* 'Teresa has made the sandwiches to/ for herself'). The fact that the reflexive clitic controls participle agreement might be due to its "light structure". In fact, it has been proposed that the dative argument is encapsulated under a K(P)-shell, which prevents it from being the controller of agreement (Rezac 2004; Atlamaz & Baker 2018; Coon & Keine 2020). Reflexive clitics might lack the K(P)-shell, perhaps because they need to be bound (or because maybe they do not need case).

As proposed in Section 3.3.3 of Chapter 3, the reflexive clitic pronoun is introduced by an applicative head. The ApplP is selected by a quirky v, which assigns dative case to the clitic and copies its π-feature, which is still unvalued because the clitic has not been bound yet. Subsequently, v introduces the external argument that binds the reflexive indirect object. Now the reflexive pronoun has acquired valued φ-features, but it is too late for successful agreement on v, since Agree has already been carried out. After this operation, there is still an unchecked feature in the complement of v, namely the [•T•] feature on the reflexive clitic. Therefore, an EF is inserted on the phase head, as the external arrow in (24) shows.

(24)

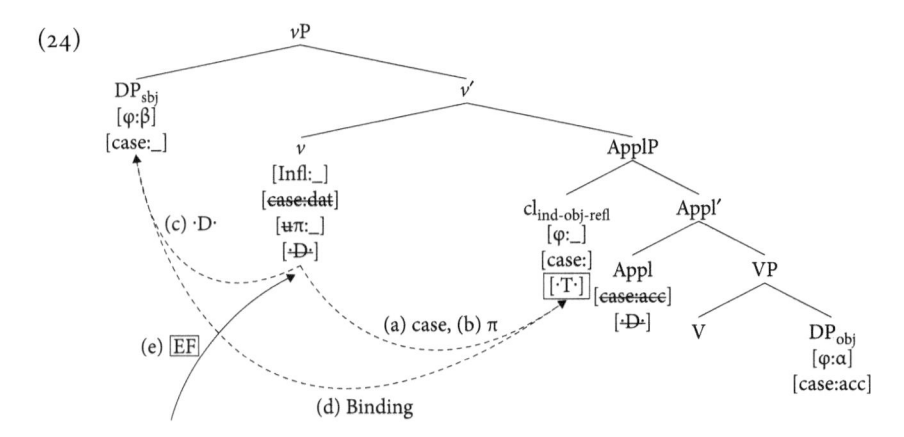

The edge feature agrees with the head bearing the unchecked feature, it copies the relevant subset of φ-features from that head (which now bears valued φ-features after binding) and it moves it to an outer specifier, as tree (25) shows. At Spell-out, the gender and number features on *v* will be overtly realized as inflectional morphology on the participle.

(25)

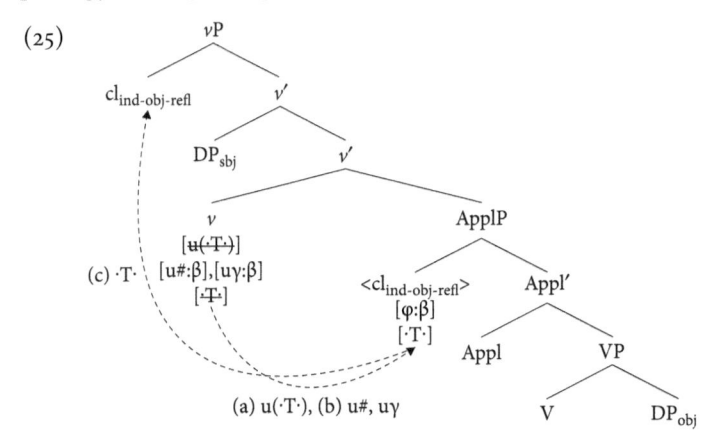

6.5.4 Transitive verbs with multiple clitics

In this section, I discuss cases where both the direct object and the indirect object are clitic pronouns. The relevant examples contain a benefactive dative argument in the form of a reflexive clitic, and a clitic direct object, as in (26).

(26) a. Teresa se=li=è   mangiat-i.
         Teresa REFL.DAT.3SG.F=ACC.3PL.M=be.PRS.3SG eat.PRTC-PL.M
         'Teresa has eaten them for/by herself.'

b. *Teresa se=li=è mangiat-a.
Teresa REFL.DAT.3SG.F=ACC.3PL.M=be.PRS.3SG eat.PRTC-SG.F
'Teresa has eaten them for/by herself.'

As (26) shows, past participle inflection is controlled by the DP that has moved last (i.e., the direct object). It is not a specific combination of person and number features that favors one set over the other one, but it is their syntactic position. In the case of multiple clitics, it is always the features of the object, or of the last moved element, that are morphologically realized.

The question is how the conflict between two different sets of φ-features (one coming from the accusative clitic, one from the dative reflexive clitic) is resolved. I propose that this is due to the presence of a single EF and to the featural make-up of edge features. Recall that an edge feature contains a set of ordered features, as illustrated in (6), repeated here in (27).

(27)   EF: [uF] > [u#], [uγ] > [•F•]

The Agree component [uF] and the φ-probes are ordered in such a way that φ-Agree must target the lowest item. I will now explain the proposal in detail.

I argue that only a single EF is inserted when there is more than one unchecked A-feature in the complement of the phase head. This is a generic EF for A-movement, EF_A, which deals with all instances of unchecked A-features in its c-command domain. Crucially, the EF can be used multiple times: it can agree with multiple goals and move multiple items (cf. *Multiple Agree*, Hiraiwa 2005; Nevins 2011; Deal 2015). Once an EF is inserted, it scans the whole c-command domain without stopping at the highest matching feature. For example, the EF inserted for the unchecked feature [•T•] can and must be used for all the instances of [•T•] that are c-commanded by the EF. The intuition behind this idea is that the function of the Agree-component [uF] of the EF is to ensure that all unchecked features are removed from the phase domain.

The derivation for clause (26a) is represented in the next trees. In (28), the complement of *v* contains two items with an unchecked [•T•] feature: the indirect object in Spec,Appl and the direct object in Comp,V. A single EF is inserted, as the external arrow in (28) indicates.

(28)

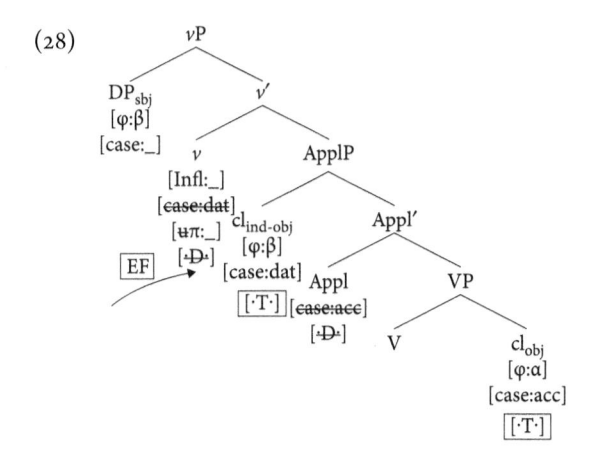

The Agree-probe [u(•T•)] of the EF undergoes Multiple Agree, as shown in tree (29) (I have omitted the features that are not crucial here). First of all, it targets the higher clitic, as minimality prescribes (arrow 1a). Then, it goes on and reaches the lower clitic, too (arrow 1b). The search domain is now exhausted, with the consequence that the Agree-component of the EF must stop. At this point, the φ-probe of the EF must be discharged. Due to Nested Agree, it must target the last checked goal, which is the lower clitic. The higher clitic lies outside the domain of this probe, instead. The EF only copies the φ-features of the lower item (arrow 2). Hence, the application of Nested Agree to the components of the EF derives the fact that it is always the lowest item that controls participle agreement, without assuming any kind of overwriting mechanism.

(29)

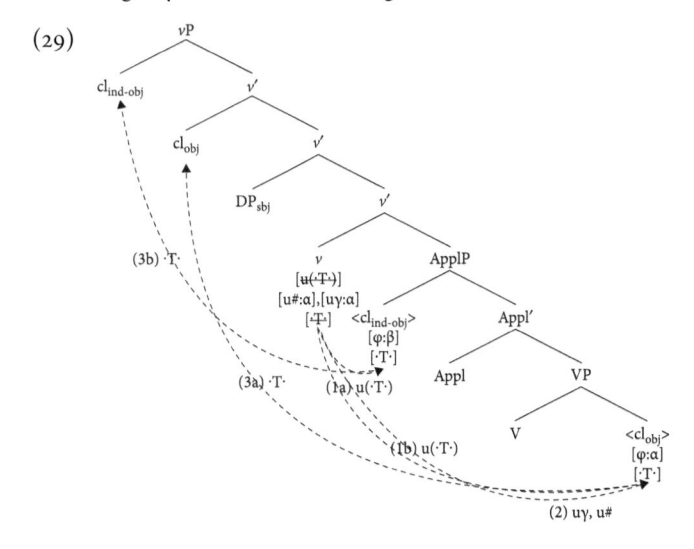

Thereafter, the Merge feature of the EF must be discharged. Due to Nested Agree, it has to start its search from the last probed item, which is the lower clitic. Hence, the [•T•] component of the EF moves the lower clitic to the outer specifier of v (arrow 3a in tree (29)). Now the last checked position is Spec,v. The downward domain of the Merge feature is not exhausted. On the contrary, it has been enlarged by the operation that has created the outer Spec,v. Hence, the EF-Merge-feature on v can scan again its c-command domain starting from v (since the last stored position is Spec,v, which c-commands v). Now [•T•] continues its search and finds the higher clitic. It moves it to another outer Spec,v (arrow 3b). Again, the Merge feature restarts its downward search from v (in fact, the last position with which v has interacted is Spec,v). However, now that the two clitics have been moved there is no other matching feature in the structure. The domain is exhausted, and the EF-Merge-feature becomes inactive.[88]

The case of participle agreement with multiple clitics constitutes evidence in favor of Nested Agree. This principle offers a simple explanation for the fact that past participle agreement is always controlled by the item that is base-merged in the lower position, when there are multiple elements that could in principle control it (see also Section 6.5.5 for another example). This happens because the domain of the φ-probe on the EF is restricted to the lower clitic by the previous Agree-component of the single EF.

6.5.5   Unaccusative verbs

Unaccusative participles agree for gender and number with the internal argument, which is the surface subject, as shown in (1a), repeated here in (30).

(30)   Teresa è   uscit-a.
       Teresa be.PRS.3SG go.out.PRTC-SG.F
       'Teresa has gone out.'

---

88. In this derivation, I have considered Merge features to be subject to Nested Agree. This is true if Nested Agree constrains all ordered operations in general, including structure-building operations. Alternatively, Nested Agree can be considered as a principle that only regulates ordered instances of Agree (further research is needed to clarify this point). If Merge is not subject to Nested Agree, then the derivation is slightly different from what is represented in tree (29). After φ-Agree with the direct object, the Merge component of the EF is discharged. Firstly, it raises the indirect object, which is the highest constituent bearing the unchecked feature. Secondly, it raises the direct object to an outer specifier. In other words, the arrows (3a) and (3b) of tree (29) must be inverted in their order. The two derivations (the one where Merge is free, the one where Nested Agree constrains Merge as well) only differ for the order of the clitics in the outer specifiers of v. The respective position of the clitics can be adjusted by some linearization rules in both cases.

This is due to the defectiveness of unaccusative v, which is not a case assigner. Tree (31) shows that the unvalued case feature on the internal argument causes edge feature insertion, indicated by the external arrow.

(31)

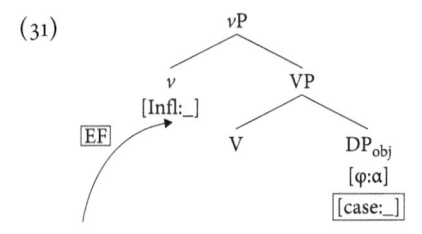

In tree (32), the EF copies the φ-features of the DP and moves it to the specifier of v. From Spec,v, the DP remains accessible for the higher case assigner T. Because of EF-insertion, v ends up bearing a value for gender and number, which will be realized by participle agreement. However, it does not bear any value for person, since it does not contain a person probe in its featural inventory. For this reason, v will not be a matching goal for person-Agree on Perf, despite the presence of the EF-related φ-feature (see Section 3.3.5 of Chapter 3 for the whole derivation).

(32)

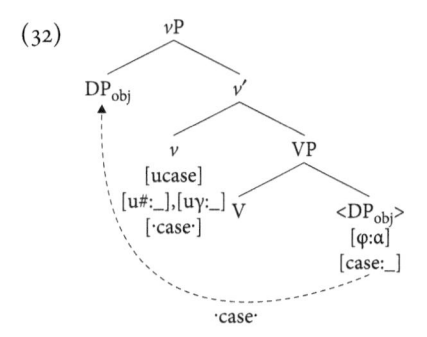

Unaccusative clauses may also contain clitic pronouns. Nominative clitic pronouns are excluded because they do not exist in Standard Italian (unlike in many Northern dialects): the unaccusative subject cannot be realized as a clitic. Given that unaccusative verbs only combine with a single argument, reflexive pronouns are excluded as arguments of these verbs (because of *Principle A*, Chomsky 1981). Accusative clitics are excluded because of the lack of accusative case from unaccusative v. The clitics that can be found here are the quantitative (partitive) *ne* 'of', the locative *ci* 'there', and the impersonal *si*. The partitive *ne* can be found with unaccusative verbs because it is related to the internal argument position (Perlmutter 1978; Burzio 1986). Similarly, the locative clitic *ci* can be an adjunct of any predicate. In addition, impersonal *si* can be the argument of any verb. Dative pronouns can also be found, as with any verb.

If one (or more) of these clitics is present in the structure, both the clitic and the nominative object move out of their base position; however, the finite verb and the participle agree with the internal argument. As Examples (33) show, participle agreement does not change in the presence of such clitics: locative (33a), partitive (33b) (cf. unaccusative postverbal subjects in Section 6.6), impersonal (33c), dative (33d).

(33)   a.   Teresa ci=è   andat-a.
            Teresa there=be.PRS.3SG go.PRTC-SG.F
            'Teresa has gone there.'
       b.   Di ragazze, ne=è   andat-a   via   una.
            of girls   of=be.PRS.3SG go.PRTC-SG.F away one.SG.F
            'Of girls, one of them has gone away.'
       c.   Si=è   arrivat-i   in anticipo.
            IMPERS=be.PRS.3SG arrive.PRTC-PL.M on early
            'People have arrived early.'
       d.   Le bambine gli=sono   scappat-e   dalla   vista.
            the children DAT.3SG.M=be.PRS.3PL run.away.PRTC-PL.F from.the sight
            'The children have run away from his sight.'

In Section 6.5.4, I have argued that only one generic EF for A-movement is inserted on a phase head, independently of the amount of unchecked A-features in the phase domain. This predicts that agreement is always controlled by the unaccusative argument, as confirmed by (33). If only a single EF_A is inserted, whenever the object must escape the phase domain, it being a clitic or an unaccusative argument, it will control participle φ-agreement.

The derivation just proposed for unaccusative verbs is also the same for quirky verbs. Example (34) contains a quirky verb in the present tense: the participle agrees with the nominative internal argument.

(34)   A Teresa   sono   piaciut-i   questi panini.
       to Teresa.DAT.3SG.F be.PRS.3PL like.PRTC-PL.M these sandwiches
       'Teresa liked these sandwiches.'

In Section 3.3.8 of Chapter 3, I have explained that the internal argument cannot receive case from v because this type of quirky v is not a case assigner. Consequently, the direct object must move to the edge of the phase v in order to remain accessible for the head T and receive nominative case. This is exactly the very same scenario as for unaccusative verbs. An EF must be inserted on v, which consequently copies the number and gender value of the moved DP. At Spell-out, an overt exponent realizes these values on v.

It is noteworthy that a sentence such as (34) shows the additional complication of the surface position of the internal argument, which seems not to have moved from its base position (this is also possible with unaccusative predicates: *è uscit-a Teresa* 'Teresa has gone out'). I will talk about this issue in Section 6.6, which deals with EF-agreement with DPs in situ.

6.5.6 Passive clauses

Example (35) shows a passive clause in the present tense and in the perfect tense.

(35) a. Teresa è   promoss-a.
         Teresa be.PRS.3SG promote.PRTC-SG.F
         'Teresa is promoted.'
      b. Teresa è   stat-a   promoss-a.
         Teresa be.PRS.3SG be.PRTC-SG.F promote.PRTC-SG.F
         'Teresa has been promoted.'

In the present tense (35a), the lexical verb appears in the form of a participle because of the feature [Infl:pass] on *v* due to the presence of passive Voice (see Section 3.3.7 of Chapter 3). Voice is a phase boundary, as shown by the presence of participle agreement. The agreeing participle is the passive participle, which has the same phonological form as an active past participle. In the perfect tense (35b), both the lexical verb and the passive auxiliary are spelled out as participles. The lexical verb shows up as a passive participle because of [Infl:pass] on *v* due to passive Voice. The passive auxiliary is realized as a past participle because of [Infl:perf] on Voice$_{pass}$ due to the presence of the head Perf.

The derivation up to VoiceP is represented in tree (36). The representation only contains the EF-components and the features relevant to participle agreement. There are two edge features because there are two phase heads, *v* and Voice$_{pass}$.

(36)

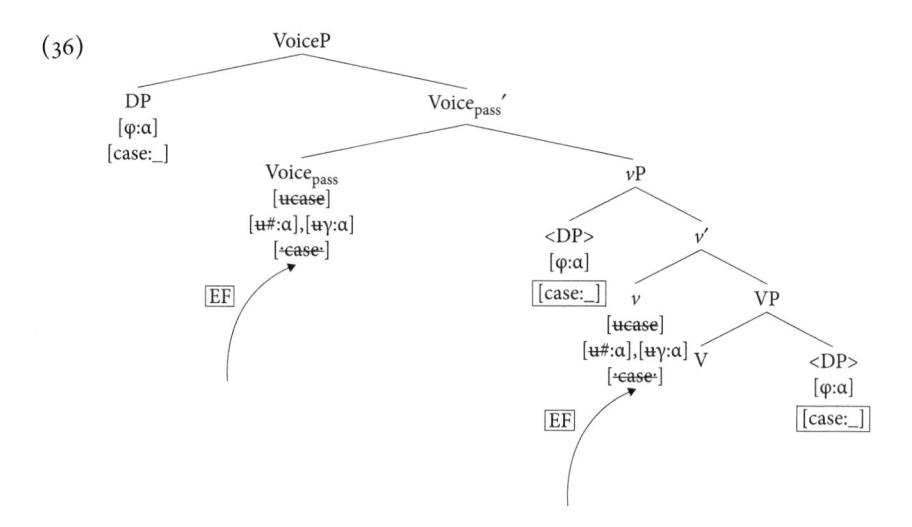

As the tree shows, the internal argument moves through Spec,v and Spec,Voice$_{\text{pass}}$ (before reaching its final landing site in Spec,T). This is because passive Voice selects for a defective v, which is not a case assigner (cf. Section 3.3.7 in Chapter 3 for details). The internal argument cannot receive case until T is merged in the structure. Therefore, it must move first to the edge of v, then to the edge of Voice$_{\text{pass}}$. This is achieved by EF-insertion first on v and then on Voice. Both edge features copy the number and gender feature of the internal argument. Gender and number inflection is realized on both participles, as Example (35b) shows. This is due to a Vocabulary Item as in (37), which is a generalization of the metarule proposed in (17), where v stands both for v and Voice (assuming that their categorical feature is the same), and [Infl] can be valued either as *pass* or as *perf*.

(37)   /participle agreement for α/ ↔ v[Infl:pass/perf],[γ:α],[#:α]

6.5.7   Impersonal clauses

Moving on to impersonal clauses, I refer the reader to Section 3.3.9.2 of Chapter 3 for the detailed derivations. Here I will only focus on participle agreement.

If the predicate is a transitive verb two scenarios are possible: in (38a), the participle does not show agreement and the finite verb is in third person singular, while in (38b) both the finite verb and the past participle agree with the internal argument.

(38) a. Si=è   mangiato gli spaghetti.
          IMPERS=be.PRS.3SG eat.PRTC the spaghetti
      b. Si=sono   mangiat-i   gli spaghetti.
          IMPERS=be.PRS.3PL eat.PRTC-PL.M the spaghetti
          'People have eaten the spaghetti.'

In Section 3.3.9.1 of Chapter 3, I have argued that this distinction comes about by means of two possible derivations: Voice$_{impers}$ may select either a transitive v or a defective v. I have proposed that cases without agreement (38a) can be explained by assuming a transitive v. If v is non-defective, it assigns accusative to the internal argument, with the consequence that no EF is needed and no participle agreement arises (unless the object is a clitic, as is expected: *la=si=è mangiat-a* 'one has eaten it(sg.f)'). In addition, the impersonal clitic *si* is introduced by v. Although it moves to the finite verb, there is no need for EF-insertion because the clitic is raised by the [•D•] feature on Voice$_{impers}$. So there is no participle agreement with either the object or the impersonal clitic.

In contrast, cases with participle agreement (38b) are due to a defective v that does not assign case to the internal argument, leading to EF-insertion. This is the very same situation as for passive predicates. Given the presence of an unchecked case feature in the complement of v, an edge feature must be inserted. This EF copies the gender and number features of the internal argument, which will be spelled out as participle agreement. In this derivation, the impersonal *si* is introduced in Spec,Voice$_{impers}$. Since there are no phase boundaries between Spec,Voice$_{impers}$ and T, its movement does not require any EF insertion.

Participle agreement in impersonal clauses with unaccusative verbs, shown in (39), can be explained in the very same way.

(39) Si=è   partit-i   presto.
      IMPERS=be.PRS.3SG leave.PRTC-PL.M early
      'People have left early.'

In impersonal unaccusatives, the impersonal clitic *si* is base-merged in the internal argument position. The only possible v is defective (because unaccusative verbal roots cannot combine with a full argument structure v). The clitic *si* in the internal argument position bears the unchecked [•T•] and [case] features. Hence, an EF must be inserted on v, giving rise to participle agreement. The impersonal clitic bears an unvalued person feature, but its number is valued as plural (cf. Section 3.2.6.2 in Chapter 3). This is why the inflection on the participle is plural (while both gender values are possible: the sentence *si=è partit-e presto* 'one(pl.f) has left early' is uttered when the impersonal pronoun refers to a female group).

6.6   Participle agreement in the absence of overt movement

As I have already highlighted throughout this chapter, there are some cases where participle agreement does not seem to originate from A-movement. In such sentences, the argument that controls agreement apparently remains in its base position. For example, the unaccusative subject can surface in the object position, and still trigger participle agreement, as (40a) shows. Another case is the impersonal transitive clause in (40b), where the participle agrees with the object in its base position. Similarly, the same configuration can arise with quirky verbs, as mentioned in Section 6.5.5, and in passive clauses (cf. Section 6.5.6).[89]

(40) a. Sono   arrivat-e   le ragazze.
          be.PRS.3PL arrive.PRTC-PL.F the girls
          'There have the girls arrived.'
      b. Si=sono   cucinat-e   le lasagne.
          IMPERS=be.PRS.3PL cook.PRTC-PL.F the lasagne
          'People have cooked the lasagne.'

Note that the in situ position of the internal argument constitutes a problem not only for participle agreement, but also for case assignment and agreement on the finite verb. In (40), the finite auxiliary in T agrees with the nominative object in situ. This should not be possible under the phase theory, which makes the internal argument position opaque for operations triggered by heads that are higher than the phase head *v*.

If the participle may agree with the object in situ, two hypotheses are possible. Either participle agreement is not due to EF, or an EF is involved but it does not seem to move the DP. If participle agreement is not due to EF, then another theory of participle agreement must be developed, such that it is able to distinguish a pattern in (40a) from agreement with a transitive object in situ (which is ungrammatical). In Section 6.3, I have already highlighted the flaws of previous analyses

---

89. A further case of participle agreement with in situ constituents is found in reduced clauses, as in (i).

(i) Mangiat-i   gli spaghetti, le ragazze uscirono.
     eat.PRTC-PL.M the spaghetti the girls   go.out.PST.3PL
     'Having eaten the spaghetti, the girls went out.'

I tentatively suggest that participle agreement in reduced clauses is not due to edge features, but rather to a φ-probe on C, as suggested by data from languages such as Spanish, where participle agreement is normally excluded, but it is instead found in reduced clauses. Nonetheless, their structure must also be defective in order to explain other properties, such as the restrictions on argument realizations. Since the syntactic structure of reduced clauses is quite controversial (Belletti 1990, 2017; D'Alessandro & Roberts 2008), I leave this case out of the discussion.

of participle agreement and the reasons for providing a new theory, which must be compatible with auxiliary selection. Hence, I will not take this route.

I argue that participle agreement in sentences where the controller DP seems not to have moved is due to edge feature insertion, exactly as in other cases with overt DP A-movement. Evidence in favor of this claim comes from the fact that sentences such as those in (40) behave as sentences with DP movement, as I will discuss in Section 6.6.1. For participle agreement with postverbal controllers as in (40), I propose an account in terms of covert movement. The postverbal DP in (40) triggers past participle agreement because it moves to Spec,v (although covertly), where it remains accessible to T. I adopt the copy-theory of covert movement (Nissenbaum 2000; Bobaljik 2002, 2008; Amaechi & Georgi 2020).[90] Movement leaves copies behind that are available both to LF and PF. Covert movement is the Spell-out of the lower copy (and PF-deletion of the higher one). This is represented in (41).

(41) <Maria> arriva <Maria>   'Maria arrives.'
 a.   Maria arriva ~~Maria.~~   (overt movement)
 b.   ~~Maria~~ arriva Maria.   (covert movement)

Optionality between the structures in (41) arises at PF, where either the lowest copy or the topmost copy is pronounced.[91]

Hence, the cases in (40) do not constitute an exception to the implicational relation between A-movement and participle agreement proposed in (2), repeated here again (and updated with the possibility of covert movement).

(42) a.   A-movement (either overt or covert) → Agree
 b.   no Agree → no A-movement (either overt or covert)

---

90. It has also been proposed that some instances of A-movement can happen at LF rather than in narrow syntax, in the same way as covert Ā-movement does (Polinsky & Potsdam 2013). I do not adopt the LF-theory of covert movement because covert movement must feed overt participle agreement. Hence, it must happen in syntax (unless Agree is post-syntactic, but I do not adopt this view).

91. There is a remaining question about which copy must be spelled out. Amaechi & Georgi (2020: 320) have shown that in Igbo there is a (non-perfect) correlation between focus position and focus interpretation: in situ focus encodes new information, ex situ focus expresses additional pragmatic meaning. This means that PF can be influenced by semantic-pragmatic factors (Bobaljik 2002: 251). Perhaps a similar explanation can be given for Italian participle agreement. One of the relevant factors for the choice of the copy to spell out is the new vs. discourse-given status of the DP (Bianchi & Chesi 2014; Schaefer 2020). In particular, there is a (non-perfect) correlation between subject position and pragmatic force. If the DP is discourse-linked, it tends to be uttered preverbally; if it is discourse-new, it should be pronounced postverbally (Schaefer 2020: 8).

If the participle agrees with the DP, the DP must have moved from its base position, even when the result of movement is not visible from the surface word order (because the lower copy is spelled out at PF).

For Ā-movement, analyses along these lines have been proposed in Bruening (2001) as an account of past participle agreement in Passamaquoddy, and Amaechi & Georgi (2020) for focus in Igbo, among others. For A-movement, Cardinaletti (1997) has argued that case assignment and finite agreement with the postverbal DP_{obj} is possible if the DP covertly moves to a preverbal position. According to Cardinaletti (1997: 532), covert movement is triggered as a last resort operation by the head T that needs to discharge its features. This movement can be either overt, as in sentences with preverbal subjects, or covert, as in sentences with postverbal subjects (in this case, Spec,T is occupied by an expletive pro that remains underspecified for case). Evidence for covert movement comes from the ability of the postverbal DP to control the subject PRO of an adjunct clause. In Example (43), the postverbal subject can control into the adjunct clause. Hence, the DP must be located in a higher position than its Merge position, since control requires c-command of PRO.

(43) Sono   entrat-i   due uomini$_i$ [PRO$_i$ senza   neanche
      be.PRS.3PL enter.PRTC-PL.M two men   without even
      identificar=si].   (Cardinaletti 1997: 524)
      identify.INF=REFL.ACC.3PL.M
      'Two men have entered without even identifying themselves.'

6.6.1 Tests for the position of the DP

I now present some tests to identify the real position of the unaccusative subject and the internal argument of impersonal clauses in sentences as (40). The results are summarized in Table 6.1. The postverbal subject of passive clauses and quirky clauses behaves as the postverbal subject of unaccusative clauses.

Table 6.1 Tests for DP movement

	transitive object	unaccusative subject	impersonal object
control	no	yes	yes?
binding	no	yes	yes?
quantifier scope	no	yes	yes?
quantifier floating	no	yes	yes?

These tests suggest that a postverbal DP that controls participle agreement is located at least in Spec,v. This is the reason why past participle agreement emerges.

6.6.1.1 *Control of PRO inside an adjunct clause*

The first test is control into an infinitival adjunct clause. The adjoined clause is merged at the vP level, if not higher, at least in case of adjuncts introduced by the prepositions *senza, prima, dopo* 'without, before, after' (cf. Nissenbaum 1998, 2000; Sheehan 2010; Narita 2011; Brown 2016 for the correlation between the extractability from adjuncts and their Merge position). Independently of the exact base position of the adjunct, it will be in any case higher than the base position of the DP$_{obj}$ (which is Comp, V). If the object can control PRO, it means that it c-commands it, since control requires c-command.[92]

The direct object of a transitive verb cannot control a PRO within an adjunct, as Example (44) shows. This is expected, since the object of a transitive verb does not have any reason to move to a higher position (unless focused).

(44)   Teresa$_j$ ha   rimproverato Paolo$_i$ [PRO$_{j/*i}$ prima di andare a casa].
       Teresa have.PRS.3SG scold.PRTC   Paolo   before of go.INF at home
       'Teresa has scolded Paolo before going home.'

In unaccusative clauses with in situ argument, the DP in its surface position is too low to control PRO in an adjunct: it is expected to behave as the transitive object in (44). In contrast, the unaccusative subject can control PRO in the adjunct clause even when it is in the postverbal position, as (45a) shows (see also Cardinaletti (1997: 524) for similar data on control). Control from the preverbal position (45b) is also possible, as expected.

(45)   a.   [PRO$_i$ prima di chiedere il   permesso] è   entrat-a
                 before of ask.INF   the permission be.PRS.3SG enter.PRTC-SG.F
             Teresa$_i$ nella stanza.
             Teresa in.the room
       b.   [PRO$_i$ prima di chiedere il   permesso] Teresa$_i$ è
                 before of ask.INF   the permission Teresa be.PRS.3SG
             entrat-a   nella stanza.
             enter.PRTC-SG.F in.the room
             'Teresa has entered the room before having asked for permission.'

---

92. Note, however, that it has been argued that PRO in adjuncts must be controlled by the matrix subject and not by the object (Boeckx, Hornstein, & Nunes 2010). This would independently explain the data in (45) where the controller is the matrix subject, although it is base-merged as an object.

This means that in sentence (45a) (and (40a)) the unaccusative subject must be located at least in Spec,v, high enough to control into the adjunct clause.

The same can be said for impersonal clauses with object agreement, as (40b). The object of the impersonal clause in (46a) can control PRO. Hence, it is higher in the structure than it seems to be: it occupies at least Spec,v. The same happens if the object overtly moves, as in (46b). The argument *si* can also control participle agreement (46c).

(46) a. #Si=sono   chiamati   i   genitori$_i$ [PRO$_i$ prima di essere
             IMPERS=be.PRS.3PL call.PRTC-PL.M the parents   before of be.INF
             pronti dalla riunione].
             ready of.the meeting
      b. #I   genitori$_i$ si=sono   chiamati   [PRO$_i$ prima di essere
             the parents IMPERS=be.PRS.3PL call.PRTC-PL.M   before of be.INF
             pronti dalla riunione].
             ready of.the meeting
             'People have called the parents before being ready from the meeting.'
      c. #Si$_j$=sono   chiamat-i   i   genitori$_i$ [PRO$_j$ prima di essere
             IMPERS=be.PRS.3PL call.PRTC-PL.M the parents   before of be.INF
             pronti da   scuola].
             ready from school
             'People have called the parents before being ready from school.'

Note that these sentences are subject to speaker variation, as the symbol # indicates. In general, the tests provided in this section do not give clear results for impersonal. Further research is needed to explore the structure of these clauses. Nonetheless, there is always a neat contrast between impersonal clauses with and without object agreement. In contrast to (46), object control inside the adjunct is always excluded in impersonal clauses without object agreement.

(47) a. *[PRO$_i$ prima di essere completamente cotti], si=è
             before of be.INF completely   cooked IMPERS=be.PRS.3SG
             mangiato gli spaghetti$_i$.
             eat.PRTC the spaghetti
      b. *Si=è   mangiato gli spaghetti$_i$ [PRO$_i$ prima di essere
             IMPERS=be.PRS.3SG eat.PRTC the spaghetti   before of be.INF
             completamente cotti].
             completely   cooked
             'People have eaten the spaghetti before they were completely cooked.'

To sum up, the postverbal DP that agrees with the participle can control PRO in the infinitival adjunct clause. Hence, even when the DP surfaces in the postverbal position, it has moved out of its base position, as participle agreement indeed shows.

6.6.1.2 *Anaphoric binding*

The second test is binding of possessives. Since a condition for binding is c-command, if the internal argument can successfully bind an anaphor, then there must have been a derivational step in which the DP_{obj} was higher in the structure than the anaphor. Since the DP_{obj} is base-merged in Comp, V, it must have moved from the base position in order to be higher than the anaphor. The transitive object cannot bind an anaphor (48a), unless it moves to a higher position (48b).

(48) a. Teresa$_i$ ha   sgridato   [al posto di suo$_{i,j,*z}$ padre] la
          Teresa have.PRS.3SG scold.PRTC at place of POSS.SG.M father the
          bambina$_z$.
          child
          'Teresa$_i$ has scolded the child$_z$ instead of her$_{i,j,*z}$ father.'

      b. Teresa$_i$ ha   sgridato   la bambina$_z$ [al posto di suo$_{i,j,z}$
          Teresa have.PRS.3SG scold.PRTC-SG.F the child   at place of POSS.SG.M
          padre].
          father
          'Teresa$_i$ has scolded the child$_z$ instead of her$_{i,j,z}$ father.'

Example (49) show that the unaccusative postverbal subject can bind an anaphor from both positions.[93]

---

93. Cardinaletti (1997) provides an example where the unaccusative subject in the postverbal position cannot bind an anaphor, despite overt or covert raising.

(i) a.$^{?(?)}$[Alcuni studenti]$_i$ sembrano   [gli uni agli   altri]$_i$ essere arrivati   in
        some   students seem.PRS.3PL the ones to.the others be.INF arrive.PRTC-PL.M late
        ritardo.

     b. *Sembrano   [gli uni agli   altri]$_i$ essere arrivati   [alcuni studenti]$_i$
         seem.PRS.3PL the ones to.the others be.INF arrive.PRTC-PL.M some   students
         in ritardo.
         late
         'Some students seem to each other to have arrived late.'   (Cardinaletti 1997: 526)

Example (i) contains an intervening dative: raising across a coindexed experiencer should be prohibited by minimality. This might be the relevant problem here, also in light of the well-formed Example (49).

(49) a.   Teresa$_i$ è   sfuggit-a   di vista [a suo$_{i/j}$ padre].
           Teresa be.PRS.3SG get.out.PRTC-SG.F of sight to POSS.SG.M father
      b.   È   sfuggit-a   di vista [a suo$_{i/j}$ padre] Teresa$_i$.
           be.PRS.3SG get.out.PRTC-SG.F of sight to POSS.SG.M father Teresa
           'Teresa$_i$ has slipped out of her$_{i/j}$ father's sight.'

Hence, the unaccusative subject has moved at least to Spec,v (probably not to
Spec, T, see Panagiotidis & Tsiplakou 2006).

   Examples (50a,b) show that the object of an impersonal clause with agreement can bind a higher anaphor, whereas this is not possible for the object of an
impersonal clause without agreement (50c). Again, these data are subject to some
speaker variation.

(50) a.   #Si=sono   giudicat-e   [per la loro$_i$ performance] tre
           IMPERS=be.PRS.3PL judge.PRTC-PL.F for   the POSS.SG.F performance three
           macchine$_i$.
           cars
      b.   #Tre   macchine$_i$ si=sono   giudicat-e   [per la loro$_i$
           three cars   IMPERS=be.PRS.3PL judge.PRTC-PL.F for   the POSS.SG.F
           performance].
           performance
      c.   # *Si=è   giudicato   [per la loro$_i$ performance] tre
           IMPERS=be.PRS.3SG judge.PRTC-PL.F for   the POSS.SG.F performance three
           macchine$_i$.
           cars
           'People have judged three cars for their performance.'

To sum up, a postverbal DP that can bind an anaphor must have moved out of its
base position. Therefore, participle agreement is expected as a consequence.

6.6.1.3 *Quantifier scope interactions*

The third test concerns scope interactions between quantifiers. If an inverse scope
reading is available next to the surface scope reading, it means that the respective
positions of the quantifiers are inverted at a relevant step in the derivation, and
the quantifier that is higher on the surface can reconstruct to a lower position.
With transitive objects, only the surface scope is available, as shown in (51a). In
the presence of an indirect object, both readings are only available if the direct
object moves above the indirect object, as in (51c), but not if it remains in its base
position, as in (51b).

(51) a.   Ogni ragazza ha   letto   una poesia.   ∀>∃; *∃>∀
           each girl   have.PRS.3SG read.PRTC a   poem
           'Each girl has read a poem.'

b. Ho   presentato   a un insegnante ogni ragazza.   ∃>∀; *∀>∃
   have.PRS.1SG introduce.PRTC to a   teacher   every girl
   'I have introduced to a teacher every girl.'

c. Ho   presentato   ogni ragazza a un insegnante.   ∀>∃; ∃>∀
   have.PRS.1SG introduce.PRTC every girl   to a   teacher
   'I have introduced every girl to a teacher.'

Instead, both readings are available with an unaccusative postverbal subject, as Example (52) illustrates.

(52) a. Ogni ragazza è   andat-a   da un insegnante.   ∀>∃; ∃>∀
        every girl   be.PRS.3SG go.PRTC-SG.F to a   teacher
        'Every girl has gone to a teacher.'

     b. È   andat-a   da un insegnante ogni ragazza.   ∀>∃; ∃>∀
        be.PRS.3SG go.PRTC-SG.F to a   teacher   every girl
        'Every girl has gone to a teacher.'

The availability of both readings in (52b) shows that the postverbal subject is covertly located in a higher position from where it c-commands the prepositional phrase. In particular, the subject covertly moves to Spec,v, but not up to Spec, T. This is confirmed by the fact that the availability of both readings disappears with negation (Bianchi & Chesi 2014: 539), as shown in (53).

(53) a. Ogni panno non è   caduto.   ∀>¬; *¬>∀
        every laundry not be.PRS.3SG fall.PRTC
        'Every laundry has not fallen down.'

     b. Non è   caduto   ogni panno.   ¬>∀; *∀>¬
        not be.PRS.3SG fall.PRTC every laundry
        'Not every laundry has fallen down.'

As far as impersonal clauses are concerned, both readings are possible when the impersonal object that controls agreement occupies the subject position (54a). When it is in the direct object position, the availability of the inverse scope reading is not straightforward and, at least for some speakers, it is out (54b). The inverse scope reading is ungrammatical for the clause without object agreement (54c), meaning that neither the object nor one of its copies is located in a position above the PP.

(54) a. #Ogni chiave si=è   dat-a   a un proprietario.
        every key   IMPERS=be.PRS.3SG give.PRTC-SG.F to a   owner
        'People have given every key to an owner.'   ∃>∀; ∀>∃

     b. #Si=è   dat-a   a un proprietario ogni chiave.
        IMPERS=be.PRS.3SG give.PRTC-SG.F to a   owner   every key
        'People have given every key to an owner.'   ∃>∀; ?∀>∃

    c. #Si=è   dato   a un proprietario ogni chiave.   ∃>∀; *∀>∃
        IMPERS=be.PRS.3SG give.PRTC to a   owner   every key
        'One has given every key to an owner.'

However, judgments are not very coherent. For this reason, no conclusive evidence for impersonal clauses can be drawn from this test.

6.6.1.4 *Quantifier floating*

DP movement may also be indicated by quantifier floating. When a DP that contains a quantifier moves, the quantifier can be left behind in one of the positions that have been occupied by the DP along the movement path. Transitive objects do not allow for quantifier floating: this is because the direct object does not move.

(55) a. Vorrei   che Teresa avesse   mangiato tutti gli
           want.COND.PRS.1SG that Teresa have.CONJ.PST.3PL eat.PRTC all   the
           spaghetti.
           spaghetti
    b. *Vorrei   che Teresa avesse   tutti mangiato   gli
           want.COND.PRS.1SG that Teresa have.CONJ.PST.3PL all   eat.PRTC-PL.M the
           spaghetti.
           spaghetti
           'I would like that Teresa has eaten all the spaghetti.'

With unaccusative arguments, the quantifier *tutti* can be located in a higher position when the DP is spelled out postverbally, as shown in (56)

(56) a. Vorrei   che fossero   venut-i   tutti i
           want.COND.PRS.1SG that be.CONJ.PST.3PL come.PRTC-PL.M all   the
           figli   di Maria.
           children of Maria
    b. Vorrei   che fossero   tutti venut-i   i
           want.COND.PRS.1SG that be.CONJ.PST.3PL all   come.PRTC-PL.M the
           figli   di Maria.
           children of Maria
           'I would like that all children of Maria have come.'

In (56), the DP has covertly moved to Spec,v, leaving there the stranded quantifier in (56b).

    Once again, impersonals do not behave so clearly, at least for some speakers.

(57) a. Vorrei   che si=fossero   mangiat-i   tutti gli
  want.COND.PRS.1SG that IMPERS=be.CONJ.PST.3PL eat.PRTC-PL.M all   the
  spaghetti.
  spaghetti

  b. #?Vorrei   che si=fossero   tutti mangiat-i   gli
  want.COND.PRS.1SG that IMPERS=be.CONJ.PST.3PL all   eat.PRTC-PL.M the
  spaghetti.
  spaghetti
  'I would like that people have eaten all the spaghetti.'

Quantifier floating has also been used by Georgi & Stark (2020: 23) to show that in French postverbal subjects that trigger participle agreement are really in situ.

(58) a. Je   voudrais   que soient   inscrit-s   tous les
  NOM.1SG want.COND.PRS.1SG that be.CONJ.PST.3PL enrol.PRTC-PL all   the
  enfants   de Marie.
  children of Marie

  b. *Je   voudrais   que soient   tous inscrit-s   les
  NOM.1SG want.COND.PRS.1SG that be.CONJ.PST.3PL all   enrol.PRTC-PL the
  enfants   de Marie.
  children of Marie
  'I would like that all children of Marie are enrolled.'

This claim is also supported by quantifier scope interactions. The narrow scope reading is preferred with postverbal subjects (Georgi & Stark 2020: 23).

(59) a. Une éprouve sera   présenté-e   à chaque candidate.   ∃>∀; ∀>∃
  a   test   be.FUT.3SG present.PRTC-SG.F to each   candidate
  'A test will be presented to each candidate.'

  b. À chaque candidate sera   présenté-e   une éprouve. ∃>∀; ??∀>∃
  to each   candidate be.FUT.3SG present.PRTC-SG.F a   test
  'Each candidate will be presented a test'

Based on these data, it can be concluded that in French postverbal subjects do not move covertly. In French, participle agreement may be due to another mechanism and not to edge features. For instance, Georgi & Stark (2020) propose as an independent probe on v, and I also suggest something similar for other languages with various patterns of participle agreement (see Section 6.7.2).

6.6.1.5 *Short scrambling impossible*

An interesting point is illustrated with a test that seems to show that the DP does not move: short scrambling. If the postverbal unaccusative subject moves to Spec,v (either overtly or covertly), then it should be possible to find sentences where adverbials that generally show up before the object can be located after the object. However, this does not seem to be the case.

In Italian, the active past participle moves above the position of the low adverbs tutto 'all' and bene 'well' (Cinque 1999:147). The adverb bene should be located in a lower position than Spec,v. In fact, in canonical transitive clauses bene can precede or follow the direct object (60). I take object movement in (60b) to be short Ā-scrambling.

(60) Transitive clause: bene > DP, DP > bene
    a. Teresa ha   fatto   bene i   conti.
        Teresa have.PRS.3SG do.PRCT well the counts
    b. Teresa ha   fatto   i   conti bene.
        Teresa have.PRS.3SG do.PRCT the counts well
        'Teresa has done the counts well.'

Quite surprisingly, in unaccusative clauses with postverbal subject the subject has to follow the adverbial bene and cannot scramble across it.

(61) bene>DP; *DP>bene
    a. Sono   arrivat-e   bene le ragazze.
        be.PRS.3PL arrive.PRCT-PL.F well the girls
    b. *Sono   arrivat-e   le ragazze bene.
        be.PRS.3PL arrive.PRCT-PL.F the girls   well
        'The girls have arrived well.'

A similar fact can be observed with impersonal clauses. Although judgments are subject to some speaker variation, short scrambling is non-fully grammatical, as shown in (62).

(62) Impersonal with object in situ: bene>DP, ??DP>bene
    a. Si=sono   fatt-i   bene i   conti.
        IMPERS=be.PRS.3PL do.PRCT-PL.M well the counts
    b. ??Si=sono   fatti   i   conti bene.
        IMPERS=be.PRS.3PL do.PRCT-PL.M the counts well
        'People have done the counts well.'

There are two possible explanations for this fact. A first possibility is that short scrambling is blocked because of improper movement (Chomsky 1973). Short scrambling cannot take place because it would bleed covert movement: once the DP is located in the scrambling landing site, which is an Ā-position, it cannot further move to an A-position, even if it does so covertly.

Alternatively, the problem might concern Spell-out. In the copy-theory of covert movement, the lower copy of the moved DP is phonetically realized. The ungrammaticality of the order DP>Adv in these examples can be explained if only the lower copy of the subject can be pronounced, ruling out (61b) and (62b). This means that in Italian either the copy in the landing position is spelled out (overt movement), or the copy in the Merge position (covert movement), and no other intermediate position is available for Spell-Out.

6.7   Participle agreement in other Italo-Romance varieties

In Italo-Romance, and in Romance in general, participle agreement is subject to much variation. Four main patterns of participle agreement are found: (i) the edge feature-agreement type, (ii) the object-agreement type, with some further variation that eventually gives rise to subject agreement, (iii) the clitic-agreement type, (iv) the non-agreement type. Each of these types can occur with each type of auxiliary selection (see Section 6.9 for a summary). I will now briefly discuss these options.

6.7.1   The edge-feature-type

There are languages where participle agreement behaves as in Standard Italian: it is related to unchecked features and can be modeled with edge features. A language of this type might be French (at least in unaccusative clauses; but see Georgi & Stark 2020 for an alternative analysis). Another example is the variety spoken in Soazza (Switzerland) (Manzini & Savoia 2005: II: 620, Manzini & Savoia 2007: 182). In this variety, past participle agreement is as Italian. The only difference is that it is optional in reflexive clauses. Similar varieties are also found in Veneto (Kayne 1993; Loporcaro 1998) and Friuli (Benincà 1985) (see Section 5.7.2 in Chapter 5).[94]

The Italian type of participle agreement is also found in languages where auxiliary selection is mixed (argument-structure-driven, plus additional person restrictions, see Section 5.5 of Chapter 5). Examples are the varieties of Ortezzano (Marche) (Manzini & Savoia 2005: II: 682) and Servigliano (Marche) (Loporcaro 1998: 103–108). Participle agreement exactly patterns as in Italian: with unaccusative subjects, with reflexive pronouns, with clitics, but not with non-clitic

---

94. The optionality of participle agreement in reflexive clauses within a single language can be explained by means of two series of reflexive pronouns in the lexicon: one with default features, one with unvalued features. When the reflexive pronoun in the object position is marked as default 3rd person masculine, participle agreement is not realized at vocabulary insertion because there is no vocabulary entry specified for default features. When the reflexive pronoun enters the derivation with unvalued φ-features, participle agreement realizes the φ-features that the reflexive pronoun has newly acquired via binding. See Section 5.7.2 of Chapter 5.

arguments of transitive verbs. This fact can be considered as further evidence for treating mixed systems as argument-structure-driven varieties rather than as subject-driven varieties. Note that in these languages overt participle agreement does not always correlate with the auxiliary BE. For instance, for transitive verbs with 1st and 2nd person subjects the auxiliary is BE (the pattern is BBH), but the participle does not agree with any argument (unless the direct object is a clitic or a reflexive pronoun).

This type of participle agreement is quite rare in subject-driven varieties. In general, these languages tend to exhibit the object-agreement type, with participle agreement with the direct object. Potential examples of languages with subject-driven auxiliary selection and edge-feature-type of participle agreement are the dialects of Pescocostanzo (Abruzzo) (Manzini & Savoia 2005: II: 698), Sonnino (Lazio), (Manzini & Savoia 2007: II: 199, 701), Carmiano (Puglia), (Manzini & Savoia 2005: II: 560,795,796). However, the available data are not enough to exclude the possibility of participle agreement with the transitive subject. Past participle agreement with the transitive object seems to be possible in almost every language where auxiliary selection is subject-driven. If the participle agrees according to the edge feature type, then it also tends to agree with the transitive object.

6.7.2   The object-agreement-type

In many varieties, the participle agrees with different arguments, including the transitive direct object. This is the case in Old Italian, where the participle behaves as in Standard Italian, but in addition it can agree with the internal argument (Egerland 1996; Loporcaro 2010; Belletti 2017; D'Alessandro 2022). Participle agreement with the transitive object is not ubiquitous, but it is well-attested, differently from the Standard Italian where it is generally excluded. Example (63a) comes from Boccaccio's *Decameron*, taken from Egerland (1996: 38); Example (63b) belongs to the collection *Il Novellino*, taken from D'Alessandro (2022: 14).

(63)   a.   (...) come che tu   abbi   perdut-i   i   tuoi
              as   that NOM.2SG have.CONJ.PRS.2SG lose.PRTC-PL.M the your
              denari (...)
              money
              '... even if you have lost your money...'   Decameron; II: 5 (1350 ca.)
        b.   Mio padre ha   offert-i   duomila   marchi.
              my   father have.PRS.3SG offer.PRTC-PL.M two thousand marks
              'My father has offered two thousand marks.' *Il Novellino*; 18, 15–16 (1525 ca.)

Other examples of this type are found in Friuli (Raetho-Romance), although in the dialects spoken in this area object agreement is optional, as shown in (64).

(64) *Friulan*
   a. O ai   comprade   / comprât una biele giachete.
       have.PRS.1SG buy.PRTC.SG.F   buy.PRTC a   nice jacket
       'I have bought a nice jacket.'
   b. Si=son   vidûs   / si=an
       REFL.ACC.3PL=be.PRS.3PL see.PRTC.PL.M   REFL.ACC.3PL=have.PRS.3PL
       vidût   tal spieli.
       see.PRTC in mirror
       'They have seen themselves in the mirror.'   (Loporcaro 1998: 80–81)

This pattern of participle agreement is widespread in those languages where auxiliary selection is subject-driven. I have already mentioned above some languages of the first group that might instead belong to this second set of languages. In addition, some dialects of Lazio show this distribution of participle agreement: Piglio, Genzano (Tufi 2003; Bentley 2003), Cori (Chiominto 1984: 179, Kayne 1993: 11,13). The dialect of Cori exhibits the auxiliaries BBBBBH, and the participle agrees with the unaccusative subject, with the transitive object, but not with the transitive subject.

(65) *Cori*
   a. Jésse èo   it-e   a vedè.
       3PL.F have.PRS.3PL come.PRTC-PL.F to see.INF
       'They have gone to see.'
   b. Ntonio è   rott-a   la brocca.
       Antonio be.PRS.3SG break.PRTC-SG.F the jug
       'Antonio has broken the jug.'   (Kayne 1993: 11, 13)

Object agreement on the past participle is found in many languages with a single auxiliary: Morano Calabro, Trebisacce (Calabria, Loporcaro 1998: 74–76). It is also quite common outside Italo-Romance. For instance, it is found in many Occitan, Gascon and Catalan dialects (Loporcaro 2016: 806–807).

   This type of past participle can be derived by means of a φ-probe on transitive v (differently from Standard Italian, where transitive v only bears a π-probe). If the participle agrees with both the unaccusative subject and the transitive object, there should be two strategies available at the same time: the edge feature system (independently needed for successive cyclic movement) and the φ-probe on transitive v. EF-insertion on v for clitics and for the unaccusative argument gives rise to participle agreement as in Standard Italian. Moreover, the presence of a φ-probe on transitive v, instead of a π-probe, leads to object agreement in the case of transitive clauses. A similar analysis, where more than one strategy for participle agreement is present within a single language, has been proposed by Georgi & Stark (2020) for French.

Hence, the object-agreement-type is due to an independent probe on *v*. This proposal is represented in (66) for Old Italian (compared to Standard Italian).

(66)   a.   *Old Italian*
$v_{trans}[u\phi{:}\_] (+ EF[u\#{:}\_, u\gamma{:}\_])$
    b.   *Standard Italian*
$v_{trans}[u\pi{:}\_] (+ EF[u\#{:}\_, u\gamma{:}\_])$

In Old Italian, participle agreement is due to two processes: φ-Agree on transitive *v*, and edge feature insertion. Standard Italian has lost the former strategy because the probe on transitive *v* has become more simplified (from $[u\pi{:}\_, u\#{:}\_, u\gamma{:}\_]$ to $[u\pi{:}\_]$). The featural make-up of *v* can also explain the optionality of object agreement in Old Italian, which is not always realized. This variation emerges if in Old Italian transitive *v* can also be equipped with a π-probe instead of a φ-probe (i.e., both grammars in (66) are simultaneously available for speakers of Old Italian). Standard Italian has lost the option of a φ-probe on *v*. However, this is still found in many dialects spoken in Lazio and Campania.

Note that these two strategies are compatible with every type of auxiliary selection. If it is argument-structure-driven, the different types of *v* remain distinguished by the presence or absence of a person probe: transitive *v* bears $[u\phi{:}\_]$, whereas unaccusative *v* does not contain any φ-probe. If it is subject-driven, the relevant feature for auxiliary selection is located on the subject in Spec,*v*, so that the featural specification of *v* does not matter at all.

This type of participle agreement can lead to complicated patterns, depending on various factors, such as the position of the probe, or its specification. If the probe is located in a higher position, the participle can agree with the external argument, against Belletti's generalization (Belletti 2017). If the probe is relativized to a specific feature value, the participle only agrees when the argument bears a particular feature value, for instance [#:pl]. A language where these two configurations coexist is Ariellese. In Ariellese, participle agreement can be controlled by the internal or external argument, as long as this is plural (D'Alessandro & Roberts 2010). The participle only exhibits overt number inflection, with the exclusion of person and gender. Agreement is morphologically realized as root allomorphy with metaphony. The controller is always the plural argument, if there is a plural DP, without considering its syntactic position (object or subject). Participle agreement is absent in (67a) because all arguments are singular; it is with the plural internal argument in (67b), with the plural external argument in (67c), with any (or both) of these two in (67d).

(67) a. Giuwanne a   pittate   nu mure.
          John   have.PRS.3SG paint.PRTC.SG a   wall
          'John has painted a wall.'
      b. Giuwanne a   pittite   ddu mure.
          John   have.PRS.3SG paint.PRTC.PL two wall
          'John has painted two walls.'
      c. Giuwanne e Mmarije a   pittite   nu mure.
          John   and Mary   have.PRS.3PL paint.PRTC.PL a   wall
          'John and Mary have painted a wall.'
      d. Giuwanne e Mmarije a   pittite   ddu mure.
          John   and Mary   have.PRS.3PL paint.PRTC.PL two wall
          'John and Mary have painted two walls.' (D'Alessandro & Roberts 2010: 58)

Since the subject can control participle agreement, the probe responsible for it should be located in a higher position than v. Such a position could be a Part head that takes the vP as its complement (D'Alessandro & Roberts 2010). The relevant feature is a probe for number that can be satisfied only by a plural value. The sensitivity of a probe to a particular value has been called *relativized probing* (Béjar 2003; Nevins 2007; Béjar & Rezac 2009; Preminger 2014). According to this theory, a DP is a potential goal for a probe only if it bears the matching value of the feature that the probe is looking for (and not just the matching feature). The distribution in (67) can be derived if Part bears a relativized probe of the form [u(#:pl):_]. If the search domain of this probe contains a higher singular DP and a lower plural DP, the probe can skip the higher DP and keep on searching, until it finds the lower plural DP, with which it agrees (without incurring a PIC violation by assuming a probe [uφ:_] on transitive v, whereas for unaccusative verbs the object in Spec,v is accessible for Part).

According to this analysis, participle agreement in Ariellese is unrelated to the presence of unchecked features and to the choice of the perfect auxiliary, as is expected if it does not depend on the defectiveness of the structure. This does not imply that the language does not make use of edge features: EFs can still be inserted for triggering successive cyclic movement. However, it might be the case that in Ariellese EFs are not equipped with any φ-probe, or that participle inflection spells out the head Part instead of v.

6.7.3 The clitic-type

In other languages, participle agreement is only found with clitic pronouns. An example outside Italy is modern Catalan: the participle agrees with clitic pronouns, but not with the unaccusative or reflexive argument (Loporcaro 2016: 807). Among the Italo-Romance varieties, an example is the dialect of Viticuso (Lazio).

Here the participle only agrees with object clitic pronouns and reflexive clitics. As shown in (68), agreement with an accusative clitic is obligatory, whereas it is optional with the reflexive pronoun.

(68)   *Viticuso*

    a. A   parl'latə   / məˈnutə.

         have.PRS.3SG speak.PRTC   come.PRTC

         'S/he has come / spoken.'

    b. ʎ=a   caˈmatə/ l=a   caˈmat-a.

         ACC.3SG.M=have.PRS.3SG call.PRTC ACC.3SG.F=have.PRS.3SG call.PRTC-SG.F

         'S/he has called him / her.'

    c. Ts=a   laˈva:tə/-a.

         REFL.ACC.3SG=have.PRS.3SG wash.PRTC/PRTC-SG.F

         'He/she has washed himself/herself.' (Manzini & Savoia 2005: II: 704–705)

Another example is the dialect of Catanzaro (Calabria). As shown in (69a,b), the participle does not agree with either the unaccusative object or the reflexive clitic; instead, it agrees (although optional) with resumptive clitic pronouns (69c,d) (Loporcaro 1998: 164–167, Loporcaro 2010: 238).

(69)   *Catanzaro*

    a. Maria avía   ǧǧa   ju:tu/*-a   a la ka:sa.

         Maria have.PST.3SG already go.PRCT/PRTC-SG.F to the house

         'Maria had already gone home.'

    b. Anna s=avía   ǧǧa   lava:tu/*-a.

         Anna REFL.ACC.3SG.F=have.PST.3SG already wash.PRCT/PRTC-SG.F

         'Anna had already washed herself.'

    c. A li   čiŋku l=avíanu   ǧǧa   kučina:tu/-a   a

         at the five   ACC.3SG.F=have.PST.3PL already cook.PRCT/PRTC-SG.F the

         pasta.

         pasta

         'At five o'clock they had already cooked, the pasta.'

    d. Ki:ḍẓi dɔlči   si=l=avíanu   ǧǧa

         these sweets REFL.DAT.3PL=ACC.3PL.M=have.PST.3PL already

         manča:tu/-i.

         eat.PRCT/PRTC-SG.F

         'These sweets, they had already eaten them.'   (Loporcaro 1998: 164)

Note that Catanzarese (and other varieties that behave similarly, such as Catalan) constitutes a counterexample to Lois's (1990) generalization, which states that the participle can agree with the clitic internal argument only in languages where there are two auxiliaries at disposal.

One hypothesis (which needs to be evaluated with further studies) is that in these varieties participle agreement results from cliticization and not from a syntactic φ-probe (neither on EF, nor inherently on *v*). This is a case of clitic reduplication: the inflection on the participle is a clitic rather than the result of syntactic Agree (Preminger 2009; Nevins 2011; Kramer 2014; Yuan 2018). This case is a bit different from canonical clitic doubling, where there is a clitic that doubles the information of a full DP. Here, there are two clitic pronouns: one is the argument of the verb, one is the copied one, incorporated into the participle.

Similar analyses in terms of cliticization have been proposed for Catalan by Vilanova (2018), and for French by Georgi & Stark (2020). Vilanova (2018) argues that in Catalan participle inflection is due to the grammaticalization of φ-features from doubled semantic features. According to Georgi & Stark (2020), French participle agreement with clitic pronouns is a case of resumption.

Other analyses are also possible. For instance, participle agreement can be due to edge features, but the only EF equipped with a φ-probe is the one specified for the unchecked feature of clitic pronouns (EF[•T•]).

6.7.4   Languages without past participle agreement

There are also languages without participle agreement. This is the case of many varieties spoken in Sicily (for example, in Calascibetta, Manzini & Savoia 2005: II: 802). Outside Sicily, we can mention the dialect of Terracina (Lazio) (Tuttle 1986), and Montebello Ionico (Calabria) (Manzini & Savoia 2005: II: 800); outside Italo-Romance varieties, Spanish (no participle agreement except in passives).

It is noteworthy that languages that lack participle agreement tend to have a single auxiliary (HAVE in Calascibetta, BE in Terracina, free alternation in Montebello Ionico). Even though there is a tendency for the correlation between lack of participle agreement and lack of auxiliary alternation, this is not always the case. There are also subject-driven dialects without participle agreement. An example is the dialect of Acquafondata (Lazio): the auxiliary follows the BBH pattern, and the participle never agrees with any argument (Loporcaro 2007: 182–183).

The lack of participle agreement can be due to different reasons. Either the lexicon does not contain any specific vocabulary entry for participle inflection, or the EFs come without a probe and there is no φ-probe on *v*. According to the former hypothesis, there is a vocabulary entry that is not specified for gender and number and that is always inserted in the absence of a specialized VI-entry for participle agreement. Under the latter approach, participle agreement can never show up because the language lacks the probe to begin with.

6.8 Past participle agreement and auxiliary selection

In this chapter, I have proposed that past participle agreement in Standard Italian is due to edge features related to successive cyclic movement. This mechanism is completely independent of the source of auxiliary selection, which is person Agree. That participle agreement and auxiliary selection are independent phenomena has already been highlighted by Loporcaro (1998); Bentley & Eythórsson (2004); Belletti (2017); Manzini & Savoia (2005, 2007); Legendre (2010), among others. It is certainly true that in Standard Italian the perfect auxiliary BE tends to co-occur with overt gender and number inflection on the past participle, but this correlation does not always take place. The account of auxiliary selection and participle agreement developed in this book have the considerable advantage of explaining not only why the full correlation between these two processes is not real, but also why there is indeed a partial correlation.

In Standard Italian, the auxiliary BE and participle agreement happen to show up together because they both depend on the features of the head v and of the arguments. The former dependency stems from the distinction between two types of v: a full-argument-structure v and a defective v. The defective v lacks a person probe, determining the realization of Perf as BE. Moreover, it cannot assign case, so that an EF must be inserted, leading to participle agreement. With unaccusative verbs, the fact that defective v is neither a probe for person, nor a case assigner leads to the emergence of BE and to participle agreement, with the expected correlation. In Standard Italian, the features [ucase:acc] and [uπ:_] cluster together on v. These two features influence auxiliary selection on the one hand, and participle agreement on the other hand. However, these two phenomena are as different as the features on v [ucase:acc] and [uπ:_] are.

As far as the features of the arguments are concerned, a defective DP (i.e., with an unchecked feature) causes EF-insertion on v and, consequently, participle agreement. This is the case of clitic pronouns. In addition, if the DP is φ-defective, it leads to failed Agree on v, with the consequence that BE must be inserted. With the reflexive and impersonal clitics, the co-occurrence between BE and participle agreement is due again to the cluster of two properties on a defective item: the argument is a clitic and is φ-defective. As we saw for v, where case and person probe cluster together, in Standard Italian φ-defective pronouns happen to be clitics. The generalization seems to be that if a D category bears an unvalued person feature (π-defectiveness), then it must also be a clitic. For this reason, it is not possible to have the auxiliary BE without participle agreement with reflexive and impersonal clitics. On the one hand, the unvalued π-feature of the clitic leads to BE insertion; on the other hand, its [•T•] feature causes participle agreement via edge feature insertion.

Thus, the frequent co-occurrence between BE-selection and participle agreement is an effect of the featural specification of the functional head v and of the arguments. Nonetheless, various factors can destroy the correlation between BE and participle agreement on the one hand, and HAVE and lack of participle agreement on the other hand. These correlations break down at least in the following cases: with impersonal transitive and unergative clauses (70a,b), with object clitic pronouns (70c), and occasionally with relativization (in formal Italian) (70d).

(70) a. Si=è   mangiato gli spaghetti.
      IMPERS=be.PRS.3SG eat.PRTC the spaghetti
      'People have eaten the spaghetti.'
   b. Si=è   lavorato   molto.
      IMPERS=be.PRS.3SG work.PRTC a lot
      'People have worked a lot.'
   c. Le=ho   conosciut-e.
      ACC.3PL.F=have.PRS.1SG know.PRTC-PL.F
      'I have met them.'
   d. Le ragazze che ho   conosciut-e…
      the girls   REL have.PRS.1SG know.PRTC-PL.F
      'The girls that I have met…'

The auxiliary BE shows up without participle agreement in impersonal clauses, with both transitive verbs without person agreement (70a) and unergative verbs (70b). The prediction that a defective clitic (reflexive or impersonal) leads to both BE insertion and participle agreement does not hold here because of the syntactic structure. In (70a) and (70b), the Merge position of the defective clitic is higher than the locus of participle agreement (which is v), but lower than the position of Perf (cf. analysis of auxiliary selection in impersonal clauses, Sections 3.3.9.2, 3.3.9.3 in Chapter 3). Participle agreement here is excluded in the same way as is excluded with external arguments in general. Hence, in those positions that can cause participle agreement (namely, in the v domain), the joint presence of [uπ:_] and [•T•] on a D category always leads to both BE and participle agreement. If the DP is in a position that is not relevant for participle agreement (i.e., if it is merged in the external argument position or even higher), then the correlation is automatically not active, since the precondition for participle agreement is not met anymore (the affected domain is not the v domain).

If a transitive verb takes a clitic as its direct object (70c), then the auxiliary is realized as HAVE because v successfully agrees with the clitic, but participle agreement is caused by the defectiveness of the clitic (indicated by [•T•]), and not of v. Example (70d) can be explained by assuming that the EF for relativization may contain a φ-probe in some grammars of Italian.

The relations between the phenomena are summarized in Table 6.2.

Table 6.2 Auxiliary selection and participle agreement

	Auxiliary	Participle agreement	Motivation	Example
i.	BE	yes	defective v / defective pronoun	(1a)
ii.	BE	no	defective pronoun above v	(70a)
iii.	HAVE	yes	clitic [•T•]	(70c)
iv.	HAVE	no	non-defective v	(3a)

The correlation between BE and participle agreement also does not hold in many Italo-Romance varieties. There are languages where the perfect auxiliary with unaccusative verbs is HAVE, but the participle behaves as in Italian (for instance, Cori (71)). In other varieties, even when the auxiliary is BE, the participle does not show agreement (for example, Colledimacine (72)).

(71) *Cori*
Au venuti.
have.PRS.3PL come.PRTC-PL.M
'They have come.' (Kayne 1993)

(72) *Colledimacine*
Semmə mənu:tə / maɲɲat:ə.
be.PRS.2PL come.PRTC / eat.PRTC
'We have come / eaten.' (Manzini & Savoia 2005: II: 695)

More in general, the correlation between a specific distribution of perfect auxiliaries and participle agreement turns out to be a mistake when one considers other Italo-Romance varieties. In Italo-Romance, almost every combination of auxiliaries and participle inflection is attested. In this chapter, I have only dealt with a subset of the possibilities that are found cross-linguistically (for additional data, see the collection by Manzini & Savoia (2005), and the literature mentioned in this chapter). Some of the possible combinations are shown in Table 6.3, which summarizes the distribution of participle agreement (ppa) and auxiliary selection (aux sel) together. Under the column 'source' I also indicate the mechanism that leads to that phenomenon, according to the analysis proposed in this book. Table 6.3 is not complete and presents some uncertainties with respect to the status of certain languages (marked with '?'). More data should be collected to complete the empirical picture.

Table 6.3 Participle agreement and auxiliary selection

Language	ppa	Source of ppa	Aux sel	Source of aux sel
Italian	with DP_{unacc}, clitics	$EF[u\#,u\gamma]$	arg. str. split	$[uInfl] > T[u\pi]$
Ortezzano, Servigliano	with DP_{unacc}, clitics	$EF[u\#,u\gamma]$	mixed split	$[uInfl] > [u\pi] + T[\varphi]$
Pescocostanzo	with DP_{unacc}, clitics	$EF[u\#,u\gamma]$	pers. split	$[u\pi] > [uInfl]$
Carmiano?	with DP_{unacc}, clitics	$EF[u\#,u\gamma]$	1 aux or free variation	lexicon
Old Italian	with DP_{obj} or others	$[u\varphi]$	arg. str. split	$[uInfl] > [u\pi]$
Tufillo	with DP_{obj} or others	$[u\varphi]$	mixed split	$[uInfl] > [u\pi] + T[\varphi]$
Arielli, Genzano	with DP_{obj} or others	$[u\varphi]$	pers. split	$[u\pi] > [uInfl]$
Trebisacce, Castrovillari	with DP_{obj} or others	$[u\varphi]$	1 aux or free variation	lexicon
	with clitics	clitic doubling	arg. str. split	$[uInfl] > [u\pi]$
	with clitics	clitic doubling	mixed split	$[uInfl] > [u\pi] + T[\varphi]$
Viticuso?	with clitics	clitic doubling	pers. split	$[u\pi] > [uInfl]$
Catanzaro, Catalan	with clitics	clitic doubling	1 aux or free variation	lexicon
Ranrupt (Gallo-Romance)?	no	no	arg. str. split	$[uInfl] > [u\pi]$
Secinaro, Colledimacine	no	no	mixed split	$[uInfl] > [u\pi] + [\varphi]$
Acquafondata	no	no	pers. split	$[u\pi] > [uInfl]$
Calascibetta, Montebello Ionico	no	no	1 aux or free variation	lexicon

6.9   Summary

In this chapter, I have argued that past participle agreement in Standard Italian is a morphological reflex of A-movement across v. Overt morphological inflection is realized on the past participle when the internal argument has moved out of its base position. A constituent must move out of a phase domain if it bears a feature that has not been checked yet (e.g., [case] for unaccusative arguments, [•T•] for clitics). This "featural defectiveness" can be inherent (as in the case of clitic pronouns), or structural (due to the presence of defective v). I have also shown that cases of participle agreement that apparently do not involve movement can be reduced to instances of covert A-movement.

The theoretical implementation of this idea makes use of edge features, which have been independently proposed as triggers for successive cyclic movement. The analysis developed in this chapter includes a new component on the edge feature: a probe for gender and number. This probe targets the φ-features of the item that bears the unchecked feature.

Participle agreement and auxiliary selection are independent phenomena. In Standard Italian, they happen to show some correlations (i.e., BE and past participle agreement; HAVE without past participle agreement) because of how features cluster together on the functional head v and on the arguments.

Participle agreement can have different sources in different languages. The inflection on the participle can be the Spell-out of an edge feature, of a φ-probe with different degrees of complexity, of a doubled clitic pronoun. The type of participle agreement does not seem to correlate with any particular configuration of auxiliary selection. Almost all combinations of auxiliary selection and participle agreement are attested.

CHAPTER 7

Concluding remarks

7.1 Why this book exists

Auxiliary selection is a very well-known phenomenon that has been studied from different perspectives. For this reason, the core data of a language such as Standard Italian are very simple and uncontroversial. Nonetheless, when one tries to understand the computation that generates the alternation between the auxiliaries HAVE and BE, no existing analysis can cover the Italian data (in simple clauses and more complex sentences), can be extended to person-driven auxiliary selection, and is compatible with other analyses of past participle agreement. The main goal of this book is to propose a new solution to the long-standing puzzle of auxiliary selection, which is relevant to many aspects of Romance linguistics and of theoretical linguistics in general.

The problem of auxiliary selection is an interesting one because it shows impressive variation among closely related varieties, although limited to two main types: the argument-structure-driven system, and the subject-driven system. Given that these two systems are attested in closely related varieties, it would be surprising if the underlying syntax responsible for these two types were not the same. For this reason, I have proposed a cross-linguistically uniform syntax, where the differences between languages are only due to different featural specifications on lexical items (the feature orderings on the perfect head) and to different Vocabulary Items (the allomorphs that spell out the perfect head). This analysis minimizes the differences between languages in accordance with the research program of Minimalism, exemplified by the *Uniformity Principle*.

(1) *Uniformity Principle*   (Chomsky 2001: 2)
    In the absence of compelling evidence to the contrary, assume languages to be
    uniform, with variety restricted to easily detectable properties of utterances.

The solution to the problem of auxiliary selection is extremely relevant not only for understanding cross-linguistic variation, but also for more theoretical and foundational issues, such as the distribution of labor between syntax, morphology and the lexicon, and the conditions on the operation Agree. Since there is no previous analysis that is able to derive all the Italian data by means of the basic operations Merge and Agree, this suggests that the inventory of the principles of grammar must be enlarged with new tools. The new theoretical contribution to syntactic theory is the introduction of the principle *Nested Agree*. By giving a new answer to a very old puzzle, this book sheds light on the theoretical tools that are needed to account for this phenomenon. In particular, it contributes to the ongoing discussion on multiple probing, locality, minimality, and Agree.

7.2   The main results

7.2.1   Auxiliary selection

In the perfect tense, many languages realize the perfect auxiliary as either BE or HAVE. This alternation depends on either the type of argument structure, or the person feature of the subject.

I have assumed that the perfect auxiliary realizes a functional head Perf located between v and T. Since the operation that transmits information across the syntactic structure is Agree, the natural way to derive the dependency between Perf and another head or phrase is to model auxiliary selection as an instance of Agree. In particular, it should be Agree for person because the auxiliary is sensitive to the φ-features of the arguments (cf. Italian reflexive and impersonal clauses). In subject-driven systems, the dependency on the person feature of the subject is realized via Agree between Perf and the DP_{sbj}, which is the highest matching goal (assuming that all types of v are phases). In argument-structure-driven systems, the dependency on argument structure and on the features of the arguments is obtained via Agree between Perf and the person feature of the lower head v (valued as a result of a prior Agree operation between v and the internal argument). Auxiliary selection is due to Cyclic Agree (Legate 2005) between Perf and a lower argument, enabled by the intermediate head v.

The difference between these two systems is achieved by different extrinsic orderings of the features on the perfect head Perf: [uInfl:perf] > [uπ:_] for argument-structure-driven systems, [uπ:_] > [uInfl:perf] for subject-driven systems. The fine-grained cross-linguistic differences are due to the morphological inventory of each language.

The selected allomorph spells out the result of person-Agree on the head Perf. The person feature on the head Perf is morphologically realized as allomorph selection (and not as person inflection). In Standard Italian, if Perf has successfully copied a π-feature via Agree, then the more specific allomorph (HAVE) is chosen; if Agree has failed, then the elsewhere form (BE) is inserted. The alternation between the two allomorphs also depends on the result of Agree in other varieties. In subject-driven systems, the more specific allomorph is inserted in the context of a specific person value (differently from argument-structure-driven systems, where the dependency is based on the presence/ absence of a person feature, rather than on its specific value). Languages that have only a single auxiliary at disposal may result from two different scenarios: either their lexicon contains just a single lexical entry for the Perf head, or their lexicon contains one allomorph that is inserted in the context of any person value and their auxiliary selection is subject-driven (meaning that Agree on Perf always succeeds in copying a value).

If auxiliary selection is considered as agreement for the person feature, the astonishing cross-linguistic variation can be accounted for by means of a simple parameter (the ordering of the features on Perf) and by assuming different inventories of vocabulary entries.

7.2.2   Auxiliary selection in Italian

Standard Italian is a language where the alternation between BE and HAVE for the perfect auxiliary depends on the argument structure. However, auxiliary selection must be also sensitive to the features of the arguments, as the presence of reflexive and impersonal arguments influences the choice of the auxiliary. Auxiliary selection depends not only on the type of argument structure (featural make-up of v) but also on the type of arguments (π-feature on v, valued as a result of a prior Agree relation between v and the internal argument). I have offered a detailed derivation of auxiliary selection in different types of clauses: transitive, transitive with reflexive direct object, transitive with reflexive indirect object, unergative, unaccusative, monoargumental, passive, quirky, and impersonal (combined with transitive, unergative, unaccusative verbs).

Whenever there is some kind of defectiveness in the structure, either in the functional head v (unaccusatives, passives), or in the DPs (reflexives, impersonals), the elsewhere form BE emerges. In the case of defective v, Agree on Perf fails because of the absence of a matching goal in the c-command domain. In the case of defective arguments, Agree with φ-defective items leads to a failure in valuation (defective intervention or failed Agree). This explains why transitive verbs exhibit BE when they are combined with defective items (reflexives, impersonals), but unaccusative verbs can never combine with HAVE (since they always involve a defective functional head). The "switch" is only from the most specific form (HAVE) to the elsewhere form (BE).

That auxiliary selection is π-Agree not only in subject-driven systems, but also in the less straightforward case of argument-structure-based splits, finds further confirmation in restructuring and in other mixed Italo-Romance varieties, whose auxiliary distribution can be derived under this specific analysis.

7.2.3   Restructuring in Italian

Restructuring clauses are complex sentences that are characterized by apparently optional transparency effects in the choice of the perfect auxiliary. The auxiliary associated with the restructuring verb can be realized either as HAVE, or as the one that the lexical verb would require (auxiliary switch).

The analysis of auxiliary selection developed for root clauses is extended to restructuring: auxiliary selection works exactly in the same way. The peculiar trait of restructuring is a special type of v, v_{restr}. This head acts as an intermediate agreeing head, thanks to the presence of a double [Infl] feature. Auxiliary selection in restructuring is the result of cyclic Agree due to the head v_{restr}: Perf agrees with v_{restr}, which agrees with the lower v. In addition, this head may select complements of different sizes: either a vP or a TP. This choice is optional and has no semantic effect (i.e., the embedded non-finite T head does not introduce any independent semantic tense feature). Evidence in favor of different complements comes from some syntactic operations that are sensitive to the size of the clause and cannot apply in clauses with auxiliary switch.

If auxiliary selection is an instance of π-Agree, as I have proposed, and if the lower portion of the clause can be of different sizes, then the distribution of the auxiliaries is exactly predicted. If v_{restr} selects a vP complement, the clausal perfect auxiliary faithfully corresponds to the one that would be selected by the lower v, since v_{restr} copies the π-information from the lower v, which is successively copied by Perf. As is the case in root clauses, auxiliary switch consists of the emergence of BE due to failed Agree or Agree with φ-defective items. Nevertheless, this effect is optional, since it depends on the size of the complement. Different complement sizes determine different search domains for Agree. By enlarging the complement, the lower v is no longer the deciding factor for the form of the auxiliary. In fact, the presence of the T head as a goal for Infl-Agree makes its c-command domain accessible for π-Agree, which always succeeds in finding a goal. In this way, the difference between the different types of v is neutralized, leading to HAVE insertion with any type of lexical verb. Hence, there is no real optionality with respect to auxiliary selection: it is the size of the complement of v_{restr} that is subject to optionality, and this influences auxiliary selection.

7.2.4   Typology

After having dealt with Standard Italian, I have also addressed the cross-linguistic variation for auxiliary selection in other Italo-Romance varieties. By modeling auxiliary selection as the result of Agree for person, I have provided a unified explanation across different languages. This reduces the distance between the two apparently very different systems of Italian and of Southern Italo-Romance varieties: not only auxiliary selection in Standard Italian is person-Agree in the same way as it is person-Agree in subject-driven systems, but also many alleged subject-driven varieties are indeed argument-structure-driven systems (mixed systems).

In addition, this approach accounts for some specific facts. For example, argument-structure-driven systems can be subject to further restrictions: tense, aspect and mood distinctions, but also person/number distinctions (resulting in so-called mixed systems). Instead, additional restrictions based on argument structure or on a different argument than the subject cannot constrain subject-driven auxiliary selection. These facts follow from minimality.

Another interesting point is that reflexive clauses show much cross-linguistic and intra-linguistic variation within argument-structure-based varieties. This fact can be explained if argument-structure-driven systems are the result of π-Agree, and if the features of the internal arguments play a role in this type of language, as I have argued throughout this book. In particular, variation is expected if in different languages reflexive pronouns may involve different features, structures, or locus of Merge.

7.2.5   Participle agreement in Italian

In this book, I have claimed that participle agreement and auxiliary selection are independent phenomena (in accordance with much previous literature). However, in Standard Italian they tend to pattern together (BE with participle agreement, HAVE without it) because of how features cluster together on the functional head v and on the arguments. These two phenomena are not directly related, but depend on different features that appear together on the heads. For this reason, the present account not only explains why there is no full correlation between auxiliary selection and participle agreement, but also why there is a partial correlation.

In Standard Italian, participle agreement is a morphological reflex of A-movement across v. Overt morphological inflection is realized on the past participle when the internal argument has moved out of its Merge position. A constituent must move out of a phase domain if it bears a feature that has not been valued, after all the operations triggered by the phase head have been carried out. Featural defectiveness can be inherent (as in the case of reflexive pronouns), or structural (due to the presence of a defective v).

The theoretical implementation makes use of edge features, which have been independently proposed as a device to trigger successive cyclic movement. The new proposal consists of the presence of a gender and number probe on the edge feature. This probe targets the φ-features of the item bearing the unchecked feature that has caused the insertion of the edge feature. Cases that do not involve overt movement, but still exhibit participle agreement, can be reduced to instances of covert A-movement.

As far as cross-linguistic variation is concerned, I have argued that participle agreement can be due to different sources in different languages. The inflection can be the Spell-out of an edge feature (Italian), of a φ-probe on a functional head with different degrees of complexity (Old Italian, Ariellese), or of a doubled clitic pronoun (Catanzarese). Almost all combinations of different patterns of participle agreement with different auxiliary distributions are attested.

7.2.6   Theoretical contribution

This analysis of auxiliary selection has required the introduction of a new principle, *Nested Agree*. Nested Agree states that, if the features on a head are ordered, the domain of each operation is reduced by the result of the previous operation triggered by the same head. In other words, the domain of Agree depends on both the syntactic structure itself and the accomplishment of previous operations. Nested Agree regulates multiple probing in a way that is subject to all the standard conditions on Agree (feature matching, c-command, minimality). It is also fully derivational, and not specificity-driven.

Nested Agree emerges from the combination of already proposed principles of syntactic theory, which are now put together in a novel fashion. The ingredients of Nested Agree are as follows: downward directionality, feature ordering, and the Agree-Link theory of Agree (Arregi & Nevins 2012). As an alternative to Agree-Link, Nested Agree also results from the combination of downward directionality, feature ordering, a specificity-driven principle such as Maximize Matching Effects (Chomsky 2001), and the Principle of Minimal Compliance (Richards 1998).

Nested Agree offers a new perspective on minimality in the context of multiple probing. If the operations are ordered, the domain of a subsequent operation may exclude an apparent intervener, if the previous operation has given as a result a more embedded syntactic position than the one occupied by the intervener. This principle is essential to derive the full pattern of argument-structure-driven auxiliary selection. Its action can be seen in two contexts. Firstly, the person probe on Perf must get past the subject of transitive verbs and agree with *v*, thereby establishing the dependency on the argument structure and on the features of the lower arguments (deriving the difference between transitive and unaccusative clauses, but also between canonical arguments and reflexive/impersonal arguments). Secondly, the raised internal argument of unaccusative verbs must be skipped by the person probe on Perf, in order to differentiate between unaccusative and transitive clauses (and this configuration cannot be achieved by any other approach, including A-over-A minimality).

7.3   Open questions

The main goal of this work is to develop an analysis of auxiliary selection in Italo-Romance within a strictly derivational approach, by means of the basic operation Agree. To the best of my knowledge, there is no other theory of auxiliary selection that has attempted to provide an explicit and coherent analysis of the whole distribution of auxiliaries in root clauses and restructuring, and has sketched a typology of other varieties.

Nonetheless, there are still many general questions that remain unanswered. Many of these questions stem from the cross-linguistic comparison. Why does the alternation only involve the two forms BE and HAVE, with the most extreme case of threefold alternation between BE, HAVE and free variation among the two? Why are there no argument-structure-driven systems where the Vocabulary Items refer to specific values of the person feature (i.e., where the perfect auxiliary depends on the particular value of the person feature of the transitive object)? Why are there no subject-driven systems in Germanic languages, differently from Romance? Why is the perfect auxiliary only sensitive to person, but not to gender and/or number with the exclusion of person? Why is participle agreement only sensitive to gender and number and not to person? Why is agreement only realized on the participle, and not just on every verbal form? Why does auxiliary selection tend to be the same phenomenon everywhere, it being the realization of the perfect head according to the person feature, whereas participle agreement is a very diversified phenomenon (involving different sources, different features, different syntactic operations)?

This book has answered only some of the questions that these linguistic phenomena pose. New works may shed light on other relevant issues, and even open up new questions.

References

Abels, Klaus. 2003. Successive cyclicity, anti-locality, and adposition stranding. Doctoral dissertation, University of Connecticut.

Abels, Klaus. 2012. *Phases: An essay on cyclicity in syntax*. Berlin: De Gruyter Mouton.

Aissen, Judith. 1999. Markedness and subject choice in Optimality Theory. *Natural Language and Linguistic Theory* 17:673–711.

Alexiadou, Artemis. 2003. On nominative case features and split agreement. In *New perspectives on case theory*, ed. Ellen Brandner & Heike Zinsmeister, 23–52. Stanford: CSLI Publications.

Alexiadou, Artemis, & Elena Anagnostopoulou. 1998. Parametrizing AGR: Word order, V-movement and EPP-checking. *Natural Language & Linguistic Theory* 16:491–539.

Alexiadou, Artemis, Elena Anagnostopoulou, & Florian Schäfer. 2015. *External arguments in transitivity alternations: A layering approach*. Oxford: Oxford University Press.

Amaechi, Mary, & Doreen Georgi. 2020. On optional wh-/focus fronting in Igbo: A SYN-SEM-PHON interaction. *Zeitschrift für Sprachwissenschaft* 39:299–327.

Amato, Irene. to appear. Auxiliary selection in Italian restructuring: an insight into the size of the clause. Syntax.

Anagnostopoulou, Elena. 2001. Two classes of double object verbs: the role of zero morphology. In *Progress in grammar. Articles at the 20th anniversary of the Comparison of Grammatical Models Group in Tilburg*, ed. Marc van Oostendorp & Elena Anagnostopoulou, 1–27. Utrecht: Roccade.

Anagnostopoulou, Elena. 2004. On clitics, feature movement and double object alternation. In *Minimality effects in syntax*, ed. Arthur Stepanov, Gisbert Fanselow, & Ralf Vogel, 15–36. Berlin: De Gruyter Mouton.

Anand, Pranav, & Andrew Nevins. 2006. The locus of ergative case assignment: Evidence from scope. In *Ergativity: Emerging issues*, ed. Alana Johns, Diane Massam, & Juvenal Ndayiragije, 3–25. Dordrecht: Springer.

de Andrade, Aroldo, & Reineke Bok-Bennema. 2017. Clitic climbing. In *The Blackwell Companion to Syntax*, ed. Martin Everaert & Henk van Riemsdijk, 1–56. Wiley Online Library.

Arregi, Karlos. 2004. The have/be alternation in Basque. Ms. University of Illinois, Urbana-Champaign.

Arregi, Karlos, & Andrew Nevins. 2012. *Morphotactics: Basque auxiliaries and the structure of Spellout*. Dordrecht: Springer.

Asarina, Alevtina. 2011. Case in Uyghur and beyond. Doctoral dissertation, Massachusetts Institute of Technology.

Assmann, Anke, Doreen Georgi, Fabian Heck, Gereon Müller, & Philipp Weisser. 2015. Ergatives move too early: On an instance of opacity in syntax. *Syntax* 18:343–387.

Atlamaz, Ümit, & Mark Baker. 2018. On partial agreement and oblique case. *Syntax* 21:195–237.

Avram, Larisa, & Virginia Hill. 2007. An irrealis BE auxiliary in Romanian. In *Split auxiliary systems: A cross-linguistic perspective*, ed. Raúl Aranovich, 47–64. Amsterdam: John Benjamins Publishing Company.

Baker, Mark. 1985. The mirror principle and morphosyntactic explanation. *Linguistic Inquiry* 16:373–415.

Baker, Mark. 1988. *Incorporation: A theory of grammatical function changing.* University of Chicago Press, Chicago.

Baker, Mark, & Jonathan David Bobaljik. 2017. On inherent and dependent theories of ergative case. In *The Oxford Handbook of Ergativity*, ed. Jessica Coon, Diane Massam, & Lisa Demena Travis, 111–134. Oxford: Oxford University Press.

Baker, Mark, & Livia Camargo Souza. 2020. Agree without agreement: Switch-reference and reflexive voice in two Panoan languages. *Natural Language & Linguistic Theory* 38:1–62.

Bech, Gunnar. 1955. *Studien über das deutsche Verbum infinitum.* Tübingen: Niemeyer.

Béjar, Susana. 2003. Phi-syntax: A theory of agreement. Doctoral dissertation, Toronto.

Béjar, Susana, & Milan Rezac. 2003. Person licensing and the derivation of PCC effects. In *Romance linguistics: Theory and acquisition*, ed. Ana-Teresa Pérez-Leroux & Yves Roberge, 49–62. Amsterdam: John Benjamins Publishing Company.

Béjar, Susana, & Milan Rezac. 2009. Cyclic Agree. *Linguistic Inquiry* 40:35–73.

Belletti, Adriana. 1990. *Generalized verb movement: Aspects of verb syntax.* Torino: Rosenberg & Sellier.

Belletti, Adriana. 1999. Italian/Romance clitics: Structure and derivation. In *Clitics in the languages of Europe*, ed. Henk van Riemsdijk, 543–580. Berlin/New York: De Gruyter Mouton.

Belletti, Adriana. 2005. Extended doubling and the VP periphery. *Probus* 17:1–35.

Belletti, Adriana. 2017. (Past) participle agreement. In *The Blackwell Companion to Syntax*, ed. Martin Everaert & Henk van Riemsdijk, 2973–3000. Oxford: Blackwell.

Belletti, Adriana, & Luigi Rizzi. 1988. Psych-verbs and θ-theory. *Natural Language & Linguistic Theory* 6:291–352.

Benincà, Paola. 1985. Uso dell'ausiliare e accordo verbale nei dialetti veneti e friulani. *Rivista italiana di dialettologia* 8:155–62.

Benincà, Paola, Mair Parry, & Diego Pescarini. 2016. The dialects of Northern Italy. In *The Oxford guide to the Romance languages*, ed. Adam Ledgeway & Martin Maiden, 185–205. Oxford: Oxford University Press.

Benincà, Paola, & Cecilia Poletto. 2005. The third dimension of person features. In *Syntax and variation. Reconciling the biological and the social*, ed. Karen P. Corrigan & Leonie Cornips, 265–299. Amsterdam: John Benjamins Publishing Company.

Benincà, Paola, & Laura Vanelli. 1984. Italiano, veneto, friulano: fenomeni sintattici a confronto. *RID. Rivista Italiana di Dialettologia* 8:165–194.

Bentley, Delia. 2003. Sur la force d'une approche non-dérivationnelle de l'analyse linguistique: quelques données de l'Italo-Roman. *Cahiers du CRISCO* 13:51–75.

Bentley, Delia, & Thórhallur Eythórsson. 2004. Auxiliary selection and the semantics of unaccusativity. *Lingua* 114:447–471.

Benveniste, Émile. 1966. *Problémes de linguistique générale.* Paris: Gallimard.

Bergeton, Uffe, & Roumyana Pancheva. 2011. A new perspective on the historical development of English intensifiers and reflexives. In *Grammatical change: Origins, nature, outcomes,* ed. Dianne Jonas, John Whitman, & Andrew Garrett, 123–138. New York: Oxford University Press.

Bianchi, Valentina. 2006. On the syntax of personal arguments. *Lingua* 116:2023–2067.

Bianchi, Valentina, & Cristiano Chesi. 2014. Subject islands, reconstruction, and the flow of the computation. *Linguistic Inquiry* 45:525–569.

Bjorkman, Bronwyn Alma Moore, & Hedde Zeijlstra. 2019. Checking up on (φ-)agree. *Linguistic Inquiry* 50:527–569.

Bjorkman, Bronwyn M. 2011. BE-ing default: The morphosyntax of auxiliaries. Doctoral dissertation, Massachusetts Institute of Technology.

Bjorkman, Bronwyn M. 2018. Ergative as perfective oblique. *Syntax* 21:321–361.

Bobaljik, Jonathan David. 2002. A-chains at the PF-interface: Copies and covert movement. *Natural Language & Linguistic Theory* 20:197–267.

Bobaljik, Jonathan David. 2008. Where's phi? Agreement as a post-syntactic operation. In *Phi theory: Phi-features across interfaces and modules,* ed. Daniel Harbour, David Adger, & Susana Béjar, 295–328. Oxford: Oxford University Press.

Boeckx, Cedric. 2000. Quirky agreement. *Studia linguistica* 54:354–380.

Boeckx, Cedric, Norbert Hornstein, & Jairo Nunes. 2010. *Control as movement.* Cambridge University Press.

Bošković, Željko. 2007. On the locality and motivation of Move and Agree: An even more minimal theory. *Linguistic Inquiry* 38:589–644.

Bouchard, Denis. 1982. On the content of empty categories. Doctoral dissertation, Massachusetts Institute of Technology.

Branigan, Phil. 1992. Subjects and complementizers. Doctoral dissertation, Massachusetts Institute of Technology.

Brown, Jessica M. M. 2016. Blackholes and subextraction from adjuncts in English and Norwegian. In *Proceedings of CLS* 51, 67–81. CSLI, Chicago.

Bruening, Benjamin. 2001. Syntax at the edge: Cross-clausal phenomena and the syntax of Passamaquoddy. Doctoral dissertation, Massachusetts Institute of Technology.

Bruening, Benjamin. 2005. The Algonquian inverse is syntactic: Binding in Passamaquoddy. Ms., University of Delaware.

Bruening, Benjamin. 2013. By phrases in passives and nominals. *Syntax* 16:1–41.

Burzio, Luigi. 1986. *Italian syntax: A Government-Binding approach.* Dordrecht: Springer.

Cardinaletti, Anna. 1997. Agreement and control in expletive constructions. *Linguistic Inquiry* 28:521–533.

Cardinaletti, Anna. 2002. Against optional and null clitics. right dislocation vs. marginalization. *Studia linguistica* 56:29–57.

Cardinaletti, Anna. 2004. Toward a cartography of subject positions. In *The structure of CP and IP. The cartography of syntactic structures,* ed. Luigi Rizzi, 115–165. New York: Oxford University Press.

Cardinaletti, Anna. 2008. On different types of clitic clusters. In *The Bantu-Romance connection,* ed. Cécile De Cat & Katherine Demuth, 41–82. Amsterdam: John Benjamins Publishing Company.

Cardinaletti, Anna, & Ur Shlonsky. 2004. Clitic positions and restructuring in Italian. *Linguistic Inquiry* 35:519–557.

Cardinaletti, Anna, & Michal Starke. 1996. Deficient pronouns: A view from Germanic. In *Studies in Comparative Germanic Syntax*, ed. Höskuldur Thráinsson, Samuel David Epstein, & Steve Peter, volume II, 21–65. Dordrecht: Kluwer.

Cardinaletti, Anna, & Michal Starke. 1999. The typology of structural deficiency: A case study in the three classes of pronouns. In *Clitics in the languages of Europe*, ed. Henk van Riemsdijk, 145–233. Berlin: De Gruyter Mouton.

Cennamo, Michela, & Antonella Sorace. 2007. Auxiliary selection and split intransitivity in Paduan: Variation and lexical-aspectual constraints. In *Split auxiliary systems*, ed. Raúl Aranovich, 65–99. Amsterdam: John Benjamins Publishing Company.

Chierchia, Gennaro. 1995. The variability of impersonal subjects. In *Quantification in natural languages*, ed. Emmon Bach, Eloise Jelinek, Angelika Kratzer, & Barbara H. Partee, 107–143. Dordrecht: Kluwer.

Chiominto, Cesare. 1984. *Lo parlà forte della pora ggente: poesie in dialetto di Cori: con una raccolta di proverbi e note grammaticali.* Roma: Bulzoni.

Chomsky, Noam. 1964. *Current issues in linguistic theory.* The Hague: Mouton.

Chomsky, Noam. 1973. Conditions on transformations. In *A festschrift for Morris Halle*, ed. Stephen R. Anderson & Paul Kiparsky, 232–286. Holt, Reinehart and Winston.

Chomsky, Noam. 1980. On binding. *Linguistic Inquiry* 11:1–46.

Chomsky, Noam. 1981. *Lectures on government and binding.* Dordrecht: Foris.

Chomsky, Noam. 1995. *The Minimalist Program.* Cambridge, Mass.: MIT Press.

Chomsky, Noam. 2000. Minimalist inquiries: The framework. In *Step by step*, ed. Roger Martin, David Michaels, & Juan Uriagereka, 89–155. Cambridge, Mass.: MIT Press.

Chomsky, Noam. 2001. Derivation by phase. In *Ken Hale. A life in language*, ed. Michael Kenstowicz, 1–52. Cambridge, Mass.: MIT Press.

Chomsky, Noam. 2008. On phases. In *Foundational issues in linguistic theory. Essays in honor of Jean Roger Vergnaud*, ed. Robert Freidin, Carlos P. Otero, & Maria Luisa Zubizarreta, 133–166. Cambridge, Mass.: MIT press.

Chung, Sandra, & William A. Ladusaw. 2003. *Restriction and saturation.* Cambridge, Mass.: MIT press.

Cinque, Guglielmo. 1988. On si constructions and the theory of arb. *Linguistic Inquiry* 19:521–581.

Cinque, Guglielmo. 1999. *Adverbs and functional heads: A cross-linguistic perspective.* New York: Oxford University Press.

Cinque, Guglielmo. 2003. The interaction of passive, causative, and 'restructuring' in Romance. In *The syntax of Italian dialects*, ed. Cristina Tortora, 50–66. New York: Oxford University Press.

Cinque, Guglielmo. 2004. "Restructuring" and functional structure. In *The structure of CP and IP*, ed. Luigi Rizzi, 132–191. New York: Oxford University Press.

Cocchi, Gloria. 1995. *La selezione dell'ausiliare.* Padova: Unipress.

Collins, Chris. 2005. A smuggling approach to the passive in English. *Syntax* 8:81–120.

Coon, Jessica, & Stefan Keine. 2020. Feature gluttony. *Linguistic Inquiry* 52:1–56.

Coon, Jessica, & Omer Preminger. 2012. Towards a unified account of person splits. In *Proceedings of WCCFL* 29, ed. Jaehoon Choi, E.Alan Hogue, Jeffrey Punske, Deniz Tat, Jessamyn Schertz, & Alex Trueman, 310–318. Somerville: Cascadilla.

Cordin, Patrizia. 1997. Tense, mood and aspect in the verb. In *The dialects of Italy*, ed. Martin Maiden & Mair Parry. London/New York: Routledge.

Cremers, Crit. 1983. On two types of infinitival complementation. In *Linguistic categories: auxiliaries and related puzzles*, ed. Frank Heny & Barry Richards, 169–221. Dordrecht: Springer.

Cruschina, Silvio. 2012. Focus in existential sentences. In *Enjoy linguistics! papers offered to Luigi Rizzi on the occasion of his 60th birthday*, ed. Valentina Bianchi & Cristiano Chesi, 77–107. Siena: CISCL Press.

D'Alessandro, Roberta. 2004. Impersonal si constructions: Agreement and interpretation. Doctoral dissertation, Universität Stuttgart.

D'Alessandro, Roberta. 2017a. Agreement in Italian impersonal si constructions: A derivational analysis. *Revista da ABRALIN* 1.

D'Alessandro, Roberta. 2017b. When you have too many features: auxiliaries, agreement, and clitics in Italian varieties. *Glossa* 2(1).

D'Alessandro, Roberta. 2022. Agreement. In *The Cambridge Handbook of Romance Linguistics*, ed. Adam Ledgeway & Martin Maiden. Cambridge University Press.

D'Alessandro, Roberta, & Ian G. Roberts. 2008. Movement and agreement in Italian past participles and defective phases. *Linguistic Inquiry* 39:477–491.

D'Alessandro, Roberta, & Ian G. Roberts. 2010. Past participle agreement in Abruzzese: split auxiliary selection and the null-subject parameter. *Natural Language & Linguistic Theory* 28:41–72.

De Alencar, Leonel Figuiredo, & Carmen Kelling. 2005. Are reflexive constructions transitive or intransitive? Evidence from German and Romance. In *Proceedings of LFG05*, ed. Miriam Butt & Tracy Holloway King, 1–20.

Deal, Amy Rose. 2015. Interaction and satisfaction in φ-agreement. In *Proceedings of NELS* 45, ed. Thuy Bui & Deniz Ozyildiz, 179–192. Amherst: GLSA.

Déprez, Viviane. 1998. Semantic effects of agreement: the case of French past participle agreement. *Probus* 10:1–66.

den Dikken, Marcel. 1994. Auxiliaries and participles. In *Proceedings of NELS* 24, ed. Mercè Gonzàlez, 65–79. Amherst: GLSA.

Dobrovie-Sorin, Carmen. 1998. Impersonal se constructions in romance and the passivization of unergatives. *Linguistic Inquiry* 29:399–437.

Doron, Edit, & Malka Rappaport Hovav. 2007. Towards a uniform theory of valence-changing operations. In *Proceedings of IATL*, ed. Yehuda Falk, 57–88.

Egerland, Verner. 1996. *The syntax of past participles: A generative study of nonfinite constructions in Ancient and Modern Italian*. Lund: Lund University Press.

Egerland, Verner. 2009. La doppia base della ristrutturazione. In *Italiano, italiani regionali e dialetti*, ed. Verner Egerland, Anna Cardinaletti, & Nicola Munaro, 99–114. Milano: Franco Angeli.

Embick, David. 2004. Unaccusative syntax and verbal alternations. In *The unaccusativity puzzle. Explorations of the Syntax-Lexicon interface*, ed. Artemis Alexiadou, Elena Anagnostopoulou, & Martin Everaert. Oxford: Oxford University Press.

Ershova, Ksenia. to appear. Phasehood as defective intervention: Possessor extraction and selective DP islandhood in West Circassian. Syntax.

Fanselow, Gisbert. 1991. Minimale Syntax. Habilitation thesis, Universität Passau.

Fanselow, Gisbert. 2001. Features, ϑ-roles, and free constituent order. *Linguistic Inquiry* 32:405–437.

Ferguson, Scott, & Erich Groat. 1994. Defining "shortest move". Ms., Harvard University.

Fischer, Silke. 2004. Towards an optimal theory of reflexivization. Doctoral dissertation, Universität Tübingen.

Franks, Steven, & James E. Lavine. 2006. Case and word order in Lithuanian. *Journal of Linguistics* 42:239–288.

Freeze, Ray. 1992. Existentials and other locatives. *Language* 68:553–595.

Friedemann, Marc-Ariel, & Tal Siloni. 1997. AGRobject is not AGRparticiple. *The Linguistic Review* 14:69–96.

Georgi, Doreen. 2014. Opaque interactions of Merge and Agree: On the nature and order of elementary operations. Doctoral dissertation, Universität Leipzig.

Georgi, Doreen. 2019. On the nature of ATB-movement: insights from reflexes of movement. In *Proceedings of NELS* 49, ed. Maggie Baird & Jonathan Pesetsky, volume 1, 291–303. Amherst: GLSA.

Georgi, Doreen, & Elisabeth Stark. 2020. Past participle agreement in French – one or two rules? In *Formal approaches to Romance morphosyntax*, ed. Marc-Olivier Hinzelin, Natascha Pomino, & Eva-Maria Remberger, 19–48. Berlin/Boston: De Gruyter Mouton.

Giammarco, Ernesto. 1973. Selezione del verbo ausiliare nei paradigmi dei tempi composti. *Abruzzo* 152–178.

Grano, Thomas. 2015. *Control and restructuring*. Oxford: Oxford University Press.

Grimshaw, Jane Barbara. 1982. On the lexical representation of Romance reflexive clitics. In *The mental representation of grammatical relations*, ed. Joan Bresnan, 87–146. Cambridge, Mass.: MIT Press.

Haider, Hubert. 1993. *Deutsche Syntax, generativ: Vorstudien zur Theorie einer projektiven Grammatik*. Tübingen: Gunter Narr Verlag.

Haider, Hubert. 2010. *The syntax of German*. New York: Cambridge University Press.

Haider, Hubert, & Rositta Rindler-Schjerve. 1987. The parameter of auxiliary selection: Italian-German contrasts. *Linguistics* 25:1029–1056.

Hale, Ken, & Samuel Jay Keyser. 2002. *Prolegomenon to a theory of argument structure*. Cambridge, Mass.: MIT press.

Hale, Kenneth, & Samuel Jay Keyser. 1993. On argument structure and the lexical expression of syntactic relations. In *The View from Building 20: Essays in Linguistics in Honor of Sylvain Bromberger*, ed. Kenneth Hale & Samuel Jay Keyser, 53–110. Cambridge, Mass.: MIT Press.

Halle, Morris. 1997. Distributed morphology: Impoverishment and fission. In *PF: Papers at the interface*, ed. Benjamin Bruening, Yoonjung Kang, & Martha McGinnis, MIT Working Papers in Linguistics, 425–449.

Halle, Morris, & Alec Marantz. 1993. Distributed Morphology and the pieces of inflection. In *The View from Building 20: Essays in Linguistics in Honor of Sylvain Bromberger*, ed. Kenneth Hale & Samuel Jay Keyser, 111–176. Cambridge, Mass.: MIT Press.

Halpert, Claire. 2012. Argument licensing and agreement in Zulu. Doctoral dissertation, Massachusetts Institute of Technology.

Harley, Heidi, & Rolf Noyer. 1999. Distributed Morphology. *Glot international* 4:3–9.

Hartman, Jeremy. 2011. The semantic uniformity of traces: Evidence from ellipsis parallelism. *Linguistic Inquiry* 42:367–388.

Heck, Fabian. 2016. Non-monotonic derivations. Habiliation thesis, Universität Leipzig.

Heck, Fabian, & Anke Himmelreich. 2016. Opaque intervention. *Linguistic Inquiry* 48:47–97.

Heck, Fabian, & Gereon Müller. 2000. Repair-driven movement and the local optimization of derivations. Ms. Universität Leipzig.

Heck, Fabian, & Gereon Müller. 2000. Successive cyclicity, long-distance superiority, and local optimization. In *Proceedings of WCCFL* 19, ed. Roger Billerey & Brook Danielle Lillehaugen, 218–231. Somerville: Cascadilla.

Heck, Fabian, & Gereon Müller. 2003. Derivational optimization of wh-movement. *Linguistic Analysis* 33:97–148.

Heck, Fabian, & Gereon Müller. 2006. Extremely local optimization. In *Proceedings of WECOL* 34, ed. Erin Bainbridge & Brian Agbayani, 170–182.

Heinat, Fredrik. 2006. Probes, pronouns and binding in the Minimalist Program. Doctoral dissertation, Lund University.

Hicks, Glyn. 2009. *The derivation of anaphoric relations.* Amsterdam: John Benjamins Publishing Company.

Hiraiwa, Ken. 2005. Dimensions of symmetry in syntax: agreement and clausal architecture. Doctoral dissertation, Massachusetts Institute of Technology.

Hoekstra, Teun. 1994. HAVE as BE plus or minus. In *Paths towards Universal Grammar: Studies in honor of Richard S. Kayne*, ed. Guglielmo Cinque, Jan Koster, Jean-Yves Pollock, & Raffaella Zanuttini, 199–215. Washington, DC: Georgetown University Press.

Hoekstra, Teun. 1999. Auxiliary selection in Dutch. *Natural Language & Linguistic Theory* 17:67–84.

Hornstein, Norbert. 2009. *A theory of syntax: Minimal operations and Universal Grammar.* New York: Cambridge University Press.

Iannace, Gaetano. 1983. Interferenza linguistica ai confini fra stato e regno. *Il dialetto di San Leucio del Sannio.* Ravenna: Longo.

Iatridou, Sabine, Elena Anagnostopoulou, & Roumyana Izvorski. 2012. Observations about the form and meaning of the perfect. In *Perfect explorations*, ed. Artemis Alexiadou, Monika Rathert, & Arnim von Stechow, 153–204. Berlin: De Gruyter Mouton.

Kalin, Laura, & Coppe van Urk. 2015. Aspect splits without ergativity. *Natural Language & Linguistic Theory* 33:659–702.

Kastner, Itamar. 2015. Factivity mirrors interpretation: The selectional requirements of presuppositional verbs. *Lingua* 164:156–188.

Kayne, Richard S. 1975. *French syntax: The transformational cycle.* Cambridge, Mass.: MIT press.

Kayne, Richard S. 1985. L'accord du participe passé en Français et en Italien. *Modèles linguistiques* 7:73–90.

Kayne, Richard S. 1989. Facets of past participle agreement in Romance. In *Dialect variation and the theory of grammar*, ed. Paola Benincà, 85–103. Dordrecht: Foris.

Kayne, Richard S. 1991. Romance clitics, verb movement, and PRO. *Linguistic Inquiry* 22:647–686.

Kayne, Richard S. 1993. Toward a modular theory of auxiliary selection. *Studia linguistica* 47:3–31.

Keller, Frank, & Antonella Sorace. 2003. Gradient auxiliary selection and impersonal passivization in German: An experimental investigation. *Journal of Linguistics* 39:57–108.

Kiss, Tibor. 2011. *Infinite komplementation: Neue Studien zum deutschen Verbum infinitum*. Tübingen: Max Niemeyer Verlag.

Koizumi, Masatoshi. 1994. Layered specifiers. In *Proceedings of NELS* 24, ed. Mercè Gonzàlez, 255–269. Amherst: GLSA.

Koopman, Hilda Judith, & Anna Szabolcsi. 2000. *Verbal complexes*. Cambridge, Mass.: MIT Press.

van Koppen, Marjo. 2005. One probe–two goals: Aspects of agreement in Dutch dialects. Doctoral dissertation, Leiden University.

Kramer, Ruth. 2014. Clitic doubling or object agreement: The view from Amharic. *Natural Language & Linguistic Theory* 32:593–634.

Kratzer, Angelika. 2009. Making a pronoun: Fake indexicals as windows into the properties of pronouns. *Linguistic Inquiry* 40:187–237.

Kučerová, Ivona. 2016. Long-distance agreement in Icelandic: locality restored. *The Journal of Comparative Germanic Linguistics* 19:49–74.

Lahne, Antje. 2008. Excluding SVO in ergative languages: A new view on Mahajan's generalisation. In *Varieties of competition*, ed. Fabian Heck, Gereon Müller, & Jochen Trommer, Linguistische Arbeitsberichte, 65–80. Universität Leipzig.

Lahne, Antje. 2012. Specificity-driven syntactic derivation. In *Ways of structure building*, ed. Myriam Uribe-Etxebarria & Vidal Valmala, 271–296. Oxford: Oxford University Press.

Lahousse, Karen. 2006. NP subject inversion in French: two types, two configurations. *Lingua* 116:424–461.

Lahousse, Karen. 2011. Quand passent les cigognes. *Le sujet nominal postverbal en Français moderne*. Paris: Presses Universitaires de Vincennes.

Laka, Itziar. 1993. Unergatives that assign ergative, unaccusatives that assign accusative. In *Papers on case and agreement*, ed. Jonathan David Bobaljik & Collin Phillips, volume 18 of MIT Working Papers in Linguistics, 149–172. Cambridge, Mass.

Ledgeway, Adam. 2000. *A comparative syntax of the dialects of Southern Italy: a minimalist approach*. London: Blackwell.

Ledgeway, Adam. 2019. Parameters in the development of Romance perfective auxiliary selection. In *Historical linguistics 2015 : Selected papers from the 22nd International Conference on Historical Linguistics*, ed. Michela Cennamo & Claudia Fabrizio, 343–384. Amsterdam: John Benjamins Publishing Company.

Legate, Julie Anne. 2003. Some interface properties of the phase. *Linguistic Inquiry* 34:506–515.

Legate, Julie Anne. 2005. Phases and cyclic agreement. In *Perspectives on phases*, ed. Martha McGinnis & Norvin Richards, MIT Working Papers in Linguistics, 147–156. Cambridge, Mass.

Legate, Julie Anne. 2014. *Voice and v: Lessons from Acehnese*. Cambridge, Mass.: MIT Press.

Legendre, Géraldine. 2007. Optimizing auxiliary selection in Romance. In *Split auxiliary systems: A cross-linguistic perspective*, ed. Raúl Aranovich, 145–180. Amsterdam: John Benjamins Publishing Company.

Legendre, Géraldine. 2010. A formal typology of person-based auxiliary selection in Italo-Romance. In *Syntactic variation: The dialects of Italy*, ed. Roberta D'Alessandro, Adam Ledgeway, & Ian G. Roberts, 186–200. New York: Cambridge University Press.

Lois, Ximena. 1990. Auxiliary selection and past participle agreement in Romance. *Probus* 2:233–255.

Longenbaugh, Nicholas. 2019. On expletives and the agreement-movement correlation. Doctoral dissertation, Massachusetts Institute of Technology.

Loporcaro, Michele. 1998. *Sintassi comparata dell'accordo participiale romanzo*. Torino: Rosenberg & Sellier.

Loporcaro, Michele. 2001. La selezione dell'ausiliare nei dialetti italiani: Dati e teorie. In *Dati empirici e teorie linguistiche. atti del XXXIII congresso internazionale di studi della Società di linguistica italiana, Napoli*, 28–30 ottobre 1999, ed. Federico Albano Leoni, Eleonara Krosbakken, Rosanna Sornicola, & Carolina Stromboli, 455–476. Roma: Bulzoni.

Loporcaro, Michele. 2007. On triple auxiliation in Romance. *Linguistics* 45:173–222.

Loporcaro, Michele. 2010. The logic of Romance past participle agreement. In *Syntactic variation: The dialects of Italy*, ed. Roberta D'Alessandro, Adam Ledgeway, & Ian G. Roberts, 225–243. New York: Cambridge University Press.

Loporcaro, Michele. 2016. Auxiliary selection and participle agreement. In *The Oxford guide to the Romance languages*, ed. Adam Ledgeway & Martin Maiden, 802–818. New York: Oxford University Press.

Mahajan, Anoop Kumar. 1990. The A/A-bar distinction and movement theory. Doctoral dissertation, Massachusetts Institute of Technology.

Manzini, Maria Rita. 1986. On italian *si*. In *Syntax and semantics: The syntax of pronominal clitics*, ed. Hagit Borer, 241–262. New York: Academic Press.

Manzini, Maria Rita. 2019. 1/2p vs 3p splits: A view from Romance and Balkan non standard languages. Talk given at GLOW 42.

Manzini, Maria Rita, & Leonardo Maria Savoia. 1998. Clitics and auxiliary choice in Italian dialects: Their relevance for the person ergativity split. *Recherches linguistiques de Vincennes* 115–138.

Manzini, Maria Rita, & Leonardo Maria Savoia. 2005. *I dialetti italiani: sintassi delle varietà italiane e romance*. Alessandria: Edizioni dell'Orso.

Manzini, Maria Rita, & Leonardo Maria Savoia. 2007. *A unification of morphology and syntax: Investigations into Romance and Albanian dialects*. London/New York: Routledge.

Marantz, Alec. 1984. *On the nature of grammatical relations*. Cambridge, Mass.: MIT Press.

Marantz, Alec. 1993. Implications of asymmetries in double object constructions. In *Theoretical aspects of Bantu grammar*, ed. Sam A. Mchombo, 113–151. Stanford: CSLI Publications.

Matushansky, Ora. 2006. Head movement in linguistic theory. *Linguistic Inquiry* 37:69–109.

McCawley, James. 1984. Exploitation of the cyclic principle as a research strategy in syntax. In *Sentential complementation*, ed. Wim de Geest & Yvan Putseys, 165–183. Dordrecht: Foris.

McCawley, James. 1988. *The syntactic phenomena of English*. Chicago: University of Chicago Press.

McCloskey, James. 2002. Resumption, successive cyclicity, and the locality of operations. In *Derivation and explanation in the Minimalist Program*, ed. Samuel David Epstein & T. Daniel Seely, 184–226. Blackwell.

McFadden, Thomas. 2007. Auxiliary selection. *Language and Linguistics Compass* 1:674–708.

McGinnis, Martha. 1998. Locality in A-movement. Doctoral dissertation, Massachusetts Institute of Technology.

Monachesi, Paola. 2005. *The verbal complex in Romance: a case study in grammatical interfaces*. New York: Oxford University Press.

Moore, John. 1994. Romance cliticization and relativized minimality. *Linguistic Inquiry* 25:335–344.

Moulton, Keir. 2009. Natural selection and the syntax of clausal complementation. Doctoral dissertation, University of Massachusetts Amherst.

Mulders, Iris. 1997. Mirrored specifiers. *Linguistics in the Netherlands* 14:135–146.

Müller, Gereon. 1995. *A-bar syntax: A study in movement types*. Berlin: De Gruyter Mouton.

Müller, Gereon. 2004. Phrase impenetrability and wh-intervention. In *Minimality effects in syntax*, ed. Arthur Stepanov, Gisbert Fanselow, & Ralf Vogel, 289–325. Berlin: De Gruyter Mouton.

Müller, Gereon. 2009. Ergativity, accusativity, and the order of Merge and Agree. In *Explorations of phase theory: Features and arguments*, ed. Kleanthes K. Grohmann, 269–308. Berlin: Mouton de Gruyter.

Müller, Gereon. 2010. On deriving CED effects from the PIC. *Linguistic Inquiry* 41:35–82.

Müller, Gereon. 2011. *Constraints on displacement: A phase-based approach*. Amsterdam: John Benjamins Publishing Company.

Müller, Gereon. 2016. The short life cycle of external arguments in German passive derivations. Ms., Universität Leipzig.

Müller, Gereon. 2017. Structure removal: An argument for feature-driven merge. *Glossa* 2(1):1–35.

Müller, Gereon. 2021. Constraints on grammatical dependencies. In *A companion to Chomsky*, ed. Nicholas Allott, Terye Lohndal, & Georges Rey. Hoboken: Wiley Blackwell.

Narita, Hiroki. 2011. Phasing in full interpretation. Doctoral dissertation, Massachusetts Institute of Technology.

Nevins, Andrew. 2007. The representation of third person and its consequences for person-case effects. *Natural Language & Linguistic Theory* 25:273–313.

Nevins, Andrew. 2011. Multiple Agree with clitics: Person complementarity vs. omnivorous number. *Natural Language & Linguistic Theory* 29:939–971.

Nie, Yining. 2020. Licensing arguments. Doctoral dissertation, New York University.

Nissenbaum, Jon. 1998. Movement and derived predication: Evidence from parasitic gaps. In *The interpretive tract*, ed. Uli Sauerland & Orin Percus, volume 25 of MIT Working Papers in Linguistics, 247–295. Cambridge, Mass.

Nissenbaum, Jon. 2000. Covert movement and parasitic gaps. In *Proceedings of NELS 30*, ed. Masako Hirontani, Andries Coetzee, Nancy Hall, & Jiyung Kim, volume 2, 541–556. Amherst: GLSA.

Noyer, Robert Rolf. 1992. Features, positions and affixes in autonomous morphological structure. Doctoral dissertation, Massachusetts Institute of Technology.

Nunes, Jairo. 2019. Edge features and phase head allomorphy. Talk given at GLOW 42.

Panagiotidis, Phoevos, & Stavroula Tsiplakou. 2006. An A-binding asymmetry in null subject languages and its significance for Universal Grammar. *Linguistic Inquiry* 37:167–177.

Pancheva, Roumyana. 2012. The aspectual makeup of perfect participles and the interpretations of the perfect. In *Perfect explorations*, ed. Artemis Alexiadou, Monika Rathert, & Arnim von Stechow, 277–306. Berlin: De Gruyter Mouton.

Pegoraro, Alessia. 2018. Some properties of restructuring in Italian and Paduan dialect. Bachelor's thesis, University of Venice.

Perlmutter, David M. 1978. Impersonal passives and the unaccusative hypothesis. In *Proceedings of the fourth annual meeting of the Berkeley Linguistics Society*, 157–191. Berkeley.

Perlmutter, David M. 1989. Multiattachment and the unaccusative hypothesis: the perfect auxiliary in Italian. *Probus* 1:63–120.

Pesetsky, David M. 1989. Language-particular processes and the earliness principle. Ms., Massachusetts Institute of Technology.

Pesetsky, David M. 1996. *Zero syntax: Experiencers and cascades*. Cambridge, Mass.: MIT press.

Pesetsky, David M. 2021. Exfoliation: towards a derivational theory of clause size. Ms., Massachusetts Institute of Technology.

Pesetsky, David M., & Esther Torrego. 2007. The syntax of valuation and the interpretability of features. In *Phrasal and clausal architecture: syntactic derivation and interpretation. in honor of Joseph E. Emonds*, ed. Simin Karimi, Vida Samiian, & Wendy Wilkins, 262–294. Amsterdam: John Benjamins Publishing Company.

Picallo, M. Carme. 1990. Modal verbs in Catalan. *Natural Language & Linguistic Theory* 8:285–312.

Pineda, Anna. 2014. What lies behind dative/accusative alternations in Romance. In *RLLT 2012*, ed. Karen Lahousse & Stefania Marzo, 123–139. Amsterdam: John Benjamins.

Platzack, Christer. 1986. COMP, INFL, and Germanic word order. In *Topics in Scandinavian syntax*, ed. Lars Hellan & Kirsti Koch Christensen, 185–234. Dordrecht: Reidel.

Polinsky, Maria, & Eric Potsdam. 2013. Diagnosing covert A-movement. In *Diagnosing syntax*, ed. Lisa Lai-Shen Cheng & Norbert Corver, 210–234. Oxford: Oxford University Press.

Preminger, Omer. 2009. Breaking agreements: Distinguishing agreement and clitic doubling by their failures. *Linguistic Inquiry* 40:619–666.

Preminger, Omer. 2011. Asymmetries between person and number in syntax: a commentary on Baker's SCOPA. *Natural Language & Linguistic Theory* 29:917–937.

Preminger, Omer. 2014. *Agreement and its failures*. Cambridge, Mass.: MIT Press.

Preminger, Omer. 2019. What the PCC tells us about "abstract" agreement, head movement, and locality. *Glossa* 4(1):1–42.

Puškar, Zorica. 2018. Interactions of gender and number agreement: Evidence from Bosnian/Croatian/Serbian. *Syntax* 21:275–318.

Pylkkänen, Liina. 2008. Introducing arguments. Doctoral dissertation, Massachusetts Institute of Technology.

Raposo, Eduardo. 1987. Case theory and Infl-to-Comp: The inflected infinitive in European Portuguese. *Linguistic Inquiry* 18:85–109.

Reinhart, Tanya, & Eric Reuland. 1993. Reflexivity. *Linguistic Inquiry* 24:657–720.

Reinhart, Tanya, & Tal Siloni. 2004. Against the unaccusative analysis of reflexives. In *The unaccusativity puzzle. Explorations of the Syntax-Lexicon interface*, ed. Artemis Alexiadou, Elena Anagnostopoulou, & Martin Everaert. Oxford: Oxford University Press.

Reinhart, Tanya, & Tal Siloni. 2005. The lexicon-syntax parameter: Reflexivization and other arity operations. *Linguistic Inquiry* 36:389–436.

Reuland, Eric. 2001. Primitives of binding. *Linguistic Inquiry* 32:439–492.

Reuland, Eric. 2005. Agreeing to bind. In *Organizing grammar: Linguistic studies in honor of Henk van Riemsdijk*, ed. Jan Koster, Harry van der Hulst, & Henk van Riemsdijk, 505–513. Berlin: De Gruyter Mouton.

Rezac, Milan. 2004. Elements of cyclic syntax: Agree and Merge. Doctoral dissertation, University of Toronto.

Richards, Marc. 2005. Object shift and scrambling in North and West Germanic: A case study in symmetrical syntax. Doctoral dissertation, University of Cambridge.

Richards, Norvin W. 1997. What moves where when in which languages? Doctoral dissertation, Massachusetts Institute of Technology.

Richards, Norvin W. 1998. The Principle of Minimal Compliance. *Linguistic Inquiry* 29:599–629.

Richards, Norvin W. 2001. *Movement in language: Interactions and architectures.* New York: Oxford University Press.

Richards, Norvin W. 2013. Lardil "case stacking" and the timing of case assignment. *Syntax* 16:42–76.

Rizzi, Luigi. 1976. Ristrutturazione. *Rivista di Grammatica Generativa* 1:1–54.

Rizzi, Luigi. 1978. A restructuring rule in Italian syntax. In *Recent transformational studies in European languages*, ed. Samuel Jay Keyser, 113–158. Cambridge, Mass.: MIT Press.

Rizzi, Luigi. 1986. On chain formation. In *Syntax and semantics: The syntax of pronominal clitics*, ed. Hagit Borer, 65–95. New York: Academic Press.

Rizzi, Luigi. 1990. *Relativized minimality.* Cambridge, Mass.: MIT Press.

Rizzi, Luigi. 1997. The fine structure of the Left Periphery. In *Elements of Grammar: Handbook of Generative Syntax*, ed. Liliane Haegeman, 281–337. Dordrecht: Kluwer Academic Publisher.

Roberts, Ian G. 2010. *Agreement and head movement: Clitics, incorporation, and defective goals.* Cambridge, Mass.: MIT Press.

Rochette, Anne. 1990. On the restructuring classes of verbs in romance. In *Binding in Romance: Essays in honour of Judith McA'Nulty*, ed. Anne-Marie Di Sciullo & Anne Rochette, 96–128. Ottawa: Canadian Linguistic Association.

Rooryck, Johan, & Guido J. Vanden Wyngaerd. 2011. *Dissolving binding theory*. New York: Oxford University Press.

Rosen, Sara Thomas. 1991. Argument structure and complex predicates. Doctoral dissertation, Brandeis University, Waltham, Mass.

Rothstein, Susan. 2004. *The syntactic forms of predication*. Dordrecht: Springer.

Sabel, Joachim. 1996. *Restrukturierung und Lokalität: Universelle Beschränkungen für Wortstellungsvarianten*. Berlin: Walter de Gruyter.

Sabel, Joachim. 1998. Principles and parameters of wh-movement. Habilitation thesis, Universität Frankfurt.

Safir, Ken. 2019. The A/ā distinction as an epiphenomenon. *Linguistic Inquiry* 50:285–336.

Schaefer, Silvia. 2020. The morpho-syntactic encoding of discourse-linked topics: an agreement alternation in inversion in North-Eastern Italian varieties. *Glossa* 5(1):1–24.

Schäfer, Florian. 2008. *The syntax of (anti-)causatives: External arguments in change-of-state contexts*. Amsterdam: John Benjamins Publishing Company.

Schäfer, Florian. 2012. The passive of reflexive verbs and its implications for theories of binding and case. *The Journal of Comparative Germanic Linguistics* 15:213–268.

Schwarze, Christoph. 1998. A lexical-functional analysis of Romance auxiliaries. *Theoretical Linguistics* 24:83–105.

Sheehan, Michelle. 2010. The resuscitation of the CED. In *Proceedings of NELS* 40, ed. Seda Kan, Claire Moore-Cantwell, & Robert Staubs, volume 1, 135–150. Amherst: GSLA.

Sigurðsson, Halldór Ármann. 1996. Icelandic finite verb agreement. *Working Papers in Scandinavian Syntax* 57:1–46.

Sigurðsson, Halldór Ármann, & Anders Holmberg. 2008. Icelandic dative intervention: Person and number are separate probes. In *Agreement restrictions*, ed. Roberta d'Alessandro, Susann Fischer, & Gunnar H. Hrafnbjargarson, 181–213. Berlin: De Gruyter Mouton.

Sorace, Antonella. 2000. Gradients in auxiliary selection with intransitive verbs. *Language* 76:859–890.

Sorace, Antonella. 2004. Gradience at the lexicon-syntax interface: Evidence from auxiliary selection and implications for unaccusativity. In *The unaccusativity puzzle. Explorations of the Syntax-Lexicon interface*, ed. Artemis Alexiadou, Elena Anagnostopoulou, & Martin Everaert. Oxford: Oxford University Press.

Spathas, Georgios. 2010. *Focus on anaphora*. Utrecht: LOT.

Sportiche, Dominique. 1989. Le mouvement syntaxique: contraintes et paramètres. *Langages* 35–80.

Sportiche, Dominique. 1996. Clitic constructions. In *Phrase structure and the lexicon*, ed. Johan Rooryck & Laurie Zaring, 213–276. Dordrecht: Kluwer.

Sportiche, Dominique. 2014. Assessing unaccusativity and reflexivity: Using focus alternatives to decide what gets which θ-role. *Linguistic Inquiry* 45:305–321.

Starke, Michal. 2001. Move reduces to Merge: A theory of locality. Doctoral dissertation, University of Geneva.

Steddy, Sam, & Coppe van Urk. 2013. A DM view of person-driven auxiliary selection in Upper Southern Italian. Talk given at NELS 44.

Sternefeld, Wolfgang. 1990. Scrambling and minimality. In *Scrambling and barrier*, ed. Günther Grewendorf & Wolfgang Sternefeld, 239–257. Amsterdam: John Benjamins Publishing Company.

Stowell, Timothy Angus. 1981. Origins of phrase structure. Doctoral dissertation, Massachusetts Institute of Technology.

Stroik, Thomas S. 2009. *Locality in Minimalist Syntax*. Cambridge, Mass.: MIT Press.

Strozer, Judith Reina. 1977. Clitics in Spanish. Doctoral dissertation, University of California, Los Angeles.

Sundaresan, Sandhya. 2013. Context and (co)reference in the syntax and its interfaces. Doctoral dissertation, Universitetet i Tromsø.

Sundaresan, Sandhya. 2016. Anaphora vs. agreement: a new kind of Anaphor Agreement Effect in Tamil. In *The impact of pronominal form on interpretation*, ed. Patrick Grosz & Pritty Patel-Grosz, 77–106. Berlin: De Gruyter Mouton.

Taraldsen, Knut Tarald. 1995. On agreement and nominative objects in Icelandic. In *Studies in comparative Germanic syntax*, ed. Hubert Haider, Susan Olsen, & Sten Vikner, 307–327. Dordrecht: Springer.

Tenny, Carol Lee. 1987. Grammaticalizing aspect and affectedness. Doctoral dissertation, Massachusetts Institute of Technology.

Tufi, Stefania. 2003. Transitivity in non-standard Italian: Three case-studies. Doctoral dissertation, University of Manchester.

Tuttle, Edward. 1986. The spread of esse as universal auxiliary in central Italo-Romance. *Medioevo romanzo* 11:229–287.

Ura, Hiroyuki. 1995. Multiple feature-checking: A theory of grammatical function splitting. Doctoral dissertation, Massachusetts Institute of Technology.

Ura, Hiroyuki. 2000. *Cheking theory and grammatial funtions in Universal Grammar*. New York: Oxford University Press.

van Urk, Coppe. 2015. A uniform syntax for phrasal movement: A case study of Dinka Bor. Doctoral dissertation, Massachusetts Institute of Technology.

van Urk, Coppe. 2016. On the distribution of reflexes of successive cyclicity. Talk given at the Brussels Conference on Generative Linguistics 9.

van Urk, Coppe, & Norvin W. Richards. 2015. Two components of long-distance extraction: Successive cyclicity in Dinka. *Linguistic Inquiry* 46:113–155.

Vergnaud, Jean Roger. 1977. Letter to Noam Chomsky and Howard Lasnik. Reprinted in 2006. Syntax: Critical concepts in linguistics, ed. Robert Freidin and Howard Lasnik, 21–34, London: Routledge.

Vilanova, Jorge Vega. 2018. Catalan participle agreement: Syntactic features and language change. Doctoral dissertation, Universität Hamburg.

Wurmbrand, Susanne. 1999. Modal verbs must be raising verbs. In *Proceedings of WCCFL* 18, ed. Sonya Bird, Andrew Carnie, Jason D. Haugen, & Peter Norquest, 599–612. Somerville: Cascadilla.

Wurmbrand, Susanne. 2003. *Infinitives: Restructuring and clause structure*. Berlin/New York: De Gruyter Mouton.

Wurmbrand, Susanne. 2004. Two types of restructuring – lexical vs. functional. *Lingua* 114:991–1014.

Wurmbrand, Susanne. 2012a. Parasitic participles in Germanic: evidence for the theory of verb clusters. *Taal en Tongval* 129–156.

Wurmbrand, Susanne. 2012b. The syntax of valuation in auxiliary–participle constructions. In *Proceedings of WCCFL* 29, ed. Jaehoon Choi, E. Alan Hogue, Jeffrey Punske, Deniz Tat, Jessamyn Schertz, & Alex Trueman. Somerville: Cascadilla.

Wurmbrand, Susanne. 2014. Tense and aspect in English infinitives. *Linguistic Inquiry* 45:403–447.

Wurmbrand, Susanne. 2015. Restructuring cross-linguistically. In *Proceedings of NELS* 45, ed. Thuy Bui & Deniz Özyıldız, 227–240. Amherst: GLSA.

Yuan, Michelle. 2018. Dimensions of ergativity in Inuit: Theory and microvariation. Doctoral dissertation, Massachusetts Institute of Technology.

Zaenen, Annie, Joan Maling, & Höskuldur Thráinsson. 1985. Case and grammatical functions: The Icelandic passive. *Natural Language & Linguistic Theory* 3:441–483.

Zeijlstra, Hedde. 2012. There is only one way to agree. *The Linguistic Review* 29:491–539.

Index